SOVIET-
AMERICAN
RIVALRY

by the same author

Disarmament and Soviet Policy, 1964–1968
Soviet Politics Since Khrushchev
(co-edited with Alexander Dallin)

SOVIET-
AMERICAN
RIVALRY

Thomas B. Larson

W. W. NORTON & COMPANY, INC.
New York

0727076   ~~42797~~

For Helen, John, and Ruth

CONTENTS

Preface   xi

1 Introduction   3
  Scope of the Study   8
  Plan of the Work   11
  Differences Yes, But Rivalry?   13
2 Geographic-Historical Background of the Rivalry   16
  Climatic-Geographic Setting and Economic Possibilities   17
  Political Geography and the Positions of the U.S. and
    USSR   18
  Population and Ethnic Characteristics   19
  Comparative Levels of Education and Urbanism   22
  Economic Development in Comparative Focus   23
  The Political Background   26
  The Background of Russian–American Relations   31
3 Soviet–American Economic Competition   33
  Dimensions of Economic Rivalry   34
  Domestic Comparisons   36
    Economic Strength of the Two Countries in 1950   36
    General Economic Trends, 1950–1975   39
    The Industrial Base in the USSR and U.S.   43
    Agricultural Organization and Trends in Output   45
    Levels of Consumer Welfare in the Two Societies   52
    Equity and Efficiency in the Distribution of Rewards   55

International Economic Rivalry   59
  Economic Underpinning of U.S.–USSR Policies in
    Europe   60
  Economic Assistance to Less-Developed Countries   63
  Economic Sanctions Against Adversaries   66
  Bilateral Trade and Soviet–American Economic
    Competition   70
  Promoting Rival Economic Models   74
  A Quarter-Century of Economic Rivalry   76
4 Rival Political Orders   78
  Unity and Diversity in American and Soviet Politics   79
  The Class Basis of Politics   86
  National Political Leaders in the U.S. and USSR   91
  Collective and One-Man Leadership   96
  Contrasts in Government-to-Citizen Relations   101
  Repression of Political Deviance   108
  The U.S. and USSR as Political Models   111
5 Contest of Ideologies: Democracy, Freedom, Human
  Rights   114
  Ideology in Soviet–American Rivalry   115
  Soviet and American Claims to "Democracy"   121
  "Freedom" in Soviet and American Ideology   129
    Class-Based vs. Universal Rights   131
    "Freedom" as Absence of Restrictions and "Freedom"
      as Capability to Exercise Rights   132
    Soviet and American Versions of Human Rights
      Deserving Protection   134
  U.S.–USSR Contention over Freedom of the Press   137
6 Ideological Struggle: "Totalitarianism" vs. "Imperialism"   144
  The American Version of a Divided World   147
    Characterizing Totalitarianism   148
    Communist Rule = Fascist Rule   151
    Totalitarian States Distinguished from Merely
      Authoritarian Rule   152

Racism and the Free World/Totalitarian Contest   153
Domestic Impact of the Doctrine   154
Two Worlds Locked in Combat: The Soviet Version   156
Impact in the USSR of the Focus on Imperialism   161
Complications for U.S. and USSR Ideologies   162

7 U.S.–USSR Military Rivalry   167
Postwar Military Trends   170
Military Personnel   171
Military Spending   174
Strategic Arms Competition   178
U.S.–Soviet Military Rivalry in Europe   187
Globally Mobile Military Forces   191
Arms Limitation and U.S.–USSR Military Competition   196
Strategic Arms Limitation   198
Arms Limitation Proposals for European Theater and
    Globally Mobile Forces   202
U.S.–USSR Rivalry in Building Military Alliances   206
U.S.–USSR Rivalry as Arms Suppliers   211
Competition for Military Supremacy   214

8 Soviet–American Rivalry in International Relations 217
The Rise and Decline of Bipolarity   219
Clashing Foreign Policy Objectives   220
Other Countries' Internal Affairs Are the Business of the
    U.S. and USSR   222
USSR Efforts to Encourage Leftist Trends in Other
    Countries   223
American Efforts to Support Favored Trends in Other
    Countries   225
Covert Operations Supplement Overt   228
U.S.–USSR Support of Democracy and Stability   230
The "Status Quo" in U.S. and USSR Foreign Policy   231
Gaining Allies and Winning Support   232
Soviet–American Bilateral Relations   239
European Developments and U.S.–USSR Relations   240

Soviet–American Relations Outside Europe   243
"Normalization" of Soviet–American Relations   252
Soviet and American International Standing After Three
    Postwar Decades   261
9 Toward the New Century: The Future of Soviet–American
   Rivalry   264
    Past Trends and Future Projections   265
    Economic Prospects   266
    The Prospective Military Balance   273
    Struggle for International Influence   277
    Ideological Prospects   284
    Challenges to Soviet and American Leadership   287
    Conclusion   290
  Bibliography   292
  Index   299

PREFACE

POSTWAR SOVIET–AMERICAN affairs have not lacked for analysts and chroniclers. A five-foot bookshelf would not begin to hold all the volumes on this topic written by American, Russian, and other authors. The collection includes works of lasting value as well as a large number of eminently forgettable books.

A "decent respect for the opinions of mankind" (well, at least for those of potential readers) requires an author to justify an addition to the formidable library of existing works. This book differs from most other treatments in two respects. First, it focuses on Soviet–American rivalry, not on the bilateral relations of the two countries. Such relations are obviously important, but they play only a subsidiary part in the overall rivalry, which encompasses activities that are immune to diplomatic or other bilateral regulation. Second, the book seeks to present Soviet–American rivalry from the standpoint of an outside observer rather than from that of an adherent of one side in the contest. Most writing on the topic, certainly in the USSR but also in the United States, is nationally oriented. Implicitly if not explicitly, the interests and values of one or the other country serve as the guiding principles of the treatment.

Both characteristics of the approach taken in this book involve difficulties. The focus on overall rivalry requires treatment of a wide range of topics and thus necessitates a bird's-eye view. A single book must omit much that is relevant. Moreover, no author, and certainly not this one, can pretend to expertise on the subject as a whole. Likewise, the adoption of the standpoint of a disinterested observer involves equal or greater difficulties. Our views of competition, conflict, and cooperation between rival countries are certain to reflect in some degree our social conditioning: we are products of one and not another society. Therefore, any attempt to shed, even temporarily, a national "skin" is bound to be at best only partially successful. Whether or not the attempt itself is worthwhile, and whether the attempt in this case is successful, are matters for the reader to judge.

To avoid monotonous repetition, words like "Russia" and "the Soviet Union" are used more or less interchangeably, as are "America" and "the United States," and also designations such as "state," "country," and "nation." Precision would require differentiation among such terms, but an interest in readability may excuse a certain looseness. I have drawn the line, however, at the prevalent American barbarism of using the term "the Soviet" (in Russian "soviet" means simply "council") to designate the USSR or, still more grating to the ear, to refer to an individual leader or citizen of the USSR.

Various chapters of the manuscript were read by Eric Willenz, Herbert Block, and Robert Baraz. Although I have benefited from their comments, it is more than usually necessary to exculpate them from any responsibility, because on occasion they expressed strong disagreement with the tenor of the discussion. I am also indebted to James L. Mairs, senior editor at W. W. Norton & Company, for perceptive comments on the manuscript as a whole.

Bethesda, Maryland   THOMAS B. LARSON

SOVIET-
AMERICAN
RIVALRY

INTRODUCTION

F OR A BRIEF MOMENT in World War II an impossible dream appeared to be realized. The Soviet Union and the United States were allies. Their collaboration was filled with strain, and barely outlasted Hitler's death in a Berlin bunker. Nazi Germany had created the basis for this collaboration, and the collapse of the Third Reich removed its raison d'être. To be sure, it survived until the end of the war in Asia. For good reason, Stalin kept to his promise to enter the war against Japan. But this entry came when the Japanese were already fighting with their backs to the wall, after almost four years in which largely American forces pushed their retreat from overseas conquests. Atomic bombs made in the U.S. were dropped on Hiroshima on August 6, 1945, and on Nagasaki on August 9, the latter day marked as well by the entry of Soviet military forces into Manchuria. No doubt these bombs were used, on President Truman's orders, to hasten Japanese acceptance of defeat, perhaps as a means of keeping Russian forces out of Japan proper. But certainly Washington saw them also as a stark demonstration to Moscow of American military muscle. The last act of World War II became the first act of a new struggle for world leadership pitting America against Russia.

History seemed to be repeating itself. For World War I had also seen a brief period of collaboration between Russia and the United States, which ended with the Bolshevik Revolution of October 1917. The "specter of communism" announced by Marx and Engels seventy years earlier was now really haunting Europe, and haunting America as well. Lenin and his Bolshevik comrades represented a challenge to everything for which leaders such as Woodrow Wilson stood. Southern-bred, devout Presbyterian, respecter of propriety and property, firm believer in the rights of the well-born over the inferior, of the Anglo-Saxons over other ethnic and racial groups (especially blacks), of the "civilized" nations over the backward, Woodrow Wilson was convinced that Bolshevism was not only immoral but unnatural. Russia would soon be rid of the uncouth subversives who were deflecting the country from the path of Christian respectability and stirring up so much trouble for rightful rulers elsewhere. Leaders with proper credentials of class and culture would soon take the Russian situation in hand (with a little help from friends at home and abroad), restoring the authority of the cultured elite.

And Lenin had as little use for the likes of Wilson, whom he was to call in 1918 "a hypocritical imperialist" and "a servant of the capitalist sharks."[1] Comfortably middle class by family status, a provincial from a small town on the Volga, Lenin chose the life of a revolutionary, a life of arrests, deportation, and exile. He led a tiny band of conspirators who managed to bring off a revolution in war-torn Russia, a success which reinforced a belief imbibed from Marxism that a revolutionary tide would clear away bourgeois rule in America as in Europe. Intoxicated by this vision, he saw signs of the coming revolution everywhere, even in the United States. Indeed, in the early postrevolutionary years Lenin based his belief in the survivability of Bolshevik rule in Russia on the spread of Communist rule to more advanced countries:

> There is no *other* alternative. *Either* the Soviet government triumphs in every advanced country in the world, *or* the most reactionary imperialism triumphs, the most savage imperialism which is throttling the small and feeble nationalities and reinstating reaction all over the world—Anglo-American imperialism which has perfectly mastered the art of using the form of a democratic republic. One or the other. There is no middle course.[2]

As the First World War ended, therefore, neither the Russian nor the American leaders expected that the others would be around for long. But Lenin's "either/or" proved wrong. And Wilson's confidence in the nonviability of Communist rule, a confidence shared by others of his generation—who delayed U.S. recognition of the USSR for six-

---

[1] "Letter to American Workers," August 20, 1918, in V. I. Lenin, *Sochineniya*, 3rd ed. (Moscow: Partizdat TsK VKP(b), 1935), 23:185.

[2] "Valuable Admissions by Pitirim Sorokin," November 21, 1918, in V. I. Lenin, *Selected Works* (London: Lawrence & Wishart Ltd., n.d.), 8:148–49.

teen years while awaiting the Soviet downfall—proved equally wrong. Russia under Soviet power and the United States under alternating Republican–Democratic leadership continued for more than half a century to go their separate ways, alive and well, or if not "well," at least showing no signs of terminal illness.

The American–Soviet rivalry which took shape after World War II was reminiscent of, and yet much different from, that characteristic of the interwar period. For by the end of World War II Wilson's America and Lenin's Russia had become great powers aspiring to world leadership on a scale barely conceivable as the First World War ended. Each country managed great resources; each constituted the nucleus of a new kind of "empire," asserting responsibility for and leadership over like-minded states which remained formally independent. And, most importantly, each was free—particularly in the early postwar years—of a serious rival except for the other.

Thus, none of the states coming under Communist rule in the aftermath of the war was in a position to vie with Soviet power until, much later, China mounted a strong challenge to Soviet dominance. And none of the other capitalist nations was in a position to challenge American dominance. Germany and Japan had been crushed and occupied, as had Italy and certain smaller countries of Europe and Asia. France had been liberated, but likewise liberated from a dominant influence on the European continent. And the French were soon to be liberated from their dependencies and possessions in the Middle East, Southeast Asia, the Magreb, and Africa south of the Sahara. Even victory did not save Great Britain from eclipse, although—unlike France—the country remained unoccupied during the war and incurred relatively minor wartime destruction. In contrast to the decline of the Axis powers and of France, Britain's postwar slippage into a role of dependence on the United States had not been generally anticipated: even sophisticated students of international affairs mistakenly believed that the United Kingdom would share postwar leadership with the U.S. and the USSR.

For most of the period under review, the three postwar decades, the United States and the Soviet Union were the only centers radiating global influence. Their rivalry would probably have been intense even if they had shared more likenesses than differences. But they represented dissimilar and antagonistic forms of society, different and clashing ideologies. It was these differences rather than simply national singularities that were decisive in creating a bipolar world. Two "camps" contested for the world as Washington and Moscow grouped behind them a congeries of ex-great, never-great, and only potentially great states.

The USSR and the U.S. occupied a place in the calculations of the other rather different from that existing in 1917 and the ensuing interwar years. Then Russia had nearer adversaries to dissipate any excessive preoccupation with America. And until the end of World War II Russia as a military-economic power did not appear to the American ruling group as the kind of threat which was visualized after 1945. To be sure, Wilson's hatred and fear of Bolshevism was made acute by the fact that communism had found a territorial base in the old Russian Empire. But Russian state power was not, and could not be, much feared. It was the revolutionary example, and the political ideology, which alarmed the American leadership. Lenin was not far off the mark when he wrote in April 1919:

> Just think: the advanced, most civilized and "democratic" countries, armed to the teeth, enjoying unchallenged military sway over the whole world, are mortally afraid of the *ideological* infection coming from a ruined, starving, backward, and, as they assert, even semi-savage country.[3]

After the war of 1939–1945, in contrast, it was precisely the strength of the USSR as a state which inspired the fear and loathing of such American leaders as Truman and Acheson. Apprehensions over communism as an ideological force had not disappeared, even if the Communist movement in advanced industrial countries displayed little revolutionary potential. But Soviet Russia had demonstrated its ability to emerge victorious from a long and bloody war with one of the strongest of these advanced states, Germany. Moreover, Stalin and his associates had also shown their capability and intention to extend the area under Communist rule. Spurred and protected by Moscow, Communist-led régimes came into being in a belt of Eastern European countries from the Baltic to the Black Sea. Washington had hoped for a restoration of the old social order in this area, minus the specific fascist elements, indigenous or German-imposed, prominent in the 1930s and war years. Instead of this, the U.S. leadership had to accommodate itself to a drastic overturn of political, economic, and social life, and to a reorientation of foreign policies in the area, as

---

[3] Lenin, *Selected Works,* 10:29.

Moscow-allied Communists assumed control and the Soviet Union became the dominant external power.

The America which Russia confronted after 1945 was also a different America from that of the interwar period. It was much stronger than it had been, both relatively and absolutely. The U.S. emerged from the war untouched by any devastation, with its population almost intact, its economy more productive than ever, and its military power vastly expanded over that of the interwar period. The United States had showed in World War II a capability of using military power at great distances from American shores, and a similar potential to use its economic resources on a world scale.

The war provided the occasion for both the United States and the Soviet Union to break out of "isolation," an isolation which the former had chosen and which had been largely forced on the latter. Before the war the two countries had been involved, of course, in international affairs, in some areas heavily involved. But most of the important decision-making in regard to both European and Asian developments in the interwar period had been carried on without their participation as major actors. This relative isolation also meant that their military forces—overall rather modest in size until the late 1930s—were maintained and deployed primarily to serve purposes geographically centered on the environs of the respective homelands.

All this changed drastically with World War II and its aftermath. "Outward Bound!" might have been inscribed on Soviet and American banners. Soviet military power flowed beyond the old borders, seemingly never to be confined again to USSR territory. This deployment facilitated, of course, the spread of Communist rule throughout most of Eastern Europe and in northern Asia. American military power also flowed beyond old limits, and even more extensively than Soviet, in Europe, Asia, and other parts of the globe. As in the Soviet outward thrust, it appeared unlikely that U.S. forces would ever again be confined to the environs of national territory. And, like the Soviet thrust, this forward stationing facilitated American efforts to preserve and promote régimes serving Washington's aims.

The Soviet outward push did not fail to excite American apprehensions, nor the American to heighten Soviet apprehensions. Soviet concern about American military power after 1945 was focused first of all on U.S. capabilities to damage the USSR proper. Russia had lived with centuries of military vulnerability, in contrast to the U.S. But Russia was now vulnerable to U.S. military power on a scale that was completely new. With the decline of the old European and Asian centers of military-political power, American replaced Muscovy's nearer adversaries as the chief force capable of threatening the destruction of the heartland. These apprehensions were immensely heightened, of course, by the demonstration over Hiroshima and Nagasaki of American success in the development of atomic weapons.

Although the war left America still invulnerable to foreign attack, U.S. interests in Europe and Asia were jeopardized by the Soviet outward thrust. And eventually Soviet vulnerability to American destructive capabilities came to be matched by American vulnerability to Soviet power, thus deepening American fear and hatred of Communist Russia. A qualitatively new element had been added, introducing a touch of Armageddon into the Soviet–American rivalry.

The role of the new military technology should not, however, be exaggerated. For the rivalry, the suspicions, and the fears would have existed even if World War II had not initiated a technological revolution in the ultimate means of warfare. The vulnerability to weapons that could destroy entire countries merely heightened fears and antagonisms and made the struggle for power and influence appear to be also a struggle for survival.

The awesome prospect of nuclear devastation set limits, however, to the world clash of the two new empires, which repeatedly edged toward but always drew back from that engagement *corps-à-corps* that threatened the ruin of both countries and of much else besides. These countries were not "too proud to fight," in Wilson's famous phrase of 1916, but both desperately longed for "victory" without paying the price newly demanded for victory. To the extent that the likelihood of a nuclear test of arms receded, the rivals confronted a prospect of indefinitely continuing struggle and competition in which world leadership would be determined by the staying power, strength, and dynamism of two dissimilar social orders.

SCOPE OF THE STUDY

This book presents an analysis of Soviet–American rivalry, struggle, and occasional collaboration in the postwar period. It is an interpretive essay reflecting on some of the most important areas of an ongoing competition, with an evaluation of trends characterizing this rivalry over the past thirty years and a projection of likely developments in the remaining years of the twentieth century. The book does not purport to be a history of U.S.–USSR relations. In fact, it devotes relatively little attention to bilateral diplomatic relations, because a focus on such direct Soviet–American interactions tends to obscure the scale of the rivalry. That rivalry goes far beyond the range of issues that have been, or conceivably could be, brought within the scope of diplomatic negotiation.

This is not to deny that Soviet–American bilateral or multilateral negotiations and agreements affect competition between the two states as they agree to undertake certain actions, or to refrain from actions that otherwise they would be free to undertake unilaterally. Such agreements have been reached in military, economic, political, and cultural affairs. Clearly the agreements so far concluded have not exhausted the possibilities of diplomatic regulation of Soviet and American behavior. At most, however, diplomatic regulation can affect only marginally the kind of U.S.–USSR competition which is the subject of this work.

The point requires emphasis in light of the considerable enlivening of Soviet–American official contacts since the early 1960s, the agreements registered, and the much discussed détente of recent years. Certainly a marked change has occurred since the period of the "cold war," a period of intense and seldom-relieved hostility between the United States and the Soviet Union lasting from the late 1940s to the early 1960s. In that period diplomatic interchanges tended to be spasmodic; often policy-makers in Washington and Moscow knew in advance that nothing in the way of agreements would come from the negotiations they entered. The latter were considered useful, at best, as a means of psychological warfare. The object of such exercises was usually not agreement but impasse, for impasse allowed each ruling group an occasion to display its own staunchness and the perfidy of the opponent, and thus demonstrate the futility of the enterprise. Often the top leaders, on one side or both sides, were averse to meeting, to the exchange of signs of civility, and especially to the compromises essential to the attainment of agreements.

That period passed, and is perhaps unlikely to return. American and Soviet statesmen became interested in contacts and even, sometimes, agreements. Diplomacy came alive. Agreement rather than impasse became the measure for evaluating the worth of negotiations. The change was most marked in the area of military affairs. Since the early 1960s Soviet and American negotiators have been almost uninterruptedly engaged in bilateral or multilateral conferences on arms limitations, sometimes more than one simultaneously. And these conferences involved more than just talk, the traditional volume-input and volume-output of disarmament negotiations. A whole series of arms limitation measures has been worked out, a result unparalleled in any other area of mutual Soviet–American concern.

At first glance this greater success in the arms field may seen surprising, because the negotiations touched upon more sensitive issues of national security than were involved in other areas where negotiations were spotty and agreements infrequent. But at second glance this is not so surprising, because the area of greatest common interest came to be seen as the avoidance of a U.S.–USSR war, one from which both countries would emerge as losers in an absolute if not in a relative sense.

Yet it would be fair to say that even in this "best" case, best in the sense that it involved the most continued activity and produced the greatest number and most significant agreements, the accords affected only a secondary part of these great powers' military programs. Soviet–American military rivalry was deflected somewhat as a few areas of existing or potential competition were placed off-limits. But as a whole their military competition remained free of any external limitations or regulation, partly because many of the agreements prohibited activities that neither the Soviet nor the American military establishment was carrying on or intended to begin. Channels of arms competition left open were often used with redoubled energy. If the object of the negotiators was to reduce the danger of war by reducing war-making capabilities, as sometimes claimed, or to reduce the waste and burden of military expenditures by shifting resources to civilian needs, then the negotiators' success would have to be rated at close to zero.

If this appraisal of the limited impact of U.S.–USSR agreements is accepted in regard to military rivalry, it can hardly be doubted in relation to other areas of competition. Even if it were to be taken for granted, on a very risky assumption, that détente will flower into a great proliferation of agreements touching economic, foreign policy, cultural, and other matters, such agreements will still be of marginal importance to the interstate rivalry treated here. For this latter encompasses everything contributing to the flourishing or fading of two differently organized societies, to their vigor or debility, to their impact on the world as forces of attraction or of repulsion. Thus, trade and other economic exchanges may be increased by bilateral agreements, but any expansion which is conceivable is not likely to have decisive impact on economic strength or rates of growth, particularly in relation to countries such as the U.S. and the USSR in which foreign trade is relatively small compared to total output. Likewise, agreements on foreign policy may ward off a drift to crisis or war, but no conceivable agreement is likely to have more than marginal effect on efforts by the U.S. or USSR to strengthen, usually at the rival's expense, its international position. Finally, ideological competition between America and Russia is beyond the scope of any diplomatic regulation.

PLAN OF THE WORK

The ensuing chapters take up some of the crucial areas of Soviet–American rivalry over the three decades 1945–1975. The plan of the work is simple. Chapter 2 briefly touches upon certain elements in the geographic setting and historical background of Soviet–American rivalry. The focus of Chapter 3 is on economic rivalry, on the changing capacities of the two countries to produce a variety of goods and services, to maintain growth, and simultaneously to provide an economic model for other countries to adopt or reject. Trends in economic capabilities are important because they determine not only the standard of living provided the population but also the rivals' military standing and their potential for influencing other states. The discussion shifts in Chapter 4 to rival political systems, where an attempt is made to explore some of the strengths and weaknesses of the dissimilar political institutions. Two succeeding chapters are devoted to ideological rivalry. Chapter 5 treats the struggle by the adversaries to appropriate symbols or concepts used in common, with "democracy" serving as the prime example. Chapter 6 centers on efforts by each power to gain dominance for unique ideological formulas, the U.S. concentrating on a "free world vs. totalitarianism" formula, the USSR on a formula posing "imperialism vs. antiimperialism."

Following these two ideological chapters, military capabilities are examined in Chapter 7, with emphasis on Soviet efforts to equal or excel the United States, efforts which have been given a higher priority in the period under review than similar efforts in any other area of competition. Chapter 8 discusses rivalry in foreign policy, that is, efforts by the U.S. and USSR to gain the support of other nations and to frustrate the rival's similar efforts, thereby creating a world environment favorable to Soviet or, alternatively, American ambitions. Finally, Chapter 9 offers some projections of likely developments in

Soviet–American rivalry in the last quarter of the twentieth century.

The thirty-year period discussed in this work constitutes a relatively brief span in history. The fate of nations contending for world dominance is usually not decided in a period of a few decades. Rome, as they say, was not built (or destroyed) in a day. The rise, hegemony, and decline of Great Britain as a world power covered a period of more than a century. Of course, war tends to speed up otherwise slow historical processes, for success at arms may catapult a state ahead just as defeat may hasten its decline or bring about its destruction. The "thousand-year" Third German Reich offers a case study of the impact of war and conquest in hurrying a state's rise and fall.

And the same war which destroyed German and Japanese hegemony was instrumental in elevating the United States and the Soviet Union to positions of world leadership. But these countries' reluctance to test each other's war capabilities probably indicates that changes in their relative strength will occur at slower tempos. The postwar generation which experienced the rise of Russia and America to the forefront of international affairs is unlikely to see the disappearance of either state as a major force on the world scene.

A book of this dimension cannot pretend to be exhaustive, in either its treatment of those subjects raised or its inclusion of all relevant topics. Thus, developments in science and technology are not covered, nor those regarding education and other means of socialization, health maintenance, control of deviance, and so forth. The discussion of ideological rivalry is focused rather sharply on a few topics to the exclusion of others equally important. Rival propaganda activities are referred to only glancingly, even though each country maintains a large apparatus for, and expends much effort and money on, propaganda and counterpropaganda. The list of areas omitted or incompletely covered could go on and on. Moreover, any chapter could be expanded to many volumes.

Nevertheless, the treatment of the rivalry is broad in scope, encompassing activities that are often considered to lie outside the boundaries of Soviet–American competition, a point considered below. It is also implicit in the approach adopted here that the rivalry is present just as much in times of relative relaxation in Soviet–American relations as in times of tension, and that it pertains as fully to activities in areas where the two states are linked by agreements as in those where they operate free of any mutual obligations. Finally, according to the approach of this work, the rivalry is not merely intergovernmental but counterposes one society to the other, a point that requires special emphasis in regard to the United States, where the sphere of governmental authority is more limited than in the USSR.

DIFFERENCES YES, BUT RIVALRY?

An objection may be raised that "rivalry" is used in this book in too loose a sense, covering areas in which Soviet and American institutions, policies, and behavior may be—and are—different, but involve nothing qualifiable as rivalry. It is certainly true that two rather different phenomena are brought here under the rubric of rivalry. The first is that of conscious, willed competition, in which each country attempts to equal or outdo the other in a specific element of power. Obviously, there is much competition of this kind in programs of armaments and other forms of military power. Soviet military developments, like American, are closely watched in the other country, and usually incite responses of one kind or another, often but not always involving imitation. This is clearly due to the possibility that Soviet and American military forces might have to prove themselves in a direct clash. Although such direct collisions are only possible in the military field, there are other areas in which conscious competition is the order of the day. Efforts directed from Washington or Moscow to gain influence in and over other countries are often spurred by calculations about what the rival is doing or might do. Such motivations, for example, have appeared to spur sales and other transfers of arms supplies held by the U.S. and USSR, the world's biggest producers. Or, to take another example, the fate of Angola scarcely preoccupied American policy-makers in the period of Portuguese rule and in the transition to independence; only the prospect of rising Soviet and Cuban influence spurred American counterefforts.

The other kind of situation treated here as part of Soviet–American rivalry involves little or no conscious or willed competition. This situation is typical in regard to domestic institutions. Thus, the political and economic systems and policies of the two countries are largely isolated from one another. Trends in one country have little impact on the other. Take the choice of the top executive in each country, the president designated at four-year intervals by means of nationwide elections, the general secretary named by a small group of high party officials on those irregular and infrequent occasions when the post becomes vacant. Anything the Soviet Union does or does not do, says or does not say, will have as little impact on the choice of an American president as similar U.S. positions and activities on selection of a Soviet party chieftain.

The same lack of reciprocal impact can be seen in the adoption of policies as in the selection of leaders. Both countries have had to deal with serious racial or ethnic problems. But developments in the United States arising from the treatment of blacks as second-class citizens have been little affected by anything happening in the USSR. While the U.S. was vulnerable to Soviet criticism, aimed at both American and foreign audiences, such criticism obviously played a minor role in changing U.S. practices.[4] On the other side, Soviet policies responding to problems posed by the existence on Soviet territory of a polyglot, multinational population are largely (again, not entirely) immune from American influence.

A similar situation prevails as to economic policy. Economic developments in the United States, including governmental activities to regulate or influence economic behavior, are only minimally affected by the economic status of, or economic trends in, the Soviet Union. This is due in part to the fact that economic decision-making in the U.S. is in the first instance a function of businesspeople responding to market signals in and outside the country. But even in the Soviet Union, where the government's economic role is far more comprehensive, the régime's day-by-day management and long-range planning of the economy are only marginally influenced by events in the United States.

The presence or absence of direct competitiveness can be illustrated in a hypothetical example. If the United States or the Soviet Union had not been forced to take account of the rival's strong military posture in the postwar years, the history of armaments programs would no doubt have been far different than it was. As to political-economic institutions and policies, however, the absence of the USSR or U.S. from each other's calculations would not necessarily have altered in any major way the course of postwar developments.

Given the minor role of willed competition in certain spheres, how is it possible to insist that rivalry exists? The answer is that rivalry in-

---

[4] It should be underlined that the argument concerns Soviet influence, not foreign influence in general. The proliferation of independent, black-run states in Africa contributed to pressures for a change in U.S. treatment of black Americans, particularly in their legal status.

volves the viability of the two states, of the social systems they champion, and of the position in the world to which they aspire. And their relative strength and stability, their dynamism and appeal, is determined as much by what happens in areas isolated from direct competition as in those dominated by such competition. Soviet and American successes and failures in dealing with ethnic or racial problems, in educating and "socializing" their youth, in eliciting popular support for leaders, institutions, and national policies crucially affect the long-term prospects of the two states. Levels of output in industry and agriculture, levels of supply of consumer goods and services, and rates of growth have an equally important impact.

It is pertinent, therefore, to discuss Soviet–American rivalry over a broad area which encompasses but is not limited to the kind of competition involving a strong element of interaction. So conceived, this rivalry counterposes two large countries of different natural and human endowments, countries molded by different historical experiences. It is a rivalry of dissimilar nations and simultaneously a rivalry of divergent social structures, modes of economic organization, antithetic systems of ideology, different ways of life. Each of the two countries and each of the social systems has elements of strength and weakness, of dynamism and stagnation, of stability and instability. Each simultaneously exerts a power of attraction and repulsion. These elements are subject to change, sometimes slow, sometimes rapid: the effect of such changes is reflected in the shifting correlation of strength between the United States and the Soviet Union and thus foreshadows their chances to prevail in a contest for world leadership.

2

GEOGRAPHIC-HISTORICAL BACKGROUND OF THE RIVALRY

I F THE END of World War II ushered in a new stage in Soviet–American relations, one marked by global rivalry, the United States and the Soviet Union entered this era from different starting points, with different resources in terms of natural endowment and population, carrying over traditions emerging from decades and centuries of prior development. A brief account can call attention to only a few elements of the geographic setting and historical background that are most pertinent to the ensuing contest for world supremacy.

It is no accident that these rivals are among the largest of the world's states in area and population. Particularly under the conditions prevailing in modern times, a large territory and population are necessary conditions for a claim to dominance. No matter how advanced, a country with a relatively small population and a relatively small area lacks the critical weight to exert a major influence on international affairs. Such a country is less likely to have the range of natural resources which large states can exploit; its smallness of territory increases military vulnerability; its industrial capabilities, even if of the highest order qualitatively, cannot reach the high quantitative threshold required to buttress a claim to world leadership; and it is sure to lack enough population to meet the needs of global power.

But a large territory and population are not decisive: they are necessary but not sufficient conditions for global pretensions. While the Soviet Union has far more territory than any other country, the United States—the most powerful country—is edged in this respect by both China and Canada, and is only moderately larger than Brazil. In population the USSR and U.S. rank third and fourth in the world, far exceeded by China and India. In other words, size counts for something but not for everything. In fact, a large population may be an element of weakness, or at least of only potential strength, as may be also a great expanse of territory which is undeveloped, especially if it is inhospitable to easy settlement. This applies to Soviet–American comparisons. From a qualitative perspective much of the putative Soviet advantage over the United States in scope of territory (almost two and one-half times as much) diminishes in significance, as does the difference in population size (that of the USSR is almost one-fifth larger than that of the U.S.).

CLIMATIC-GEOGRAPHIC SETTING AND ECONOMIC POSSIBILITIES

A great sweep of Soviet territory is inhospitable (and therefore expensive) for human habitation and exploitation, while the U.S. has comparable frozen wastes only in Alaska. Both countries extend, to be sure, over climatically varied regions, including subtropical areas, the latter larger in the U.S. than in the USSR. But most of the Soviet population and most Soviet industry and agriculture are concentrated in areas at latitudes well north of those of the United States. In its location, therefore, Soviet Russia is more nearly like Canada than the United States.

The impact of this northerly location is most dramatically felt in agriculture. For crop production the northern setting means a generally shorter growing season, with especially negative consequences on production of corn, legumes, fruits, and vegetables. For animal husbandry it means more expensive maintenance of animal herds and equipment, and—other things being equal—lower yields. American agriculture is favored not only in temperate climate but also in availability of moisture and richness of soils. There is, for example, no area in Russia comparable to the American corn belt where sun, moisture, and soils conspire to yield relatively consistent high returns. Nature is less kind to Russia, generally providing sufficient precipitation only to areas of poor soils, and providing better soils only to areas of frequently insufficient moisture.

The climatic disparity also has negative consequences on Soviet economic activities outside agriculture, as in industry, mining, and transportation. Heating requirements are greater; construction and upkeep of buildings and equipment are more difficult. Rivers and ports are frozen for long periods. Maintenance costs of rail and motor vehicle roadbeds are high. The impact of the northern location also affects adversely the housing and provisioning of the USSR's working population, both in urban and rural settlements.

Disparities between the U.S. and the USSR in natural endowment of resources, particularly forests and subsoil resources, are less marked. While neither country can produce tropical products such as rubber and certain foodstuffs, like coffee and cocoa beans, both have substantial resources for mining coal, iron ore, and a variety of other metal-bearing ores, and for extraction of large quantities of oil and natural gas. In fact, reserves of subsoil resources and timber are considerably greater in the Soviet Union than in America. But the location of such reserves is generally less favorable in the USSR than in the U.S.: they are often very far from processing and consuming areas, require costly transportation, and in many cases are located in forbidding and at best thinly inhabited regions. Their exploitation requires, therefore, an onerous transplantation of the labor force and costly development of an infrastructure of transportation, housing, and other facilities.

POLITICAL GEOGRAPHY AND THE POSITIONS OF THE U.S. AND USSR

If economic geography generally favors the United States, so does political geography. Spreading westward from original settlements on the eastern seaboard, the United States eventually enveloped the North American continent on an east–west axis. It thus gained borders on two major oceans while establishing lines of demarcation north and south with two countries, Canada and Mexico, which could neither threaten the U.S. militarily nor rival it in politico-economic power. Atlantic and Pacific ports have given the United States free access to all the world's oceans, and the two oceans have also served as barriers to invasion. The development of capabilities for air flight and more recently for flight in space have reduced, of course, the country's invulnerability to attack. But they have not eliminated its invulnerability to invasion by a hostile great power.

In contrast to this favorable physical-political location, Russia's was and is much less advantageous. In the course of its expansion over several centuries from a small principality centered on the dusty little town of Moscow to a gigantic empire stretching from east-central Europe to the Pacific, Russia never ran out of strong and often hostile powers at its borders. These adversaries changed, of course, as some old rivals and foes were bypassed and others were conquered and incorporated into the expanding empire. But replacements were always near at hand. Except in the Caucasus, Russia's frontiers on land were very permeable, and the sea margins have not provided the kind of security that ocean borders provided for the U.S. Sea access for both commercial and naval vessels is blocked during long months each year because of the icing of ports, European and Far Eastern alike, and access by water, to the Mediterranean especially but elsewhere as well, is vulnerable to interference by other powers even when ports are ice-free.

These differences in political geography contributed to differences in Russian and American development as world powers, and the influence of such geographical differences continues to be felt. Russian history was thus marked not only by a struggle against nature that was more difficult than anything Americans faced, but also by intermittent armed conflict with neighboring nations. In contrast, war scarcely interfered with the buildup of American overall strength, either by bringing destruction or by diverting efforts from economic development to military preparedness.

Armed struggle, to be sure, played an essential part in American as in Russian expansion. Fulfillment of what American leaders were pleased to call the nation's "manifest destiny" led to the forceful dispossession of European and indigenous claimants to what became U.S. territory. But these were skirmishes involving small commitments of manpower and resources, for the opposing forces were weak. Unlike the American experience, Russian expansion involved major engagements against opponents north and south, east and west, scarring the land and imposing a heavy price in blood-letting and destruction. Even when Russian territory was not a battleground, the politico-military situation encouraged the maintenance of large military forces, notably a large standing army, to deal with hostile neighbors. Unlike the U.S., Russia was not allowed to concentrate single-mindedly on economic development, even if its rulers had chosen to do so.

POPULATION AND ETHNIC CHARACTERISTICS

Historical circumstances dictated that the American population would be constituted in a manner quite different from that determining the population of the Russian state. In its expansion by conquest, the Moscow-centered state incorporated many long-settled areas, including some peoples who had maintained independent states. The process of expansion brought under Muscovite rule not only other Great Russian–inhabited lands and lands inhabited by closely related Slavic peoples such as the Byelorussians and Ukrainians, but also those peopled by Armenians, Georgians, and Azerbaizhani in the Caucasus, and by Turkic-speaking peoples in Central Asia, to name only some of those incorporated.

There was, certainly, a parallel between Russian expansion into Siberia and the American expansion into and settlement of North America, not an "empty continent" but a thinly inhabited one, in which the native dwellers were conquered and shunted aside. Measured, however, in terms of the population numbers and the eventual importance of areas peopled in this manner, such expansion was far less important in Russian than in American history. Russian expansion involved much more incorporation of existing ethnic groups and much less settlement of free land. Moreover, because of the unimportance of immigration in Russian history, even the settlement of the more or less empty lands coming under Russian rule took the form principally of an eastward movement of population from the western part of the Russian Empire rather than of an influx of settlers from outside the country.

In contrast, immigration was decisive in American expansion of both territory and population. The U.S. population grew considerably more rapidly than the Russian in the last half of the nineteenth century and the early part of the twentieth; it was large-scale immigration to the U.S. plus much greater Russian population losses in war that made the difference.

Ethnic diversity in America, unlike that in Russia, was also a result of immigration on a large scale. Despite restrictions on the entry of nationalities considered exotic or inferior, American lands were filled by great waves of post–Civil War emigrants from various European cultures. This process altered the earlier ethnic structure composed principally of colonists and their descendants from England, and Negro slaves purchased or abducted from Africa, plus their descendants. Along with the spread of native- and foreign-born settlers to all sections of the country, urban and rural concentrations of one or another ethnic group emerged in the United States. Such ethnic concentrations were less important, however, than those in Russia, and in any case were of uprooted people rather than of long-settled groups.

Thus, the ethnic pluralism of both the United States and Russia, while in contrast to the relative homogeneity of countries such as Poland, Germany, France, England, and Japan, presented different problems and opportunities to the two countries. And, in fact, ethnic multiplicity elicited rather different policy responses. In both countries, naturally, there was an attempt to unify the population. In Russia, however, even under tsarism, there was no comprehensive, sustained effort to "Russianize" the minority ethnic groups, particularly non-Slavs, even though the superior position of the Great Russians and of the Russian language was ordained as state policy. On coming to power the Bolsheviks renounced this "Great Russian chauvinism," and replaced the unitary state structure characteristic of tsardom with a federal structure of government whose components were territorial units (the principal ones called "republics") delimited to take account of major ethnic concentrations. Minority languages were given recognition rather than disparagement. But recognition of ethnic diversity and autonomy did not go much beyond linguistic-cultural matters. Offsetting, moreover, whatever diversity Soviet federalism allowed, the ruling Communist party was organized on a unitary instead of a federal basis.

For this and many other reasons the Great Russians have always retained a dominant role in the USSR, as of course earlier in prerevolutionary Russia, that went beyond their numerical preponderance in the population. In addition, command of the Russian language has remained indispensable for accession to all but local positions of influence, for professional careers and the like. The Russian language serves as a kind of *lingua franca* for the political-cultural elite as well as the mother tongue of the leading nationality.

Ethnic diversity, however important in American history, has played no role in U.S. federalism. The U.S. federal structure involves simply a geographic division of power between the national government and the governments of the constituent states. In fact, the federal structure came into being with national independence, when the population that counted politically (i.e., excluding blacks) was relatively homogeneous ethnically.

In the United States the problem of welding people of different cultures and different mother tongues into a unified nation, one having as its motto "E pluribus unum" (from the many, one), led to an insistence on "Americanization." The latter had as its principal component the establishment of English as the language of instruction in schools and as the language of business and government. Americanization involved more, of course, than dropping old languages. It meant dropping old ways of behavior and old ideas and the inculcation of a new ideology—Americanism.

U.S. policy was thus distinct from that of Russia. In Soviet Russia, particularly, ideological indoctrination and retraining of the population in new values became extremely intense and pervasive, engaging a level of effort previously unknown in any country. But promotion of the Russian language, and Russification in general, played a much smaller role in this attempt to unify the country than Americanization, including instruction in English, played in the United States.

COMPARATIVE LEVELS OF EDUCATION AND URBANISM

In the period after World War II the population ratio between the U.S. and the USSR stabilized as both countries grew at about the same rate, with the USSR attaining about 255 million people in 1975 to 214 million in the United States. In the three postwar decades rates of natural increase were not only relatively low, a consequence of industrialization and urbanization, but approached equality. No major war losses occurred to inflect population trends, and immigration to the U.S.—subject to quantitative restrictions since the period of the First World War—no longer added large cohorts of new residents.

But other population characteristics were changing. The population of the USSR, since 1917 as before, has remained much less educated than the American. To be sure, heavy Soviet investment in education, including literacy programs for adults, narrowed the marked gap existing at the time of the Revolution. Less than 30 percent of the Russian population was then literate, as against over 90 percent in the United States. By 1945 the USSR also had reached a 90-plus percent rate of literacy. But if literacy could be promoted by crash programs, raising the educational level of the population required both prolongation of schooling and the gradual disappearance of the older, less educated generations. Thus, the Soviet population at the war's end still lagged far behind the American in median years of schooling (for the U.S. population sixteen years of age and older, about nine years; for the Soviet population, less than half that). The disparity in proportion of persons with higher education was, of course, still greater in the U.S.'s favor. As in the prewar wars, so in the postwar years there was to be a further narrowing of the U.S.–

USSR education gap, with many more Soviet youth completing not only the eight years of compulsory education but also finishing secondary education (through Grades 10 or 11). Still, these and other advances were insufficient to bring the Soviet population as a whole up to the American level three decades after the war ended. Both countries were expanding, and at much the same rate in increase, the number of trained natural scientists; in view of the initial U.S. advantage this meant that in 1975 there were still twice as many such scientists in the U.S. as in the USSR, though the ratio of engineers is more favorable for the Soviet Union, which emphasizes engineering training. This continued lag in the level of higher education and specifically in the availability of natural scientists has contributed to the continued lag of the USSR behind the U.S. in scientific discovery and technological innovation, although there were other causes as well.

To take another dimension of the population situation, that of rural–urban proportions, the Soviet Union had a long way to go to approach the level of urbanism of the United States. By the First World War less than one-fifth of the Russian population lived in urban areas, as compared to one-half of the American. At the end of World War II the Soviet figure had risen to about 35 percent, but the U.S. by then was 58 percent urban. Only in the succeeding decades did the population of the USSR become more urban than rural (60 percent in 1975), a point reached in the United States over half a century earlier.

Ever-higher rates of urban preponderance are, of course, not necessarily advantageous to a country—unlike higher educational levels and other indices of development—nor are they necessarily sought by national authorities. Nevertheless, urbanization is closely linked to the growth of industry and the proliferation of cultural and education opportunities. Certainly the greater ratio of urban dwellers in the United States to those in the Soviet Union is associated with a more advanced economy, the lesser importance of agriculture, and the greater availability of secondary and higher education.

ECONOMIC DEVELOPMENT IN COMPARATIVE FOCUS

The U.S.–USSR population characteristics summarily discussed above offer a point of departure for a consideration of other pre-1945 conditions affecting the two states' prospects in the postwar world. The next paragraphs will focus on the development of economic capabilities, and will be followed by a consideration of political evolution in the two countries. In both areas the weight of the past bore very heavily on the courses adopted by the rivals in the years after 1945.

Even if there had been no World War II, in 1945 the Soviet Union would have lagged far behind the United States in the kind of economic power necessary to give substance to ambitions for world leadership. The heart of the matter lay in industrial potential. Industrial development in Russia was not a recent, Soviet phenomenon. It began in Russia even before America was settled. But the early start did not lead to sustained or rapid progress. In both Russia and America a transition from manual to machine production assumed substantial proportions in the first half of the nineteenth century, and in both countries the decade of the 1860s represented a turning point. Reforms centering on the abolition of serfdom and slavery reduced the role of patriarchal landowners in affairs of state and removed obstacles to the development of a free labor force, a wage-earning proletariat without ties to the land. Hence these reforms spurred industrial development along capitalist lines. In Russia, but not in the U.S., however, the agricultural aristocracy continued to be very influential because it was a main prop of tsarist autocracy.

American industrial development, and economic development in general, from the 1860s to the First World War proceeded at such a rapid pace that the rates of growth achieved were subsequently never to be matched over a long period. There were recurrent crises, of course, but they were short-lived. In Russia there were also spurts of rapid but uneven development in this same period, but the pace was generally slower and the interruptions more severe. It was in this era that the United States pulled away from Russia in enlargement of productive capacity, above all in industry. On the eve of World War I Russian industry produced only one-eighth of American, somewhat less in machinery, about the same percentage in steel and cement, more in petroleum, and a still higher percentage in cotton cloth and certain other consumer products. These are country-to-country ratios; on a per capita basis the comparison would be a good bit more unfavorable to Russia. Even before the First World War, of course, the United States had become the greatest industrial power in the world, a status never subsequently lost. Russia at that time occupied a status below that of smaller but more advanced European states such as Great Britain, France, and Germany.

Russian agriculture was also far less productive than American. True, the ratio of Russian to American farm output on the eve of the war of 1914–1918 was in the neighborhood of two-thirds, i.e., considerably greater than the ratio in industrial output. The country could not have sustained its large population had it produced at the industrial ratio of one-eighth U.S. output. But feeding and clothing the population required the overwhelming mass of the active population to engage in farming, because productivity per worker was very low. In the U.S., by contrast, farmers were a minority from the closing decades of the nineteenth century, and yet this minority of the active population was able to produce more than the peasantry of Russia, partly because of the favorable natural conditions, but mainly because of more efficient methods and higher capitalization of agriculture.

If the trend in the late nineteenth and early twentieth century went toward a widening of the economic gap between Russia and the United States, the subsequent period, after the Bolshevik Revolution, saw mixed trends. This period began with war and ended with war (World War I and the ensuing civil war in Russia, and World War II), and these initial and terminal years set Russia back and pushed the United States ahead. In the intervening years of peace in the 1920s the USSR restored pre–World War I levels of output, and then, in the 1930s, undertook a strenuous program of industrialization. The latter enabled the Soviet Union to reduce the large American lead in industrial capabilities, an accomplishment to which the U.S. contributed by its slide into the Great Depression. The latter idled factories and labor on a scale and for a length of time never recorded earlier or since. In the four worst years, U.S. unemployment ranged between 20 and 25 percent of the labor force, and it never dropped below 10 percent until 1941, when the U.S. entered the war against Germany and Japan.

Russian gains in industry vis-à-vis the United States in the interwar period were not matched in agriculture, however. For American farmers, to be sure, the 1930s ushered in hard times, particularly because the world capitalist depression deflated prices of agricultural commodites much more than prices of industrial goods. But the 1930s brought real disaster to Soviet peasants, suddenly ordered to abandon individual farming on lands redistributed to them as part of the revolutionary process. Collectivization was decreed from on high, and a great majority of the peasants, not only the "kulaks," resisted this one way or another. Many died, many were exiled, some escaped to the cities, and most of those who became members of the new collective farms did so because there was no alternative way of keeping alive.

The country paid a heavy price for collectivization, or, more precisely, for the manner in which it was carried out. Human losses inflicted a special toll on the more knowledgeable and enterprising, but there were also great losses resulting from destruction of livestock and other agricultural capital. Output declined, sometimes sharply, as did yields. A sullen, incentiveless agricultural labor force came into being. Although conditions for farmers improved in the last half of the decade, the negative consequences of collectivization continued to be felt long after this "revolution from above" ran its course.

The economic gains made by the USSR in the 1930s relative to the United States (and there were gains, despite the agricultural debacle) were largely wiped out in 1941–1945. As a consequence, the beginning of the postwar period found the USSR, in comparison to the U.S., back again in important respects where Russia had been toward the end of tsarist rule.

THE POLITICAL BACKGROUND

By 1945 much had changed in the status of the two countries that emerged from the war as rivals for world leadership, including changes in their political organization and practices. It is to the political background of the rival states that this section is devoted.

It is possible to imagine, of course, that Russia might have modernized as a society under other auspices than Bolshevik, developing institutions more or less similar to those of other advanced states. And it is possible to imagine, also, that Russia, with its large and talented population, its great territory and wealth of resources, might have advanced by a non-Bolshevik route to a position allowing the country to overshadow the other developed countries of Europe and Asia and rival the United States for world leadership.

But the Russia that eventually came to challenge American dominance was a Communist-ruled country professing to have established a socialist society and to be en route to a communist order. This made Russian–American rivalry something quite different from merely a rivalry between two states differentiated by nationality and location but linked by similarities of social order and ideology.

Still, the national traditions in both countries, the institutions and patterns of behavior rooted in the past, a sometimes distant and sometimes repudiated past, continued to exert their influence. To take an example, slavery in the U.S. and serfdom in Russia were abolished in the 1860s. But their residues lingered on. It is impossible to understand, for instance, the challenge that the movement toward racial equality posed to the United States in recent years without taking account of attitudes and practices perpetuated from the time of slavery. Likewise, the treatment of the collectivized peasantry in Soviet Russia can only be understood in the light of the legal status and socioeconomic position of peasants under serfdom.

Of course, there was a major break in the history of Russia in 1917 which has no analogue in the American past; the revolutionary struggle of 1776 and after involved much more national liberation than social upheaval. Consequently, though Russia has a much longer history as a country, the United States has a much longer history as a continuous state. In fact, the nearest parallel in American history to the Russian Revolution of 1917 was the American Civil War of 1861–1865, though this was not in any sense a revolution. The two events were similar only to the extent that the Civil War in the U.S. and the October Revolution in Russia represented decisive turning points of history in which large groups of fellow-countrymen were pitted against each other in fierce conflicts of ideology and arms.

Whether or not interrupted by revolution, the political systems of both countries are products of traditions extending into a very distant past. This is most obvious in the case of the United States, where the present form of constitutional government has survived for almost two centuries. In addition, the American two-party system—although not envisaged by the founding fathers—dates back almost to the establishment of the government. And even the two parties which currently alternate in power, the Republican and Democratic, originated in the mid-nineteenth century, although their loci of support, especially that of the Democratic party, underwent a subsequent transformation.

Except for the Civil War, when resistance to the nationwide extension of capitalist industry and agriculture was beaten down, the U.S. political order has never been in jeopardy either from domestic or foreign enemies. Regular changes in executive and legislative policymakers resulted from national and local elections held at fixed intervals, and such changes were accepted without question, i.e., there were no attempts at coups d'état. Certainly U.S. presidents were targets of assassins about as often as tsars and Soviet leaders. But political assassinations in the U.S., unlike those in Russia, were usually attempted by individuals giving vent to private grievances rather than by members of opposition groups.

Russian history did not know this kind of stability. Monarchical rule did not give way to republican until the revolution of February 1917. Then, for a period of less than six months, a republic was in existence whose class basis and animating purposes were congenial to the West. In contrast, America had had its "February Revolution" almost a century and a half earlier. The American republic emerging from the war of independence was then a radical departure from the pattern of rule in the major European states; by 1917 the Russian try at a bourgeois republic represented nothing radical in Euro-American practice, for the Romanov attempt to maintain a three-century-old autocracy based on a hereditary monarchy had become anachronistic. The principal European dynasties had been either defanged or deposited in the dustbin of history.

After the short-lived February republic fell victim to the much more profound revolution of October 1917, a state emerged that was decidedly uncongenial to the United States and like-minded countries. For the Bolsheviks saw their revolution as ushering in a period in which Communist rule would spread over the world, sweeping away capitalist institutions, including "bourgeois democracies" such as the United States. They saw themselves as inaugurating a new era of world history just as surely as the Americans of 1776 saw themselves in the vanguard of human progress.

The Bolsheviks seized power in the name of the proletariat, a class to which most of the leaders, including Lenin, did not belong. Their avowed aim was to replace capitalism and private ownership of productive facilities by a socialist order based on public ownership. Rejecting the idea of a parliamentary republic, they created a state centered on "soviets," that is, councils of representatives of industrial and other workers, poor peasants, and ancillary groups. Unlike those countries, again including the U.S., which proclaimed equality of rights for all citizens, the Soviet state was designed to be an instrument of class struggle, committed to the defeat and elimination of capitalists and landowners. The founders sought not stability, but change; not a government which would interfere as little as possible in the lives of the citizenry, but one actively engaged in the administration of the economy and in the creation of a new society and, not incidentally, a new human being. These were the hallmarks of the Soviet order.

To achieve such goals the Bolsheviks came to insist, somewhat tentatively at first, on a monopoly of power for the Communist party, and thus to reject the kind of two-party or multiparty pluralism characteristic not only of Western states but, to a degree, of Russia in the years immediately preceding the October Revolution. Still more gradually the leadership came to demand, under Lenin and even more drastically under Stalin, not only that the Communist party have a monopoly but that the party be monolithic, with factions outlawed and the airing of intraparty differences banned.

However great the transformation in Russian political life produced by the October Revolution, the old order in Russia left its marks on the new. These were evident in both institutions and policies. Of course, no revolutionary upheaval could transform the political-geographic situation of the country in relationship to other countries, nor alter overnight its economic capabilities and population characteristics. But even the new, revolutionary institutions carried the signs of an ancient heritage.

Thus, in comparison to the situation in the United States, the state in tsarist as in Soviet Russia played a leading role in economic affairs, in the management of industry, commerce, transportation, even in agriculture. Naturally, Communist economic direction was qualitatively different from that of the *ancien régime*, and the new economic decision-makers, enterprise managers, and agricultural officials were of a different stripe from the tsarist authorities, capitalist owners, and landowners who were ousted. But Russia was accustomed to a centralized government involving itself deeply in economic affairs, even though the particular role assigned to the Soviet government was novel and the abolition of private ownership was unprecedented.

Likewise, the Russian state traditionally had assumed a much more active tutelary role in regard to society in general than was ever claimed or attempted by the government in the United States. There was no idea in Russia, as there was in the U.S., of strict limits to governmental intervention. To cite only one small example, not only governmental censors in the old Russia but even tsars at times read books—belles lettres as well as political writings—to see if they were fit for public dissemination. Certainly, Soviet control of publishing and other media was much more complete than that exerted earlier, because the Soviet régime, through its control of publishing houses and the like, could make sure that materials were published supportive of party–government institutions and policies; it did not have to make do, as did the tsars, merely with government censorship to prevent circulation of harmful materials, although censorship continued. Despite these and other important differences, the tradition of governmental responsibility for the "mental health" of the population was well-rooted in Russian history.

Again in contrast to American practice, no right of opposition found secure recognition in tsarist Russia or came to be established in Soviet Russia. The idea of a loyal opposition was foreign to both societies. It is true that the last tsar, Nicholas II, bending before revolutionary pressure in 1905, issued a manifesto promising recognition of civil liberties and of the legislative authority of the Duma (parliament). But backtracking soon began to undercut these concessions after the ebb of the revolutionary tide. And in the Soviet period the eventual inclusion in the 1936 Constitution of clauses on free speech, freedom of publication, and so forth did not mean any toleration for expression of views contrary to those put forth by the leadership.

Finally, there is some resemblance between the position of the tsar at the apex of the old order and the role of successive supreme party leaders under the Soviet system, and between pre-1917 veneration of the tsar and the veneration of party chieftains inculcated in the Soviet population. Both are in rather sharp contrast to the treatment accorded American presidents. The continuity between the tsarist and Soviet periods should not be exaggerated as to either concentration of power or deference paid, and there were great differences between one supreme leader and another. No tsar and no other Soviet leader could wield the arbitrary power that Stalin exercised in the last twenty-odd years of his life, and none received the extremes of reverence accorded Stalin.

Both under the tsarist and under the Soviet order, however, the political structure emphasized the role of one person at the pinnacle, a leader whose tenure was indefinite and who was subject to no process of replacement involving the population at large, two respects among others making the Russian leader's role unlike that of a U.S. president. Tsarism exalted a hereditary monarchy, investing the tsar with a mysterious kind of potence as the *tsar-batushka*, or "little father of the people." The hereditary principle disappeared in 1917, and under the theory of the successor Soviet régime collective leadership was to replace one-person leadership. But the collectivity got short shrift under Stalin, and has had only limited application at other times as well. Tsar veneration also disappeared in 1917, but, even if the Stalin period is excluded as aberrant, the focus on the top party leader as the unique personification of authority and practically the sole living source of doctrinal exegesis found expression in the deference paid Lenin, notably after his death, Khrushchev until his deposition, and Brezhnev subsequently.

THE BACKGROUND OF
RUSSIAN–AMERICAN RELATIONS

To the preceding brief notes on the geographical and historical background of postwar Soviet–American rivalry a few words should be added on Russian–American relations prior to 1945. Over a century before 1945 Alexis de Tocqueville had anticipated rivalry between the two countries. In an often-quoted passage from his work entitled *On Democracy in America* (1835), Tocqueville wrote:

> There are today on earth two great peoples who, starting from different points, seem to advance towards the same goal. . . . All the other peoples appear to have about reached the limits fixed by nature, and can only keep what they have; but these [America and Russia] are in growth: All the others have stopped or advance only with a thousand tries; these alone march in easy and rapid steps on a course whose limits cannot yet be seen. . . . Their point of departure is different, they follow diverse paths; nevertheless, each of them seems called by a secret design of Providence to hold in its hands one day the destiny of half the world.[1]

Despite this display of Gallic prescience, in Tocqueville's time and long afterward there was absent from Russian and American consciousness any sense of rivalry. The two countries moved in largely separate spheres. The Russian heartland was distant from American territory, contacts were limited, commercial exchanges were modest in volume and value, few Americans ever saw Russia just as few Russians joined the wave of European emigrants crossing the Atlantic, though the westward migration included a substantial number from minority nationalities living under tsarist domination. Moreover, neither country had designs on the other's territory; Russian settlements on the American west coast were abandoned and Alaska was sold in 1864 to the United States. On an ideological plane, Russia under tsarist autocracy represented no attraction and no challenge to the

---

[1] Alexis de Tocqueville, *De la Démocratie en Amérique*, in *Oeuvres Complètes*, ed. J.-P. Mayer (Paris: Gallimard, 1966), 1:430.

United States. Similarly, Russian rulers had enough problems checking domestic opponents and unfriendly foreign states to be much concerned about distant America.

The year 1917, however, brought decisive change to Russian–American relations. By drawing in the U.S. on the side of the Entente, the war made Russia and the United States temporary allies, but the October Revolution made them permanent adversaries. Soviet support for world proletarian revolution alarmed Washington policy-makers, who feared the attraction and influence—withal rather modest—of Russian-based communism as they had never feared the appeal of tsarism. U.S. military intervention in Russia against the new government and continued refusal to establish diplomatic ties with the USSR heightened animosities. This antagonism between the two countries came to be muted, however, in the 1930s and 1941–1945 as a result of U.S. recognition of the Soviet Union in 1933, Soviet adoption of a more nationalist orientation, and, above all, common resistance to the threat which Hitler's Germany presented to the survival or welfare of the two societies.

Irrespective of the suspicion and hostility which underlay U.S.–USSR relations from 1917 to 1945, i.e., even in periods of *rapprochement*, Soviet–American rivalry on a world scale cannot be said to have begun before 1945. That it did not exist in the 1920s and 1930s is indicated by the fact that American policy was not averse to the program of Soviet industrial development—a program highly relevant to the emergence of Soviet Russia as a rival to the United States—initiated at the end of the 1920s. Even before, as well as after establishment of diplomatic relations in 1933, the United States put practically no obstacles in the way of transfers to the Soviet Union of machinery and equipment and of technological "know-how" designed to assist this buildup, nor did it block flotation of Russian loans in America aimed at the same purpose. Similarly, despite adherence to an ideology foreseeing the eventual triumph of communism over capitalism everywhere, including the United States, as a practical matter the Soviet leadership had to focus on rivalry with, and threats from, the lesser capitalist states of Europe and Japan. Only World War II was to clear the tracks for a contest of strength, staying power, and dynamism between a Soviet Union buttressed by new Communist states and a United States heading up a coalition of capitalist states.

3

SOVIET-AMERICAN
ECONOMIC COMPETITION

ECONOMIC CAPABILITIES are likely in the long run to determine the outcome of rivalry between the United States and the Soviet Union, if—a big if—these states manage to avoid a nuclear war, raining destruction on good capitalists and good communists alike. Economic strength is crucial because productive capabilities undergird capabilities in other areas—political, diplomatic, ideological, and especially military.

Well before the First World War the United States succeeded in outproducing the United Kingdom, the dominant power of the nineteenth century, and all other European countries. This achievement laid the groundwork for an eventual assumption of world leadership by the U.S., effectively asserted, however, only in the post–World War II period. But America's emergence as No. 1 economic power was soon followed by the appearance in Russia of an economic order challenging the very bases of the system entrenched in the United States and other advanced countries. At first the challenge was utterly ideological, and would have remained a piddling affair had the USSR remained as economically weak as it was in the 1920s.

To be sure, the Russia conquered by the Bolsheviks had substantial industrial capacity, particularly for extraction of petroleum and mineral ores, for manufacturing textiles, and for processing food products like sugar. But if Russia was in the big league of developed countries, it occupied a place near the bottom in league standings. For Russia under Communist rule to mount any kind of challenge to U.S. economic supremacy required first the restoration of pre-1917 capabilities and then an intense effort to build a heavy industry base.

It is in Moscow that the primacy of economic competition in overall Soviet–American rivalry is recognized most explicitly. Without neg-

lecting other means of advancing USSR power, Soviet leaders absorb
from Marxism the view that economic relationships ultimately determine the course of historical development, not only within individual
countries but also among different societies. Ever since Lenin's time
it has been standard Soviet doctrine that the USSR can assure its position in the world and contribute most to the world victory of communism by building a powerful economy in the Soviet Union.

The primacy of economic rivalry has been less explicitly accepted
in the United States. But the bad memory of stagnation in the 1930s,
in contrast to rapid industrial growth and full employment in the
USSR, led to an increased recognition that the Soviet economic challenge was real. This recognition contributed its share to the acceptance by all U.S. administrations from 1945 on of governmental responsibility for the overall functioning of the economy, above all for
the maintenance of growth and avoidance of a second Great Depression.

DIMENSIONS OF ECONOMIC RIVALRY

U.S.–USSR economic rivalry takes multiple forms. Basically it involves the relative capabilities of the two countries to turn out a large
volume of goods and services, and to expand this output from year to
year. A measure such as "Gross National Product," or GNP, is used in
Western countries to take account of this total economic effort; a less
inclusive measure, National Income, focused on material products
and omitting most services, is used in the USSR. In this respect Soviet economists are following the tradition of classical economists like
Adam Smith, who did not regard services as part of national income,
and also earlier U.S. practice. None of these adherents of the ma-
terial-product approach deny the social utility of such services as passenger transport, communications, health care, education, and cultural activities; in fact, USSR economists regard as progressive the
trend, found in the Soviet Union as in the United States, toward an
increase in the proportion of workers engaged in service "industries"
to those engaged in material production.[1]

---

[1] The growing role of services, which led to their inclusion in U.S. accounts of
GNP, is also causing a reevaluation of Soviet practice. A prominent Soviet economist
recently suggested that the USSR needed a general measure, which he called "an integral index of the economic activity of society," to cover both material production and
"nonproductive" spheres. See A. Yefimov, *Kommunist*, no. 12 (August, 1975): 31.
There are problems with each approach. Should the armed forces, for example, be con-

Changing levels of production are one thing, but patterns of distribution of rewards are also important in a discussion of economic rivalry. This involves the relative level of supply of consumer goods and services, some of which are allocated socially as more or less "free" goods (education in the USSR and to a considerable extent in the U.S., health care in the former but only exceptionally in the latter), or made available for purchase (most personal and household products in both countries, health care in the U.S.). Distribution of rewards also involves issues centering on the justice or expediency of unequal rewards to various individuals and groups in the population, whether this inequality is viewed in terms of contribution to production or of satisfying needs for consumption.

Another dimension of this economic competition concerns the external linkages of the two economies, that is, the capabilities of the U.S. and USSR to exert (or suffer) economic influence in relations with other countries, developed and less-developed. Both the U.S. and USSR play significant roles in the world economy, though that of the United States is much greater. These roles include buying and selling abroad—or refusing to sell or buy—dispensing or withholding economic assistance, and, in the case of the U.S., exporting and importing capital.

There is one other area of economic rivalry to be considered. Though related to the output and distribution of material goods and of services, it is more metaphysical than physical. This is the contest of economic models, of capitalism and socialism. The USSR proclaims itself socialist, although the claim is challenged; the United States is described as capitalist, although spokesmen often prefer other terms. When discussion of the merits of capitalism and socialism descends from disembodied ideal types to the real world of existing institutions, it must inevitably center on the achievements and failings of the Soviet and American economies. This is not because they are "representative" of states organized on the one basis or the other: the very fact that they are the most advanced and powerful of such unlike groups of countries makes them atypical. The tendency to focus on the Soviet and American alternatives is fortified by each country's efforts to present its economy as a model worthy of emulation and to depict the adversary's as one to be shunned like the plague.

---

sidered as contributing to *economic* output, as they are in the U.S. but not in the USSR? Should Igor Oistrakh's new violin be included in the account, but not his fee for a recital, as in Soviet practice?

DOMESTIC COMPARISONS

Economic Strength of the Two Countries in 1950

This discussion of comparative economic development takes as its starting point the year 1950 rather than 1945, because the first five postwar years were for the USSR, but not for the U.S., years of recovery from wartime losses. Inclusion of these five years would unduly exaggerate Soviet capabilities for growth: reattainment of previous levels of output is always and everywhere easier than expansion beyond achieved levels. The period 1950–1975 offers a sufficiently long span of years to minimize short-term fluctuations, and a period uninterrupted by any major warfare. As to this latter characteristic, it is appropriate to note that any long-term comparisons of the American economic record to that of Russia from the time of the tsars or even from 1917 are likely to have almost no predictive value. This is because wars had such negative consequences for Russia and the USSR but not for the U.S. If another general war were to break out it seems most unlikely that it would leave the United States unscathed and only the USSR heavily damaged.[2] Therefore comparisons showing that the USSR was at the same economic level in relation to the United States after World War II that Russia had been at in 1913 are only useful for propaganda purposes, and certainly offer no sound basis for anticipations of the future.

Well before 1950 the United States had completed its postwar reconversion to a peacetime economy, albeit with a level of military spending unprecedented before World War II, and by 1950 the Soviet Union had regained, on the whole, prewar levels of production, somewhat earlier in industry, a little later in agriculture. By no means had all of the economic effects of the war been overcome in the USSR; some persist to this day. The 20 million war dead obviously included a high proportion of eighteen- to thirty-year-old males, an age group now in the older ranks of workers, who display a disproportion of males to females on the order of two to three.[3]

---

[2] For a rather different view, see Herbert Block, "Soviet Economic Power Growth—Achievements under Handicaps," in *Soviet Economy in a New Perspective*, Joint Economic Committee, U.S. Congress (Washington, D.C.: Government Printing Office, 1976), pp. 243–68.

[3] Frederick A. Leedy, "Demographic Trends in the USSR," in *Soviet Economic Prospects for the Seventies*, Joint Economic Committee, U.S. Congress (Washington, D.C.: Government Printing Office, 1973), p. 434.

In 1950, at the beginning of the period under review, the United States had a Gross National Product about three times that of the Soviet Union. This represents a U.S. calculation, but Soviet calculations in terms of material product come to the same figure.[4] The mix of goods and services was rather different in the two economies, of course, for industry contributed a much higher proportion to U.S. output than in the USSR. *Ipso facto,* agriculture bulked larger in Soviet than in American output, a sure sign of Soviet relative underdevelopment. By 1950, in fact, the proportion of agricultural workers in the total labor force of the USSR had just dropped for the first time below one-half, a stage reached in the U.S. by the 1870s.[5]

The tremendous lead of the United States in total output reflected a wide gap in productivity of labor, which in turn was principally a result of a much higher level of mechanization in industrial and agricultural production, though differences in the education, skills, and motivation of workers were contributory factors. In order to produce its much smaller GNP the Soviet Union had to employ about the same number of workers in industry, mining, and construction as did the U.S., and an astounding seven times as many in farming. In agriculture the labor productivity gap was enormous, with the very much larger Soviet farm labor force producing only three-fifths the farm output produced in the United States.[6]

In spite of this general backwardness, by 1950 the USSR had in certain respects acquired the structural characteristics of an advanced industrial economy. A recent study has shown that on the eve of the 1930s industrialization drive, the Russian economy—compared in historical context to countries with similar levels of income, population, and natural resources—was skewed in the direction of consider-

---

[4] The Soviet estimate is 31 percent of American output. See *Narodnoye Khozyaistvo SSSR. 1922–1972 gg., Yubileinyi Statisticheskii Yezhegodnik* (Moscow: Statistika, 1972), p. 64. The 1950 Soviet GNP is estimated at $173 billion compared to U.S. output of $519 billion, both figures in deflated U.S. dollars of 1972. See Peter G. Peterson, "U.S.–Soviet Commercial Relationships in a New Era," U.S. Department of Commerce, 1972), p. 30; and Herbert Block, "The Planetary Product in 1972: Systems in Disarray," Department of State, RESS–46 (Washington, D.C., 1973), p. 23.

[5] *Narodnoye Khozyaistvo SSSR, 1922–1972 gg.,* p. 343; *Historical Statistics of the United States, Colonial Times to 1957* (Washington, D.C.: U.S. Bureau of the Census, 1960), p. 72.

[6] F. Douglas Whitehouse and Joseph F. Havelka, "Comparison of Farm Output in the U.S. and USSR, 1950–1971," in *Soviet Economic Prospects for the Seventies,* pp. 355–358.

ably above-norm capacity for production of consumer goods (food and light manufactures) and of considerably below-norm output of machinery and other heavy-industry products. At the end of the 1930s these proportions had been drastically altered. Similar structural shifts had occurred in the advanced capitalist countries; indeed, they were essential to the great augmentation of productive capacity in Europe and North America in the nineteenth and early twentieth centuries. But a process which lasted half a century or so in the United States and Europe was accomplished in about a decade in the Soviet Union.[7]

This structural shift facilitated postwar recovery and expansion in the USSR. Overcoming efforts by the U.S. and its allies to block Soviet recovery and expansion, the Soviet leadership again put into effect a fast-growth program which involved, as in the 1930s, limitation of the population to a relatively spartan mode of life. Despite the comparatively meager total product which the economy could yield, Soviet leaders in Stalin's time and after allocated to investment a share of the national product significantly greater in proportion than that devoted to investment in the much richer United States. Their economic model presupposed that the high ratio accorded investment would permit, at best, a slow rise in consumption levels in early years, but with the prospect of more rapid increases in the future as productive capacities expanded. In other words, betterment of consumption levels was supposed to result principally from enlargement of total output rather than from a shift of emphasis to consumer goods production.

The United States faced different problems in the early postwar years. Although intent on growth and avoidance of stagnation, the leadership was under no special pressure to give priority to rapid growth, to postpone current satisfactions for the sake of future consumption. The U.S. advantage in wealth and level of production over the USSR (and indeed over advanced capitalist countries) was never greater than at the end of World War II. To maintain a modest momentum of growth and to prevent cyclical fluctuations from passing the point of peril on downswings, U.S. policy-makers were prepared to have the government intervene in economic affairs more or less

---

[7] Paul Gregory, *Socialist and Nonsocialist Industrialization Patterns: A Comparative Appraisal* (New York: Praeger Publishers, 1970), pp. 140–57.

continuously. Such intervention was designed to keep the economic machinery operating, not to deal with the problem of persistent poverty in the midst of plenty. Improvement in the lot of the lowest "one-third of the nation" was largely dependent on sustained growth of the economy as a whole, just as in the very different Soviet setting improvement in the generally meager standard of living was dependent on a rise in total output.

General Economic Trends, 1950–1975

Much American discussion, whether by specialists or others, of Soviet economic trends, and almost all Soviet writing on American economic affairs, portray a scene of gloom and doom, portrayals not unconnected with the fact that it is the rival "establishments" which sponsor most of the research, through intelligence agencies or otherwise. Indeed, many U.S. and USSR postwar economic objectives failed to be realized, and some major problems became more rather than less acute as the postwar years rolled by.

Yet the tone of gloom and doom is inappropriate. Both countries achieved major objectives, first of all in avoiding repetition of the traumas of the 1930s, those associated with collectivization in the USSR and those associated with the Great Depression in the United States. They both maintained growth, though with fluctuations. In the U.S., growth was interrupted by four periods of actual decline in output as cyclical conditions reduced consumer demand and business investment. In the Soviet Union, downswings took the form of growth slackening rather than actual decreases of total output, and were principally due to physical causes: crop failures had ripple effects on agriculture as a whole, on trade, and on industrial sectors dependent on raw materials from farms.

If the post-1950 decades showed that both capitalist America and socialist Russia could ride curves of expansion, they also demonstrated the potential of the Soviet economy to grow more rapidly than the American. For the period 1950–1975 as a whole, Soviet national product grew at an average rate of over 5 percent annually, in contrast to a U.S. rate of little more than 3 percent, according to U.S. semiofficial estimates. As a result of this differential, Soviet output over the quarter-century increased by more than three and one-half times, while American GNP grew by little more than two times. Put another way, an economy which had produced less than one-third the Ameri-

Table 1
U.S.–USSR Economic Strength

U.S.		USSR	USSR as % of U.S.
(U.S. estimates of Gross National Product—GNP)[b]			
$ 660 billion	1950	$ 216 billion	32.7
$1516.3 billion	1975	$ 865.3 billion	57
(Soviet estimates of National Income)[c]			
(na)[a]	1950	(na)[a]	31
$ 849 billion	1975	$ 569 billion[d]	67
(US estimates of GNP per capita)			
$4334	1950	$1199	28
$7097	1975	$3400	48
(Soviet estimates of National Income per capita)			
(na)[a]	1950	(na)[a]	26
$3975	1975	$2235[e]	56

[a] (na) = not available.

[b] In U.S. dollars of 1975. Estimates derived from those of CIA in *Soviet Economy in a New Perspective*, Joint Economic Committee, U.S. Congress (Washington, D.C.: Government Printing Office, 1976), p. x, and in Peter G. Peterson, "U.S.–Soviet Commercial Relationships in a New Era," Department of Commerce, August 1972; and from estimates of Department of State (Herbert Block), "Soviet Economic Power Growth—Achievements under Handicaps," *Soviet Economy in a New Perspective*, p. 246.

[c] The concept of GNP is not used in Soviet statistics, and the Soviet concept of National Income differs from the U.S. concepts of GNP and National Income in various ways, notably by excluding most services from national income accounts. Soviet estimates are, therefore, basically confined to material product. *Narodnoye Khozyaistvo SSSR v 1975 g.* (Moscow: Statistika, 1976), pp. 120–23.

[d] The $569 billion figure is purportedly in comparable prices. At the official (Soviet-established) ruble/dollar exchange rate, the Soviet estimate for USSR national income is $503 billion, or 59% of the U.S. total.

[e] At the official exchange rate, this figure drops to $1975, or 50% of the U.S. per capita figure.

can at the beginning of the period could produce something like three-fifths at the end.[8] These estimates originate from an adversary source, i.e., in the United States; estimates from Soviet sources claim a more marked advantage for the USSR in rate of growth, 8 percent average annually compared to 3-plus percent for the U.S., and in narrowing the lag behind the United States in total output (the USSR

---

[8] Peterson, "U.S.–Soviet Commercial Relationships," p. 30; Herbert Block, *The Planetary Product at Near Zero Growth in 1975* (Washington, D.C.: Department of State, March 1977), p. 32; Block, "Soviet Economic Power Growth."

producing in 1975—a poor year, incidentally, for both economies—about two-thirds of American output).[9] Of course, by either Soviet or U.S. calculations the USSR is farther behind in per capita production figures because of its larger population.

The Soviet gain was substantial. It had consequences in diverse areas of Soviet–American world rivalry. But the fact that it took a quarter-century for the USSR to make the gain indicated the unlikelihood that the Soviet Union could equal or surpass American levels of output in any near future. Moreover, the Soviet rate of growth, high in the 1950s, dropped in the 1960s and still further in the first half of the 1970s. American growth rates, in contrast, were very low in the 1950s but rose in the 1960s before falling back in the next quinquennium. In each of these periods, it should be noted, the U.S. rate of expansion was below the Soviet.

Both countries, in fact, faced seemingly intractable problems as they entered the 1970s. The persistent downward trend of USSR growth rates indicated that the traditional methods of spurring expansion by additions to the labor force and to the capital stock of machinery and equipment no longer sufficed. Soviet spokesmen acknowledge that increments to the labor force can no longer occur, at least in the near future, on anything like the scale of the past. Nor can increases in the proportion of output directed to investment, which already rose from about 20 percent of GNP in 1950 to over 30 percent two decades later.[10] Even in the 1960s investment did not expand by as rapid rates as earlier.[11] So far, however, more efficient use of labor and machinery has not compensated for the retardation in growth of inputs in these areas.

American problems were different, but equally serious and even more dramatic than those facing the Soviet Union. The creeping inflation of the first two postwar decades gathered momentum during the war in Vietnam and reached a double-digit pace for a brief spell in the 1970s. This inflation contributed to a weakening of the international

[9] *Narodnoye Khozyaistvo SSSR v 1975 g.* (Moscow: Statistika, 1976), p. 120. The Soviet figures are based on the material product concept of national income.

[10] Stanley H. Cohn, "General Growth Performance of the Soviet Economy," in *Economic Performance and the Military Burden in the Soviet Union,* Joint Economic Committee, U.S. Congress (Washington, D.C.: Government Printing Office, 1970), p. 169.

[11] See Abram Bergson, "Toward a New Growth Model," *Problems of Communism,* no. 2 (March-April 1973): 1–9.

Table 2
U.S.–USSR Growth Rates

U.S.	Average annual rate of growth 1950–1975	USSR
	(U.S. estimate based on GNP)[a]	
3.3%		5.3%
	(Soviet estimate based on National Income)[b]	
3.2%		8.1%
	Trend in growth rates	
	(U.S. estimate of growth in GNP)[c]	
4.3%	1951–1955	6.2%
2.2%	1956–1960	5.9%
4.8%	1961–1965	5.2%
3.2%	1966–1970	5.6%
2.1%	1971–1975	3.5%

[a] Based on data from Herbert Block, "Soviet Economic Power Growth—Achievements under Handicaps," *Soviet Economy in a New Perspective*, Joint Economic Committee, U.S. Congress (Washington, D.C.: Government Printing Office, 1976), p. 268.

[b] *Narodnoye Khozyaistvo SSSR v 1975 g.* (Moscow: Statistika, 1976), p. 122.

[c] Slightly adapted from data in Herbert Block, "The Planetary Product at Near Zero Growth in 1975," Department of State, March 1977, p. 32.

standing of the dollar, the prize currency of the world after World War II, forcing two devaluations. The U.S. faced increasing competition at home and abroad from other advanced capitalist powers, while both the U.S. and these powers suffered, much more than the Soviet Union, from a shift in world market prices favoring producers of primary products, notably the oil-producing nations. As a result of these and other blows the United States underwent a short-lived recession in 1970 followed by an equally short-lived recovery, and then plunged into an economic crisis at the end of 1973 which turned out to be the most severe and prolonged downturn in thirty years. Unemployment reached a level without precedent in the postwar period, though far from the level of the Great Depression years. A new word, "stagflation," had to be invented to describe the unholy combination of falling production and rising prices which the U.S. confronted, and for which there proved to be no easy solution. Suddenly, silence descended on claims that the U.S. government was capable of "fine-tuning" the economy: measures to spur business activity and counter unemployment threatened to worsen inflation, and measures to slow inflation threatened to reduce production and increase unemployment.

Despite these difficulties facing the Soviet and American economies, doomsday does not appear to be at hand for either. Both possess capabilities for recuperation and expansion. The United States was able to arrest the pace of inflation and the downward production slide of 1974–1975, even though it could not reduce inflation or unemployment to easily manageable proportions. And the Soviet Union has been able, despite a slower pace of expansion, to satisfy some of the overdue demands for consumption increases while unstintingly building up Soviet state power, especially military power. Moreover, there is certainly no visible threat to the continuity of the capitalist system in the United States or the socialist system in Russia.

The Industrial Base in the USSR and U.S.

While a consideration of trends in total output gives an appreciation of how the rival economies are generally faring, a focus on such aggregate measures as GNP or national income tends to obscure significant shifts in sectors crucial for one or another national objective. Hence, here we turn from the general to the particular, with a discussion first of changing capabilities for the output of producer goods, followed by a consideration of trends in agriculture, and then a focus on the production and supply of consumer goods and services.

Notwithstanding its inheritance of industrial capacity from tsarist times, mostly in consumer-oriented industry, and despite the surge of development in the 1930s, the Soviet Union in 1950 had a backward industrial base from which to mount a challenge to the United States. Soviet industrial output, like total output, came to less than one-third of American. In the ensuing quarter-century industrial output expanded in both countries more rapidly than total output, but the Soviet rate of increase substantially exceeded that of the United States. At the end of the period Soviet industrial production was more than six times that at the beginning, while the comparable figure for the U.S. was less than three times. As a result, whereas in 1950 the USSR produced about 30 percent of U.S. production, by 1975 this was in the neighborhood of 75 percent.[12]

---

[12] The Soviet claim is over 80 percent, *Narodnoye Khozyaistvo SSSR v 1975 g.*, p. 120. See also Rush V. Greenslade and Wade E. Robertson, "Industrial Production in the USSR," in *Soviet Economic Prospects for the Seventies*, p. 275.

Table 3
Commodity Production

Commodity	Year	U.S.	USSR	USSR as % of U.S.
Crude oil	1950	270.7	37.9	14%
(million metric tons)	1975	412	491	111%
Natural gas	1950	177.8	6.18	3%
(billion cubic meters)	1975	569	270	49%
Electricity	1950	389	91.2	22%
(billion kilowatt-hours)	1975	2100	1039	49%
Coal	1950	560	261.1	47%
(million metric tons)	1975	585	645	110%
Crude steel	1950	91	27.3	30%
(million metric tons)	1975	109	141	130%
Cement	1950	39.3	10.2	26%
(million metric tons)	1975	63.1	122	193%
Iron ore	1950	99.7	39.7	40%
(million metric tons)	1975	82.6	233	282%
Trucks and buses	1950	1337.1	294.4	22%
(thousands)	1975	2272.2	763	34%

SOURCE: *Soviet Economy in a New Perspective*, Joint Economic Committee, U.S. Congress (Washington, D.C.: Government Printing Office, 1976), p. x; *Narodnoye Khozyaistvo SSSR v 1975 g.* (Moscow: Statistika, 1976), pp. 132–124, 138–141; *Narodnoye Khozyaistvo SSSR v 1956 g.* (Moscow: Statistika, 1957).

These figures pertain to total industrial production, however, including the share designed for consumer purchase (especially large in the United States). But Soviet emphasis in planning and in allocation of resources was directed mainly to expansion of the industrial base by proliferation of the supply of producer goods—machinery, raw materials, and fuels. And it was in this sphere that the USSR made noteworthy steps toward equaling American capacities. In a well-known speech of February 6, 1946, Joseph Stalin singled out four industrial products whose expanded output was said to be crucial in guaranteeing the Soviet Union protection "from any accidents," a delicate reference to the possibility of a Third World War. These were pig iron, steel, coal, and oil. In three of the four the USSR attained the level of production set as a goal by Stalin in the fifteen-year period he mentioned, and in all four the USSR was to exceed U.S. output by 1975. These gains are significant even if discounted by the fact that the U.S. was substituting—much more than the Soviet Union—other metals as well as plastics in products formerly made of iron and steel, other energy sources for coal, and imports for domestically produced supplies of oil and steel.

The emphasis placed by Soviet authorities on heavy industry is reflected in the fact that 1975 output of oil, gas, electricity, chemical products, and machinery was eight to twelve times more than 1950 output, i.e., above the average increase of 6.2 times for industry as a whole; increases in output of the food and light industries producing for consumers fell below the industrial average. Even in output of producer goods, however, the U.S. retained a lead which was especially marked in more sophisticated and complex types of machinery and other products. Computers are an example: the U.S. produced 20,000 digital computers in 1971 to 1000 in the USSR.

While Soviet emphasis on producer goods at the expense of consumer goods was somewhat relaxed toward the end of the period under review, the burden on the population remained heavy. Soviet priorities were directed to enhancement of the state's military and other capabilities for international influence, and to expansion of an industrial base slated to generate only in the future (a future which tended to recede as the years crept by) an abundance of consumer satisfactions.

Agricultural Organization and Trends in Output

No area of U.S.–USSR economic rivalry is the subject of more contention than agriculture. So, it is necessary to examine the issues somewhat more fully than might otherwise seem appropriate for a sector originating only one-twentieth of America's total output and one-fifth of Soviet. Discussions of agriculture are especially polemical because the organization of farming in the two countries is much more sharply divergent than the organization of industry or most other economic sectors. The presence or absence of private entrepreneurs responding to market forces differentiates American from Soviet enterprises in industry, construction, and transportation just as in agriculture. But factories in both countries have similar hierarchical structures and similar routines of production; in both countries those involved in producing goods rely mostly on salaries or wages for their rewards. In agriculture, however, organizational differences leap to the eye. American farming is one of the last bastions of small entrepreneurs. While large agrobusinesses play a greater role than extollers of family farms usually recognize, no enterprise or group of entrepreneurs is large enough to dominate the market and administer prices. Soviet farming, in contrast, is a bastion of collectivism, with little play of market forces and little private entrepreneurship.

As noted earlier, the Soviet Union in 1950 was relatively backward economically compared to the United States not only because the country was much more dependent on agriculture but also because its agriculture was much less productive than that of the U.S. This is not in the least surprising: countries that are overwhelmingly agricultural typically have low agricultural productivity, because high labor productivity on farms is associated with access to supplies of power, machinery, fertilizer, and other industrial products.

In the USSR, however, there were unique conditions which contributed to the lag. Even in 1950 the country had not fully overcome the disinvestment resulting from the costly process of collectivization in the early 1930s, when the Soviet people, as a Russian writer put it, "ploughed sorrow and sowed disaster." Moreover, as long as Stalin lived Soviet policy not only emphasized industrial development, especially expansion of heavy industry—that policy continued after Stalin—but treated agriculture and the farming population with malign neglect. The post-Stalin régimes of Khrushchev and Brezhnev made strenuous efforts to promote agricultural expansion by means of increased allocations of investment and returns to agriculture, and by means of organizational changes such as the abolition of Machine-Tractor Stations, which left untouched, however, the basic structure of collectivized agriculture.

In 1950 Soviet agriculture produced roughly three-fifths of the ouput produced in the United States; a quarter-century later this had risen to four-fifths. The improvement was accomplished as the USSR doubled farm output while the output increased by one-half in the U.S. Expansion of production was not, of course, a primary objective in the United States, as it was in the USSR; certain governmental policies aimed at restriction of output. In the postwar years there was a slight reduction of sown acreage in America which contrasted to the substantial expansion, by almost one-half, of such acreage in the Soviet Union. This expansion resulted largely from the virgin lands program, which sought both an increase in grain output and a broadening of the geographical scope of grain growing so as to counter regionally diverse climatic conditions.

In both countries the period saw a reduction of the farm labor force. This dropped in the United States from the 10 million of 1950

Table 4
Agriculture

	Year	U.S.	USSR	USSR as % U.S.
Agriculture as % of GNP	1950	5.5	38.4	
	1975	2.6	26.3	
Agricultural labor force [a] (millions)	1950	9.9	49.9	
	1975	4.4	34.6	
—as % of total labor force, including military	1950	12	51	
	1975	4.6	25	
—labor productivity USSR as % of U.S.	1975	(US estimate) [b] (Soviet estimate) [c]	11 20– 25	
Net output agriculture [d] (average yearly in billion U.S. $)	1950–55	26.6	15.9	60
	1966–71	35.1	29.2	83
Output food grains [e] (million metric tons)	1950	30.6	50.2	164
	1974	43.5	89.9	207
Output feed grains [e] (million metric tons)	1950	103	31	30
	1974	133.9	72.6	54
Output meat [f] (million metric tons)	1950	(na)	4.9	(na)
	1975	23.7	15	63
Availability of machinery [g]				
Tractors (thousands)	1955	4480	840	19
	1974	4376	2267	52
Trucks (thousands)	1974	2906	1336	46
Combines (thousands)	1974	698	673	96

[a] U.S. estimates. Soviet statistics use higher figures for U.S. agricultural labor, in order to take account of unpaid family labor. This difference lies behind the wide divergence in estimates of relative labor productivity.

[b] F. Douglas Whitehouse and Joseph F. Havelka, "Comparison of Farm Output in the U.S. and USSR, 1950–1971," in *Soviet Economic Prospects for the Seventies*, Joint Economic Committee, U.S. Congress (Washington, D.C.: Government Printing Office, 1973), p. 354.

[c] *Narodnoye Khozyaistvo SSSR v 1975 g.* (Moscow: Statistika, 1976), pp. 120–21; see also *Narodnoye Khozyaistvo SSSR v 1970 g.* (Moscow: Statistika, 1971), where Soviet farm labor force is estimated at 30 million to 7 million for the U.S., the former much lower and the latter much higher than U.S. estimates.

[d] *Soviet Economic Prospects for the Seventies*, p. 345.

[e] *Soviet Economic Prospects for the Seventies*, p. 374; and David W. Carey, "Soviet Agriculture: Recent Performance and Future Plans," in *Soviet Economy in a New Perspective*, Joint Economic Committee, U.S. Congress, (Washington, D.C.: Government Printing Office, 1976), p. 578.

[f] For 1975, see *Narodnoye Khozyaistvo SSSR v 1975 g.*, pp. 132–135. Cf. *Soviet Economy in a New Perspective*, p. 578.

[g] *Soviet Economy in a New Perspective*, p. 578, 618. It should be noted that the average horsepower of U.S. farm tractors exceeds considerably that of Soviet tractors.

to 4.4 million in 1975. The Soviet reduction was smaller in ratio, one-quarter rather than one-half, but larger in absolute numbers, from almost 50 million to slightly less than 35 million. The result of these shifts was an actual increase in the relative number of Soviet to American farm workers, and this despite the fact that agriculture in the USSR absorbed a much greater proportion of total fixed investment than it did in the United States.[13]

The point deserves reiteration here that climatic and soil conditions are such that it will always be necessary, other things being equal, to put more live labor or capital ("dead labor") into Russian agricultural production in order to obtain an output on U.S. levels. But Mother Nature cannot be held responsible for the Soviet–American productivity gap. Differences in organization, equipment, and incentives have been crucial, as is indicated by the fact that the American margin of productivity is even greater in animal husbandry than in crop raising, although the former is somewhat less affected by climatic and soil conditions than the latter.

Probably the decisive factor in the superior American agricultural record is the greater availability to U.S. farmers of machinery for field and barn work and for transport, of electricity and other sources of power, of fertilizers, herbicides, and pesticides. (This is not the orthodox opinion in the U.S., which blames collectivism, on which more will be said shortly.) As to availability of tractors, for example, there is one for every fifteen farm personnel in the Soviet Union while in the United States there are almost as many tractors as farmers; if calculated in terms of sown acreage the U.S. has three times as many tractors. Measured in terms of grain acreage harvested, American farmers have nine times the number of combines. In transport the Soviet situation is worse, with 39 trucks per thousand farm workers compared to 660 per thousand in America, a ratio of one to seventeen. And the farm-to-market road network in Russia is primitive. Though availability of fertilizers has grown rapidly in the USSR, per acre availability is still only about half that in the US.[14]

---

[13] On this general topic, see Whitehouse and Havelka, "Comparison of Farm Output," pp. 340–74, esp. p. 355.

[14] Ibid. These figures concern inputs to agriculture, and since sane policy in agriculture as in industry aims at maximizing output, not inputs, the figures would not be decisive if Soviet farms made more efficient use of equipment and supplies than American farms. But the opposite is generally the case.

As a result of these and other conditions, agricultural labor productivity is much lower in Russia than in America. The output per Soviet farm worker is estimated by U.S. specialists at 11 percent of the American figure; the Soviet claim is 20–25 percent.[15] But the main divergence of opinion is not on the exact degree of Soviet agricultural backwardness but on the reasons for the gap. American observers mostly blame the ills of Soviet agriculture on sinful collectivism; Soviet writers say that the deficiencies are in spite of collectivism. They see collective agriculture as superior to private production geared to market conditions, whether carried on as a family affair or by large enterprises hiring farm labor. The presumed superiority derives from the possibility of longer range and more integrated planning, and from the possibility of more rational use of labor and capital stock. Needless to say, this theoretical supremacy has yet to be demonstrated in practice.

U.S. critics see the weakness of Soviet agriculture in the collective structure (whether of state farms, where the workers are paid wages and the product belongs to the government, or of collective farms, whose members have some control of the output and are rewarded, either in cash or kind, in relation to yield). Such critics may deplore the absence of private entrepreneurship in industry as well, but consider that agriculture suffers especially because farm enterprises and farmers do not marshal their efforts to make profits by responding to changing market conditions, as in the United States. They point out that to a greater degree than industry farming requires many timely, informed, on-the-spot decisions by experienced hands for which intervention by distant planners and administrators is no efficient substitute. Moreover, they assert, the labor of farmers is more difficult to keep under constant control than that of workers concentrated in factories and similar enterprises. And they see this problem of production discipline made acute by the generally poor incentives and low returns motivating the USSR's farm labor force.

An assessment of the prospects of collective agriculture must distinguish, however, between collectivization as a historical process and collective agriculture as an ongoing institution. There can be no doubt that the way collectivization was carried out in the 1930s resulted in disastrous effects. Nor can there be much doubt that the subsequent use of the collective farm system, to squeeze as much ag-

---

[15] Ibid., p. 354; *Narodnoye Khozyaistvo SSSR v 1975 g.*, p. 121.

ricultural "surplus" as possible from an already disenchanted rural population, prevented agricultural progress.

In pushing through massive collectivization, Stalin and those who abetted him had one principal goal: to get administrative control of farm output, and not be forced to rely any longer on making prices attractive to peasants in order to get hold of this output. They wanted to be in a position to use the agricultural surplus (output above a bare minimum needed for peasant subsistence) to feed a rapidly growing urban population of industrial and other workers. But even if some such program was dictated by the need to industrialize rapidly, for both domestic and foreign policy reasons, actual collectivization was carried out with such haste, severity, violence, and irrationality that the costs were very high.

There was, however, another reason behind the adoption of a collectivist agricultural organization, even if this reason did not dictate choice of the method of collectivization used. This was the desire to establish a farm structure appropriate for creation of a modern mechanized agriculture. On the eve of collectivization Russian agriculture was mechanically very backward. In relation to need, even the greatly increased supply of tractors, combines, and other equipment and supplies that industry was expected to produce in the first Five-Year Plan was a drop in a bucket. But this machinery promised to yield the greatest returns if allocated for use on farms of fairly large scale rather than on the much smaller parcels of land cultivated by individual peasants. Moreover, selling such machinery and equipment to individual proprietors would have meant adding to the economic and political power of the richer peasants, a consummation devoutly abhorrent to the Communist leadership.

There is nothing inherent in collective agriculture which requires squeezing of the peasantry. The mechanism can be applied with a heavy or a light hand, just as state control of industry is compatible with alternative policies regarding emphasis on producers or consumer goods or concerning wage structures. Post-Stalin agricultural policy illustrates the point. Previously weak economic incentives were strengthened by measures to raise farm income, notably by increasing prices paid to collective farms for output sold to the state, by transfer payments to collective farmers, and by increasing the wages of state farm workers and adding to their numbers through creation of new state farms, usually as a result of consolidation of several small collective farms into a larger state farm. Such state farm workers now constitute about 40 percent of the agricultural labor force, up from less than 10 percent in 1950.

This sweetening of incentives has been accompanied in recent years by heightened efforts to modernize and industrialize agriculture. Greatly increased investment has gone into farm machinery, electrification, chemicalization, irrigation, and reclamation. Between the first and last Five-Year Plans of the quarter-century, the ratio of investment in agriculture to investment in the favored heavy industry sector went up from 38 to 56 percent. In the same period the total energy endowment of agriculture increased sixfold.

While none of this negates the fact that Soviet agriculture is still very backward compared to American, the lag is not of itself proof that collective agriculture is inherently less productive than private farming. Not only are American farms better equipped with machinery, power, and transport than those of the USSR, but American farmers are also better educated and better rewarded. It was industrialization which made U.S. farming highly productive, as industry brought to farms ample quantities of power, machinery, and soil- and feed-additives. Collectivism certainly does not block, and may even favor, attainment of the American level of mechanization in the USSR. Nor does it hinder improvement of the educational level of Soviet farm managers, specialists, and workers. And there is no structural obstacle to betterment of farm income and incentives. Furthermore, there are possibilities for economies of scale in the Soviet system that are not present to the same extent in the American, at least in that part dominated by small family farms. Such economies would involve greater specialization of personnel and machinery and an optimum ratio of machinery and transport to acreage or unit of output.

It was once suggested that Russia and the United States could simultaneously solve their farm problems, of shortages and surpluses respectively, by a population transfer: send all the American farmers to Russia and the Soviet farmers to the United States! But the previous discussion implies that less drastic measures may do. Certainly, Russia's catching up with the United States in agricultural productivity is not, at best, for tomorrow. But neither is Soviet agriculture condemned to an eternal lag behind that of the United States, except to the extent that nature dictates. Even unfavorable and ineradicable natural conditions might be circumvented, rather than directly overcome, if the Soviet Union were to rely more in the future than in the past on substitution of imports for those farm products which are disadvantageously expensive, because of natural conditions, for the USSR to produce domestically.

Levels of Consumer Welfare in the Two Societies

Russia's poverty at the time of the October Revolution, plus the course of unbalanced growth chosen by Soviet leaders in the post-recovery years, with emphasis on expansion of producer rather than consumer goods, meant that a linkage between socialism Soviet-style and a high standard of living could not be established. Not only agriculture but production of clothing and foodstuffs, consumer durables, and soft goods got short shrift. The existing stock of housing, passenger transport, and other amenities was exploited to the maximum so as to require as little new investment as possible. The Soviet citizen as producer was the object of lavish attention; as consumer, of little.

In America the story was different. Living in a generally richer country, whose progress was uninterrupted by catastrophes, natural or, like war, man-made, the American as consumer was the object of great attention, although scarcely the sovereign sometimes portrayed. This focus on guiding and satisfying consumer demand derived from the fact that a high level of consumer spending was required to propel the economy.

The difference between the Soviet and the American standard of living in 1950 was tremendous. Per capita consumption in the USSR was barely one-fifth of the U.S. level, and not much above the level reached in Russia on the eve of the First World War. In ratio to the United States, food consumption was more like two-fifths, because the tempo of work required sufficient calories to fuel heavy physical labor. The diet emphasized grain products and potatoes and was light on meat and fresh vegetables. In soft goods, like clothing, the USSR to U.S. ratio was below the one-fifth average, and still worse in consumer durables. Housing was notoriously bad: housing space per capita in Russia after World War II was less than that available before the Revolution, and the Russians then had lived under more crowded conditions than most Europeans. Per capita space in 1950 was only one-sixth of the average in the U.S., and housing in the USSR was inferior to that in the U.S. in quality (lack of privacy, of electricity and gas, of running water) as well as in quantity.

In the following quarter-century the Soviet standard of living improved substantially. Per capita real income increased by four to five times over the period. But real income in the United States also rose substantially in 1950–1975, though at a slower pace. As a result the Soviet gains were translated into a gain from the 20 percent level of U.S. consumption in 1950 to about 35 percent in 1975. Food consumption increased to about 60 percent of the U.S. intake per capita, and qualitatively followed a trend established earlier in America with a shift from starchy products to meat, fats, and sugar. In other words, socialist man was on the route to, but still a distance from, the rich diet and increased heart attacks of advanced capitalism. Sharp gains were registered in the supply of consumer durables, such as radio, TV, and household appliances, though from an extremely low 1950 base; gains relative to the U.S. were significant but less marked in soft goods and personal services. In housing, per capita space doubled over the twenty-five-year period, and housing units per thousand population reached 80 percent of the American level. Nevertheless, USSR housing space (in urban areas it was largely in apartments) remained much smaller and less well-equipped than that in American houses and apartments.[16]

One of the most striking differences between the Soviet and American standards of living centers on the role of passenger cars. Already in 1950 some 50 million cars were registered in the U.S., and that figure almost doubled by the end of the period. The ubiquity of the automobile exercised a dominating influence on almost all aspects of American life, including, *inter alia*, the direction of industrial development, the use of natural resources, the location and character of housing, and the state of public transportation. Not so in Russia. Only a few of the relatively small number of cars operating in 1950 were in private ownership, and even twenty-five years later the number was still small, with only one car per twenty-five families. Nevertheless, passenger vehicle production shot up in the 1970s, passing 1 million a year, as compared to about 7 million in the U.S., with an increasing proportion of these sold to private individuals.[17]

Of course, an abundance of cars is not an unmitigated blessing. For a time it looked as if Soviet planners might associate increased avail-

[16] David W. Bronson and Barbara S. Severin, "Soviet Consumer Welfare: The Brezhnev Era," in *Soviet Economic Prospects for the Seventies*, pp. 376–403; and Willard S. Smith, "Housing in the Soviet Union—Big Plans, Little Action," in *Soviet Economic Prospects for the Seventies*, pp. 404–26.

[17] Imogene U. Edwards, "Automotive Trends in the USSR," *Soviet Economic Prospects for the Seventies*, pp. 291–314.

Table 5
Consumer Goods

Item	Year	U.S.	USSR	USSR as % of U.S.
Automobile production [a]	1950	6,666	64.6	<1%
(thousands)	1975	6,713	1,201	18%
Radio output	1950	13,468	1,083	8%
(thousands)	1975	34,516	8,400	24%
Television set output	1950	7,464	(negligible)	<1%
(thousands)	1975	10,637	7,000	66%
Telephones installed (thousands)	1974	143,977	15,782	11%
—per hundred population	1974	67.7	6.2	9%
Daily newspapers total circulation	1974			
(thousands)		62,147	93,243	150%
—copies per thousand population		300	373	124%
Railroad passenger travel (million kilometers)	1974	16,629	306,298	1,842%
Roads and highways (thousand kilometers)	1971	5,095	1,363	27%
—of which paved		1,925	224	12%

SOURCE: *Statistical Abstract of the United States, 1976* (Washington, D.C.: U.S. Department of Commerce, 1976); *Soviet Economic Prospects for the Seventies;* Joint Economic Committee, U.S. Congress (Washington, D.C.: Government Printing Office, 1973); *Soviet Economy in a New Perspective;* Joint Economic Committee, U.S. Congress (Washington, D.C.: Government Printing Office, 1976); *Narodnoye Khozyaistvo SSSR v 1975 g.* (Moscow: Statistika, 1976).

[a] The stock of passenger vehicles is far greater in the U.S. than in the USSR, because the latter has only in recent years attained volume production in the millions, whereas several million cars have been produced yearly in the U.S. over a long period.

ability of private cars with novel social arrangements to avoid some of the ills of the automobile age. But no such arrangements have emerged. Probably Soviet authorities are in a better position than their American counterparts to mitigate some of the negative consequences of automobile proliferation, such as the decay of central cities, through administrative control of housing construction. The results are not yet in.

Partly because of the very low density of automobile ownership, the USSR has had to maintain a rather thick network of public transportation, reversing the situation of the United States. The Soviet

Union is so backward, in fact, that it even operates an extensive railroad system which actually carries people and goods from one city to another! However, the American intercity bus system is far superior to the Soviet, partly because of a much better road network, and for other reasons this is also true of air transport. But large-city subways, electrified trains, city buses, and streetcars give Soviet urban and suburban dwellers a public transport option often unavailable to their American counterparts.

The citation of data on consumers' welfare has been very partial, omitting such important areas as education, health care, and cultural institutions, to name only a few, but a broader and more detailed treatment would not alter the conclusion that this is the sphere of greatest difference between American and Soviet achievements. American spokesmen like to dwell on U.S. superiority in this realm, a superiority admitted, if grudgingly, by Soviet spokesmen. The latter are critical of a focus on the acquisition and enjoyment of consumer goods as the be-all and end-all of human life, but simultaneously point with pride to Soviet advances toward U.S. levels of consumption. And they recognize, at least implicitly, that the USSR's slowness in improving citizen welfare has had a deleterious effect on the appeal of Soviet socialism, a subject to be examined later.

Equity and Efficiency in the Distribution of Rewards

Soviet–American economic rivalry in respect to consumer welfare has another dimension in addition to that expressed in per capita availabilities of consumer goods and services. The latter are not distributed on an average, per capita basis in either country. Some of the population get more, most get a lot less than per capita data might suggest. The justice or equity of the pattern of distribution of rewards thus enters intersystem rivalry, as does the effectiveness of each distribution system in promoting maximum output.

Both countries defend unequal distribution of rewards, though from somewhat different perspectives. Advocates of American capitalism justify the inequality of income and wealth built into the system of private ownership and entrepreneurship, because they see the struggle for advantage, and particularly the profit incentive, as a powerful force for economic expansion. Usually accepting with pride or resignation the necessity of measures to mitigate the most extreme forms of inequality by redistributive devices, they are hostile both to equality as an ideal and to equalization steps impinging on the right to be rich, which implies a "right" to be poor. They often profess their support for "equality of opportunity," but mean by this merely the absence of legal barriers to class mobility and acquisition of property and income. Obviously, equality of opportunity in any other sense is unrealizable in a society characterized by great differences of wealth and of other advantages passed on from generation to generation.

For the United States there are abundant data to show the extent of inequality of income and wealth. As to wealth, the top fifth of Americans owns over three-quarters of all personal wealth, that is, three times the amount owned by the other four-fifths of the population. Within this top group the richest 1 percent owns about 25 percent of all wealth, including, for example, a great and increasing proportion of all corporate stock, now about three-quarters. This concentration of corporate ownership must be juxtaposed to the more than tripling in postwar years of the number of individual stockholders, a statistic often cited in support of the concept of "people's capitalism."

A similar inequality pervades the income picture. The richest fifth of American families receive considerably more income than the total received by the lower three-fifths, and well over seven times the income received by the bottom fifth. The top 5 percent of families, in fact, receive almost as much income as the lowest 40 percent. Neither government transfer payments, like welfare and Social Security assistance, nor progressive income taxes substantially alter the disparity in income shares.[18] The formalism already mentioned in regard to equality of opportunity is equally characteristic of taxing according to "ability to pay." Federal tax laws are written so that the top 1 percent of income receivers pay an effective tax rate of only 26 percent, despite levies on paper running up to 70 percent; the phenomenon is not unconnected with the great political influence that wealthy individuals exert.

If equality as a goal for distribution of rewards, and redistributive measures toward this end, find little support among proponents of

---

[18] See Lester C. Thurow and Robert E. B. Lucas, *The American Distribution of Income: A Structural Problem*, Joint Economic Committee, U.S. Congress (Washington, D.C.: Government Printing Office, 1972), pp. 4–9; Frank Ackerman, Howard Birnbaum, James Wetzler, and Andrew Zimbalist, "The Extent of Income Inequality in the United States," in Richard C. Edwards, Michael Reich, and Thomas E. Weisskopf, eds., *The Capitalist System* (Englewood Cliffs, N.J.: Prentice-Hall, Inc., 1972), pp. 207–17.

capitalism, some form of equalization was explicit in Marxist theories of socialism, whose appeal was designedly to those disadvantaged by existing modes of property ownership and income distribution. Without denying the inevitability of human inequalities rooted in biology, socialism was supposed to eliminate the major manifestations of inequality stemming from social structure, and particularly the great inequality represented by the coexistence of an affluent minority and a deprived majority. Even if the revolution bringing socialism were to occur in a backward country rather than, as expected, in a country of advanced capitalism, it was anticipated that socialism would abolish inequality, that is, relative poverty and relative affluence, despite an inability of a poor country to achieve at once a high standard of living.

The Russian Revolution did abolish certain kinds of inequality by eliminating the classes deriving wealth and income from ownership of landed estates and productive enterprises. But the goal of equality faded as emphasis centered on restoration and expansion of production rather than on the most equitable distribution of current product. A new structure of inequality appeared, particularly as Stalin's drive against wage leveling in the 1930s took effect. Highly differentiated wages and other perquisites were designed to spur increases in production and to encourage veteran and novice workers to acquire technical skills. Such wage differentials were also used to attract labor to the so-called growth-producing industrial sectors at the expense of light industry, agriculture, and trade, i.e., sectors centered on consumption. Thus, marked wage differentials separated high- and low-paid workers within enterprises; and these differentials overlapped those between enterprises of different economic sectors.

The fact that intraenterprise wage spread in factories, for example, may be greater in the Soviet Union than in the United States does not mean, contrary to a widely held belief, that there is greater income inequality in the USSR than in the U.S., still less that there is greater inequality in wealth. Although data are scarce on wealth and income distribution in the USSR, it is known that personal wealth is far less important under the Soviet system because of the absence of income-producing property. The upper ranks of American managers, technical personnel, and professionals usually enjoy income, in addition to their salaries or fees, from property for which there is no Soviet equivalent. And there are other conditions limiting the range of income differences. Hence income inequality in the USSR, which is especially marked if account is taken—as it should be—of the low returns to the farming population, is significantly less than that characteristic of the United States.

Moreover, in the postwar period there has been in the Soviet Union, but not in the United States, a strong trend toward greater equality of income. Studies of American developments have shown that in terms of their proportions of wealth and income the rich and the poor have retained roughly the same position over the postwar years. Both upper- and lower-income groups have made gains, of course, while staying at roughly the same distance apart on the economic ladder. In fact, the paucity or ineffectiveness of redistributive measures has meant that the absolute gap in average income has increased. For example, over the decade 1958–1968 the gap between the highest and lowest fifths of income recipients widened from about $14,000 to$19,000.

In the Soviet Union, in contrast, price changes and changes in wages and other payments have worked to narrow income differentials. Productivity gains were frequently translated into price reductions on consumer goods (initially very high, with a few exceptions), and, to the extent that such changes involved common rather than luxury goods, they had an equalizing effect. The low-income rural population benefited from such price reductions, but benefited more from increases in wages and other payments. In fact, the reduction of the income differential between the farming and nonfarming population was the most marked trend of the postwar decades. In 1950 farm families constituted three-fifths of the population but received only one-sixth of total money incomes; they did have, however, income in kind which most of the urban dwellers lacked. Wage payments to collective farmers increased in the postwar years by over eleven times, from a very low base to be sure, while wages in general increased less than five times.

Other low-income groups in addition to farmers also improved their position relative to the better paid as a result of increases in the minimum wage, in the wages of such low-paid categories as service personnel, including those in education and health care, and in pensions. Moderate changes in income taxes worked in the same direction. And in the 1970s the Soviet government instituted a program of direct grants to supplement the income of the most poorly provided families.

Despite grumbling and sporadic outbursts of discontent, in neither the Soviet Union nor the United States did consumer dissatisfaction assume a threatening guise in the postwar period, whether directed toward insufficiency in the level of consumption or toward inequity in the pattern of distribution. Inequality persisted in the United States but was mitigated by general, and generally rising, standards of consumer welfare. And in the Soviet Union the low level of consumption was mitigated by steady if unspectacular improvements and by the trend toward more equal sharing of the smaller pie. Moreover, in both countries those most disadvantaged by consumption levels or consumption policies were precisely those least able to affect public policy.

INTERNATIONAL ECONOMIC RIVALRY

The areas of rivalry already discussed relate to the internal economic strength and arrangements of the U.S. and USSR. But both countries are able to project their economic power abroad to forward national objectives; reciprocally, each is subject to economic influences from world economic trends and from individual states or groups of states. This international side of American–Soviet economic rivalry is the subject of the following sections, which consider in turn the role of the United States and the Soviet Union in world economic affairs; their capabilities of using economic power to buttress foreign policy, especially in the struggle over the future of Europe; their programs of assistance to less-developed countries; and their bilateral trade, more generally East–West trade.

The United States emerged in 1945 in such a strong economic position that for many years it was able to dominate international economic affairs outside the Communist sphere. This preponderance was gained at the expense of capitalist rivals rather than of the Soviet Union, which also was enabled by the war to expand modestly its economic influence abroad, mainly in Eastern Europe. U.S. trade, capital, and economic influence penetrated freely into areas formerly oriented on the weakened states of Western Europe and Japan, and into these advanced countries as well. The U.S. dollar reigned supreme.

America's role in the first postwar decade depended greatly on the fact that the U.S. was the single large, undamaged storehouse upon which the rest of the world could draw, or hope to draw, for postwar reconstruction and development. Consequently, Washington was in a position to use its economic assets to promote its foreign policy objectives. These included the stabilization of the capitalist order and the prevention of anticapitalist shifts, the creation of alliances linking non-Communist countries with the United States under U.S. leadership, and the concomitant spread of American influence through both the industrially developed and underdeveloped countries.

In contrast, the Soviet Union was weaker economically at the end of the war than at the beginning in absolute terms (if not relative to other war-damaged countries), and especially in comparison to the United States. Specifically, the USSR was in no position to use economic assistance as a means of consolidating its position in states coming under Soviet influence, still less to use economic reprisals against adversaries. Russia was itself in need of aid. This it sought from the U.S., without success, and had to be content with whatever it could extract from those ex-enemy and other states in regions of Soviet military preponderance.

Economic Underpinning of U.S.–USSR Policies in Europe

The disparity in U.S.–USSR economic capabilities had worldwide ramifications, but nowhere made itself felt more forcefully than in Europe. As armies from the East and West approached their meeting on the Elbe, the countries liberated or occupied were subject to extremely divergent policies. American authorities sought to restore the vitality of a war-shaken social order, and to thwart radicalizing tendencies which were present wherever resistance movements—in which Communists played a large role—were prominent. Everywhere in Europe the U.S. favored those groups which sought a restoration of the status quo ante Naziism, even where such groups were tainted by complicity with the fascist "New Order."

Soviet policy went in an almost diametrically opposed direction, toward a basic overturn of the old social order and a leading role for Communists. It favored a thorough purge not only of officials connected with the National Socialist, Fascist, and similar parties, but of those who had collaborated with them.

Policies toward Germany showed the divergence of aims. American authorities had no stomach for a German denazification so comprehensive as to undermine the old ruling class. And the U.S. needed no transfer of wealth from Germany, and soon put a stop to West German reparations to the East. U.S. officials did not want German deprivations to create fertile ground for radical political movements, nor German deliveries to aid recovery in the Soviet Union and other countries falling under Communist control. In contrast, Russia wanted a great deal from Germany and Germany's wartime allies, hoping to use deliveries to aid Soviet reconstruction. In Russia, sympathy for German woes was not strongly felt, to put it mildly, not only because Russians had suffered greatly at German hands but also because defeated Germany at its lowest point lived much better than victorious Russia. In the areas of Soviet domination there were few inhibitions on denazification. This was not motivated primarily by an abstract pursuit of justice: rather, it appealed to popular sentiments among the peoples most victimized by Nazi rule at the same time that it contributed to the discrediting and uprooting of an old ruling class.

If Germany was a special case, it illustrated the cleavage between Soviet and American objectives regarding Europe as a whole. No less a disparity existed in the means available for the realization of these divergent objectives. The United States could rely on the cooperation of entrenched local elites. The Soviet Union had to get rid of these in order to lodge securely in place pro-Soviet governments of Marxist-Leninist persuasion. The USSR had a parsimony of economic means to facilitate the achievement of ambitious goals; the United States had a wealth of such means to accomplish rather modest objectives. The USSR thus relied, and had to rely, on a good measure of force and compulsion to gain its ends; for the U.S., economic means provided a substitute.

The outstanding demonstration of American use of economic capabilities to promote U.S. objectives in Europe occurred in the late 1940s and early 1950s with the Marshall Plan, for which there was no Soviet analogue. Large-scale U.S. resources, eventually totaling over $12 billion, were transferred in 1948–1951 to cooperating European countries, mostly on a grant rather than credit basis, so as to restore a traditionally high level of economic activity. Sixteen states received aid under this plan, including all thirteen of those joining with the U.S. and Canada to form the North Atlantic alliance, plus three neutrals. Though billed as the "European Recovery Program," the Marshall Plan was a recovery plan for capitalist Europe, not Europe as a whole. Geographically, it was confined to Western Europe, except that Greece and Turkey also participated, as they subsequently did in NATO.

The political thrust was unconcealed: it was not so much anti-Soviet as anti-Communist. To be sure, the USSR accepted an invitation to attend a conference of foreign ministers considering the initial U.S.

proposal, but soon withdrew, insisting that aid should be administered by recipient countries without U.S. intrusion. In any case, it is doubtful that the U.S. government, particularly the Congress, was actually prepared to aid the USSR and other Communist-controlled countries. Had participation of the latter come to pass, however, the United States would have gained considerable leverage over the economic policies of these states. For it turned out that the aid program was based on the readiness of the recipient states to cooperate with U.S. plans for Europe and to accept U.S. supervision not only over the use made of the assistance but also over their economic policies in general.

The absence of the USSR and like-minded states certainly removed a complication to the program's avowed anticommunist orientation, which stemmed from fears in Washington and other capitals that radical changes might ensue unless the private enterprise system regained momentum. But the absence of Russia and Eastern European states meant that there would be no preference for wartime allies in postwar rebuilding, or, indeed, for the countries which had suffered the most from wartime destruction. As a result the ex-Axis states of (West) Germany and Italy were major recipients, as well as countries suffering relatively little physical destruction in the war.

Given its real objective, not "European" recovery but restoration of capitalist health in Europe, the Marshall Plan proved outstandingly successful. It contributed to the economic recuperation of the participating nations, and thereby to the solidification of their socioeconomic institutions. It weakened the appeal of communism and other leftist tendencies in these countries, where attempts at obstruction were smothered. And it opened wide the door to the entry and consolidation of American economic influence, which was to continue to grow as U.S. investments expanded long after grants-in-aid had stopped.

In contrast, the firming of Soviet influence and Communist power in Eastern Europe was not eased by any comparable aid transfers from the USSR. On the contrary, this was achieved in spite of involuntary "aid" transfers from Eastern Europe to the Soviet Union. The USSR had no largesse to distribute, and made its will effective by crude and stern methods quite different from those that the United States could use.

Economic Assistance to Less-Developed Countries

Economic aid to the more or less developed European nations could be a relatively short-term affair, because its aim was recuperation rather than expansion of attained levels of production. In contrast, assistance to underdeveloped countries in Asia, Africa, and Latin America had to be a long-term proposition if it was to be meaningful in aiding countries to escape from backwardness. It became a permanent element first in American and later in Soviet efforts to advance foreign policy objectives. (Both countries also provided large amounts of military assistance to such countries under programs discussed elsewhere.)

American economic aid of this kind began in 1949 with Truman's "Point Four" program, which emphasized technical aid, but subsequently expanded to a much larger scale in terms of funds allocated, variety of programs, and aims sought. Over the period ending in 1973 the U.S. spent about $60 billion in assisting non-European LDCs (Less-Developed Countries), two-thirds in grants and one-third in loans. On a per capita basis Israel has been the favored recipient, along with Taiwan, South Vietnam, and South Korea. The last two also appear, along with Pakistan, at the head of the list arranged in terms of absolute sums, but India was the recipient of the greatest amount, $7.5 billion.[19]

Soviet assistance to countries outside Europe has involved a shorter list of recipients and much smaller magnitudes, even including aid to Communist-led states as well as non-Communist. Assistance to the latter began only in 1954–1955, well after the U.S. was in the field. A total of about $20 billion, almost all credits rather than grants, has been authorized over the postwar years. More than $11 billion of this economic assistance was directed to Communist-led countries outside Europe; the remaining $9 billion involved non-Communist states, usually those pursuing policies of nonalignment and frequently accepting aid from both East and West.

These amounts represent authorizations, as do the U.S. figures cited above, but in the Soviet case there is a substantial difference be-

---

[19] Data extracted from *U.S. Overseas Loans and Grants, July 1, 1945–June 30, 1973* (Washington, D.C.: Agency for International Development, 1974). These figures are for non-European countries only; they exclude Spain, Yugoslavia, Greece, and Turkey, which AID includes in the LDC totals.

tween aid authorized and aid delivered. Thus, of the $9 billion in commitments to non-Communist states the estimated deliveries total not much more than $4 billion. Probably deliveries to Communist LDCs were much closer to authorizations. All of the assistance was "tied" economically to Soviet sources of supply, as most American assistance came to be tied to U.S. suppliers. Moreover, as a result of the preponderance of loans in the Soviet aid totals (over 95 percent), repayments have reduced the net cost to the USSR of foreign assistance to a much greater extent than in the U.S. program, where nonreimbursable grants have predominated. The net outflow under the Soviet $9 billion program for non-Communist LDCs is thus estimated to be in the neighborhood of $2.5 billion.[20] Repayments have probably reduced Soviet costs to a still greater degree in programs to help other Communist-ruled countries: Marxist-Leninist states have generally been the incarnation of staid bankers' dreams, clients who pay their debts and pay them on time!

Under the Soviet as under the U.S. aid programs, India has received more than any other non-Communist country in absolute terms (though not on a per capita basis), followed by Egypt, Iran, Iraq, and Pakistan. Among Communist recipients, Cuba heads the list, followed by North Vietnam and the Mongolian People's Republic.

In popular conception, aid transfers from advanced states are supposed to bring about development in industrially and agriculturally backward countries, and aid givers do little to disabuse supporters of this conception. But much American and Soviet economic aid is arranged with other purposes in mind. The U.S. and USSR both have given economic support to allied or comradely states engaged in military or paramilitary struggles against internal or neighboring adver-

---

[20] There appears to be no justification for the common U.S. practice of excluding Soviet aid to North Korea, Cuba, etc., from estimates of aid to less-developed countries, particularly because U.S. aid to such allies as South Korea, South Vietnam, etc., is always included in American figures. The USSR, unlike the U.S., publishes little hard data on foreign aid. The estimates are more solid for the aid flow to non-Communist countries, which make data public, than for the flow to Communist states. Estimates from the Department of State, "Communist States and Developing Countries: Aid and Trade in 1973" (Washington, D.C.: October 10, 1974); Leo Tansky, "Soviet Foreign Aid: Scope, Direction, and Trends," in *Soviet Economic Prospects for the Seventies*, pp. 775–76; and George S. Carnett and Morris H. Crawford, "The Scope and Distribution of Soviet Economic Aid," Joint Economic Committee, U.S. Congress, *Dimensions of Soviet Economic Power* (Washington, D.C.: Government Printing Office 1962), pp. 471–74.

saries. Such "Security Supporting Assistance" bulked large, for example, in U.S. grants to Taiwan, South Vietnam, South Korea, and other Asian countries. On the Soviet side, similar assistance, though not labeled as such, went to embattled Communist régimes in North Vietnam, North Korea, and Cuba.

Another form of economic aid having little to do with development was also present in the U.S. programs, but not in the Soviet, in transfers of surplus food stocks. These amounted to over one-fourth of the U.S. total of aid to less-developed countries. Such supplies alleviated pressing needs in countries temporarily or habitually unable to feed their populations; most aid to India fell in this category. But such commodity aid carried little impetus for speeding development. It was lavish because the United States found this a useful way of disposing of agricultural commodities that it could not sell advantageously; this kind of aid dwindled as the surpluses disappeared. Aid by means of transfer of surplus agricultural products, called the PL–480 program, is an extreme example of a more general phenomenon in both American and Soviet aid programs, namely, the goods and services transferred are frequently not those that receiving nations most need, but those easiest for the aid givers to relinquish.

The contributions of aid programs to realization of American and Soviet foreign policy aims were mixed, and in the decade 1965–1975 policy-makers in both countries displayed much less enthusiasm for foreign aid than they had in the preceding decade. To the extent that economic development was the goal, the results were disappointing. There were successes here and there, but neither of the powers was willing to allocate resources on the scale necessary to substantially narrow the gap in productive capabilities between "Third World" and advanced states. And neither of the aid givers could be satisfied with the domestic efforts (or lack of efforts) of recipient countries to promote development, though U.S. and Soviet reasons for dissatisfaction were rather different. Moreover, even if Soviet and American leaders could dismiss development as a goal, they could not always be sanguine about the effects of their aid in solidifying the position of the régimes they favored, in assuring the international orientation they sought on the part of the aided countries, or even in guaranteeing their own influence within these states.

There were bitter disappointments for each. For the United States the worst came with the collapse of pro-American régimes in the three Indochinese states, despite huge expenditures to support them.

Even in countries where U.S. military aid and military participation was a less crucial factor, there were glaring failures of the U.S. to achieve more than minimal goals. Thus, U.S. aid to India was large, and far exceeded that of the USSR, but Indian relations with the U.S. deteriorated—at least until Indira Gandhi's fall—as those with the USSR improved.

Moscow also had its full share of such disappointments. A major program of developmental assistance to China did not prevent the drift of the Chinese People's Republic into a more and more virulent anti-Soviet stance. In the late 1950s and early 1960s the USSR supplied much economic as well as military aid to Indonesia, but the overthrow of the Sukarno régime in 1965 left the USSR without influence over the successor government and in possession only of a bag of IOUs. Rather lavish material backing of Egypt did not prevent recurrent Soviet–Egyptian conflict and an eventual turn of the Sadat government from a pro-Soviet to a pro-American orientation.

Had these failures been the whole story, however, they would have resulted in a renunciation rather than a reduction of foreign aid by the U.S. and USSR. There were successes as well. American grants helped solidify the sometimes shaky hold on power of governments in the Philippines, Thailand, and South Korea, and contributed to economic advances on Taiwan which enabled an anticommunist government to retain possession of a Chinese base. For the USSR, also, foreign aid facilitated Soviet objectives in various countries and areas. Notably, it allowed the USSR a means of entry into Middle Eastern and South Asian affairs that it had previously lacked. Like the U.S., the USSR did not place all its eggs in one basket: if Egypt soured, there was a chance with Syria and Iraq; a setback in Ghana could be compensated by a gain in Nigeria. Foreign aid also allowed the Soviet Union to present itself to less-developed countries, at least on a limited scale, as a material and not merely ideological alternative to "imperialism."

Economic Sanctions Against Adversaries

The discussion has centered on the rival use of foreign economic assistance to promote American and Soviet world objectives. But economic capabilities also give the power to deter or penalize wayward or hostile states. An economically powerful country can put pressure on weaker nations by use of mild sanctions, such as refusal of assistance, or stronger sanctions, such as interruption of normal trade rela-

tions; it may be able to compel the support of other countries in puni-
tive measures. American capabilities to apply economic sanctions
have been incomparably greater than those of the USSR, not merely
because the U.S. is stronger economically but because it plays a big-
ger role in international economic affairs.

It was against the Soviet Union that the United States made its first
postwar use of economic sanctions. Even before the "cold war" became intense, Washington saw to it that Moscow's requests for reconstruction credits were misplaced or rejected. This was followed in
1947 by institution of restrictions on American exports to the USSR,
and these were made more severe in succeeding years, notably in
1951. A ban on the sale of military supplies would not have seriously
inconvenienced the Russians, but U.S. restrictions applied to a very
broadly defined category of "strategic goods," export of which to the
USSR and Eastern Europe was either completely forbidden or subject to severe quantitative limitations. The definition of such goods
embraced almost all of the machinery and materials that the Kremlin
leaders hoped to obtain abroad to rebuild and expand their economy.
The Soviet Union was forced not merely to do without imports of
needed equipment but, because Eastern Europe was also included in
the ban, to supply, insofar as it could, such goods to its allies.

Furthermore, Washington was in a position to close off not only the
American market for Soviet and other Communist purchasers but
Western European and Japanese sources of supply as well, a restriction that became increasingly important as these countries recovered
from the war. It was U.S. economic power that made this possible,
because Washington linked receipt of Marshall Plan aid and similar
benefits with adoption of U.S.-approved controls on deliveries to the
Eastern countries. In addition, the United States handicapped the
Soviet Union as an exporter to the U.S. by withdrawing in 1951 the
so-called "Most Favored Nation" tariff treatment, i.e., the U.S.
levied above-normal tariffs on Soviet and Eastern European goods.
But the U.S. restrictions on imports from the USSR and its allies
were far less important than the restrictions on exports.

Although Soviet spokesmen regularly denounced the trade restrictions, they simultaneously claimed that such measures could not
seriously affect their economic programs. But this was simply an
application of the maxim, "faire bonne mine à mauvais jeu." Certainly
Washington policy-makers were to be disappointed insofar as they
hoped to prevent Soviet recovery and expansion by keeping East–

West trade to very low levels. Nevertheless, the U.S.-promoted closing of industrial nations' markets to Soviet purchases complicated and
slowed USSR economic advances, especially in the first postwar decade or so. It is still not clear, however, whether the Western boycott
had its greatest impact in slowing USSR military development or in
retarding improvement in the standard of living in the Soviet Union
and other Communist states. For obvious reasons, the former was advertised as the U.S. goal, but Washington planners could regard the
measures as successful even if the latter were the result.

After the mid-1950s the effectiveness of sanctions declined, largely
because the United States no longer gave aid to Western Europe and
Japan and therefore had a diminished capability of controlling their
trade policies. Most of these countries had a greater dependence on
foreign trade than did America, and specifically a greater interest in
buying from and selling to Russia. They brought about a relaxation of
the jointly agreed restrictions on exports to the East.[21] This made
possible a considerable expansion of Soviet trade with Western
Europe and Japan, much of it financed by credits to the USSR,
vigorously opposed by Washington. Although the embargos and controls still exist, they no longer play a major role in blocking East–West
trade in general. U.S. national restrictions, always more exclusionary
than those jointly agreed with Western Europe and Japan, continue
to be used to prevent sales to the USSR of American goods embodying advanced technology.

Outside Europe the United States moved beyond selective restrictions to impose an almost complete ban on transactions with China,
North Korea, and North Vietnam, and later with Cuba. This boycott
was relevant to the USSR to the extent that the latter was interested
in the consolidation of Communist power in additional areas, and all
of these régimes had to depend on the Soviet economy for supplies
for varying periods of time. In none of the cases did the American embargo prevent perpetuation of Communist control. Economic warfare
against Cuba was viewed in Washington as more promising of success
than measures against the others because of the pre-1959 dependence
of Cuba on the U.S., unique among countries coming under Communist control, as a source of imports and a market for exports. But the

---

[21] A Coordinating Committee (Cocom) has existed since 1950 to police embargoes
and restrictions on exports to Communist-led countries. All of the NATO states except
Iceland are represented, plus Japan.

embargo failed to dislodge Castro despite the difficulties it caused Cuba. Soviet economic aid was crucial: in fact, Cuba was the only Communist state in which Soviet economic aid, as distinct from military aid, was of a magnitude to spell the difference between collapse and survival.

Thus, use of economic sanctions against Communist régimes showed that the U.S. could complicate but not terminate their existence. And American capabilities of inflicting damage lessened as time went on, partly because of a declining ability to bring about a united front of the advanced capitalist nations and partly because of increasing Soviet capacity to bail out comrades in difficulty. But the United States had more success in and better prospects of deterring a Marxist drift in capitalist countries characterized by private enterprise and political pluralism. Chile was the most notable of many examples. By a combination of economic pressure from outside the country and economic support to anti-Allende forces within, the United States was able to destabilize the leftist government sufficiently to pave the way for a rightist military coup d'état which ended, temporarily at least, a threat to the capitalist order by liquidating pluralist democracy. While there were some negative repercussions that might discourage frequent repetition elsewhere of the tactics used, the affair confirmed the efficacy of U.S. sanctions to block attempts at a peaceful transition to a socialist order.

A treatment of Soviet capabilities for use of economic sanctions to promote international goals can be very brief. The USSR, unlike the U.S., had few resources for this kind of economic warfare. The situation had been clear enough in bilateral relations, where the U.S. could seek to deflect Soviet policy by economic reprisals but the USSR could not even hope to reverse the roles. It was significant that even in the 1970s it was the U.S. rather than the USSR which sought to impose a political price for resumption of more or less normal trade relations. Nor was the Soviet Union in a much better position to use economic sanctions against other advanced and not-so-advanced capitalist countries if they followed courses of action inimical to Soviet interests.

It was only in relations with other Communist-ruled countries, almost all of which were less industrially developed than the USSR, that Soviet leaders had any capabilities of employing aid and trade restrictions to penalize them for policy divergences. Such efforts were employed against Yugoslavia in the late 1940s and again in the 1950s, and against Albania and China from the 1960s on. The USSR and its Cominform partners cut trade relations with Yugoslavia to a minimum after Yugoslavia's expulsion from the Cominform in 1948, and later, following a thaw and refreeze, suspended agreements for development assistance. But the Yugoslavs found other sources of supply and of markets for sale in Western countries, and accepted American economic and military aid. On neither occasion did the pressure result in a change of Yugoslavia's orientation.

As Soviet–Chinese relations deteriorated in the late 1950s, the Khrushchev leadership suspended economic assistance and withdrew technicians in 1960–1961. Because the technicians took home with them plans and blueprints for building or rebuilding a large number of industrial enterprises, some half-completed, the Chinese suffered a serious setback. Their position was worse than that of the Yugoslavs because neither the U.S. nor any other major advanced country provided an alternative source of supply at that time. Soviet–Chinese trade also fell off after 1960, but this was probably a reflection of the cutoff of aid rather than of specific trade restrictions as such. In any case, if the Kremlin authorities thought that their economic pressure would force a change of Peking's ideological and political stance, they were doomed to sore disappointment.

Thus, where the Soviet leadership tried to deploy economic power against recalcitrant Communist states it found itself repeating the American experience: it could inflict some damage but could not overturn adversary governments or deflect their policies into acceptable channels. And outside the Communist sphere the Soviet capabilities were still less. Anticommunist or anti-Soviet shifts found the USSR unable to respond with economic pressure. Thus, when Sukarno was overthrown in 1965 in Indonesia and the country made a dramatic change of course, USSR policy-makers had little recourse except to swallow the bitter pill and attempt to preserve whatever assets remained. They knew that the United States was already waiting in the wings, ready, willing, and able to lavish support on a country saved from pro-Communist rule.

Bilateral Trade and Soviet–American Economic Competition

International trade in general expanded after World War II *pari passu* with economic recovery; this trend characterized the foreign trade of both the capitalist "West" and the socialist "East." But East–West trade followed a different route, sliding down until it bottomed out in the early 1950s. Subsequent to the Korean War this trade began an upward climb with an increased tempo in the 1960s and particularly in the 1970s. Until these last years, however, the United States continued to buy little from and sell little to the Soviet Union, whose major Western trade partners were Japan, West Germany, the United Kingdom, Italy, and France, plus—a rather special case— Finland. All of these latter countries had a greater interest in imports from the USSR, because of their smaller domestic resources, than did the United States; and all were more dependent than the U.S. on foreign trade in general, because their home markets were not as large. Consequently, Soviet trade with these countries assumed a volume that made it important for both sides.

As Soviet–American relations became more civil, and intermittently amicable, Washington officials came to agree with their Moscow counterparts that expansion of Soviet–American commerce was desirable. U.S.–USSR trade turnover shot up markedly in the early 1970s from what were admittedly abnormally low levels; this resulted mostly from an increase in Soviet purchases, because Soviet exports to the U.S. increased only modestly. This enlivenment of commerce, while reflecting less hostile political relations, did not mean any diminution, let alone a cessation, of the economic rivalry between the two countries. American policy shifted from discouragement to tolerance and fitful encouragement of trade with the USSR for two reasons. First, U.S. policy-makers sought to improve the functioning of the economy and the world economic position of the U.S. in a period when the economy was buffeted by a variety of negative forces, including strong pressure from America's competitors in Western Europe and Asia. Second, U.S. officials, no longer counting on efforts to isolate the USSR, looked to the possibility that an increased Soviet dependence on the American market would give the U.S. political leverage; that is, they counted on Soviet concern about jeopardizing a continued flow of goods to discourage the Kremlin's adoption of policies adverse to American interests.

Soviet policy on trade with the United States required no such shift of position, because the USSR had sought throughout the postwar period to spur bilateral trade. No doubt Soviet planners eyed American sources of supply with heightened interest, of course, after traditional methods of increasing production proved insufficient to maintain fast growth rates. In any case, while Soviet leaders always referred to the mutual advantages of increased U.S.–USSR trade, they made it clear that they expected that Soviet utilization of imports embodying advanced technology would speed the country's economic development and thereby assist it in eventually overtaking the United States economically.

Of course, Soviet–American trade, like trade in general, involves exchanges that are rated equal in the marketplace, the standard of measure internationally being found in "world market prices."

Classical economics teaches that both countries may be better off as a result of such exchanges than in their absence. And this is no less true if the trading requires credit extended on prevailing terms of payment. "Friendly sellers" extend credit to purchasers at home or abroad not out of the goodness of their hearts but because they find it advantageous to make sales that could not otherwise be consummated, and to be paid "extra" for their willingness to postpone reimbursement.

There is, however, a characteristic of American–Soviet trade to which the market is oblivious; it inheres in the somewhat different role played by international transactions in the two economies. Individual exporters and importers in the U.S. are principally interested in making profits. Individual deals are not planned as part of any overall national program. Trade with the USSR is subject, to be sure, to various regulations which embody considerations of national policy. But these restrictions merely fix certain limits within which businesses are free to act, and they do not replace private calculations of advantages by calculations of national welfare. As in Bernard de Mandeville's *Fable of the Bees,* the governing assumption of American policy is that individuals seeking none-too-lofty ends contribute unwittingly to the general good.

No such assumption pervades Soviet trading; Soviet planners do not believe in the innocent goodness of buzzing bees. Each transaction is evaluated in terms of its contribution to overall Soviet goals, and above all to the rapid growth of the Soviet economy. Grain purchases apart, USSR policy-makers have been particularly anxious to acquire industrial machinery, plants and equipment, and other advanced products from the technologically superior U.S. to spur the productivity of Soviet industry and agriculture.

Even with the spurt of trade in the 1970s, over $1 billion in 1973 and 1975, the impact of this U.S.–USSR trade must be kept in proportion. In relation to GNP, foreign trade as a whole constitutes in both countries only a small percentage—though more in the U.S.

than in the USSR—and in neither country does trade with the other amount to more than 1 to 2 percent of total foreign trade. This conclusion requires qualification, however. No doubt the possibility exists for a greater expansion of Soviet trade with the United States (particularly of imports, which already far outweigh exports) than is true of Soviet trade with Western Europe or Japan, which has been less hindered by political obstacles. Moreover, trade totals may obscure the significance of specific transactions for individual sectors of the economy, whether in the USSR or the United States.

Although the notion that trade will promote at least limited political dependence has surfaced in the United States rather than in Russia, interdependence in trade obviously cuts both ways. If the Soviet stake in maintenance of access to the American market becomes important enough to influence the Kremlin's domestic or foreign policies, there is almost certain to be a parallel interest in the United States, if not directly on the part of the government then indirectly on the part of various enterprises and economic groups. Such "special interests" have a more open field of operation in American than in Soviet political life, and therefore a greater chance of bending national policy to serve their particular needs. Thus, "farmer power" (more precisely, the power of grain farmers) has already shown its capability of deflecting U.S. administrations away from using embargos on grain exports to the USSR as an instrument for effectuating Washington's policies toward Moscow.

All told, the prospect that increased bilateral trade will basically alter Soviet–American rivalry is distant and chancy. History offers a good many examples against the proposition that nations which trade together stay together. Equally chancy are the prospects that either of the powers will gain sufficient leverage from the other's trade dependence to exert more than marginal influence on the rival's behavior.

In addition to those elements of international economic affairs that have been mentioned, there are a host of others that are certain to influence Soviet–American economic competition. Trends in prices of goods traded on international markets, to cite one example, are likely to have a different impact on the two countries, partly because, as noted, the U.S. is more dependent on international trade than the USSR (though neither is highly dependent), and partly because the two countries have a different mix of primary and manufactured goods in their imports and exports. Zooming prices of petroleum products thus discommoded the U.S. much more than the USSR; in fact, the latter benefited to a degree. Or, in a quite different area, changes in the climate of acceptance for foreign investment and in the conditions under which multinational corporations operate obviously have a differential impact on the economic positions of the U.S. and USSR. Even phenomena of nature, like a drought in Africa or in India, present different problems and opportunities to a large food exporter such as the U.S. than to a USSR which imports more foodstuffs than it exports.

Promoting Rival Economic Models

The discussion so far has centered on the "material" side of U.S.–USSR economic rivalry. There is, however, a different kind of rivalry which involves the competition of economic "models," of the version of socialism represented in Soviet institutions and of the version of capitalism represented in the United States.

This competitive promotion of divergent social models constitutes merely one area of a wide-ranging ideological competition touched on later in this work. Although the contest pits capitalism against socialism as "ideal types," i.e., rival utopias, it is not divorced from the here and now of the U.S. and USSR economies. The accomplishment and failures of these latter provide the data to be exploited or explained away by true believers and inveterate adversaries, East and West. In promoting its own model as worthy of respect and imitation, each side depicts defects and failings as mere specks on a picture of bright todays and brighter tomorrows. Similarly, in disparaging the rival model, each side relies heavily on the ills and iniquities of the existing economic system, Soviet in the one case, American in the other.

The discrepancy between the real and the ideal has been particularly painful for the advocates of socialism, because socialism was a utopia before it became a reality, whereas capitalism was a reality before a utopian capitalism was invented. The fact that the first Communist accession to power occurred in one of the most backward of the industrial states dealt an initially severe blow to visions of socialism as a society to bring abundance to the masses. Had consumption risen dramatically despite this untoward choice of birthplace, socialism might have regained glamor. But over the decades progress in raising living standards was episodic and slow, partly because of unfavorable developments over which Russia had little control, partly because of choices imposing many sacrifices and much regimentation on the population. In the mid-1930s Stalin and his associates claimed that in Russia a socialist society had been built "in the main." Perhaps the system could be called socialism, but it was not the socialism dreamed of by generations of European workers and intellectuals imbued with Marx's vision.

If, however, socialism Soviet-style could not be associated with abundance, it was associated in the 1930s with a dynamism in economic growth that was in sharp contrast to the capitalist stagnation of the time. Moreover, Russia's capacity to emerge victorious from a trying war with Germany, and to recover from the onslaught not only without aid from wartime allies but against their pressure, testified to the strength of the Soviet system. The USSR's subsequent success in narrowing its economic lag behind the leading capitalist countries and in functioning as a world power softened the image of Soviet backwardness.

Nevertheless, the pull of affluence worked in favor of the United States and against the Soviet Union, and therefore, to the extent that the former symbolized capitalism and the latter socialism, in favor of the American model rather than the Soviet. Maintenance of relatively steady growth by the U.S. and maintenance of technological supremacy in the postwar years reinforced this attraction. Almost all of the innovations characterizing postwar life were developed first in the U.S. and only gradually spread to the other industrial nations, sometimes last to Russia: use of nuclear energy, automation, electronic devices, transistors, computers, television, xerography, jet propulsion.

Affluence and technological advancement allowed the economic model represented by the United States to hold its grip particularly in the developed countries, where the socialist model typified by the USSR made no striking gains. For many underdeveloped countries, however, the contest of rival models had a different meaning. American power and wealth exerted their pull in this area also, as illustrated, for example, by the migration of skilled people opting for the easier life in America.[22] But for the nations they left behind, the So-

---

[22] Preferences embodied in American immigration policy are very relevant to the subject of U.S.–Soviet rivalry. One preference goes to immigrants with advanced training, and serves to increase U.S. economic competitivity by transferring the burden of training specialists to other developed and less-developed countries. A second preference has been accorded persons fleeing Communist-ruled countries, especially Hungary, Cuba, and Vietnam, and serves to bolster the ranks of professional anticommunist cadres in the United States as well as to bring in persons with needed economic skills.

viet model provided a more relevant example than the American of a country lifting itself by its own bootstraps from backwardness to industrial power within a brief span of time. The much higher American living standard was less relevant for countries far below even Soviet standards. And such countries were constantly reminded of their powerlessness by the presence within their borders of American or other foreign capitalist enterprises (but not Russian) which often controlled important sectors of their economies.

For important population groups and for some modernizing elites, in many underdeveloped countries socialism gained a favorable image that it had lost or never acquired in the advanced countries. It suggested a way to economic progress and independence by means of indigenous control of industry and commerce, of mining and agriculture. Certainly this attraction to the socialist model implied no inclination to install institutions and practices copied from those of the Soviet Union. Third World socialism frequently bore little resemblance to the "scientific socialism" honored in Moscow; usually it alloted no role to an indigenous Communist party. In fact, Moscow ideologists sometimes bemoaned the popularity of "socialism" in Africa and Asia because the *ersatz* was often confused with the *echt* socialism of which the USSR considered itself guardian. Still, a common characteristic of the pro-socialist régimes in less-developed countries was opposition to imperialism and rejection of capitalism; another was a striving to bring economic activities under national control by squeezing out foreign ownership; a third was preference for the state sector over the private sectors of the economy. Such tendencies, however inconsistently expressed, were more in consonance with the Soviet economic model than with the American.

A QUARTER-CENTURY OF ECONOMIC RIVALRY

The future prospects of U.S.–USSR economic rivalry are reserved for discussion in a later chapter. Here it is only necessary to note that the USSR has made significant gains over the postwar decades in improving its economic position relative to that of the United States. This has narrowed the gap in the productive capabilities of the two economies and in the rivals' capabilities of exerting economic influence abroad. But the gap, though smaller, remains substantial. It is reflected in gross economic power and in production levels and productivity of industry and agriculture; it remains particularly large in consumption. The latter in turn has militated against efforts to invest the model of Soviet-style socialism with the drawing power that American-style capitalism enjoys (especially in developed countries, less so in the underdeveloped) as a result of relative U.S. affluence.

If early Soviet hopes, and early American apprehensions, that the USSR would soon overtake the U.S. economically were dissipated, the postwar trend has nevertheless witnessed a change favoring the Soviet Union in the correlation of economic strength.

4

RIVAL POLITICAL ORDERS

A QUESTION raised earlier has particular pertinence to the subject of this chapter. Can political systems like the Soviet and American be considered as rivals? Clearly they fall into a category in which mutuality of response is at a very low level; that is, organizational patterns and trends of change in each country are basically autonomous. Each has its distinct pattern of structuring relationships between authorities and citizens, of selecting and changing leaders, of organizing such functions as rule making in policy-making bodies, including legislatures, administering governmental and other operations, and settlement of disputes, to name only a few of those functions inherent in both orders.

Still, there is a competitive element. The effectiveness of the Soviet and American political institutions in satisfying popular needs and aspirations, in enlisting support and deflecting opposition, in adapting policies and structures to meet external challenges and opportunities—all this is a crucial element in the overall rivalry of the two states. A specific example may make clear the kind of rivalry that is present. The highest political leaders of the U.S. and USSR, the president and the general secretary of the Soviet Communist party, are selected in unlike ways, represent different "constituencies," are vested with dissimilar authority, leave office by divergent routes. In neither nation is the selection, functioning, and changing of the supreme leader much influenced by the leadership practices of the rival. Yet the importance of these dissimilar offices, and of their changing occupants, on the fate of the two countries, on national achievements and failures, and particularly on the international standing of the respective states, is not likely to be disputed.

Discussion of this political rivalry begins with a consideration of pluralism and monolithism, diversity and unity, in Soviet and American theory and practice of politics. This is followed by an examination of the "class" basis of the two systems, of the extent to which the American can be described as "bourgeois" and the Soviet as "proletarian." The previously mentioned subject of political leadership is then taken up, the appointment and replacement of the officials vested with varying amounts and kinds of authority. A subsequent section treats the relationship between régime and population, the governors and the governed. This discussion involves not only a look at citizen participation in political processes but also at nonparticipation and opposition to the ruling system. Finally, the roles of the American and Soviet political systems as models for other countries is examined in an effort to assess efforts of the rival elites to gain support for or encourage emulation of their particular order.

UNITY AND DIVERSITY IN AMERICAN AND SOVIET POLITICS

Even a casual observer is struck by the difference between the pluralism institutionalized in American political life and the monolithism promoted in the Soviet Union. The former is exemplified by the existence of two major political parties contesting elections and alternating in control of the White House and the bicameral Congress; the latter by the existence of only one party whose continued dominance is never threatened in any of the periodic elections. But it is misleading to apply the same term, *party*, to the Communist organization in the USSR and the Republican and Democratic organizations in the United States. The Communist party of the Soviet Union (CPSU) is a ruling party in a sense that is not true of either U.S. organization, even if the Republicans or Democrats happen to control both the presidency and the two houses of Congress. The Soviet party is heavily involved in directing national and local affairs; for this purpose it requires a large, permanently functioning bureaucracy. The latter supervises the parallel but even larger governmental bureaucracy and other nongovernmental organizations, some of which, like the trade unions, perform quasi-governmental functions. In contrast, the U.S. parties are loose organizations held together (if at all) principally as vehicles for winning elections: they lapse into near somnolence between these contests. Basically, aspirants for office use the party as the means of gaining power, but a party in the U.S. has no way of "using" adherents in office to promote party objectives. Party machinery, ramshackle at best, becomes a mere skeleton between elections, and the party as such is not in any way involved in direction of national or local affairs.

These differences are linked to differences in the relationship of Soviet and American parties to members or adherents. It is misguided to speak of "membership" in either the Republican or Democratic party as a whole, though there are a few local party clubs with membership rosters. Most party adherents are not enrolled in any organization, seldom if ever attend any party meeting, almost never pay any dues, and have no party duties or privileges. Their role is limited to a declaration of party affiliation in registration for voting and to voting for party candidates in periodic elections. At the national level there are no party channels by which they can determine the policies of officeholders elected on party tickets.

In contrast, party membership is meaningful in the Soviet Union, even though the electorate is much larger than the 15-odd million adults enrolled in the single party. CPSU members are selected with some care, must attend meetings and pay dues, are given various party assignments absorbing a good deal of free time, and are subject to party discipline affecting their personal life and wage-earning work as well as their behavior in party contexts. Rewards and privileges gained through party membership, and the sanctions which the party can impose, serve as the most important means of making this party discipline effective. Almost all of the important positions in the society involving leadership or administrative responsibility are reserved to Communist party members, a situation of particular significance in the armed forces, where a very high percentage of officers and other permanent cadres is party members. While nonparty status is perfectly respectable in the USSR, there is no concept of nonpartisanship in application to the judiciary, for example, or other functions.

Soviet emphasis on unity goes beyond the establishment of a single legal party and the rejection of a multiparty system; it is also expressed in the cultivation of monolithism in the only party permitted. Factions are prohibited in the CPSU, and dissent is repressed within the party as well as outside its ranks. All members are required to accept the tenets of Marxism-Leninism, and this means in practice acceptance of the interpretation of Marxism-Leninism and of the party "line" on ideology and policies which is promulgated by the party leadership. The party stands for something definite, and this something can be described with fair precision.

It is very difficult, in contrast, to say what either the Republican or Democratic party stands for, except perhaps to put partisans in office. If a thousand adherents of either party were asked what their party stood for, they might well produce almost as many answers as members queried. American parties are congeries of widely dissimilar individuals and groups committed to different, even opposed, policies. Because party identification means so little, adherents can freely migrate from one party to the other, and, although the phenomenon is rarer, even elected officials and other party leaders can switch allegiance without any switch of ideology.

It is unnecessary, though it would be possible, to go further in cataloguing differences between the U.S. and USSR political systems associated with the existence of plural parties or a single party. Note must be taken, however, of certain conditions which mitigate the sharpness of contrast between the pluralist character of the American system and the monolithic quality of the Soviet system. The alternatives represented by the two major U.S. parties are, as suggested above, often rather indistinct. Moreover, to the extent that they are distinct, usually they are not widely divergent, if viewed against the world background of contesting political ideologies. To paraphrase Dorothy Parker, as a rule Republican–Democratic differences run the gamut from A to B. This is partly a result of the fact that both parties depend for their material support on basically the same sources and cater in identical ways to the same media of communication; both adjust their appeals so as to gain the support of groups with divergent, even inimical interests. Looked at from a different direction, it is not uncommon for the moneybags capable of supplying parties and candidates with the wherewithal for expensive campaigns to insure protection for their interests by buying into both parties, a phenomenon itself indicative of the cloudiness of party differences.

To be sure, minor parties representing more extreme positions on the political spectrum are allowed to exist in the United States. They confront, however, many legal, administrative, and other barriers to their activities. Endorsement of pluralism in American politics is nothing more than endorsement of the two-party system, and reaches its limit where major-party orthodoxy ends. Pluralism in regard to alternatives in foreign policy has an even more constricted range than in domestic policy: politics is supposed to stop, as the saying goes, at the water's edge. A "bipartisan" foreign policy is designed to make alternative viewpoints in this area appear illegitimate and unpatriotic.

If the pluralism of American political life is less open to variety among contending viewpoints than is often advertised, the monolithism of the Soviet system is made to seem more complete than reality justifies. Despite legal, administrative, and social pressures mobilized against divergence and dissent, i.e., against unorthodoxy, such phenomena persist. In fact, against the perspective of the postwar period as a whole, the boundaries of tolerated pluralism have been enlarged. Spokesmen and media in the USSR referring to the unanimity of the Soviet "people" indulge in a hyperbole that is rather disingenuous. Even the CPSU is less unified than is suggested by the image presented to the world; within the party, different currents are expressed, different interpretations and emphases of common doctrine come to light. On occasion the curtain of secrecy is drawn open a crack as losers in intraparty disputes are bounced from their posts, thus revealing the existence of divisions unacknowledged until the moment of truth occurred. And differences come to light in other ways.

Promoting an image of unity, it is party policy to conceal not only such explosive differences but the entire process of decision-making in which the pros and cons of alternative courses of action are weighed by policy officials at different levels. In any system of rule, choices have to be made day by day, week by week, year by year. The ruling ideology may frame the issues, and certainly rules out various alternatives, but no precepts of Marx or Lenin can determine specific decisions of national or local policy, whether on domestic or foreign policy questions. They cannot do so on "yes or no" questions, like the advantage or disadvantage of the 1968 intervention in Czechoslovakia, or the appropriateness of receiving President Nixon in Moscow for the 1972 summit meeting in the face of American bombing and mining of North Vietnamese cities. They can do so even less on questions of "how much," as in the allocation of resources to competing military and civilian claimants. Yet Soviet practice shields from public view this inevitable process of weighing and debating the choices that must be made. Nor is there as a rule any ex post facto reference to the possibility that a different decision might have been adopted.

This silence about alternatives stems from two considerations. First, reference to rejected alternatives would be contrary to a public posture implying that Soviet policy flows inevitably from the creative application of Marxist-Leninist postulates. Second, reference to choices among alternatives might encourage those outside the circle of policy-makers to debate the merits of a decision rather than to accept, propagandize, and help implement such a decision.

Especially in the post-Stalin period in the Soviet Union there have been issues of public policy on which expression of divergent points of view has been allowed or encouraged, usually discussions by specialists in specialist journals rather than in the mass media by nonspecialists. School organization and curricula, relations between research and development bureaus and industrial ministries, the use of profits and similar criteria to measure and influence the performance of enterprises—these are only some of the problems addressed in such discussions. There have been other, more formal nationwide discussions, one of which, for example, centered on the revised Third Program of the CPSU. Such discussions have appeared to aim primarily at arousing interest in and propagandizing already prepared documents rather than at eliciting a spectrum of variegated opinions. Even in the freer type of discussions, however, the range of permissible expression is limited, and all public discussions avoid entirely questions of foreign policy and the more sensitive issues of domestic policy.

Although Soviet publications circulate much material critical of government and party operations, of bureaucratic, self-seeking, or immoral behavior on the part of various officials, the highest party and government officials are immune from such criticism, as are party and government decisions and policies, especially at the national level. This immunity does not always protect USSR ministers from individual criticism, but such criticism—as well as that implicating lower officials and institutions—is usually phrased in terms of deficiencies in implementing intrinsically praiseworthy party or government policies. All this is in marked contrast to American practice, where the president and other high officials are freely criticized (and also caricatured visually or verbally, in good-natured or hostile strokes, an absolute taboo in Soviet media).

It is no accident, to adopt an expression familiar in *Pravda* editorials, that pluralism in political life has only flourished under advanced capitalism, in the industrially developed countries of Europe, North America, and Japan, while Communist-ruled states have all gravitated toward monolithism in ideology and organization. Political pluralism recapitulates the competitive aspect of capitalism; monolithism, the collectivist economic order. American pluralism reflects a society oriented toward the search by more or less self-reliant individuals for riches, power, and security; it is rooted in a structure of private ownership of productive wealth and personal possessions. Characteristically, there is absent in the U.S. any overarching national goals which give direction and meaning to the strivings of individuals and groups. The state exists so that individual citizens, well- or ill-placed, can work out their own destinies.

Soviet monolithism is the natural outgrowth of a society in which all but personal property is public property, one which stresses community values and the individual as being fulfilled through various collectives of which he is a part, above all the very largest collective, Soviet society. The end-all and be-all is not the individual struggling for gain in competition with his fellows but the welfare of the society, a society whose goals are defined by the avant-garde party.

The fate of the pluralist political order in the U.S. appears to depend, therefore, on the viability of American capitalism, just as the fate of the Soviet monolithic order depends on the fate of Soviet socialism. It is difficult to imagine a combination of socialism and political pluralism or of a flourishing capitalism and a monolithic political order. The words *flourishing capitalism* should be underlined, because there are countries with economies based on private ownership which have sought to spur development or to compensate for weakness in their bases of support by attempting to create and maintain a monolithic political structure. For a variety of reasons, however, the combination of capitalism and monolithism appears to involve irreconcilable contradictions, and régimes of this kind seem to be ultimately unstable.

The major strength of Soviet monolithism derives from its capability of harnessing the efforts of a large population behind programs, strenuous, demanding programs, to lift the country by its own bootstraps, to transform Russia from a lagging European state of the second rank to a front-rank world power able to command respect and either admiration or fear. Struggle has been the key word in Soviet politics, whether struggle against foreign adversaries or struggle to implement ambitious programs of socioeconomic transformation. It may be noted that in general, and not only in Russia, the appeal of monolithism and unity is strengthened and the hold of pluralism and diversity is weakened when nations or groups accept onerous challenges of development or face struggles against strong opponents. This is true of nations engaged in war against other nations, of opposed population groups fighting civil wars, and, on a more modest level, of trade unions carrying out strikes against employers.

Soviet struggles paid off. Soviet power was sufficient to survive foreign intervention and domestic resistance in the civil war, to defeat an invading Germany in World War II, and to overcome U.S.-led postwar efforts to isolate and weaken the USSR politically and economically, and to prevent its emergence as a major force in the world. Likewise, programs to make over the country, to raise its productive power, to make the population literate and raise its educational level, to develop science and technology, were also successful. Had such international and national programs failed, it is doubtful if Soviet monolithism could have survived.

The other side of the coin was that the unitary emphasis of Soviet politics had the negative effect of engendering considerable lip-service, much apathy, and even some dissent among the population precisely because of the high demands asserted for unanimous popular support. Demands on the population were rigorous; rewards to the population were meager. Soviet citizens who could derive psychic income from achievements of the community or nation (or, still more broadly, from Communist gains abroad) might be satisfied, but an unmeasurable but significant section of the population was not sufficiently "socialized" to rejoice in such achievements and not regret the sparseness of progress in individual material welfare. Moreover, there is evidence that sizeable numbers of people in the USSR experience a sense of powerlessness resulting from the absence of opportunities to make individual choices of word and deed, to express individual whims in ideology and behavior.

American pluralism is by definition much more tolerant of human diversity, and this is one of its greatest strengths, probably next in importance to the association of the pluralist mode with the world's highest standard of living. Since the United States, unlike the Soviet Union, is not a goal-directed society, apathy and even dissent are not viewed with the alarm that such phenomena register in Moscow. With the mass political parties and the mass media in safe hands, dissent can be relatively easily absorbed or neutralized. Such toleration, combined with the fact that real choices (if not always very meaningful choices) are presented to citizens as voters and as consumers of mass media output, has succeeded in inculcating among most Americans a confidence in citizen autonomy and power. Alongside there also exists, to be sure, much apathy, expressed for example in the low turnout for elections, but this kind of apathy may actually be as functional in the American system as it would be dysfunctional in the Soviet.

Another strength of the American system which is linked to pluralism derives from the treatment of political life as a game (a spectator sport) or a drama, in the last case intermittently tragedy, morality play, comedy, and farce. This characteristic is present not only in the periodic extravaganzas of election campaigns but also in the everyday clashes among executives, legislators, and judges. In both kinds of contest the spectacles focus to a high degree on personalities rather than issues. This attention-focusing and emotion-rousing feature of the American political system is almost totally absent from the Soviet system, with its sober rejection of personalia and concentration on impersonal issues and programs. For the American, politics is like going to the movies; for the Russian, like going to a class in civics.

The major weakness of the American pluralist system is the reverse of the Soviet strength, that is, the difficulty of unifying the country behind any national effort. With power dispersed and competing interests strongly entrenched, "moving the nation" has to overcome formidable obstacles. Community ethos is weak; the relevant standard of judgment is expressed in the question "What's in it for me, Jack?" To deal with individualism and conflict, the order of the day becomes compromise, sometimes lauded as the genius of the American nation, but a mode of resolution which militates against any marked shift from the status quo. The United States has not, of course, faced any major challenge to its existence or progress since the Civil War, nor have unified national efforts been required to create the advanced economy of present-day America. But with American power no longer as dominant in the world, an external or internal challenge would test the viability of pluralism under new conditions.

THE CLASS BASIS OF POLITICS

The examination of pluralism and monolithism in respect to Russia and the United States has been rooted in a distinction regarded as basic in American approaches to political structures. A consideration of the class basis of the rival systems employs categories fundamental in Soviet writings. Needless to say, the concept of the class basis of politics, and especially of a ruling class exploiting other classes, using state power to preserve its position, even of the existence of classes as such—all this is generally rejected in American writings, just as the pluralism concept is rejected or minimized in Soviet writings. However, even those who disparage the validity of political analysis stressing class rule and class conflict usually do not deny a connection between economic and political power, between economic and political powerlessness. And this is the essence of the topic under consideration.

Stress on the class basis of politics means a minimization of the importance of differences among forms of government, between monarchies and republics, between democracies and dictatorships, and a consequent focus on the economic groups dominant in a given country who adapt one or another form of rule to their specific needs. The class approach also rejects the concept of the state as something standing above society, the embodiment of a "national" interest separate from the partial and partisan interests of the various groups and individuals composing the society.

In answer to the question "Who rules Russia?" the orthodox answer in the USSR is simple: the workers. Having abolished private ownership of productive enterprises and gradually constructed socialism, the proletariat is said to have become the dominant class in a two-class society, the senior partner in an alliance with a collectivized peasantry. In this view, the ruling party, the CPSU, was merely the avant-garde of the proletariat, although including not only workers but representatives of the peasantry and of the intelligentsia (the latter classified not as a class but as a "stratum" of society, derivative of workers and peasants).

The theory of the dictatorship of the proletariat underwent a certain modification in the 1960s with the announcement of the advent of the "state of all the people" and of a Communist party "of all the people." Much earlier, however, the régime had dropped certain preferences accorded workers over other population groups in regard to voting and admission to the ruling party. Adoption of the formula regarding the "state of the whole people" and deemphasis on proletarian dictatorship, however, brought about no change in the way the political system operated. This absence of change was due to the fact that proletarian dictatorship is defined in the Soviet lexicon as meaning workers' democracy, and has nothing to do with absolute rule by one person or a small group, the meaning usually associated in the West with the concept of dictatorship.

Certainly, the absence of private ownership and of profit-oriented enterprises in the USSR has important consequences for the political life of the country. No individuals or classes possess self-sustaining economic power which can be exerted to deflect government or party policy in their favor; all officials and officeholders are ultimately dependent on satisfactory performance to maintain their position in the society. Most political-economic leaders, for example those who are members of the party Central Committee or the USSR Supreme Soviet, have emerged from modest family backgrounds and have had experience and training in industrial or other forms of material production. This is in sharp contrast to the United States, where leading executives and legislators generally come from more affluent backgrounds and have had training and experience in business management, the law, publishing, and similar pursuits. Those with experience as rank-and-file workers are few and far between. Another contrast with the U.S. is that production workers with records of high performance are given honors and publicity on a scale reserved in the United States for movie stars, athletes, and the beautiful people of the jet set.

When all this is said, however, it is still difficult to regard the Soviet Union as a workers' state, if by that is meant a state in which the workers as a class determine policy. The top leaders are at most ex-workers, and their ties to ordinary workers of bench and field are remote and tenuous. The representation of rank-and-file workers and peasants steadily lessens from the bottom to the top of the hierarchy of party and state organs. In the party Central Committee and the USSR Supreme Soviet, for example, there are only token representatives of the rank-and-file, obviously selected for symbolic or decorative purposes rather than to reflect their real power. The Central Committee is a collection of over 400 leading officials of the USSR, a power elite in which a welder from Simbirsk or a milkmaid from Krasnodar has no real place.

This situation would not of itself disprove the claim that the working people constitute the ruling class of the country if the political structure ensured that the decision-makers at the top were dependent for their continuance in office and for the policies they adopt on expressed preferences flowing upward through channels of representatives. But the representative quality of the leading party and governmental organs is attenuated. Soviet "democratic centralism" is strong on centralism and weak on democracy. The average Soviet citizen, worker or farmer, like the rank-and-file party member, is largely powerless to influence decisions taken at higher levels. No one asks his opinion; he is told what to think about decisions coming from above, and these decisions often come as a surprise. Moreover, the representatives or officials that the citizen or party members "elect" are usually those assigned by higher authorities.

It was clearly not preferences of the mass of citizenry but those of top Soviet planners that caused priority to be given to the growth-producing sectors of the economy, and, for different reasons, to military preparations, at the expense of allocations to sectors promising more immediate returns to citizens as consumers and producers. Such planners' preferences could be defended rationally, but they were never put to either the party membership or the citizenry as choices on which expression of grassroots opinions was elicited.

The "proletarian" stamp on the Soviet state has, in other words, little to do with any special role played by industrial or other workers in running state affairs. It comes down to an ideological orientation which exalts workers as the salt of the earth, stressing their contribution to society through the production process and also the value and satisfaction which labor provides for the individual, even its healing and redemptive value. This is exemplified in a hundred ways. In addition to the aforementioned honors paid individual workers and groups of workers, including so-called labor dynasties, i.e., families in which two or three generations in one family work at the same trade or in the same factory, Soviet ideology promotes the image of labor as the most important part of a healthy lifestyle. Work is necessary not merely for the sake of eating; it is work which makes the whole man— and the woman, too! On a therapeutic level the beneficial effects of labor are emphasized in both penal and psychiatric practice in the USSR. Thus, maintaining the mentally ill in jobs during treatment, or restoring them to work as soon as possible after hospitalization, is regarded as the best kind of therapy. But these varied forms of respect paid to productive labor do not include any obeisance in practice to individual workers or workers collectively as the rightful decision-makers of the country.

If it is difficult to describe the proletariat plausibly as the ruling class of the USSR, it is a good deal easier to acknowledge the dominance of the capitalist class in the United States. Ownership of productive property is concentrated in a group which is relatively small compared to the population as a whole, but is in a strategic position to dominate public policy. Business people and property owners are protected by a legal system (of common and statutory law) that favors their interests, and enjoy great capabilities to deflect governmental policy to serve their needs. At the same time they operate on a day-by-day basis with a large degree of autonomy from governmental "interference." Of course, the situation should not be oversimplified. Individuals and individual enterprises, no matter how well-placed or powerful, may be unable to block government policies which they deem noxious, and the business and propertied interests as a whole may have to accept reforms to alleviate discontent, guard stability, or mitigate the economic anarchy to which the "free enterprise" system often gravitates.

But these business and propertied interests are in a much better position to control political institutions than are other groups to use governmental organs to control business behavior. The point is eloquently illustrated in the history of government regulation of business in the United States, where for the most part regulation has been taken over by the "regulated" for their own welfare and profit.

This class domination is realized in two principal ways. Class ties between capitalists and their representatives (lawyers, for instance) on the one side, and leading cadres of the American government in all branches, on the other side, are reinforced by a circulation of the elite between policy-making posts in the government and similar posts in the "private" sector. The pattern is well illustrated in the flow of officials back and forth between the foreign policy and military establishments and large industrial firms, banks, Wall Street law firms, and similar organizations. The flow is little affected by governmental shifts between Republicans and Democrats: the rhetoric may change, but the faces remain familiar.

In addition, the concentration of economic power characteristic of twentieth-century capitalism gives owners and managers enormous capability to control governmental policy, entirely apart from class links and personal ties between the business and political elites. Economic powerholders control funding of political parties and of election campaigns, supporting in different degrees both major political parties. A candidate for major office in the U.S. has to be either independently wealthy or, more typically, find wealthy supporters in order to make a serious bid for office.

Still more important, the mass communication media are almost entirely in the hands of large corporations or wealthy individuals whose values and preferences determine the content and context of the information and images disseminated daily to mass audiences. Controlling the flow of communications, they are able to define what is important and what is not, to inculcate attitudes overtly or subliminally, and also, as in election campaigns and other political contests, to define the nature of the issues confronting the population.

The class nature of the American and Soviet political systems is indeed paradoxical. In the USSR there is a proclaimed ruling class which does not rule. In the U.S. it is proclaimed that there is no ruling class, or even that no classes exist, and yet it is difficult to avoid the conclusion that the capitalist-propertied group is the dominant force in American political life. Which contradiction is the more explosive only time will tell. Perhaps neither is explosive, for living with contradictions is the human fate. And both systems have survived, even prospered, and seem likely to continue for an indefinite future.

NATIONAL POLITICAL LEADERS IN THE U.S. AND USSR

It was earlier asserted that the viability of the dissimilar Soviet and American political systems hinges to a significant degree on the quality of leadership emerging in the two countries. An examination is appropriate, therefore, of the ways of selecting and replacing national political leaders, the kind of authority vested in them, and the conditions under which they function in policy-making and administration of national affairs. The focus will be on the top political leaders, the president of the United States and the party general secretary in the Soviet Union, plus a small number of their associates. The positions of the top two leaders are in many respects not comparable, of course, and the problem of comparability becomes more difficult below the apex of the systems. Because of the broad scope of party–government authority in the USSR, a focus on the several hundred members of the Central Committee of the CPSU would bring into view almost all of the most important leaders and officials of the country, national and regional, not only "political" leaders in the American usage but those responsible for industrial and agricultural production, trade, construction, transportation and communications, trade unions, education, health care, and culture. No comparably defined group exists in the U.S., and certainly one limited to elected or appointed government officials would miss many powerful persons who would be the nearest U.S. equivalent to those represented in the party Central Committee. Thus, it is not among department secretaries in the president's cabinet that one can find the American version of the numerous Soviet ministers who direct various economic sectors, and who constitute a majority of the Soviet "cabinet," or USSR Council of Ministers. These could only be found, *mutatis mutandis*, among businessmen in charge of General Motors, American Telephone and Telegraph, U.S. Steel, and other corporations on *Fortune*'s list of the 500 largest.

If groups of the 500 most powerful figures in the two countries could be delineated and compared, such a comparison would probably soften certain sharp contrasts that appear when the generally aged and long-tenured group of Politburo leaders is compared to the younger and changing group of U.S. government heads serving with the president in the cabinet.

In the USSR, selection of the party general secretary, the most important leader in the country, is for all practical purposes a function of the Politburo, a group of twenty-odd key figures of the Soviet régime. And the Politburo itself is selected by cooption; that is, the dominant element in this group decides who is to be added, promoted, or dropped. Formally, the election is held in the Central Committee, but this is usually merely a ratification of a Politburo decision.[1] While the full members of the Politburo (of whom there were sixteen in 1976, plus six nonvoting or "candidate" members) have equal voting rights, the Politburo is not an organ of equals but a herarchically differentiated council in which the top party secretary is the dominant figure and various members are subordinated to others in the full-time jobs to which they are assigned by the Politburo.

The result of this system is that there is no participation by any large population group in the selection of the country's top leaders. Apart from "elections" by party organs, these top leaders also stand for election, in individual constituencies, to the USSR Supreme Soviet and similar quasi-legislative bodies; like other nominees, they face no opposition and therefore receive almost 100 percent of the vote. In any case their membership in the Supreme Soviet is not the source of their power but a reflection of their status.

Cooption, or self-renewal, of the highest leadership group has several important consequences. One is a tendency toward geron-

---

[1] An exception occurred in 1957, when Khrushchev assembled a majority in the Central Committee to prevent his ouster as First Secretary even though his opponents had a majority of the Politburo.

tocracy. With no fixed term of office and no fixed retirement age, a long service record assumes critical importance in leadership selection. And the Politburo as constituted in postwar years shows this tendency in full force: in the mid-1970s the leading figures of the régime were over or near seventy years of age.[2]

Since the general secretary and his associates are chosen within a very limited group and do not have to participate in electoral popularity contests involving the population as a whole, there is no premium on youthful vigor, good looks, charm, adeptness in use of the mass media, or projection of appealing images with which the citizenry can identify. The selection occurs within a group all of whom know each other on a face-to-face basis, without the necessary mediation of publicity channels and secondhand communication. Of course, the relative intimacy of the selection process does not mean that the personal relations of the participants are characterized by fondness or even respect, that rivalry of ambitions and disagreement on methods or goals are absent. It simply means that the Soviet "electoral college" is dealing with well-known quantities.

The contrast with the mode of selecting U.S. presidents is sharp. Serious candidates for nomination by one of the two major parties, and subsequent election, must have an appeal both for a wide public, since state primaries and a final national election determine the choice, and for key "power brokers," that is, city and state party bosses, moneybags interested in funding campaigns, and controllers of access to publicity media. If standing with such power brokers is indispensable, so is public appeal: a crucial factor is the candidate's natural or synthetic charisma, his ability to persuade millions of people to identify with him or with his program, at least in preference to rivals. Experiences in common and face-to-face contacts are crucial in the Soviet process; in the American system, face-to-face contacts are required only to smooth the way of a successful candidate, but it is the media-ted contacts that are decisive.

To be sure, seniority and experience in national affairs, even a touch of worldliness, often play a certain role in a presidential can-

---

[2] Cooption did not have this impact in the early revolutionary period because the leading Bolsheviks were predominantly young, like revolutionaries everywhere: the October Revolution was in part a revolution of youth against age. The tendency to an aging leadership was temporarily reversed in the Stalin-directed purges of the late 1930s, which took their greatest toll among Old Bolsheviks and other senior figures of the régime.

didate's appeal, though executive-administrative experience has proved dispensable, as indicated by the postwar prevalence of senators among presidential candidates. The need to win the support of voters ranged over a wide age span, now from eighteen years up, discourages selection of aged candidates, and, coupled with the limitation to a maximum of eight years in office, results in somewhat younger presidents than Soviet general secretaries. All three of the latter in the postwar years have held office into their seventies; only one of seven postwar presidents, Eisenhower, reached this age while in office.

A marked contrast also can be noted between the perpetuation of the top Soviet leadership collective and the rotation in the American. American practice is determined, of course, by fixed terms of office and the contested quality of quadrennial elections. There have been more than twice as many presidents as general secretaries in the three postwar decades, and the pattern is repeated in other posts. In the USSR, for example, from Khrushchev's ouster in 1964 to June 1977, only one change occurred in the posts held by the five highest-ranking Politburo members: General Secretary Brezhnev, Chairman of the USSR Council of Ministers Kosygin, Chairman of the Presidum of the Supreme Soviet Podgorny (replacing Mikoyan on the latter's retirement), and senior Party Secretaries Suslov and Kirilenko. Only four individuals have been ministers of foreign affairs since 1945, in contrast to ten secretaries of state. The current minister holding that post, Gromyko, has dealt since 1957 with six successive U.S. secretaries of state. One Soviet minister set some kind of record by staying in the same position over almost three postwar decades.

It is pertinent at this point to note the qualifications of those rising to the topmost posts in the two systems, the presidency of the U.S. and the general secretaryship of the CPSU.[3] The difference in executive experience has already been noted. Of the six U.S. presidents in 1945–1975, most were career "politicians," having made their names in the U.S. Congress, usually as senators, and most lacked any experience in running large organizations prior to the presidency. (Vice-presidential experience is not, and should not be, counted.) President Eisenhower is the exception on all counts: he was not a career politi-

---

[3] Technically, the post is described as the "General Secretary of the Central Committee of the CPSU." Between 1953 and 1966 the top official was called "First Secretary."

cian, never served in Congress, and had extensive administrative experience, almost all in military organizations.

Generalizations about Soviet party chiefs have to rest on a slim number of cases, and only two of the three postwar incumbents provide relevant examples. Stalin's biography has no predictive value in regard to subsequent top party leaders. No successor could have Stalin's credentials as a member of the Old Bolshevik revolutionary generation, nor could he—because of the combination of cooption and trend to gerontocracy—have the long tenure of Stalin, who became general secretary as a relatively young man of forty-three and died in office at seventy-three, and transformed the post from which he operated, originally of modest stature, so that he became the unchallenged and unchallengeable ruler of Russia.

Nevertheless, something can be said about the qualifications required for elevation to the general secretaryship in the post-Stalin period, qualifications likely to pertain to future general secretaries. These qualifications are no less pertinent if the promotion process is considered as one of self-selection rather than selection by others. Obviously, the pool of candidates is very small, being limited to Politburo members, in contrast to the much larger number of possible candidates, even serious candidates, for the White House post. The crucial area in a possible replacement's biography is administrative experience, operational responsibility for running affairs in an important area. This means essentially experience in a key party administrative post, because in all areas from cities and regions to the country as a whole it is the highest party official of the area, not the top Soviet (state) or government official, who has final responsibility for coordination and management of public affairs.

It follows from this that the pool of possible general secretaries is not even as large as the entire Politburo. For the Politburo is likely to include, as at present, leaders of great experience and standing—Kosygin is an example—whose experience has been entirely in government posts, or—like Suslov—whose experience has been almost as completely limited to "staff" work at party headquarters. Also ruled out are Politburo members with still more narrow specialties, for example in foreign affairs or military establishments. (Leaders as old as Kosygin and Suslov would probably not now be considered for elevation because of age, but the qualification described has nothing to do with age.)

What this boils down to is that eligible candidates among Politburo members are those who have had—whatever their current job assignment—substantial experience as responsible party leaders in large cities, regions, or republics of the USSR. A first secretary in such an area directs party activities and coordinates the work of party, governmental, and economic agencies, keeping control over ideological, scientific, educational, and similar affairs. While subject to considerable control from Moscow, executives of this kind are the closest analogue to the general secretary at the All-Union level, even though most foreign and military affairs are beyond their purview.

In the selection of chief executives, the difference between the American emphasis on ability to galvanize the support of a large population behind his personality and program and the Soviet emphasis on administrative experience stems from more fundamental differences in the way the two societies function. An American president heads a large administrative organization, but in view of limitations on his authority and governmental authority in general, skill on conciliation and negotiation and persuasive public appeal are essential to his role as leader of the country. The Soviet leader has less need of these latter qualities and more need to be able to manage and coordinate a huge administative apparatus covering all aspects of Soviet life.

In particular, the Soviet government manages industrial and agricultural production, transportation and commerce, and numerous other economic, cultural, and social activities; the U.S. government administers few enterprises and exercises limited authority over such spheres. The differences in function result in requirements for different talents. It is as unthinkable for a lawyer to rise to the top in the Soviet hierarchy as it is common in the United States; it is almost as unlikely that an engineering or production background would help propel an American into the top political ranks as it is common in Soviet practice.

Obviously, the discussion above merely points to the kind of qualifications and experience that are relevant to the choice of top leaders, for in both systems an infinitesimal number are chosen from among the many who may possess both the appropriate qualifications and the aspirations for high office. Aspirants need other qualities than those singled out, qualities that are difficult to define but certainly include a strong drive for power.

COLLECTIVE AND ONE-MAN LEADERSHIP

After a consideration of the selection of top leaders, it is appropriate to examine the way in which national leadership is organized in the U.S. and USSR, particularly as to the difference, more marked in theory than in practice, between single-person and collective leadership. In the United States, national executive authority is vested in one person, the president, who has great freedom in choosing his associates, the heads and high-ranking personnel of government departments, and in filling vacancies on the Supreme Court and other federal courts.[4] Formally, he has also almost unlimited authority to depose national officials at will, except for the vice-president, judges, and certain others. Although the vice-president, like the president, is nationally elected (the only other national official so elected), he has little power by right; most of whatever authority and influence he commands, normally not very much, is delegated by the president, who in fact if not in theory is responsible for his selection.

Entrustment of executive authority to one person has persisted almost unchallenged for two centuries of American history, despite erosion of some of the conditions which inspired the principle. Believing that government should have a very limited scope, the makers of the Constitution expected that the federal government would have a smaller scope of activity—though higher authority—than that of the constituent states. The president's primary role was conceived as the carrying out of policies, that is, the execution of laws, that were made elsewhere, i.e., in the Congress (though normally with the consent of the president). The need for unity and promptness in the administration of such laws was thought to be best served by concentrating authority under a single administrative head. As Alexander Hamilton wrote in one of the *Federalist Papers* (No. 70, March 18, 1788), "decision, activity, secrecy, and despatch will generally characterize the proceedings of one man in a much more eminent degree than the proceedings of any greater number."

In fact, the assumptions of a do-little federal government, of lesser federal than state activity, and of Congress's making policy for the president to execute did not stand the test of time. The president's role was aggrandized as a result of the expansion of "executive" functions and of a shift away from the Congress to the White House even of initiatives for legislation. The president has become chief legislator and chief policy-maker as well as chief executive. And the post-1945 expansion of the American role in world affairs has contributed much

---

[4] Most of these appointments require Senate approval, but such approval tends to be routine—somewhat less so in the case of Justices of the Supreme Court—because the final choice is always with the president.

to this growth of an "imperial presidency," because in foreign affairs the president has to share less authority with the Congress (and courts) than in domestic activities.

However expanded the role of the president, he is subject to limitations for which there are no Soviet parallels. These are a consequence of the constitutionally fixed autonomy of the states and of the Congress and courts. Despite inroads, this autonomy is still considerable. Therefore, the concentration of national executive leadership in the hands of one person is counterbalanced by the existence of independent centers of governmental power, as well as by other characteristics of the American political system to which the discussion will revert.

Emphasis on collective leadership is as pronounced in Soviet political arrangements as is stress on single-person leadership in American. Soviet theory distinguishes, to be sure, between policy making and policy execution in a manner somewhat reminiscent of the American constitutional distinction between legislative and executive functions. Responsibility for administration, for carrying out decisions, is to be precisely fixed, i.e., one person is to be accountable. Government departments operate on this principle of *yedinonachaliye*, or one-person control, under responsible ministers. The same is true of military organizations, economic enterprises, and the like.

In contrast, party and trade union organs, as well as government and state (Soviet) organizations of broad scope, operate under the principle of collective leadership, that is, are headed by a group of the most senior officials who have the decision-making authority. Collective leadership is the rule at all geographic levels from the smallest district to the country as a whole. Though such leadership collectives have an officially designated chairman or, in the case of the party, a de facto chairman in the person of the senior secretary (Brezhnev is referred to as the "head" of the Politburo), the chairman in theory has no special right to command or to make decisions; he is the presiding officer and spokesman of a group which theoretically at least functions by consensus or majority rule. The chairman is supposed to be merely the first among equals.

The rationale for collective leadership rests heavily on the policy-making functions of the leadership group. Collective discussion and resolution of issues is portrayed as the appropriate means of reaching sound decisions: each member of the collective brings to policy-making a different perspective derived from different past experiences, different administrative responsibilities, different personal strengths and weaknesses. One-sidedness is presumably avoided because personal quirks are canceled out and individual strengths are amalgamated.

If the theory underlying the role of the U.S. chief executive scarcely conforms to present-day facts of executive policy-making, the Soviet theory of collective leadership, particularly at the national level of Politburo operations, is often in contradiction with the real-life situation. Obviously this was so under Stalin, including the postwar years to 1953. Stalin's dictatorial form of one-man rule was in glaring contradiction with the theory of collective leadership, a theory which in application at the national level was deemphasized though not renounced under Stalin. Even if this particular kind of rule died with Stalin, many difficulties stand in the way of realizing the premises of collective leadership at the Politburo level and perhaps at lower levels as well.

In the Politburo the position of the general secretary is so formidable that the formula of "first among equals" is hardly applicable. Under Khruschchev and since 1964 under Brezhnev, the general secretary has been the only Politburo member routinely cited as an authority on ideology and practice, on domestic and foreign affairs. Of all the other present and past occupants of the top party and top government posts, only the long-dead Lenin shares this status as a fount of wisdom: this is partly due to the fact that all the former occupants of the two posts have been repudiated as unworthy of honor.

Moreover, the absence of equality among the members of the Politburo militates against the collectivity principle. There are gradations of status, as mentioned, among members of the Politburo, with some subordinate to others, some having national responsibilities, others regional.

Members of the leadership collective are supposed to engage in free discussion before decisions are taken, but afterward all are supposed to be good soldiers and carry out the group will. In theory the members can decide matters even against the will of the party chief, because the latter's vote counts for no more than that of any other member. Possibly this has occurred at the Politburo level, as it certainly has occurred at lower levels. But a case of this kind is not known, and some past episodes suggest its unlikelihood. Lenin opposed a Politburo majority on acceptance of the onerous Brest-Litovsk peace terms, and continued to defend his position until he won a Politburo majority. In a more recent affair, Khruschchev's colleagues went along with policies on agriculture and party structure that they opposed until October 1964, when they finally acted to bring about Khrushchev's ouster. The general secretary's position is so dominant that thwarting him requires a mini-revolt.

The failure of collective leadership at the top to work according to the letter of the theory does not mean that the principle counts for nothing. Penalties for dissent have been considerably lessened, so that Politburo members need no longer fear for their lives or freedom; since 1953 oblivion is the worst fate that unsuccessful dissent holds in store. Collective leadership at the Soviet apex, even if limited by the considerations mentioned, has contributed since 1953 to stability of personnel and has probably improved the quality of high-level policy-making. But it still offers no built-in safeguard against abuse of power on the part of the leadership collective as a group (though it offers some protection against individual abuses) because the top leadership controls the legislature and the courts, and is free from public criticism by the media or citizenry.

Survivability of collective leadership is also jeopardized by the felt need to focus public attention on a single leader as the incarnation of the political order. It is next to impossible to achieve popular identification with a group or committee; it is easier with a single flesh-and-blood person. The president serves this function in the United States, even though occupancy of the White House changes frequently, each time forcing a refocusing of efforts to endow the resident with "presidential" attributes, however modest or ample his personal charisma.

In the USSR this same need for symbolic incarnation is met by centering public attention on the general secretary, leaving in relative obscurity his associates in the leadership collective. To be sure, much less attention is paid in the USSR than in the U.S. to the personal life of the top leader or leaders. Family, health, vacations, recreation, unofficial travel are all considered inappropriate for public mention. It is all strictly public business. But in both systems there are attempts to associate the person of the head man with an image of a leader tirelessly working for the good of the country and of the world. Under Soviet conditions this spotlighting of a single leader not merely reflects, but widens the discrepancy between political reality and the theory of collective leadership.

CONTRASTS IN GOVERNMENT-TO-CITIZEN RELATIONS

Like other political orders, those in the USSR and U.S. must try to maximize support for and minimize resistance to the ruling groups, their programs and objectives, the established institutions and practices. To buttress support and disarm opposition, both systems find a place for persuasion and repression, the carrot and the stick, but in widely different combinations.

One major difference centers on the degree of concern about activities and attitudes of the population. American leaders are much more relaxed than their Soviet counterparts about the extent of popular participation in political life and about the existence of dissent. They react differently to apathy. Total involvement of the citizenry in supportive activities and total commitment to the orthodox ideology are sought in the USSR. Spasmodic displays of interest, approval, and loyalty are all that is expected in the United States, where repression of dissent is spasmodic and much milder than in the Soviet Union. Soviet authorities systematically use strong measures to root out or submerge disaffection and dissidence.

Although this dissimilarity of approach reflects in part diverse historical backgrounds and traditions, it is intimately associated with the different roles assigned to the political sphere in the two societies. In the one, the role of the political order is modest and preservative; in the other, expansive and transformational. The party–state régime of the USSR adopted early and maintains now a mission of guiding the transformation of society from the old order through socialism to an eventual communism, the transformation of a country poorly developed by Euro-American standards to one with a high level of economic capabilities, the transformation of a power relatively weak militarily and therefore a born loser in contests with advanced states to one of first-rate capabilities, the transformation of a citizenry largely illiterate and in other ways backward to one with new skills and new values. The emphasis, therefore, is overwhelmingly on achievement of developmental goals, to which are subordinated all other elements of political life, especially the exercise of individual political rights. The major concern involves the making of the omelette, not the cracking of eggs that accompanies the process.

No comparable developmental goals are built into the American political structure. In the U.S., unlike Russia, whatever utopian thinking finds expression centers less on anticipations of the future and more on nostalgic reconstruction of a long-gone past. The state's role is ambiguous, at once protective and threatening. As guardian, government is necessary in order to defend and promote social stability and national interests, especially against foreign rivals and hostile un-American forces. Simultaneously, government is often conceived as a menace to the liberty and property of the citizenry. This dualism is reflected in the constitutional practice of empowering governmental authorities to act in certain areas or in certain ways and at the same time prohibiting actions in others. This mixture of start and stop signals derives in turn from the private property base of the economic structure, a structure maintained by legal and administrative support of the government and yet protected from extensive governmental "interference" as private corporations and individuals administer in their own interest the production, exchange, and distribution of goods and services, i.e., the most important sphere of social activity.

Of course, the assignment of limited powers to the U.S. government, and the ambivalent mixture of trust in and distrust of the government's role which is so characteristic of American political attitudes, have consequences outside economic relationships. They create the framework under which citizens are normally protected against governmental interference in property and economic dealings, but also against such interference in the exercise of freedom of speech, publication, assembly, and religious worship. This situation is a striking contrast to that prevailing in the USSR, where régime activities are depicted as an unambiguous good, not something threatening to popular welfare, and where civil liberties are justified only so far as their exercise contributes to realization of the transformational missions assigned to the political order.

In any case, both persuasion and repression are less needed in America than in Russia to maintain support of and minimize opposition to the social order because of the incomparably greater material benefits that can be routinely provided to the American population than to the Soviet. Even if such material benefits are distributed less equally in the U.S. than in the USSR, the average level is so much higher in the former as to mitigate the relative deprivation of those living near the poverty line. Providing affluence mutes discontent and dissent in the U.S.; inability to provide abundance on the same level impels Soviet authorities to depend much more on nonmaterial rewards and penalties to keep their people in line.

Thus, "psychic" rewards, such as various kinds of honors involving no transfer of material resources, are manipulated by the Soviet state to encourage socially desired behavior, and "psychic" pressures are applied to those straying from approved behavior, with such pressures supplemented by harassment and occasional incarceration of militant dissidents. In addition, Soviet media of communication carry heavy loads of indoctrinational material to convince Russians that they live, if not in the best of all possible worlds, at least in the best of existing societies. Soviet media of communication are deadly serious about their instructional vocation, if not plain deadly.

The American picture is quite different. Mass media in the U.S. also indoctrinate their audiences, if less openly and less relentlessly than their Soviet counterparts. They focus more on diversion and entertainment, and in addition reinforce an absorption in material welfare by functioning as part of a vast apparatus for selling consumer goods and services. Consciously or not, they tend to mold a populace whose basic concerns and satisfactions revolve around eating well, dressing in style, driving the latest model car, prettying the home, spraying away bad odors, and, if worse comes to worst, taking pills for headaches, arthritis, and insomnia. It would be easy, but unwise, to scoff at a tactic of engaging loyalty and undermining disaffection by concentrating on individual consumption, a tactic that may be described as materialist but not dialectical materialist. Populations can probably be induced to conformist behavior more easily and reliably by a focus on, and abundant provision of, material rewards than by attempts to substitute psychic rewards and penalties.

Whatever the role of materialist persuasion, the ruling elements in the U.S., as in the USSR, have to provide ideological justification for both the political-economic system and social order of the country and the day-by-day policies and behavior of the ruling group. In both countries this inculcation of basic values and molding of opinions are accomplished through the educational system and the mass media.

This is not to say that civic indoctrination is the main function of either schools or communication media. They serve other purposes. In both societies the major function of schools is the reproduction among the youth of socially necessary physical and mental skills so that they can serve as a replacement shift for elders gradually dropping out of productive activity because of retirement or death. Simultaneously, the educational system serves, somewhat more so in the U.S. than in the USSR, to reproduce the class structure of society. This occurs because differences in the quality, length, and orientation of the schooling children receive are generally correlated with the economic status of their families: children are "taught" to take over the social roles of their parents.

Even if the indoctrinational function is secondary, it is an essential part of the schools' role. In the United States this indoctrination is particularly pronounced at secondary levels where pupils are instilled with the values approved by society, including approved attitudes on American democracy and Soviet totalitarianism, on communism and free enterprise. Youth organizations like the Scouts and family-oriented institutions like churches supplement school efforts to inculcate habits of patriotism, obedience to laws, respect for leaders, and religious reverence. In an unorganized way families also play a major part in transmission of such attitudes. This civic function is less prominent in American higher education, for universities and professional schools, as well as individual faculty members, have considerable autonomy from external control, and there is greater emphasis on scholarship and less on citizenship training. As a result, students in higher education encounter greater diversity of thought, though there is little to support the notion sometimes advanced in the U.S. that the basic role of the university is to provide a free forum of ideas.

In the Soviet Union the ideological component in education is avowed and omnipresent, with far less fall-off in higher education than occurs in the United States. Moreover, this ideological thrust in the USSR is supplemented by a much more comprehensive system of extraschool organizations, beginning with the Pioneers for young children, among whom universality of membership is sought, and continuing with the Komsomols for older youth. As an adjunct of the party, the Komsomols are more selective in membership, though still a very large organization. Indoctrination in Marxism-Leninism, Soviet patriotism, and other approved values pervades all education and training, including programs concerned with manual skills, technical knowledge, medical care, and the natural sciences in which the curriculum is otherwise not basically different from that of similar programs in the U.S. No tolerance is sanctioned toward freethinkers among faculty or students who might question or oppose officially ordained values. Whereas in America an occasional Marxist or other radical critic of the established order can survive in a public or private educational institution, a heterodox professor or student could survive in a Soviet institution only by concealing his views.

If the focus of indoctrination in schools is on implanting basic values, the focus of indoctrination in the communication media is on influencing attitudes toward day-by-day domestic and international developments. Films are an obvious exception, but newspapers and magazines, radio and television in their indoctrinational aspect play a large role in fixing attitudes toward current events and national policies. Such media have other functions as well. One, unique to the United States and almost absent in the USSR, is the proliferation of advertisements for (mostly) consumer goods, a kind of publicity which appears to play an essential part in maintaining a high level of demand for new and old products.

This combined indoctrinational-commercial characteristic of American communication media is connected with the fact that they are privately owned and are operated for profit; those in the USSR are operated by various party, governmental, and other approved organizations, all under the immediate or ultimate direction of the Communist party. No government censorship exists in the United States to control content of communications, in contrast to the complete and rigorous censorship in the USSR affecting all channels of communication. This censorship by a government agency, Glavlit, is aimed more at what should not be publicized than at what should be disseminated, and therefore does not serve, contrary to a widespread opinion abroad, as the major instrument for implementing regime control of media content.

A consideration of the role played by U.S. and Soviet media in attitude formation will not go very far if it rests on the idea that the American press and other media are "free" while the Soviet media are "controlled." Newspapers in the U.S. and, to a large degree, radio and TV are free from government control, and only to that extent is the contrast valid.[5] But "uncontrolled"? No organ of communication is uncontrolled; someone always has to decide what is to be published, broadcast, or pictured. The American mass media are not controlled by government, but by big business. Immediate responsibility for management may rest with editors and the like, but their autonomy is in turn fixed by owners of communication enterprises. Even if everyone has a formally equal right to publish a newspaper or

---

[5] There is a mild degree of federal supervision of radio and TV programming, and some control by states of film showings.

magazine, under present-day conditions only those commanding very great assets can hope to exercise this right.[6]

The commercial orientation of American mass media naturally affects the attention they give to civic indoctrination. Their primary aim is to deliver a large audience to advertisers, and hence they emphasize entertainment in order to maximize that audience. As a result, the media in the U.S. are not highly political, either in emphasizing political topics or in pushing a specific political line. Either course would interfere with audience building and thereby weaken the competitive position of any communication enterprise that tried it.

Nevertheless, these mass media still play a crucial role in civic indoctrination, in maintaining mass support for the existing social order and the values it embodies, and in implanting views of national and international developments congenial to the ruling elite. This is no less true if the latter is divided into competing groups and tendencies. The press and other media faithfully inculcate the idea that these orthodox or traditional parties and tendencies exhaust the spectrum of acceptable alternatives. Insofar as such differences are slight, and particularly in relation to foreign policy where bipartisan orthodoxy is the rule, the media can unambiguously build support for American orthodoxy as defined by national leaders.

Soviet mass media are organized quite differently, but play a similar role in organizing ideological support for the ruling group and the established order. And they play this role very vigorously. Although commercial considerations affect media operations, such considerations are very much subordinated to requirements for indoctrination. Moreover, such commercial aspects do not include the use of mass media as an essential part of the system for distributing consumer goods: advertising is minimal. Although entertainment is not entirely absent from the fare presented by mass media (as in the United States it is stronger on TV and radio than in the press), it occupies a minor place in media programming. The diet is heavy with instructional and hortatory materials.

The Soviet goal of presenting a single, consistent budget of communication materials, a single line of ideas and interpretations to a diverse population spread over a huge territory is implemented

---

[6] Radio and television broadcasting requires a government-issued license, but otherwise the point is still valid that great resources are needed for control of major channels of communication.

through national TV and radio networks (as in the U.S., but inclusive of all stations), nationally circulated magazines (again as in the U.S.), and also through several national newspapers, not only *Pravda* and *Izvestiya* but several others designed to appeal to various occupational or other groups of the population. No parallel American national newspapers exist, because prestige papers such as the *New York Times*, *Washington Post*, and *Los Angeles Times* are basically limited to a regional clientele, and nationally circulated papers such as the *Christian Science Monitor* and the *Wall Street Journal* have relatively small readerships.

In both the USSR and the U.S. there is greater diversity of opinion, and greater opportunities for expression of unorthodox slants, among communication enterprises reaching small or specialized segments of the population than in the mass media, but the discrepancy is particularly marked in the United States. Under American conditions this results from the fact that the economic threshold for dissemination of such communications is much lower than in the case of the mass media. In a very attenuated form a similar phenomenon occurs in the Soviet Union, even in the "legal" press. However, because the Soviet régime controls in one way or another all publishing houses and other communication enterprises, and all mechanisms for reproducing and disseminating written materials (even down to mimeograph machines), opportunities for unorthodox and especially dissident messages to be circulated are very slight. The Soviet underground press (*samizdat*, or self-publication) not only has to rely on carbon copies of typed material but has to be more or less clandestinely passed around; in contrast, the so-called underground press of large American cities is not really concealed, although those responsible for publication and distribution may encounter harassment or opposition.

With all due recognition of the differences between the systems of education and mass communication in the United States and the Soviet Union, particularly as to the role of the government, it is still necessary to insist on the similarity of their functions in political-social education and indoctrination. Despite the greater pluralism of the former and the monolithic quality of the latter, schools and media serve the same purpose of fortifying the existing order in the two states by inculcating in the population proper attitudes of support for national policies and institutions and of rejection of alternatives. The sharpness of Soviet–American rivalry highlights these characteristics, because in each country the most intense efforts at civic indoctrination focus precisely on those institutions and policies which are at issue in the U.S.–USSR contest for world influence.

REPRESSION OF POLITICAL DEVIANCE

Efforts to build popular support for the ruling order, discussed in the previous section, are supplemented in both the United States and the USSR by efforts to disarm, contain, or repress dissent. The problem has been more serious in the USSR than in the U.S. for reasons cited earlier, the insufficiency of material inducements to conformity and the grandiosity of the objective sought by Soviet rulers, namely, an active and complete identification of the population with the régime on a scale unimaginable in pre-Bolshevik Russia and foreign to the practice of countries like the United States. Alienation, if expressed merely in passivity, scarcely ruffles Western ruling groups; such alienation appears as threatening to those of the USSR.

Soviet officials make no claims of a permissive attitude toward opponents of either the social order or the policies of the party and government. An intolerance to hostile words and activities, to "anti-Soviet propaganda," for example, is reflected in Soviet criminal legislation, and under such laws dissidents are occasionally tried in courts and confined to compulsory labor camps, exiled to remote areas, or otherwise punished.

Of course, the situation in the USSR regarding control of disaffection has changed greatly over the postwar years. Until 1953 the security police had legal authority to confine or exile persons without judicial trial and without any need to charge or prove any violation of law. Large numbers were "repressed," that is, executed or kept for long periods in forced-labor camps under the Stalin régime on mere suspicion of anti-Soviet behavior, or because they belonged to a suspect social category, basically, for no reason at all. It would have been unthinkable in the early postwar years for such displays of anti-Soviet hostility to occur as took place repeatedly in later years: press interviews in Moscow for denunciation of Soviet policies, publication abroad of heretical works by writers living in the USSR, circulation in the USSR of *samizdat* writings condemning official behavior. In those years, also, almost no one was allowed to emigrate.

Post-Stalin relaxation of the most severe measures against disaffection and opposition had the somewhat paradoxical effect of allowing dissent to become both more common and more visible, a consummation decidedly unpleasant for the Soviet rulers. Yet the latter found no effective means of averting these results. They could not go back to the extreme harshness of the past or move toward greater permissiveness without endangering other objectives. So they maintain pressures for conformity, including spasmodic application of criminal laws, while acquiescing in—or forcing—the departure of a considerable number of discontented or rebellious citizens, the majority Jews, but a good many others as well.

The Soviet authorities can arrange for the harassment of malcontents without resort to criminal sanctions, not only by choking off expression of noxious views but by dispersing and arresting demonstrators, by searches of living quarters and seizure of papers, by dismissals from jobs and other economic pressure. And the statute books are well supplied with legal provisions allowing prosecution in closed or semiclosed trials if that option is taken.

The persistent display of disaffection is, however, more embarrassing than threatening to the Soviet régime. It is embarrassing because of official pretensions that the population is solidly behind the social order in Russia. It is not especially threatening because the dissent is confined for the most part to a small and disorganized part of the population, mostly intellectuals whose complaints center on concerns felt strongly by the intelligentsia and whose programs for change slight the bread-and-butter issues of importance to the masses.

Political deviance is a less serious problem in the United States than in Russia because American ruling circles are not as concerned about national unity and active participation of the population in the political life of the nation. Malcontents and dissenters threaten no cherished values. Dissent in this context does not mean, of course, the usual criticism of the "ins" by the "outs" characteristic of the American two-party system. The "outs" constitute a loyal opposition; the traditional congratulations of losers to victors after an election reflect the sporting character of a contest in which nothing vital is usually at stake. By the problem with dissent is meant, instead, extrasystem challenges, those which call into question the basic economic and political order of the country, that founded on private property and capitalist relations.

Theoretically, political and intellectual life in America is open to all tendencies, and there are in fact important barriers to governmental efforts, particularly by way of legislation, aimed at quashing heresy and opposition. In any case the problem of dealing with radical political movements has not been very serious. Economic abundance, even though it passes by sizeable elements of the population, has weakened the appeal of those seeking basic changes, and ethnic heterogeneity, especially white–black racial animosities, militate against coalescence of disaffected individuals and groups. In general, therefore, the American elite has been able to rely on nonrepressive measures or lightly repressive administrative harassment to control dissent without invoking harsh tactics. And this reliance has been facilitated by confidence that the powerful private interests controlling the means of mass communication will find it in their own interest to limit circulation of heretical materials.

This does not mean that the authorities have followed a "hands off" policy in relation to subversive elements, i.e., those going outside the limits of two-party orthodoxy to push for radical changes in American institutions. Various laws are on the books to restrict the activities of Communists and other left-wing groups, and Communist leaders have been imprisoned for teaching subversive doctrines. In addition, various forms of administrative and legislative harassment have been mounted against leftist and black militants: investigations, penetrations, surveillance, wire-tapping and "bugging," anonymous letters of denunciation, pressure on employers, and others. A powerful and largely autonomous FBI has played a central role in such efforts, but local police and other investigative agencies also have participated.

As in the USSR, in America pressures against dissidents diminished after the first postwar decade along with a declining intensity of "cold war" hostilities. Some of the more extreme legislative measures were declared unconstitutional; others, including establishment of concentration camps for confinement of subversives in case of national "emergency," were abandoned. Political leaders whose appeal centered on anticommunism, of whom Senator McCarthy was the most notorious, found a dwindling response to this focus. Again, a certain parallelism to the trend of events in the USSR marked the lightening of anticommunist, antiradical pressures in the United States. Dissent did not disappear; instead it was heightened in the 1960s with the stirring of the large, previously quiescent black population, especially in urban ghettos, and with the eruption of antiwar movements as the war in Vietnam, strongly supported by almost all Democratic and Republican leaders, lost its popularity. Nevertheless, dramatic expressions of disaffection receded in the 1970s, despite (or because of?) a serious economic decline and despite revelations of malfeasance in Washington (on a scale that only radical critics had suggested earlier) culminating in the Watergate-related affairs of the Nixon administration but extending back over Democratic administrations as well.

In the United States no more than in the Soviet Union did ineradicable dissent threaten the bases of society or the hold of the ruling establishment on power. Both ruling elites had reserve capabilities of mobilizing communication media and instruments of repression if needed to counter any challenges to the social order. Such challenges could conceivably arise from dissatisfactions of minority ethnic groups, such as the blacks in the U.S. or nationalist Ukrainians in the USSR. But there seems little doubt that dissident movements based on ethnic identification could be crushed by the ruling powers, if push came to shove, by activating racial chauvinism among the white majority in the U.S. or ethnic chauvinism among the dominant Great Russians of the USSR.

In dealing with these and other sources of possible dissidence, moreover, the ruling groups in both countries have shown a capability of solidifying domestic support by focusing on the "threat" posed by the principal adversary, Russian communism for the U.S. and American imperialism for the USSR. Anti-U.S. propaganda in the USSR and anti-Soviet propaganda in the U.S. have become, certainly, less virulent and pervasive in recent years. But propaganda disparaging the rival remains indispensable. The two powers maintain cadres of academic and other specialists who produce the materials to be drawn on for this propaganda and also train the *apparatchiki* and ideologists who staff those government agencies, newspaper offices, and educational institutions involved in the Soviet–American ideological struggle. In addition, a focus on the distant threat of American imperialism or Russian communism always carries a certain appeal to the powers-that-be in each society, because it diverts attention from domestic ills that the ruling groups are unable or unwilling to alleviate.

THE U.S. AND USSR AS POLITICAL MODELS

Being world rivals, the USSR and U.S. each has incentives to present its political system as a model worthy of commendation and emulation, the rival's as deserving of condemnation and avoidance. The model endorsed is in each case an idealized version of reality, strained of all but minor blemishes; in the adversary portrayal, each model is strained of all but minor virtues. This contest of political models is an integral part of a larger rivalry in which the two states vie for world leadership by maximizing material power and ideological influence.

Because this ideological rivalry is discussed at some length elsewhere in this book, it suffices here to say that the American self-portrait presented to the world is totally at odds with the portrait of the United States presented by Soviet media, and the Soviet self-portrait is similarly opposed to the depiction of the USSR in American output. The existence of this contest of models does not mean, however, that it is a first priority of either Moscow or Washington policy-makers to push for immediate and widespread adoption of their political systems by other countries. The situation is somewhat complicated.

In some ultimate sense, no doubt, Soviet leaders look toward a world of states under monolithic Communist direction which are bound together in some form of "socialist commonwealth" by ties of proletarian internationalism. Likewise, American policy-makers unquestionably would prefer a world of capitalist democracies with pluralist features of the kind common in Europe and North America. Certainly in Eastern Europe the Kremlin has shown a determination to see maintained, with some adaptation to local conditions, the basic features of the Soviet political model, especially the domination of a single Communist (workers') party. This has required a degree of Soviet involvement in Eastern European affairs, and a willingness to intervene militarily in extreme situations, that has been far greater than any involvement required of the United States in order to secure the maintenance in Western Europe of liberal capitalist institutions. For in these latter countries, shaken though they were by the rise and fall of fascist régimes, the pluralist model had deep roots which monolithic Communist rule in Eastern Europe lacked.

In most areas of the world, however, and especially in underdeveloped countries, Soviet and American policy-makers seek more modest goals than the implantation of political orders modeled on those of the USSR or U.S. Russian leaders have bent most of their efforts toward encouragement of an antiimperialist, anti-U.S. orientation on the part of these countries. This stance was dictated by the fact that in many such countries there was little industry, few proletarian elements, few if any Communists. The immediate priority in such countries was nation building, not class struggle. The effective criterion for the USSR came to be not the local political order but the international slant of the country. Whether the particular country had a semifeudal or tribal structure, a monarchy or a military dictatorship, a single party or a multiparty structure was a matter of less concern than the orientation of the given régime toward the U.S. or the USSR. Even countries in which Communists were not allowed to function legally were viewed with favor in Moscow if their foreign stance was sufficiently antiimperialist and anti-U.S.

American leaders have been even more reticent, even ambivalent, about the export of American pluralism. Countries of Western Europe, Japan, some in Latin America and the Middle East, could afford this kind of pluralist order without endangering either the private enterprise system or a pro-American orientation. But in many, perhaps most, countries outside the sphere of developed states pluralist democracy appeared as a danger to American interests, and American authorities did not in fact encourage a trend toward its adoption. Authoritarian governments, military or civilian, of centrist or rightist hue but committed to the protection of private property and of U.S. investments in particular, supplying America with strategically placed real estate for military bases, and following a pro-American and anti-Soviet, anticommunist policy line, what more could Washington possibly want? Opening up political life to diverse currents would threaten the continued hold on power of faithful friends of the American establishment.

Preaching the virtues of pluralism to the Russians, the Czechoslovaks, and other Eastern Europeans was one thing, for a trend in this direction would have opened up possibilities for anticommunist forces. Defending the virtues of pluralism in Western Europe and other advanced states was also sensible, because most of these countries showed that they could allow Communist or other left-wing parties to function while keeping them as a harmless minority with bleak prospects for coming to power. (Even in Europe American authorities were content with the Salazar–Caetano dictatorship in Portugal and that of Franco in Spain, being apprehensive about the consequences of pluralist democracy, and welcomed in 1967 the overthrow of the more or less pluralist democracy in Greece by a group of rightist colonels.) But promoting pluralism in countries under right-wing dictatorships was regarded by Washington as most inappropriate, particularly in less-advanced societies which elsewhere had provided the most favorable terrain for Communist advances.

5

CONTEST OF IDEOLOGIES: DEMOCRACY, FREEDOM, HUMAN RIGHTS

IDEOLOGICAL STRUGGLE occupies a crucial dimension of the Soviet–American contest for world supremacy. This is a struggle to persuade people the world over, within the United States and the Soviet Union and outside their borders, that the cause represented by the U.S. or the USSR is just, beneficial to the welfare of individuals and nations, and destined to final triumph. In the cliché employed by U.S. authorities in Vietnam, the contest involves "Winning Hearts And Minds," or WHAM! But ideological struggle is also part of a larger struggle to gain or maintain control over levers of power, to possess or occupy and use such instruments of power as government headquarters, communications networks, productive facilities, and valuable real estate for positioning military bases. In other words, the rival ruling groups promote systems of ideas designed to buttress their own position at home and abroad and to undermine the power and influence of their rivals.

The acerbity of ideological conflict has had ups and downs over the postwar years, but ideology gained in importance in U.S.–USSR competition as war became more risky. In the age of nuclear weapons and of rapid delivery systems that laughed at frontier defenses, neither the USSR nor the U.S. was in a position to afford a battlefield test of relative strength, the traditional means of measuring the power of rivals. Even resort to conventional warfare was discouraged by the prospect of escalation into a conflict likely to devastate both countries.

Ideological conflict cannot be sharply distinguished, of course, from the contest of rival propaganda and counterpropaganda. The emphasis here is on ideas at issue, not on the totality of communications disseminated to target audience or on the techniques of their dissemination. A treatment of propaganda agencies, technical means of dissemination, themes, and targets would clearly be relevant to this study of great-power rivalry, but is reluctantly omitted.

In fact, only a very small segment of Soviet–American ideological opposition is dealt with in this work, either in the two chapters which center on the topic or in other parts which touch on ideological aspects of economic, military, and similar areas of rivalry. The treatment of ideology in this chapter and the next begins with an introductory section on ideology in general and in relation to Soviet–American rivalry. The proposition that there are, indeed, "national" ideologies of both the U.S. and USSR is defended; this underlies all the subsequent discussion. A fundamental distinction is then drawn between two kinds of struggle apparent in Soviet–American ideological contention. One involves certain venerable and valuable concepts of which both sides seek to gain exclusive possession. "Democracy" is the first example discussed of such value symbols that are regarded positively in both American and Soviet ideology and are targets of conflicting claims to ownership. A discussion of other concepts which both ideologies seek to appropriate, namely "freedom" and "human rights" (inclusive of "civil liberties"), concludes this chapter. The next chapter is focused on concepts unique to either Soviet or American ideology and rejected in the other. The examples used are the dichotomous formulas "free world vs. totalitarianism" and "imperialism vs. antiimperialism." The first formula is prominent in U.S. ideology; the second, characteristic of Soviet ideology. In maneuvering with such formulas the aim of each side is not to wrest control of concepts used in common but to establish dominance for one kind of formula over that promoted by the rival.

IDEOLOGY IN SOVIET–AMERICAN RIVALRY

What is ideology? The word has a long history, dating back to the eighteenth century, and the concept has accumulated a large and contentious literature. Ideology became of major importance in the nineteenth century as the masses were increasingly brought into political life in advanced countries. This process intensified in the twentieth century with the development of new forms of mass communication, radio and television, to supplement and partially replace the printed word, and with the spread of mass-participation régimes from advanced to less-developed countries.

The term *ideology* here means merely a more or less systematic aggregation of views and ideas: political, economic, legal, aesthetic, moral, religious, and philosophic. A system of ideas has importance, however, only to the extent that it is shared by a large or strategically placed group of people, i.e., becomes a movement. The Soviet and American ideologies of interest in this context are national (though not necessarily or avowedly nationalist) ideologies. That is, they may aspire to universalism, carrying an appeal designed to go beyond national frontiers, but are national ideologies in the sense that their strength derives from their hold on two powerful nations. They are systems of ideas that have acquired armies and navies.

The Soviet and American ideologies discussed subsequently are the dominant idea systems in each country, those supported by the rival establishments and propagated through the mass media. Especially in the United States, but even in the USSR, there is less than complete acceptance of the dominant ideology. The latter is challenged by fringe groups openly in the U.S. and more covertly in the USSR. But minority ideologies will be ignored here because the dissenters do not control the main institutions and channels for thought molding. In both countries the unorthodox mostly communicate with one another; it is the defenders of orthodoxy who control newspapers, radio, and TV, who administer schools and universities.

Some deny that there is anything like an American ideology. They prefer to use the term only for systems like Marxism-Leninism. In contrast, Marx—the great popularizer, though not the originator, of the term *ideology*—excluded scientific socialism, or what is now called Marxism, from the scope of ideology, which he defined in terms of "false consciousness," that is, distorted and tendentious reflections of social reality. This aversion to the term *ideology* as applied to socialist doctrine eventually disappeared. Retaining the notion of false consciousness for opposing doctrines, Lenin and all succeeding adherents of Soviet Marxism have also applied the term to their own "scientific" views. Thus, the USSR is forthrightly said to be guided by an ideology.

Not so the United States. American reluctance to admit the existence of a ruling ideology stemmed in part from the bad odor of the word. For it was associated with Marxism, a tainted commodity from which U.S. intellectuals recoiled. Just as propaganda appeared more innocent and honorable if called "information," so ideology could be rebaptized as "value system" or "political beliefs."[1] Definitions fol-

---

[1] The words quoted, typical of the genre, are from Zbigniew Brzezinski and Samuel P. Huntington, *Political Power: USA/USSR* (New York: Viking Press, 1963), p. 23.

lowed suit. Ideology was identified with revolutionary or action-oriented belief systems. Put baldly, ideas of radical change, and particularly those espousing the replacement of the capitalist order by socialism and communism, were called ideological; ideas serving to justify and preserve the status quo, or to validate only incremental change, were said to be nonideological.

No purpose would be served in this work, however, by adopting a preference for quietist over activist belief systems. A ruling elite may yearn for passive acceptance of the established order, perhaps accented by occasional signs of deference, as did the Russian tsars. Or another ruling group, as in the U.S., may allow or encourage a higher level of political activity, provided that this is safely channeled into forms not threatening maintenance of the existing system. Finally, a ruling group, as in the Soviet Union, may seek to achieve a very high level of mass political participation rigorously confined within predetermined bounds. Whatever the precise ingredients of the formula, systems of ideas designed to produce the required combination of activity and passivity in support of a given social order appear just as ideological as systems of ideas aiming at disintegrative or revolutionary purposes. Capitalist institutions require an ideological basis of support fully as much as socialist institutions.

Earlier there was reference to ideology as a "more or less systematic aggregation of views and ideas." Clearly, emphasis cannot be placed on system if the American ideology as well as the Soviet is to be included in the discussion. Undoubtedly the former is less crystallized, more loosely defined, less formal than the latter. As a consequence, an outline of American ideology is more troublesome to flesh out than its Soviet counterpart. The fundamentals of U.S. ideology—those shared by all the different segments of the ruling elite—become clear enough, however, if placed in contrast to Soviet ideology. In other words, differences between conservatives and liberals, however significant in certain contexts, pale in importance if the focus shifts from the internal American scene to the world contest of opposing forces.

Moreover, even in the heyday of the claim voiced in America that ideology was dead ("There's nobody here but us pragmatists!"), Americans were told often enough that there was definitely an "un-American ideology." Un-American ideas were regularly denounced and proscribed by presidents, legislators, and judges. Congressional committees actively ferreted out, harassed, and denounced those suspected of holding or circulating un-American ideas. No uncertainty regarding the existence of an American ideology hampered efforts to suppress un-American doctrines, if necessary by imprisoning those who were active in their dissemination.

As the 1960s gave way to the 1970s, and as the American consensus came under challenge, there was less insistence that America was nonideological. The result was somewhat paradoxical. Heretical challenges to the dominant principles of the American system made it patent that yes, indeed, the United States had a ruling ideology. By the time of the Nixon administration, the president would often refer to "American ideology," and—pertinently anticipating the theme discussed here—sign official documents with Soviet and Chinese leaders contrasting the American ideology to that of the USSR and the Chinese People's Republic.

Although ideologies often serve a perceptual function for leaders as well as for the masses, concern here centers on the instrumental uses that the two ruling groups make of ideology to aid them in efforts to consolidate strength at home and gain influence abroad. For this reason, there is little need to bother about questions of sincerity, i.e., whether or not the ruling elite really believes in the propositions at the core of the established ideology. It does not matter all that much. Political leaders have an interest in persuading their clienteles, for instance, that all their people enjoy equal rights. They may even believe this, though the hypocrisy of successful politicians should not be underestimated. Obviously, the powerful would not be where they are if they had not learned to dissemble skillfully, and the large powerless masses in all societies would not be where they are if they had learned to pierce the pretences of the powerful. But that is another story.

The subsequent discussion of ideology emphasizes the ongoing competition of opposed viewpoints and shies away from judgments on the validity of either side's ideological standpoint. Some notice must be taken of the extent to which Soviet or American formulas correspond to "reality," because discrepancies between theory and practice affect the course of ideological struggle. There is no attempt, however, to say that one version of "democracy," for example, or of "liberty," is correct and the other wrong.

It is clear that even when the same concepts appear in Soviet and American ideologies, as with "democracy," they have sharply different referents. "When I use a word," Humpty Dumpty said in *Through the Looking-Glass*, "it means just what I choose it to mean—

neither more nor less." As long as the USSR and the U.S. remain ideological adversaries, there will be a contest between rival meanings attached to concepts used in common. Ultimately, the decision on what "democracy" means, on what practices and institutions are accepted as democratic, will be made by history, a judge unmoved by sentiment, tradition, or logic, caring only for survivability. If the ideology (and social system) currently championed by the United States eventually supersedes that identified with the USSR, history will describe the outcome as a victory of American-style democracy over Soviet-style totalitarianism. If the reverse happens, history will describe a victory of Soviet-style democracy over American "bourgeois" institutions. Or the contest may continue indefinitely. Whatever happens, and other possibilities are conceivable in history's bag of tricks, the point remains valid that the judgment of the future on twentieth-century ideological rivalry will be pronounced in terms of the tradition with the superior staying power.

Common usage of venerable concepts like "democracy" and "freedom" is understandable. Soviet and American ideologies are rooted in the same European intellectual tradition, although they followed somewhat divergent lines of development as a result of the nineteenth-century bifurcation associated with the name of Karl Marx. Despite this separation, the U.S. and USSR operate with political vocabularies having more similarities than differences. That this adherence to tradition should be asserted about the United States will raise no eyebrows, because American history has been undeflected by revolution since the founding of the nation.[2] But the USSR? The fact that in 1917 Russia underwent a profound social revolution affects, of course, the current language of political discourse in the USSR. Despite innovations, however, the revolutionary order in Russia had enough problems in legitimizing its discontinuity, that is, in gaining acceptance as the rightful régime of the country, without taking on the added burden of attempting to supersede, rather than merely reinterpret, values deeply embedded in European and therefore in Russian ways of thinking.

---

[2] This is to ignore the "revolutions" periodically announced in the United States by everyone from fashion designers to presidents. Of the latter, the latest to proclaim a revolution was President Nixon in 1971, who announced a "New American Revolution . . . as exciting as that first revolution almost two hundred years ago." This revolution was characterized by the introduction of revenue sharing between national and local governments!

The extent of ideological overlap can be appreciated by considering ideas glorified in celebratory Soviet rhetoric: peace, democracy, friendship of peoples, popular welfare, scientific-technical progress, universal education, social development, national independence, international security. These can all be found in similar American statements. There is a comparable overlap in the negative symbols used: war, reaction, aggression, racism, oppression, exploitation.

Consider, for example, the USSR's "moral code of the builder of communism," consisting of the following principles:

Devotion to the Communist cause; love of the socialist motherland and of the other socialist countries.

Conscientious labor for the good of society—he who does not work, neither shall he eat.

Concern on the part of everyone for the preservation and growth of public wealth.

A high sense of public duty; intolerance for actions harmful to the public interest.

Collectivism and comradely mutual assistance: one for all and all for one.

Human relations and mutual respect between individuals—man is to man a friend, comrade, and brother.

Honesty and truthfulness, moral purity, modesty, and unpretentiousness in social and private life.

Mutual respect in the family, and concern for the upbringing of children.

An uncompromising attitude to injustice, parasitism, dishonesty, careerism, and money grubbing.

Friendship and brotherhood among all peoples of the USSR; intolerance of national and racial hatred.

An uncompromising attitude to the enemies of Communism, of peace, and of the freedom of nations.

Fraternal solidarity with the working people of all countries, and with all peoples.[3]

Probably the National Committee of the Republican party in the United States would not adopt this code, but suppose the document were retouched to eliminate the few specific references to communism, the USSR ("socialist motherland"), and other socialist countries. Twelve commandments to righteous conduct would remain,

---

[3] Program of the Communist Party of the Soviet Union, 1961.

the USSR having already in 1961 surpassed by 20 percent the old world's Ten Commandments. They would sound a bit archaic but otherwise largely familiar to American ears, though lacking any reference to ecological concerns and phrased in typically Soviet male-chauvinist language. The twelve injunctions might then appear as a code of ethics propounded in America by a perfectly patriotic but somewhat pompous religious leader, with the silence about God suggesting one of the Unitarian persuasion.

Even in discussions more explicitly focused on social-political questions than on individual behavior, many of the frequently encountered concepts are identical in Soviet and American materials. It is to these commonly used political concepts that the discussion now turns, beginning with "democracy."

SOVIET AND AMERICAN CLAIMS TO "DEMOCRACY"

In both Soviet and American ideology "democracy" is a plus word. In both, the concept of democracy is closely linked to conceptions of freedom and liberty, of human rights and the special subdivision called civil liberties. It must be kept in mind, therefore, that the treatment of democracy in separation from that of liberty (or liberties) is dictated by convenience rather than logical necessity.

American ideologists describe the United States as a democracy and deny Soviet claims to be democratic. Soviet ideologists describe the USSR as democratic and repeat Lenin's claim that "Soviet government is a million times more democratic than the most democratic bourgeois republic."[4] Democracy, in fact, has become one of the prevalent plus words of the twentieth century. Except for a few states attempting to remain isolated from the trend toward mass participation in political affairs, there is scarcely a régime anywhere that does not call itself democratic, whatever the form of its institutions.

It was not always so. Historically, democracy was regarded as merely one of several alternative forms of state organization, and usually not the form preferred by state architects and theorists. Rulers and commentators could and did reject democracy in favor of a different order. Nevertheless, through a long evolution democracy has come in modern times to be viewed almost universally in a posi-

---

[4] V. I. Lenin, "The Proletarian Revolution and the Renegade Kautsky," (1918), in *Selected Works* (London: Lawrence & Wishart Ltd., 1937), 7:135.

tive sense. The Russia of the tsars was one of the last major states to explicitly deny the virtues of democracy and celebrate those of (monarchical) autocracy, a tradition not broken until 1917.

In the United States the adoption of democracy as a preferred symbol was a more gradual process, unconnected with revolution but certainly linked to incremental changes in political institutions. With few exceptions the men of 1776, and especially those who became the framers and populizers of the Constitution of 1787, did not believe in democracy, though they wanted to establish a republic. At that time, democracy generally meant rule by "the masses," especially those at the lower end of the social scale. It usually meant, also, a form of government unmediated by representatives. The word "democracy" does not appear in either the Declaration of Independence or the U.S. Constitution. Nor did the founding fathers desire that the American republic evolve into a democracy. The Constitution was grounded in a political order that gave preference to the propertied over the property-less, to men over women, and to whites over blacks (the Constitution recognized the legitimacy of human slavery). Universalism and equality did not appeal to the most influential of these late-eighteenth-century political leaders: they were republicans but not democrats (small r, small d).

The dismantling of explicit or informal restrictions on political participation was a long process extending into the nineteenth century. Progress in this direction was particularly marked in the latter half of the nineteenth century, in America as indeed in Europe. It accompanied the discovery on both continents that universal suffrage and mass participation need not, at least in economically advanced states, jeopardize the status of the propertied elite. This discovery at once alleviated the fears of the privileged and disappointed the hopes of those seeking to undermine the status quo. Karl Marx is a classic example of one among many who expected much more radical change to result from broadening of the suffrage than was to happen.

Along with this creeping universalization of political rights, the concept of democracy in the U.S. and similar states acquired a new content. It ceased to mean rule by the largely property-less poor and came to describe a political order involving electoral competition between different groups vying for control of public office under conditions allowing generally for the exercise of people's rights to combine in political parties and assemble freely, speak and write for or against the party or government in power. Democracy, in other words, lost its former class content.

The Soviet concept of democracy harks back to Aristotle's defini-tion of democracy as "government in the interest of the poor," a formula which retained currency for many centuries. Even in the nineteenth century the well-known theorist W. E. H. Lecky asserted in *Democracy and Liberty* that democratic theory held that "the ul-timate source of power, the supreme right of appeal and of control, belongs legitimately to the majority of the nation told by the head—or in other words, to the poorest, the most ignorant, the most incapable, who are necessarily the most numerous."[5] (It might be pointed out that Lecky erred, as far as majority rule is concerned, both logically and, as it turned out, factually. He linked majority rule with rule by the poor, ignorant, etc., but in theory a majority can begin at the top and include the rich, best-informed, etc.; and, in fact, privileged groups have shown their capability of assembling such majorities.)

In a historical survey of the way in which "democracy" has been used, it was shown that up to the mid-nineteenth century in almost all usage, whether by those favorable or those opposed to democracy, the concept "denoted a revolutionary force, the unrestricted rule of the masses, or the raising of the proletariat to the ruling class."[6] The last variant is the specific Marxist concept, derived from a more gen-eral proposition that portrayed all states as dominated by one or another economic class. To the extent that Soviet Marxism identifies democracy with rule by the working people, the oppressed and de-prived masses, it is firmly placed in one strand of traditional demo-cratic theory. Even the justification in Soviet ideology of measures against capitalists and landowners is not inconsistent with the earlier emphasis of democratic theory; traditionally, democracy was not as-sociated in any special way with the idea of civil liberties for all or with pluralist political institutions.

In Soviet Marxist usage it is not only proletarian-ruled states that are described as democratic. Even states dominated by exploiting classes are so described, provided that majority rule exists within the

---

[5] W. E. H. Lecky, *Democracy and Liberty* (New York: Longmans, Green and Co., 1900), 1:25–26.

[6] Arne Naess, *Democracy, Ideology and Objectivity* (Oslo: University Press, 1956), p. 119.

ruling class: classical Athens, where democracy was real enough for slaveowners if not for slaves; bourgeois democracy, where democracy is real enough for the capitalist ruling class, but not for exploited workers and farmers, e.g., the U.S. The difference between pre-bourgeois and bourgeois societies, Soviet Marxists claim, is that the latter pretend to be universal democracies, extending equal rights to all citizens, whereas the former made no such pretences.

"Democracy for whom?" is the question always asked by Soviet ideologists. Democracy for the exploiting minority, or democracy for the masses of the population? The American system qualifies as only a very limited form of democracy, according to this view, because political power is actually, though not overtly, in the hands of the capitalist rulers. If a Soviet professor of sociology were called upon to grade political orders, he would give the United States and other "bourgeois democracies" no better than a C minus, and other varieties of rule by exploiting classes Ds or Fs. Even proletarian states would receive only a B plus, because As are reserved for classless and stateless societies, as yet nonexistent but anticipated in the future evolution of proletarian democracy.

If U.S. democracy gets a low grade from Soviet ideologists, according to American lights the Soviet political order flunks the test of democracy, utterly and hopelessly. The prohibition of other parties beside the Communist and the lack of respect for political minorities are decisive. In the American book, even states which severely discriminate against and repress three-quarters or more of their population, like Rhodesia and the Republic of South Africa, score better as democracies than the USSR because some pluralism and right of opposition exists within the privileged minority. Something similar is true of run-of-the-mill dictatorships, civilian or military, in countries whose economy rests on private ownership.

The mention of dictatorship brings up the point that American and Soviet ideology treat differently the relationship between democracy and dictatorship. Historically, dictatorship meant a temporary concentration of power in the hands of one person (or a small group) selected to deal with some emergency. Modern usage departs from this meaning because the phenomenon—so defined—has ceased to exist: modern dictators seize power rather than having it thrust upon them, and they rarely relinquish power voluntarily. Nevertheless, dictatorship in modern Western usage always retains the idea of more

or less unlimited personal power, usually exercized by a single dictator gaining office through irregular means.

To American and Western thought the notion of a dictatorship
without a dictator is completely foreign, but it is central to one variety
of Soviet usage (the other will be mentioned shortly). This is the concept of class dictatorship, whether of the proletariat or another class.
According to this view, "every state in a society with antagonistic
classes represents an organ of the dictatorship of the ruling class."[7]
Proletarian democracy is compatible with proletarian dictatorship,
and bourgeois democracy with dictatorship of the bourgeoisie. The
democratic element is said to exist within the ruling class, the dictatorial in the relations of the ruling class to opposing classes. In any
case, by dictatorship of the proletariat Soviet ideologists do not mean
a personal dictatorship of the kind that evolved in Russia as Stalin
came to exercise unchecked authority. In fact, the concept of dictatorship of the proletariat originated with Karl Marx and was orthodox
in Soviet Russia long before Stalin's near-absolute rule; it remained in
force after Stalin passed from the scene.[8] The example of Stalin, however, obscured for most of the world the neat distinction elaborated in
Soviet theory between a class dictatorship and a dictatorship of one
person.

Soviet ideology also uses dictatorship in a sense approximating that
characteristic of American ideology which stresses maximum concentration of power in a few hands and suppression of opposition. In neither Soviet usage is dictatorship unqualifiedly a "bad thing." Class
dictatorship of the proletariat is good, that of the bourgeois is bad; so
dictatorships in the sense of concentrated authority are good if
directed to progressive or revolutionary tasks and bad if used for reactionary, counterrevolutionary purposes.

American ideology is less ambivalent in treatment of dictatorship,
which is a negative symbol and is often, especially in popular usage,
regarded as the opposite of democracy. If democracy is characterized

---

[7] *Sovetskaya Istoricheskaya Entsiklopediya* (Moscow: Izdatelstvo 'Sovetskaya Entsiklopediya,' 1964), 5:201.

[8] Marx expressed the idea as early as 1850 in his articles on class struggles in
France, 1848–1850, and restated it in his 1875 "Critique of the Gotha Program" (the
program of the German Social Democratic Party). See *Marx & Engels: Basic Writings
on Politics & Philosophy*, ed. Lewis S. Feuer (Garden City, N.Y.: Anchor Books, 1959),
pp. 315–17, 126–29.

by pluralism and respect for opposition rights, and dictatorship is associated with concentration of authority and suppression of dissent, the two are at opposite poles. Indeed, were American ideology free to take account of the United States and Russia alone, it could simply contrast praiseworthy American democracy to blameworthy Soviet dictatorship. But the world is not so simple. There are numerous other dictatorships (by U.S. definition) besides those of the USSR and Communist states, and many, perhaps a majority, of these régimes are fast friends of the U.S. and fixed foes of the Soviet Union. Consequently, sophisticated American ideologists, like Prof. Carl J. Friedrich of Harvard, prefer to describe the USSR as totalitarian—a concept on which more will be said later—rather than "merely" dictatorial. The distinction allows for a partial exculpation of good dictators, no longer seen in the bad company of the totalitarians. Although this usage is particularly cherished by right-wing theorists of the Friedrich–Brzezinski type, it has entered the mainstream of American ideology.

One post-Stalin change in Soviet political ideology affected the doctrine of proletarian dictatorship. Marx had portrayed the latter as the transitional form of state between the overthrow of bourgeois rule and the emergence of classless, stateless communist society. Under Khrushchev's sponsorship, however, the CPSU in 1961 introduced into a revised Party Program a formula holding that the dictatorship of the proletariat in the USSR had given way to a "state of the whole people." It was not claimed that the Soviet Union had become a classless society or that the state was withering away; the new formula merely indicated that the USSR had become a mature socialist society without class conflict. Dictatorship of the proletariat was not ejected from Moscow's version of Marxism, for such a dictatorship continues to be regarded by Soviet ideologists as necessary in countries moving from capitalist to socialist institutions. (Some other Communist parties, e.g., the French, have renounced the need for proletarian dictatorship even in this transitional period.)

This doctrinal shift, and an accompanying change in the designation of the party from a party of the proletariat to a party of "the whole people," led, as mentioned earlier, to no marked alteration in the functioning of the Soviet political system. Unlike other Khrushchevian innovations, neither was repudiated by the successors, although the latter placed a shade more emphasis on the continuity of the "state of the whole people" with the preceding dictatorship of the proletariat, and have seldom used the new designation for the party.

For the most part the doctrinal modifications reflected the fact that workers had long since ceased to enjoy any special privileges in Soviet society, as had once been formally true in both state and party affairs (greater weight in state elections, easier admission to the party). The deemphasis on the proletariat and the accent on the people as a whole, i.e., the formal universalization of rights of all citizens, allowed a neater portrait of the USSR to be displayed. This depicted the society as integrated on a new basis, that of socialism, in which there was no discrimination or privilege because of class origin or status, race, nationality, or gender. Lenin had insisted that in every country there were two nations, one of the bourgeoisie and one of the working population (toilers). Now the Soviet Union was depicted as one nation, united and indivisible, not under God but under the Communist party. The last institutional traces of class conflict were wiped off the books.

This universalization of formal political rights in the USSR had its parallel in the United States, where in the postwar period ethnic barriers to political participation, discriminating particularly against blacks, ceased to be justified in American ideology. A process was thus completed that had involved in earlier decades the knocking down of formal barriers to the participation of the property-less and of women. In both countries, therefore, ideologists were enabled to portray their political orders as open, as far as formal prerequisites are concerned, to the equal participation of all citizens.

This limited convergence has in no way attenuated Soviet–American ideological struggle for possession of the key symbol "democracy." Ideologists of each country disparage adversary claims to be democratic, doing so principally by contrasting reality to theory. They have easy sledding, because in both countries the democracy of the books is far from the democracy actually practiced. Although space does not permit exploration of many topics centering on democracy, one central issue, that of elections, offers an illustration. Elections—in this case national elections—are viewed in both ideologies as a principal means by which the citizenry can shape national policy through choice of representatives sent to the capital and, in the U.S., of a chief executive.

At this point agreement ends. From the U.S. standpoint, elections are meaningful only when they are contests of rival candidates and, ordinarily, of candidates representing rival political parties. Most elections in the U.S. involve choices between the two major parties, whose policy stands and candidates reflect the differing preferences of most citizens. At the polling booth all are free and equal, free to vote representatives and administrations in and out of power, equal because each person's vote generally counts for as much as the vote of anyone else.

From this same U.S. perspective, Soviet elections are charades. No one need stay up late for election returns; the results are known in advance. Without a contest of parties, or even of individuals belonging to the same party, no real alternatives of policy or personality are presented to voter. Candidates are not selected by voters in primary elections but through a nomination process in which a consensus on only one name is somewhat mysteriously arranged. Pressure then brings almost 100 percent of the electorate to vote in elections, and brings almost 100 percent of voters to endorse the single candidate on the ballot in any one constituency. Even the theoretical possibility of a candidate's receiving less than a majority vote, and therefore losing, never comes to pass in national elections (but only, and then seldom, for the most minor local offices).

Soviet ideology on elections is, not surprisingly, class-oriented. According to this view, elections reflect the class character of society. Under socialism, Soviet elections express the unity of the two friendly classes that continue to exist in Russia, the working class and the collectivized peasantry. Under capitalism, as in the United States, elections reflect the divisions of society, within classes and between classes.

There is no place in the USSR, it is argued, for multiple parties because there is no class antagonism to be given political form in rival parties. And there is no room for opposition to the régime because the CPSU serves as the vanguard of a united population working to achieve goals on which all, a few recidivists aside, are agreed. The practically unanimous endorsement received by the slate of party and nonparty candidates in elections is evidence not of compulsion and repression but of the broad support rendered party-sponsored programs to make Russia strong and prosperous—and communist.

Soviet ideologists describe elections in America as contests between different sectors of the ruling, capitalist class. American working people and other "progressives" may, or may not, have an interest in the victory of one party over the other; they certainly have an interest in maintaining capitalist democracy against possible tendencies on the part of the most reactionary forces to institute dictatorial, "fascist" rule. But this does not mean that either major U.S. party is any the less controlled by business and other propertied groups.

The focus on personalities in American elections is designed, according to this view, to divert attention from important issues, which in any case are obscured in Democratic and Republican rhetoric. And sometimes there are no differences of importance to the people between the two parties. Moreover, the voting public has no certainty as to the results to be expected from a vote for a given party or candidate, a condition aggravated by the fact that winning candidates can with impugnity disregard in office the assurances proffered in election campaigns to win popular support.

Soviet writers dismiss the notion that the Republican and Democratic parties are class-free organizations shaped by whatever ideas and policies find popular support and expression. They also disparage the importance of the formal equality of citizen participation in elections and political life generally. The crucial element is the dominating role of monopoly capitalists whose control of economic resources and channels of communication, frequently passed on from generation to generation, enables them to manipulate elections and between-election national policy-making.

Each model of democracy has its distinctive strength and appeal as well as its vulnerabilities. The American system appeals especially to those whose primary concern is to limit the harm that governments can do, who envisage the future largely in terms of individual advancement, and who are habituated to, even glory in, the freest expression of diverse, even contradictory interests. They are particularly numerous in advanced countries, though not limited to these. The Soviet system appeals to those (more numerous in less-developed countries) who place primary value on collective action under state guidance and envisage the aim of political life as the forging of national or supernational unity, a unity essential for mobilization of a population to accomplish programs of social and economic development.

"FREEDOM" IN SOVIET AND AMERICAN IDEOLOGY

Like "democracy," "freedom" is a traditional value symbol which both American and Soviet ideology seek to appropriate. Freedom and liberty have been defined historically in a multitude of ways, and placed in apposition or opposition to an equally numerous collection of cherished or disparaged values. It is not feasible to discuss the tradition here. Even if earlier usage is the source of manifold echoes in present-day discussions, the focus in this work must be on the function of these concepts in American–Soviet ideological struggle.

An objection may be raised. Is not freedom similar to justice, which is omitted from discussion on the ground that justice is a purely rhetorical term, in the sense that by definition justice is to be praised and injustice condemned? Not quite. True, the usage of the concept has moved in that direction. As contrasted to slavery, or other forms of human bondage, freedom was always regarded as a higher, preferred status. Historically, however, slavery and serfdom were defended and even praised as fit institutions at various times and places. Curiously, or perhaps significantly, the United States and Russia were the last of the "civilized" countries to abolish slavery and serfdom, and the last to harbor ideologies justifying human servitude.

The disappearance of property in human beings made the dichotomy "freedom vs. slavery" a purely rhetorical device, though one that still resounds in contemporary ideological battles. When Soviet Marxists speak of "wage slaves" and American ideologists of "slave nations," they are giving voice to echoes of vanished institutions. Clearly they are not asserting that workers under capitalism or nations under communism are the property of others, subject to purchase and sale, as were slaves and serfs in the U.S. and Russia before the 1860s.

While human freedom is now a universally endorsed value, the deprivation of liberty and indeed of life is also approved under certain conditions. Whether deprivation of liberty is permanent or temporary, however, it is justified as a punishment for offenses against others or against society, rather than as a due consequence of birth in a slave or serf family, purchase, or capture.

The freedom celebrated in current ideological writings has to do with enjoyment of certain human rights; it goes beyond mere freedom from bondage or incarceration. The human rights deserving protection are in dispute between the opposing ideologies, American and Soviet, or more generally Western and Communist. Both sides try to appropriate such broad symbols as liberty and freedom as well as narrower concepts such as freedom of speech and freedom of publication. In doing so, ideologists of each society vaunt their society's, and disparage the rival society's, claim to unique or superior realization in practice of these various rights and liberties.

The subsequent discussion of contesting positions on human rights is organized around three major distinctions between the Soviet and American approaches. The first part deals with the contrast between the focus on classes and class struggle in Soviet ideology and the concentration on the individual citizen in U.S. ideology. The second concerns the contrast between American treatment of human rights as freedom from governmental interference and the Soviet emphasis on material capacity to make use of approved rights. The third points to differences between Soviet and American ideology in specifying and defining rights worthy of respect, and also discusses the Soviet emphasis on economic rights as against the American emphasis on political rights (civil liberties).

Following the elaboration of these broad differences of approach to human rights issues, attention in the concluding section is directed to a specific area, that of freedom of the press. Although exercise of this freedom involves certain unique characteristics, the circumstances affecting the right of publication are only marginally different from those affecting the exercise of other traditional civil liberties, freedom of speech, freedom of assembly, and freedom of religion. Concentration on one specific right, freedom of publication, allows a somewhat fuller portrayal of the differing Soviet and American principles on exercise of citizens' rights and also of the ways in which these principles are translated into practice.

Class-Based vs. Universal Rights

In Soviet ideology, human rights are viewed in the context of an overriding class struggle that penetrates both national and international life. Rights are recognized as valid only for working people and their organizations, not for their class antagonists. In other words, it is not human beings as citizens who are the legitimate bearers of these rights, but people in their socioeconomic status as members of nonexploiting classes. The citizenry and the working population coincide only after the triumph of socialism and the elimination of capitalists, landlords, and other exploiters.

Soviet Marxists claim that the USSR has attained this status, and it would appear, therefore, that the once-felt need to deny rights to capitalists and their ilk had passed into history. But if class struggle inside the Soviet Union has disappeared, Soviet ideology portrays it as very much alive within bourgeois states and within countries where the building of socialism has not been completed. Hence class struggle marks the international relations linking socialist and capitalist states. This condition explains, according to Soviet ideologists, the emergence in the USSR of individuals venting anti-Soviet views or indulging in other anti-Soviet behavior. And such renegades require suppression, even though they have no class support within the country, but plenty outside it.

All this adds up to the fact that Soviet ideology puts forward no doctrine of universal rights; *ipso facto* it has no doctrine of minority rights as such. Adversaries who see a contradiction between Soviet criticism of repressive measures against Communists in capitalist countries and Soviet repression of anticommunist (or anti-Soviet) elements in the USSR completely miss the point, according to the view of Moscow ideologists. American Communists and "progressives" should be free of restrictive measures not because they are a minority, but because they speak the truth, represent the vanguard of the population, stand for good things like peace and welfare of the people. Anticommunists in the Soviet Union deserve to be silenced, however, because they utter falsehoods and slander, engage in antisocial behavior, represent forces of reaction.

Under American doctrine, in contrast, rights are attributes of individual human beings, of men and women as citizens. The rights they enjoy have nothing to do with their economic role or status in society, with their being owner or worker, rich or poor. All are equally entitled under the law to exercise their individual rights; no one is to be especially aided or hindered in this exercise.

From this perspective, human rights are inalienable, necessary to the fulfillment of the individual personality. To make exercise of such rights dependent on standards of truth or utility, or dependent on socioeconomic status (class membership), necessitates the establishment of governmental or other external control, and thus inevitably leads to a decline of individual autonomy. For even the best of governments—*rara avis*—cannot be trusted to avoid abuse and arbitrariness in exerting such control.

"Freedom" as Absence of Restrictions and "Freedom" as Capability to Exercise Rights

In the U.S. system of values, citizens have freedom if there are no governmental barriers to exercise of various guaranteed rights. This point of view finds reflection in the wording of constitutional guarantees, the first amendment to the U.S. Constitution serving as the most celebrated example. It provides that "Congress shall make no law respecting the establishment of religion, or prohibiting the free exercise thereof; or abridging the freedom of speech, or of the press; or the right of the people peaceably to assemble, and to petition the government for a redress of grievances." In general, however, American spokesmen defend a broader conception of citizens' rights; the latter should be free of governmental interference from any quarter, from state and local laws and ordinances as well as federal laws, from executive-administrative activities, and from other legislative activities as well as lawmaking.[9]

In any case, the point is clear. Protection of human rights does not go beyond prohibition of state interference; interference from other sources is scarcely mentioned. In terms of constitutional guarantees, the only exception at the federal level is contained in the thirteenth amendment, adopted in 1865. This forbids slavery and involuntary servitude save, in the latter case, as a punishment for crime; clearly this was, and had to be, aimed at "private parties." On the whole, therefore, the American approach puts the emphasis not on guaranteeing that rights can be utilized but on protection against governmental "meddling" if citizens have the material capabilities of exercising guaranteed rights. People must find their own means of implementing their rights: society's duty is done if the state keeps hands off.

The Soviet approach has sharply contrasting emphases. An identity of interest is asserted between the proletarian state and the rights-bearing citizenry; therefore, no need exists to protect the Soviet citizen against the government. The task in facilitating observance of guaranteed rights is not that of preventing state interference but of seeing to it that the material prerequisites for exercise of rights are provided to the appropriate groups. As in the United States, the point of view is reflected in the wording of constitutional clauses. Provisos on citizens' rights were introduced into the second USSR Constitution, that of 1936; curiously, neither the original USSR Constitution,

---

[9] Certain of these types of governmental interference are in fact subject to constitutional prohibitions. On the federal level, the fourteenth amendment to the Constitution, adopted in 1868, bars states from making or enforcing any law abridging "the privileges or immunities of citizens of the United States" and from depriving "any person of life, liberty, or property without due process of law. . . ." In addition, various state constitutions incorporate provisions protecting citizens' rights from interference on the part of state legislatures.

made effective in 1924, nor the original U. S. Constitution of 1789, included any mention of such rights. The Soviet list of rights, to be discussed shortly, is introduced by a general clause stating that the
rights of Soviet citizens are guaranteed by law "in conformity with the
interests of the working people and in order to strengthen the socialist system. . . ." Although technically not phrased as limitations on
the subsequently enumerated rights, the introductory clauses have in
fact served to circumscribe those rights. The attention to material
necessities is spelled out in a clause stating that printing presses and
paper, public buildings and streets, communication facilities and
other prerequisites needed for the exercise of rights of publication,
assembly, etc., are to be placed at the disposal of "the working people
and their organizations." (The phrases quoted are taken from the 1936
Constitution, but the clauses on civil rights in the new Constitution of
1977 are similarly worded.)

Soviet and American Versions of Human Rights
Deserving Protection

The discussion up to this point has omitted mention of a central
issue: What are the human rights that, according to the contesting
ideologies, deserve protection? The Soviet and American answers dif-
fer; one of the main differences concerns the emphasis given to economic rights as compared to political rights. In Soviet discussions the
former are stressed more than the latter, and certainly economic
rights are accorded more importance in Soviet than in American
treatments of human rights. The differences of approach and emphasis are reflected in constitutional provisions which in turn emanate
from differently organized economic systems.

The American Constitution is not explicit on property rights; in the
document as originally framed, only one kind of property guarantee
was singled out for special mention, that of property in human beings,
i.e., slavery, but this occurred because even in the eighteenth century slavery was under challenge. There was less need to specify the
rights of other property owners because their protection was assumed. Respect for property ownership underlay, and continues to
underly, the whole political structure.

In the *Federalist Papers,* for example, the propagandists for the
new Constitution argued for creation of a strong federal government
precisely on the ground that its creation would reduce the already-felt
danger of radical economic measures, such as "a rage for paper

money, for an abolition of debts, for an equal division of property, or for any other improper or wicked project." The authors recognized that society was divided into "different classes, actuated by different sentiments and views," but believed that a strong national government would facilitate class collaboration at the expense of class conflict.[10]

While the forms of property ownership have changed substantially since the late eighteenth century, defense of rights to ownership of property used for production as well as personal (nonproductive) property has remained an integral part of the American case on individual liberties, largely because of the central role of "free enterprise" (private ownership of productive property) in the U.S. social system. The justification for private property rights is usually cast in somewhat different terms from those common in the approach to political rights. The Lockean tradition in U.S. ideology has stressed individual rights as essential to personality fulfillment, to the realization of each person's potential. Although this principle enters the case for property rights as well as that for civil liberties, the justification for the former rests more on the social benefits accruing from an economic system founded on private enterprise. Free enterprise is said to maximize production and efficiency, that is, economic welfare. Private owners of productive property may aim at narrowly selfish individual advantage, but willy-nilly create social benefits.

Given this economic foundation, there is no room in American constitutional practice or American ideology generally for delineation of other economic rights beyond that of property ownership. In contrast, economic rights are featured prominently in Soviet discussions of human rights and in the USSR Constitution's catalogue of citizens' "fundamental rights." Needless to say, the list does not include any right to ownership of productive property (as against personal property, i.e., objects for personal use). Unlike the U.S. Constitution, which omits any general reference to the economic system of the country, the USSR Constitution describes the "socialist system of economy" as "the economic foundation of the USSR." Since Soviet socialism implies a dominant government role in economic management, it is feasible for various economic rights to be formally recognized.

The list is long. It includes the right to work, that is, to "guaranteed

---

[10] No. 10 (James Madison).

employment"; the right to rest and leisure; the right to maintenance in old age, sickness, or disability; the right to education. It is specified in the clause on leisure that annual vacations at full pay are provided industrial, office, and professional workers; in the clause on sickness that medical service is free; and in the educational clause that education of all kinds is free. Although workers, sick people, retirees, students, and other citizens can make claims on governmental or quasi-governmental agencies by virtue of these proclaimed rights, the constitutional provisions are basically statements of policies that the government follows, or is supposed to follow.

Nevertheless, economic rights of this type, focused on bread-and-butter issues, are of importance to common people in other countries as well as the Soviet Union, people who often experience less frustration from restrictions on civil liberties than from unemployment, inadequacy or costliness of medical care, lack of educational opportunities. Such economic rights have received recognition in international declarations and treaties on human rights along with political rights of the type enshrined in the U.S. "Bill of Rights." (Of course, none of these international instruments can be enforced against government violators in respect to either economic or political rights.) The fact that in American ideology these economic issues fall outside the orthodox conception of valid human rights is neither here nor there; Soviet ideologists more than make up for American inattention, while simultaneously engaging in polemics regarding civil liberties of traditional vintage.

The latter are given deference in both U.S. and Soviet ideology, and consequently in the constitutions of both states. The crucial, not-to-be-forgotten difference is that the familiar rights of freedom of speech, freedom of the press, freedom to assemble and demonstrate—honored in both ideologies—are treated as more or less unconditional in American ideology; in contrast, Soviet doctrine and legislation condition their exercise on contribution to the progress of socialism, with the régime rather than the individual citizen as the judge of that contribution.

Religious freedom is in a somewhat different category. In the United States, religious freedom is considered to involve separation of church and state and absence of governmental interference with religious activities. In Soviet ideology religious freedom means simply the right to worship. It does not include propagation of a faith, religious training of the youth, or other activities associated with churches in most countries. The narrow definition stems from the Marxist view that religion is inherently antiscientific and antiprogressive, therefore to be discouraged. Freedom of religion is thus distinguished from freedom of the press and similar freedoms in that speech, publications, meetings, and demonstrations can be progressive (pro-Soviet) as well as subversive (anti-Soviet).

There are other Soviet–American differences in specifying and defining rights purportedly guaranteed to citizens.[11] Some of these differences concern the rights of persons accused of crimes (a topic emphasized in the U.S. and very much deemphasized in the USSR); others center on equality of rights of men and women or of persons of different races and nationalities. But enough has been said to indicate the gross discrepancy between the American and Soviet approaches to human rights in this ideological context.

As mentioned earlier, there are also significant discrepancies between, on the one hand, the general principles advanced by rival ideologists in discussions of human rights and, on the other hand, the actual practices of the rival states. A full treatment of such discrepancies is beyond the scope of this work. In the next section of this chapter there is, however, a somewhat fuller discussion of principles and practice in the area of press freedom.

U.S.–USSR CONTENTION OVER
FREEDOM OF THE PRESS

Freedom of publication is singled out here for special treatment not because it is more important than, say, freedom of speech, but because exercise of the right to publish almost always involves the problem of access to material facilities in the form of printing presses and means of distribution. Free speech (oral communications) can be realized in face-to-face encounters without use of specialized structures or equipment: the human voice, perhaps a bull horn, and a spot on which to stand or sit are all that is required. Something similar prevails with the right of assembly. Of course, oral communications to large or scattered audiences require access to specialized communications facilities like radio-TV stations and networks, just as large

---

[11] Throughout the discussion, references have been made to rights of citizens. Particularly in the case of the United States, however, guarantees of rights usually do not differentiate citizens from other residents.

assemblies require access to meeting halls or other suitable places. The point is simply that reaching people in numbers depends on much more than an individual's or group's right to speak or publish, to be heard or be read. It requires possession of, or access to, material facilities, to equipment and buildings and supplies. This requirement is most evident in connection with the freedom of the press.

Soviet and American approaches in this area share little beyond parallel endorsement of "freedom of the press." But this freedom, as earlier noted, is considered more or less absolute in the U.S. approach, but in the Soviet hinges on the value of the content. The standard of measurement in the USSR is the contribution of writings to the strengthening of socialism; the judges are party–state authorities.

In U.S. doctrine, freedom of the press has come to mean that there should be neither prior censorship of, nor ex post facto retribution for, comment on public affairs.[12] The theory is founded on a belief that freedom from governmental intervention allows the satisfaction of individual yearnings for expression and simultaneously brings about the socially valuable circulation of a broad range of ideas and opinions. The communications arena becomes a true marketplace of contending ideas. It is admitted that shoddy and silly, even false and noxious ideas will enter circulation along with the creative, objective, and socially beneficial. But it is believed that a reverse Gresham's law will operate; instead of bad currency driving out the good, true and useful ideas will win in a contest with the false and harmful.

Soviet doctrine has no more truck with the free market of ideas than with the free market in commodities. It would be flippant, but not too far wrong, to assert that the Soviet position recognizes no right to be wrong, only a right to be right. The position is not new. Three centuries ago Thomas Hobbes described in *Leviathan* (1651) the duties of a "sovereign":

> Judge of what Opinions and Doctrines are averse, and what conducing to Peace; and consequently, on what occasions, how farre, and what, men are to be trusted withall, in speaking to Multitudes of people; and who shall examine the Doctrines of all bookes before they be published. For the Actions of men proceed from their Opinions; and in the well governing of Opinions, consisteth the well governing of mens Actions. . . . It belongeth therefore to him that hath the Soveraign

---

[12] Penalties for libel, especially libel of "private" persons, fall outside the scope of this discussion, as do measures against pornographic publications.

> Power, to be Judge, or constitute all Judges of Opinions and Doctrines, as a thing necessary to Peace; therby to prevent Discord and Civill Warre.[13]

Hobbes lives on in the Soviet Union. According to the Soviet approach, no encouragement or even permission should be given to error or to socially retrograde communications. The authorities are unabashedly partisan rather than neutral in respect to the flow of ideas and opinions, facts and quasi-facts. Not hands off, but open intervention to frustrate the adversaries and assist the friends of socialism is the principle enforced.

These thumbnail sketches of basic U.S. and USSR doctrine on freedom of the press invite some additional comment, particularly in the light of actual practice. These comments will center first on American and then on Soviet press affairs.

The case for America as the true homeland of press freedom is based, as already noted, on the absence of government control. The rather flat constitutional prohibition against any federal law abridging freedom of the press, and similar prohibitions of interference on the part of the states, have not entirely warded off governmental intervention against unpopular publications in periods of public agitation over domestic or foreign threats to U.S. security and stability. Such intervention occurred during the two World Wars and in their aftermath; in the postwar periods they were directed principally against Communists or other radicals. The latter served as the only available targets on which to vent American frustration over undesired consequences of the two wars, the Bolshevik victory in Russia in 1917 and the expansion of Soviet power, especially in Europe, resulting from World War II. Federal and state intervention of this type involved legislation as well as various executive and administrative activities to inhibit radical publications and organizations; they also included legislative "investigations." By and large these governmental efforts were upheld in the Supreme Court and other courts, though often court decisions were accompanied by eloquent tributes to the virtues of freedom of the press and freedom of speech. A doctrine of "clear

---

[13] Thomas Hobbes, *Leviathan* (London: J. M. Dent & Sons, Ltd., Everyman edition, 1937), Part 2, Chapter 18, p. 93. Although the Soviet state follows principles reminiscent of those deduced by Hobbes, the rationale is different. Soviet control is justified in terms of the class struggle and promotion of the inevitable triumph of socialism, not in terms of the nature of state power per se.

and present danger" gained prominence as support for suppression. The apolitical rejection of the psychopath's right to falsely shout "Fire!" in a crowded theater, and thereby cause a panic, served as the analogy for the very political suppression of publications and speech deemed by authorities to be especially noxious.

Despite this shading on the absoluteness of rights to free press and free speech, the absence of censorship has meant that a great variety of printed material circulates freely in the United States, including publications condemning the government and government officers, the socioeconomic system of the United States, and American policies at home and abroad. Efforts by the U.S. government and other forces may discourage but, times of stress excepted, not prohibit circulation of unorthodox views, not even those of Communists and other radicals.

It was suggested earlier that the question of freedom of the press cannot be confined solely to the existence or absence of governmental control. This is a central issue in debates over press freedom between American and Soviet ideologists; the latter assert that even if there were a total absence in the U.S. of official intervention, this would not mean that freedom of publication exists for the population as a whole. It exists, according to this view, principally for the capitalist class.

American ideology treats as largely irrelevant the material aspects of communications. Anyone is free to write what he pleases, to publish a newspaper or magazine, books or articles. The free market in ideas functions within a free market of publications, with entry to and continued operation within this market subject to no permission from any authority.

In fact, of course, great economic resources are required to establish, win control of, or maintain any newspaper, magazine, or other publishing enterprise capable of reaching large numbers of people. Those publishing enterprises reaching more modest numbers of readers—a category that includes almost all book publishers—are clearly not as demanding of great financial resources. Still, possession or access to substantial capital is essential for utilization of freedom of the press on anything above the most limited scale.

The necessity of wealth to make good claims for realization of freedom of the press affects in various ways the content of printed matter. As mentioned, publications reaching mass audiences under the American system must, almost without exception, function as part of the system for distribution of consumer goods. (Soviet publications are not dependent on advertisers; they are financed by subscriptions and sales, augmented in some cases by régime-controlled subsidies.)

The business base of the American publishing world means that it is the newspaper publishers and other communications magnates, motivated by considerations of profit and ideology, who decide what is to be printed, not the writers, reporters, editors, and commentators who fill the pages. Writers and editors, to be sure, enjoy a considerable but varying degree of autonomy, but they can make use of their freedom of expression only to the extent that they conform to or internalize the standards set by publishers and owners. In the United States, therefore, freedom of the press is not widely dispersed: it is freedom for those who have enough resources to maintain publishing enterprises, and in the case of the mass media, freedom for those who control tremendous financial assets.

In the Soviet Union the situation respecting freedom of the press is rather different, but not because exercise of the right is widely dispersed. It is freedom for party–government moguls, not for magnates of business, and writers and editors enjoy this freedom only to the extent that they, like their American counterparts, conform to or internalize criteria set by the authorities. Economic calculations, particularly profitability, play a secondary role. While mass readerships are sought for major newspapers, magazines, and even books, there is much less emphasis on giving the public what it "wants" in the way of diversion and entertainment, and much more on giving the public what it "needs." These needs include much socialist uplift; much attention to inspirational examples and techniques of production successes ("Go thou and do likewise") or to production difficulties and ways of resolving them; and much in the way of heavy theoretical (and polemical) articles on internal and external affairs.

The formalism noted in the discussion of the American doctrine of freedom of the press is matched, and then some, by the formalism inherent in Soviet doctrine. The latter avers that, although class enemies are deprived of entry to communications channels, the door is open wide to the mass of working people and intelligentsia, who are not only granted freedom of expression but are provided with the material conditions to allow utilization of these rights. In fact, even simon-pure workers and other cherished members of society have only the most modest opportunities to exercise such rights. For the latter can be used only in ways approved by the party and government, in publications established by these same authorities, and for purposes that the authorities endorse. Newspapers, journals, and other publications may or may not represent the views of the "people," but certainly the average citizen has no more effective access to the print media than does the average citizen in countries like the United States. Even rank-and-file members of the ruling party find that access to the media is dependent on staying within the fairly narrow boundaries of permitted expression.

In a sense the abstract formalism of Soviet ideology on the subject of freedom of the press (or of freedom of expression in general) is somewhat un-Marxian. In its critical mode, not only with Karl Marx and Friedrich Engels in the nineteenth century but with twentieth-century successors in Russia and elsewhere, Marxism proved to be a very powerful instrument for the demythologization of abstract formulas, such as those on human rights or on the state as the guardian of the general interest of society. Long ago Marx was asking, in effect, "Who gets what, when, and how?" Marxism showed a capability for exposing the truly enormous gap between grandiose political formulas and the real uses to which such formulas lent themselves, between, for example, the *liberté, égalité, et fraternité* espoused in slogans and the degree of liberty, equality, and fraternity that trailed in the wake of the slogans.

The critical method employed by Marx, if not his analysis of the socioeconomic order, can be applied to all states, proletarian as well as capitalist. And it can serve to demythologize the grand formulas erected in the ideology and constitutions of the one variety of state as of the other. A state such as the USSR with its doctrine of proletarian rights is thus as vulnerable to challenge as is the U.S. with its doctrine of popular sovereignty and universal rights. The challenge can be mounted from the same vantage point, namely, the contrast of doctrine with "reality," the contrast of doctrinal deference to honorific entities such as the "proletariat" or the "people" with the reality of effective rule in the hands of a small group, who accompany their dominance by occasional genuflections before the "proletariat" or the "people," genuflections as meaningless as they are cynical.

Be that as it may, one of the main functions of the ideology promoted by each of the big-power rivals is to sustain myths that it finds useful while undermining those of its adversary. The kind of ideological contest discussed in this chapter has centered on efforts by each power to gain dominance for its version of commonly used concepts such as democracy and freedom, economic rights and civil liberties. That struggle will not end as long as the two states are in a position to vie for world leadership. Equally in prospect is indefinite continuance of ideological conflict involving promotion of formulas unique to one or the other side. It is to this second variety of ideological struggle that the next chapter is devoted.

6

IDEOLOGICAL STRUGGLE: "TOTALITARIANISM" VS. "IMPERIALISM"

TO REPEAT earlier remarks, much of the Soviet–American ideological contest consists of efforts by each side to gain predominance for concepts and formulas that are emphasized in one of the rival ideologies and are used sparingly, if at all, in the other. Many examples could be cited, but the outstanding illustrations are rival formulas to describe how the world is divided and to place the contending superpowers on a political map of the world.

American ideology presents the world as divided between totalitarian states and a heterogeneous collection of "free world" countries. The corresponding Soviet practice is to contrast the imperialist states to a varied group of socialist, national democratic, and other "antiimperialist" countries. Needless to say, Soviet ideologists avoid entirely the totalitarian/free world dichotomy, and never describe the USSR, even for the period of Stalin's most arbitrary rule, as totalitarian.[1] Similarly, orthodox American ideologists make little use of the concept of imperialism in any context, and never describe the United States as imperialist or the world as divided between imperialist and antiimperialist states.

Soviet avoidance of the concept of totalitarianism and American avoidance of the imperialist description can be easily explained. Each side invests great capital in the circulation of its unique symbols, and it is likely to be unprofitable for the adversary, the target, to add to the currency of such concepts. As nasty labels they can be hurled

---

[1] Although totalitarianism is not a frequent term in Soviet discussions, it has sometimes been used to describe "fascist" and "semifascist" régimes: Hitler's Germany, Mussolini's Italy, Franco's Spain, and Argentina under Péron. See, e.g., F. M. Burlatskii, *Lenin, Gosudarstvo, Politika* (Moscow: Izdatel'stvo 'Nauka,' 1970), pp. 221–24. It also appears in anti-Chinese polemics.

back to their point of origin, a practice followed occasionally by American ideologists in labeling the Soviet Union as imperialist. But such counteruse is infrequent because the use in retort may add to the popularity of the description without any assurance that the label will really stick on the originator.

It should be noted that these specific dichotomies are not parallel in detail, because the totalitarian formula is focused on the internal order whereas that of imperialism emphasizes international aspects. Other concepts are used to supplement U.S. discussion of Soviet foreign relations and Soviet discussion of American internal structure. Moreover, it is a little unjust to speak of these formulas as locating *countries* on a political map of the world. In neither theory is a nation as such totalitarian or imperialist. American theorists allow that there are nontotalitarian elements in the USSR, and, conversely, they describe Communist political parties in so-called free world countries as totalitarian. Nor do Soviet theorists identify American imperialism with the American nation, for the latter is said to embrace antiimperialist as well as imperialist forces.

The rival formulas are heavily charged with "affect," that is, loaded to provoke strong emotional responses: each describes the world in terms of adversary camps of which one is composed of the forces of light and the other of the forces of darkness. In addition, each formula is designed to emphasize strength and minimize weakness by presenting a picture in which a majority of countries are associated with the good side and only a minority with the bad side. Thus, Soviet ideologists portray the USSR as the leading force in a worldwide movement of socialist and other nations and groups linked in opposition to imperialism, especially American imperialism. In contrast, American ideologists attempt to show the United States as the leading element in a similarly global aggregation of peoples and states, advanced and backward, all sharing one attribute, rejection of Communist (totalitarian) rule. If the two formulas were to be displayed graphically on a world globe, the Soviet version would color most of the world in bright red or pinks shading into red, leaving rather small dark blotches to mark imperialist strongholds. An American version would color most of the world in the true-blue of anti- or noncommunism, leaving patches of dirty red for the dirty Reds.

These ideological strategies reflect policy orientations, for each superpower tries to organize the world so that its influence is widespread and that of the rival minimal. The ideological constructs are models of desired institutional organization. In the American formula, all peoples who do not live under Communist rule are considered part of the free world, that is, natural allies of the United States against Russia. In the Soviet formula, all countries except the imperialist powers are considered as natural allies of the USSR against the North American adversary. Of course, neither the United States nor Soviet Russia has ever come close to organization of a world order in which its preferred formula took institutional form. It seems unlikely that either will be able to achieve this, at least in the twentieth century. Ideology is ahead of reality. But the clashing formulas indicate the direction of U.S.–USSR policy aspirations.

In neither Soviet nor American thinking, moreover, are the rival's centers of power regarded as invulnerable to disintegrative change. There are hopes in Moscow for a further retrenchment of imperialism, and in Washington for the decay of Communist rule. Such ambitions are uncomplicated on the part of Soviet ideologists, because Soviet Marxism had always rejected the possibility of anything more than a very temporary capitalist stabilization. It was more difficult for Soviet theorists to explain the absence of convulsion in the world of capitalism and imperialism than its occurrence. The problem was a little bit more difficult in respect to American ideology. There was a certain contradiction between expectations of Communist disintegration and the central features of the theory of totalitarianism. The latter emphasized a kind of stabilized evil, as though Dante's inscription were carved over the gates to the Communist hell: "Abandon all hope, ye who enter here." Attribution of a static quality to totalitarianism appeared almost to rule out the possibility of change, at least autonomous change.

In fact, the difficulty of reconciling the totalitarian concept with postwar changes in the Soviet Union and the Communist world has been partly responsible for a drift away from reliance in American ideology on the theory of totalitarianism. Other theories have been advanced, including that positing a convergence of all industrial societies; most of these foresee an evolutionary distintegration of Communist institutions and their replacement by institutions more congenial to the West. Despite this backsliding, especially marked in academic circles, the notion of a world divided between totalitarianism and free world countries remains a dominant tenet of orthodox American ideology.

THE AMERICAN VERSION OF A DIVIDED WORLD

The formula describing the international scene as a contest between totalitarianism and the free world originated after World War
II, but the key term, *totalitarianism*, is of older vintage. It came into
circulation in the 1920s as a characterization of the Italian Fascist
régime headed by Benito Mussolini. Originally used in Italy with positive connotations, the term was soon taken over by adversaries, who
used it widely in the 1930s as a critical label for both Fascist Italy and,
especially, Nazi Germany. Use in a laudatory mode languished; Mussolini abandoned the concept; Hitler did not use the term, nor did
Stalin, of course. Except, therefore, for a brief period under Mussolini, the term has been used only as a nasty epithet.[2]

Prior to the beginning of World War II there was ambivalence in
America about linking Russia with Germany and Italy as totalitarian.
Such linkage was not unusual, but the more common pattern was to
treat totalitarian and fascist as almost interchangeable designations.
Because of the key role assigned to "terror" in the theory of totalitarianism, it might have been expected that application to Soviet Russia
would have been especially common in the latter half of the 1930s,
when Stalin unleashed his most ferocious purges. Such was not the
case. References to the USSR as totalitarian increased after the Nazi–
Soviet Nonaggression Pact of 1939, even though the terror had passed
its zenith. Entry of Russia into the war against Germany brought
another shift. In the years of de facto U.S.–USSR alliance,
1941–1945, description of the Soviet Union as totalitarian almost disappeared from U.S. pronouncements, even though there was no dis-
mantlement of the institutions and practices considered characteristically totalitarian.[3] After the war American ideologists focused
discussion of totalitarianism on the USSR and other Communist-ruled
countries, and the theory occupied a prominence that it had never

---

[2] See Leonard Schapire and John W. Lewis, "The Roles of the Monolithic Party
under the Totalitarian Leader," *The China Quarterly*, no. 40 (October–December
1969): 39–42; and Hans Buchheim, *Totalitarian Rule: Its Nature and Characteristics*
(Middletown, Conn.: Wesleyan University Press, 1968), p. 11.

[3] An examination of all references to totalitarianism in articles published in *Foreign
Affairs* and the *American Political Science Review* in 1938–1945 supports these conclu-
sions. There were a few exceptions to the silence about Soviet totalitarianism in the war
years: Rep. Martin Dies, the most vocal anticommunist legislator of the period, and
Thomas Dewey, the Republican presidential candidate in 1944, both made references
to the USSR in this vein.

enjoyed earlier as a description of the Axis states alone or the Axis states plus the USSR.

This résumé suggests that American application of the totalitarian concept to the USSR is correlated more closely with the animosity present in Soviet–American relations than with any internal developments in the Soviet Union, and this despite the theory's focus on internal structure. In the period when Stalin's terror was at its height the Soviet Union appeared as the arch-opponent of expansionist Germany and a bulwark of antifascist resistance. The subsequent changes in the popularity of references to the USSR as totalitarian were closely correlated with changes for the better or worse in Soviet–American international relations.

The postwar "cold war" years brought a full flowering of American theories of totalitarianism. Scholars were enlisted to develop weighty theoretical structures buttressing the use of the concept in elite and mass media by giving it a Teutonic scientific flavor. American students were indoctrinated with the theory from the elementary grades through high school, college, and graduate school. The dominance of the theory was not unconnected with the prevalence in postwar America of a fervent anticommunist agitation to which political leaders of all stripes contributed, notably Democratic President Truman and Secretary of State Acheson and Republican Secretary of State Dulles, Senator McCarthy, and Representative (later Senator and President) Nixon, with the "nonpartisan" assistance of FBI Director Hoover.

This virulent anticommunism was itself somewhat paradoxical, because the American Communist movement had been stronger in prewar than in postwar America. But in the 1930s the Roosevelt administration could only have jeopardized its efforts at domestic reform and at prevention of Axis expansion abroad by mounting an anticommunist crusade. In contrast, postwar Soviet and Communist gains in Europe and Asia created a climate in the U.S. favorable to preoccupation with the Communist "menace," particularly since no postwar administration in Washington was committed, as Roosevelt's had been, to economic and social reform. Liberals and conservatives, Democrats and Republicans, vied to prove that each was more anticommunist than the other.

Characterizing Totalitarianism

What does totalitarian mean in the contraposition of totalitarian vs. free world? The question is all the more necessary to pose because the word has become so commonly used as often to serve simply as a hair-raising "boo" label, applicable to anything and everything. One author describes as totalitarian the part of speech "I"; another speaks of the oceans as totalitarian; even God in one of his guises, Jehovah, has been described as totalitarian. A professional basketball coach once told his players when they complained of his methods: "Cry me no tears. I am a totalitarian dictator."

Naturally, this casual use of the term drives purists up the wall, because they would like to save the concept for exclusive use against Communists. In American political discussions, despite some variations and looseness of usage, the dominant pattern has followed the line advanced by Carl J. Friedrich and Zbigniew Brzezinski in *Totalitarian Dictatorship and Autocracy*[4] and by Hannah Arendt in *The Origins of Totalitarianism*.[5] Though differing on various points, these authors center their approach on an identification of Communist Russia with the extinct German Nazi and Italian Fascist régimes, and of Stalin with Hitler and Mussolini; and they set off these states from other autocratic or dictatorial governments. In much American discussion Imperial Japan is excluded from the totalitarian category, partly because the post-1945 Japanese state represents a less sharp break with militarist Japan of prewar and war years than is true of either Germany or Italy. Moreover, in much postwar writing on totalitarianism (though not in Friedrich) the totalitarian credentials of Fascist Italy are placed in doubt, an ironical result in view of the origin of the term. There was a tendency, in other words, to describe as totalitarian only Nazi Germany and, of course, Soviet Russia; the prominent American diplomat and expert on Russia, Charles E. Bohlen, carried this tendency to its logical conclusion by challenging the totalitarian *bona fides* of the Hitlerite order in Germany.[6]

In any case, for the postwar period—when the contrast between totalitarian and free world countries became the dominant theme of American ideology—the totalitarian box was empty except for Marxist-Leninist states. These included not only the archetypical USSR and the Communist-dominated countries of Eastern Europe but also China, North Korea, and North Vietnam, and—as soon as its

---

[4] (Cambridge, Mass.: Harvard University Press, 1956® 2nd ed. revised by Carl J. Friedrich, 1965).

[5] (New York: Harcourt, Brace & World, Inc., 1951; new edition, 1966).

[6] Charles E. Bohlen, *The Transformation of American Foreign Policy* (New York: W. W. Norton & Co. 1969), p. 111.

Marxist-Leninist character was established—Cuba. Differences among these various countries, whether of party-state or economic institutions or of internal and foreign policy, are only minimally acknowledged; they are not allowed to disturb the neat arrangement. One concession Friedrich and Brzezinski make to possible doubters concerns Eastern Europe: "In the Soviet satellites," they say, "numerous survivals of a non-totalitarian past continue to function. In Poland, Czechoslovakia, Hungary, and Yugoslavia we find such institutions as universities, churches, and schools."[7] Yugoslavia and other (!) "satellites" are thus differentiated from fully totalitarian Russia, where, *kak izvestno*, there are no universities, no churches, and no schools!

A cluster of six basic features is considered by Friedrich and Brzezinski to constitute the distinctive character of totalitarian rule.

> The "syndrome," or pattern of interrelated traits, of the totalitarian dictatorship consists of an ideology, a single party typically led by one man, a terroristic policy, a communications monopoly, a weapons monopoly, and a centrally directed economy.[8]

The crucial features are usually said to be the "totalist" ideology, the dominance of a single ruler, and the systematic use of physical and psychic terror against not merely enemies but the population as a whole. These three elements are central to the treatment of totalitarianism by Hannah Arendt, who emphasizes the totalitarian "movement" rather than what she describes as the "so-called totalitarian state." This kind of movement, she writes, transcends all geographical bounds and is uneasily stabilized within the territorial limits of individual nations.

In view of the central place accorded terror in these theories, the drastic curtailment after Stalin's death of the role of the security police, and the abandonment of large-scale terror caused complications for proponents of theories of totalitarianism. Some preferred to jettison the concept in its application to the Soviet Union, a course eventually taken by Arendt. She wrote in the 1966 edition of *The Origins of Totalitarianism* that totalitarian government "came no less to an end in Russia with the death of Stalin than totalitarianism came to an

---

[7] Friedrich and Brzezinski, *Totalitarian Dictatorship*, 2nd ed. (New York: Frederick A. Praeger, Publishers, 1965, paperback), p. 20.

[8] Ibid., p. 21.

end in Germany with the death of Hitler."[9] But her position was exceptional if not unique; most American ideologists found the concept too useful in the battle of ideas to abandon merely because of changed circumstances.

Communist Rule = Fascist Rule

The dominant variety of totalitarian theory emphasized that the phenomenon was *sui generis*. There are all kinds of venerable concepts for categorization of régimes that are despised, hated, or feared: authoritarian, autocratic, despotic, dictatorial, tyrannical. But reliance on such ancient terms of disapproval would have had a leveling effect on anticommunist and anti-Soviet diatribes, by subsuming these contemporary embodiments of evil under familiar labels, as merely the latest in a long series of noxious states that humanity has endured. As a new concept, totalitarianism could be invested with extremely modern, and peculiarly sinister, attributes.

There was a more specific association that was crucial to the central role of totalitarianism in postwar American ideology. The theory offered a means of bracketing the Soviet order with the Nazi and fascist political systems. Before the war U.S. official attitudes toward Italian Fascism and German Naziism had been ambivalent. Both attracted sympathy for having saved the two countries from Bolshevism, though their dictatorships elicited some disapproval and their expansionist courses aroused alarm.[10] Condemnation increased, of course, with the coming of war. In particular, the Third Reich was seen as the organizer of aggression and conquest directed against Western as well as Eastern European countries, implementing in Germany and occupied territories a program of genocide that took most blatant form in the extermination of 6 million Jews.

By identifying Soviet Russia with Nazi Germany and Fascist Italy under the totalitarian rubric, postwar American ideologists sought to deflect revulsion toward Hitler's crimes to Joseph Stalin, who had a sizeable number of his own. This aspect of American ideological strategy was especially important in the immediate postwar years, because the war had left a strong residue of anti-German and pro-Soviet

---

[9] Arendt, *Origins of Totalitarianism,* p. xxi.

[10] For an account of American ambivalence in regard to Fascist Italy, see John P. Diggins, *Mussolini and Fascism: The View from America* (Princeton, N.J.: Princeton University Press, 1972).

sentiments in the U.S. and Western countries. Germany had to be decriminalized and Russia desanctified in one fell swoop, and in such a manner that anti-Nazi sentiment could be divorced from Germany and transmuted into an anti-Soviet form. The theory of totalitarianism provided the mechanism for this psychological operation.

Totalitarian States Distinguished from Merely Authoritarian Rule

If postwar totalitarian theory sought to link the extinct Nazi and Fascist states with existing Communist states, it simultaneously sought to differentiate the latter from "merely" authoritarian régimes. Totalitarianism was not viewed as part of a continuum separated only in degree from other kinds of authoritarian rule. On the contrary, a deep divide was posited between Communist states and all others. The former were assigned to the category of "totalitarian" governments, the latter—whether democratic or dictatorial—to the category "free world." In this dichotomy freedom came to mean nothing more nor less than freedom from Communist rule.

This formula served as a nearly perfect organizing concept for U.S. domestic and foreign policy. If the doctrine had not already existed, it would have had to be invented. Why? The reason lies in the fact that one-party, and no-party, governments of authoritarian hue have been a dime a dozen outside the industrially developed countries of Europe, North America, Japan, and, to a lesser extent, Latin America. They could be found among states long independent and among those gaining independence with the postwar collapse of colonial empires. Most of these authoritarian régimes have many common interests with the United States; many of the countries are formally allied to the U.S. Generally, they welcome foreign and especially American investment and economic influence. Above all, most share with the United States a preoccupation with the threat of communism, sometimes from external but more often from internal sources. Their parochial interests thus mesh with the global interests of postwar America, which sought to solidify a position of world leadership by finding bulwarks of anticommunism, a role into which such authoritarian states fit like the hand into the glove.

This is why the imputed division of the world between totalitarian and free world countries in American postwar ideology largely replaced the older distinction between democracy and dictatorship. The latter dichotomy was not banished. American ruling circles and ideological mentors felt an affinity for countries with genuine parliamentary institutions, such as England, France, and Italy. And this affinity outweighed the fact that such states allowed Communist and leftist parties to function, and that in some—Italy and France in particular—Communist parties were solidly entrenched. These democracies had demonstrated, however, their capability to allow Communist parties to exist while keeping them out of power.

In many parts of the underdeveloped world a different situation prevailed. Individual dictators or small ruling cliques maintained themselves in power by authoritarian measures, suspecting that any opening up of the political system to mass participation, multiple parties, and opposition activities would give opportunities for Communists or radical nationalists. Both local leaders and their Washington benefactors understood that democratic institutions might jeopardize the anticommunist, pro-American orientation of the country. Why spoil a good thing? Washington saw no profit in encouraging democratic trends under such circumstances. On the ideological plane, American emphasis on a democracy–dictatorship dichotomy would have separated from the U.S. the very countries whose firm linkage to the Washington-led international bloc was the object of U.S. policy.

The preference accorded the totalitarian vs. free world formula over the democracy–dictatorship formula thus stemmed from the fact that if a choice had to be made between democracy on the one hand and stable anticommunism on the other, Washington invariably opted for the latter. In postwar U.S. history there is scarcely an episode in which the U.S. used its great influence, military, political, or economic, to promote democratization of political life in the direction called for in the U.S. definition of democracy. U.S. statesmen and ideologists often denounced the lack of pluralism, the absence of choice in elections, and the denial of opposition rights in Communist-ruled countries. But these were precisely the countries in which the U.S. had the least capabilities of encouraging change. In regard to the states where the U.S. did have much influence, Washington manifested strong scruples against interference in domestic arrangements that institutionalized authoritarian rule.

Racism and the Free World/Totalitarian Contrast

The free world/totalitarian formula justified not only general support by the United States of anticommunist authoritarian régimes abroad, but also support of white rule in Africa against challenges from national or black liberation forces. On issues of colonial rule in

Africa, for example, the United States by and large sided with the European colonial powers whether they resisted or acceded to independence movements. For more than a decade after 1945 the U.S. maintained a line enunciated first in the Truman–Acheson administration to the effect that black populations were not ready for self-rule; the totalitarian/free world dichotomy served to justify this position. For it was suspected that black governments would be, at the minimum, less anticommunist than the local administrations maintained by London, Paris, Brussels, and Lisbon. In any case, the formula held that the black populations were "free," despite their subjection to white domination, because they were free from Communist control.

The colonial issue faded as colonial rule faded, but the issue of rule by a white minority over large black populations remained very much alive in southern Africa. Here again the doctrine under discussion facilitated U.S. accommodation to the white racist régime in the Republic of South Africa and in Southern Rhodesia (the latter presented a special problem because of its generally unrecognized declaration of independence from the United Kingdom). To be sure, the early warm support of the South African republic changed to a more critical attitude. But as late as 1960 the State Department could not bring itself to criticize South African racism when that nation "strongly supports the United States in the overriding issues of our times," i.e., the issue of communism vs. the free world.[11]

The Pretoria and Salisbury governments had logic on their side in defending themselves as bastions of the free world. South Africa in particular kept an open door for the investment of American capital, and very profitable investment, and both régimes severely repressed "communist activities," i.e., any challenge to the rule of the white minority. South African and Rhodesian leaders made much of their fidelity to the free world, and they could portray their social orders as the very epitome of freedom in the sense in which freedom was understood in the contrast between the free world and totalitarianism.

Domestic Impact of the Doctrine

It might be noted in passing that the doctrine portraying the world as divided between totalitarian and free world forces had conse-

---

[11] Joseph C. Satterthwaite, then assistant secretary of state for African affairs, later ambassador to the Republic of South Africa, quoted in Rupert Emerson, *Africa and the United States Policy* (Englewood Cliffs, N.J.: Prentice-Hall, Inc., 1967), p. 100.

quences on the internal political scene in the United States as well as on foreign policy. Though generally accepted, the theory received its strongest support from conservative and right-wing political elements, who found the doctrine congenial to their efforts to defend the status quo in the U.S. not only against a rather weak radical movement but also against reform efforts supported by liberals. The popularity of the doctrine also helped these same right-wing elements to maintain an environment in the United States favorable to a militant foreign policy stance, one involving use of military, economic, and other instruments, unilaterally if necessary, to police the world and arrest Communist, radical, or anti-American advances. Conservative–liberal differences on the point should not be overblown, because there were few foreign policy issues on which liberal–conservative consensus broke down. Vietnam policy was one, and it was not coincidental that this breakdown occurred in a period when the totalitarian/free world formula no longer received practically unanimous adherence (though it remained dominant).

The American right profited most from the contrast of the free world to totalitarianism because the formula focused attention not on internal tasks but on threats from outside the country, from Communist aggression and Communist subversion. In addition, because the United States was regarded not only as part of the free world but the leader of the free world, the "freedom" of the free world was seen a reaching its finest expression in America, in American institutions and practices.

White racism can serve as an example here, as it served earlier in relation to the foreign policy applications of the theory of totalitarianism. For generations American political leaders and ideologists, and most American citizens, found no contradiction between celebrating America as the land of freedom and keeping blacks in subjection. Even when actual slavery of blacks existed, Americans sang about the "land of the free" in the "Star-Spangled Banner" and about their "sweet land of liberty" in "America, My Country 'Tis of Thee." Nor did this attitude fundamentally change after slavery gave way to other forms of institutionalized subjection. Even in post–World War II America, it could be argued, and was so argued by some white Southern political leaders, that freedom, as in the "free world," was not at all inconsistent with maintenance of white supremacy over blacks. Even those less forthright on the racial issue—probably the major issue in postwar America—found the totalitarian menace a useful intellectual device to divert attention from demands for reform in the United States, if not to rationalize black subjugation.[12] Obviously, however, the popularity of the doctrine did not prevent gradual elimination over the postwar years of a structure of laws and policies discriminating against blacks. It would be injudicious, in any case, to assign decisive importance to a doctrine of this type in determining the internal trend of events, particularly in respect to a problem as significant in American life as black–white relations.

Especially in academic circles, the doctrine contrasting totalitarianism to the free world no longer enjoys the almost unanimous support it received in the years of intense cold war, and in U.S. ideological pronouncements generally it no longer is propounded with the verve of those years. Its decline resulted from changes in perceptions of both the Soviet Union and the United States. But that decline is only relative; the doctrine continues to occupy a major role in U.S. ideology and in U.S. psychological warfare. In other words, the formula contrasting totalitarianism to the free world is alive and well in the Washington of the 1970s, the Washington of Nixon, Ford, and Carter, just as it was in the Washington of Truman and Acheson.

TWO WORLDS LOCKED IN COMBAT: THE SOVIET VERSION

Despite obvious dissimilarities, "imperialism" plays a role in Soviet ideology that is in many respects like the role of "totalitarianism" in American ideology. Imperialism has a more ancient lineage, and even in the meaning defined by Lenin it dates back to the end of the nineteenth century.

In Soviet usage imperialism is not directly connected with empires,

---

[12] The point is illustrated in the writings of Professor Friedrich, the leading theorist of totalitarianism. See especially Carl J. Friedrich, *Man and His Government: An Empirical Theory of Politics* (New York: McGraw-Hill Book Co., 1963). In this book, which includes substantial discussion of the American political system, Friedrich avoids all treatment of racial factors except for a few references that tend to justify black exclusions and restrictions. Mentioning an increase in black political participation, Friedrich writes (p. 296): "masses of people often completely devoid of all qualifications for political participation are nonetheless permitted to vote and even to let themselves be elected." And in discussing voting, Friedrich argues (p. 308) that blacks and other "permanent minorities" are represented even though they may not choose their own representatives. They are "represented but by unasked-for representatives who represent them because they exist and occupy the position they do." Senator Bilbo's black constituents never had it so good!

ancient or modern: possession of colonies is not a necessary attribute. There is, of course, a vast literature on the subject of imperialism in general and the Leninist analysis in particular. The focus here is on the use made of imperialism in Soviet ideological strategy. But this requires a brief summary of Lenin's approach as advanced in a "popular outline" of 1916 entitled *Imperialism, the Highest Stage of Capitalism*. [13]

Lenin wrote:

> Imperialism is capitalism in that stage of development in which the domination of monopolies and finance capital has established itself; in which the export of capital has acquired pronounced importance; in which the division of the world among the international trusts has begun; in which the partition of all the territories of the globe among the great capitalist powers has been completed. [14]

In Leninist (Soviet) usage imperialism is not a *policy* adopted by one or another capitalist state but a phase of capitalist development. It is the highest stage because the contradictions of capitalism become most acute under imperialism, and therefore this phase is the prelude to proletarian revolution. No possibility exists, according to the theory, for resolving these contradictions through creation of a kind of superimperialism whose world scope would eliminate struggle between rival imperialist powers. " 'Inter-imperialist' or 'ultra-imperialist' alllances," Lenin wrote, "no matter what form they may assume, whether of one imperialist coalition against another, or of a general alliance embracing *all* the imperialist powers, are *inevitably* nothing more than a 'truce' in periods between wars." [15]

Although Lenin used terms such as *parasitism, stagnation,* and *decay* to characterize monopoly capitalism in its imperialist phase, he did not rule out the possibility that capitalist countries might continue to advance economically in the imperialist period. "It would be a mistake to believe that this tendency to decay precludes the possibility of the rapid growth of capitalism. It does not. In the epoch of imperialism, certain branches of industry, certain strata of the bourgeoisie and certain countries betray, to a greater or less degree, one or another of these tendencies. On the whole, capitalism is growing," Lenin wrote

---

[13] V. I. Lenin, *Selected Works* (London: Martin Lawrence, Ltd., n.d.), 5:3–119.

[14] Ibid., p. 81.

[15] Ibid., p. 110.

in 1916, "far more rapidly than before, but . . . this growth is becoming more and more uneven. . . ."[16] Needless to say, the formulas presenting alternatives of stagnation or decay and of rapid growth allow Soviet ideologists to display fidelity to Lenin while taking account of either prosperity or recession in the capitalist West, the former grudgingly, the latter glowingly.

In present-day usage, imperialism, like totalitarianism, identifies something that is loathsome. The term is applied to the United States in Soviet ideology with automaticity, and since World War II the U.S. has been treated as the dominant imperialist power. Description of the U.S. as imperialist is not new, but Lenin and prewar Soviet ideologists gave much more attention to British, German, and French imperialism than to American. None of these European (or Japanese) varieties received the priority that American imperialism has been accorded since the war.

It was noted earlier that the concept of imperialism is not exactly parallel to that of totalitarianism. The former stresses international relations, the latter internal structure; the former economic affairs, the latter political. Imperialism has little meaning outside the context of international affairs, though it is sometimes applied to majority–minority ethnic relations within a country, in the U.S. or in the USSR. In contrast, description of a society as totalitarian requires no reference to its position vis-à-vis others. In fact, however, most U.S. ideologists who concentrate on totalitarianism describe states of this type as inherently expansive, aggressive, and hegemonistic.

As to the emphasis on economics or politics, theorists of imperialism subsume political structure within the general theory of imperialism as theorists of totalitarianism subsume economic structure within the basic framework of totalitarian institutions. Nevertheless, there is a basic difference. Soviet ideologists portray imperialism as compatible with a variety of political orders ranging from the bourgeois democratic at one end of the spectrum to the fascist at the other. The only counterpoint to this in the U.S. discussion of totalitarianism is that a variety of ownership systems is recognized as compatible with totalitarianism provided that there exists, in Friedrich and Brzezinski's words, "a centrally directed economy."

The Soviet concept presents the world as divided between imperialist and antiimperialist states (or nonimperialist), in other words,

---

[16] Ibid., p. 116.

applies a dichotomy similar to the totalitarian/free world dichotomy of American ideology. The United States, Great Britain, France, Japan, and a few other advanced capitalist countries are alone in the first camp. The Soviet Union (naturally!) and other socialist states are placed in the second camp, which also includes, however, a large number of other countries more or less hostile to the imperialist powers, especially the newly independent countries of Asia and Africa but generally those adopting a stance of nonalignment. This grouping is ascriptive in the sense that it involves no organizational structure and no necessary self-identification of the member countries with the grouping; here also it is similar to the free world grouping posited in U.S. ideology. In Khrushchev's time the grouping of these states was called the "zone of peace," but that expression has been retired from circulation.

Clearly the formula applied by Soviet ideologists is somewhat fuzzy at the edges because—like the free world formula—it includes such a wide variety of states in the nonimperialist camp that they defy any easy characterization. Nevertheless, the purpose is clear: to portray the Soviet Union linked by common interests with an overwhelming majority of the countries and peoples of the world.[17] It depicts the United States, in contrast, as encircled within a tightening net of antiimperialist forces (and simultaneously compelled to struggle against other "imperialist sharks").

In relationship to the international scene the formula pointing to imperialism as the enemy has tended to crowd out the formula stressing capitalism as the adversary. The formula contrasting socialism to capitalism has by no means been abandoned; in Soviet discussion of ideological and social systems the choice is said to be either socialism or capitalism. No third alternative is possible. According to this view nonalignment in ideology is ruled out; there is no intermediate system, no "zone of peace" in ideological struggle.

But portrayals of the world stressing the capitalism–socialism dichotomy, more common under Stalin than under his successors, have the effect of "ideologically" isolating the USSR and fraternal socialist states from the rest of the world. The capitalist–socialist formula thus

---

[17] To be precise, Soviet ideology depicts the world as divided on a class basis rather than a country basis. Socialist nations, uniquely free of class conflict, are thus said to be united in a common movement with progressive antiimperialist states and with groups of working people and others in nonsocialist countries, even in imperialist states, who oppose imperialism.

tended to emphasize socialist weakness and capitalist strength. In fact, Stalin's Russia was more or less isolated from all but Communist-run countries, and this isolation was partly willed by the Soviet leadership, then rather hostile toward the leadership groups in newly independent and other less-developed countries.[18]

If Stalin saw mostly disadvantages in Soviet attempts to play the new "third world" against the old imperialist world, opportunities loomed larger to his successors, who allowed the passivity of Stalin's foreign policy to be criticized.[19] In any case, economic recovery from the war permitted the post-Stalin leadership to give material backing to a more forward policy respecting underdeveloped countries. Thus, changes in both leadership and resource availability facilitated a change in foreign policy that found ideological reflection in a shift of emphasis from the socialist–capitalist dichotomy to the imperialism vs. antiimperialism formula.

Just as the totalitarian formula served American policy needs in the postwar years, so the imperialism concept fitted to a tee the needs of Soviet policy. World War II had opened opportunities for the spread of Communist rule to Eastern Europe, northern Asia, and Indochina. But prospects for further advances were dim. In most areas Communists were not strong enough to gain power on their own momentum; the USSR had few capabilities to help; and not only in Europe but elsewhere the United States had the capability and, as the Korean War showed, the determination to intervene militarily to block Communist advances.

The formula centering on imperialism sanctified a Soviet opening to countries in Asia, Africa, and Latin America that had long been politically and economically dependent on the U.S. or other advanced capitalist powers. These "third world" countries were (in varying degrees) economically underdeveloped; most were basically agricultural; some had almost no industry. They were not, therefore, good

---

[18] The contrast between Stalin's policy and that which followed should not be exaggerated. The "two-camp" formula associated with the Cominform (established in 1947) depicted an imperialist and antidemocratic camp under American domination opposed by an antiimperialist and democratic camp. Although the latter included not only the USSR and other Communist-dominated countries, and even Finland, developing countries were significantly omitted.

[19] The beginning of this shift occurred, however, in Stalin's last years, when India and some other newly independent countries began to stake out a neutralist position in response to Korean War developments.

prospects for socialism in any near term; and the USSR could not hope to make common cause with them on this basis. They had, however, bundles of grievances, old and new, against the Western states, old colonial masters or not. Such grievances were reinforced constantly by evidence of their poverty and powerlessness in comparison to such rich nations as the United States. Thus, they offered good prospects to be potential allies of the USSR in an antiimperialist cause.

In practical terms the formula meant that the Soviet leadership was willing to subordinate the USSR's role as a bellwether of socialism to a role in promoting a world bloc against the U.S. and other imperialist powers. If a state displayed at least a minimal anti-U.S. orientation, Soviet leaders and ideologists were perfectly willing to overlook almost everything else: oppression of the masses, dictatorship resting on a narrow class base, domination by the military, perpetuation of a stagnant economy, even suppression of Communist activities—all sins in the Marxist-Leninist bible.

Soviet foreign policy managers no doubt calculated that the logic of an antiimperialist (and anti-U.S.) orientation would lead such countries eventually to take the road to socialism. The rationale of antiimperialism as such does not go beyond measures limiting or eliminating foreign economic penetration, rejection of alliance with the U.S. and refusal of U.S. military bases, adoption of a posture of nonalignment; such measures can gain the support of varied population groups, including native businessmen, the so-called national bourgeoisie. But Soviet expectations are that a vigorous antiimperialism leading to the "expropriation of the foreign expropriators," to adapt Marx's terminology, would be merely the prelude to a socialist "expropriation of the indigenous expropriators." In most of the targeted countries the main problem is one of development rather than redistribution, and Soviet policy-makers apparently expect that a focus on antiimperialism will result in programs to build up the state sector rather than the private economic sector, again paving the way for transition to socialism. Even if a socialist pattern were not followed, local measures against foreign (i.e., American) economic and political influence offer satisfaction to the USSR sufficient for the day.

Impact in the USSR of the Focus on Imperialism

Parallel to the situation in the United States, emphasis in the USSR on the imperialist/antiimperialist struggle has certain domestic consequences. The doctrine receives its strongest support from, and simultaneously buttresses the position of, the more reactionary elements in Soviet political life.[20] It serves this purpose by stressing the threat represented by imperialism and particularly by the USSR's archrival, the United States. Calls for domestic reform in the Soviet Union, for more attention to the population's material needs, for relaxation of pressures for citizen conformity, and for a more conciliatory foreign policy were shunted aside so as not to divert attention from the need to carry on a determined struggle against imperialism.

The evidence is scanty at best, but it appears that the elements of the Soviet elite who are most anxious to preserve the status quo, build military strength, heighten vigilance against enemies, and push an aggressive foreign policy line are precisely those most inclined to emphasize the dangers of imperialism, of imperialist ideology and imperialist agents. In contrast, those seeking reform of Soviet domestic policies and practices and a more conciliatory foreign policy are naturally led to minimize the threat stemming from imperialism; they prefer to focus on homegrown evils and deficiencies, including, since the late 1950s, the threat of a revived "Stalinism."

COMPLICATIONS FOR U.S. AND USSR IDEOLOGIES

Postwar developments created a number of complications for the American and Soviet ruling orthodoxies, including the key formulas discussed in this chapter. The American focus on the totalitarian challenge aroused few questions in the first postwar decade, when the "cold war" flourished and bilateral relations with the USSR fluctuated back and forth between intense animosity and icy reserve. In the period beginning in the middle 1950s, however, changes went against ideologists' anticipations. Theorists of the totalitarianism such as Friedrich and Brzezinski posited in 1956 a tendency for "totalitarian dictatorships . . . to become more total."[21] Any kind of stability was out of the question: these régimes "oscillate between an extreme of totalitar-

---

[20] In American parlance, these could be called rightist elements. But in the Marxist-Leninist movement, rightists are those tending to reformism with a "softness" on bourgeois opponents; leftists are those tending to ultramilitancy in promoting orthodox values with a "hard" line toward opponents.

[21] Friedrich and Brzezinski, *Totalitarian Dictatorship*, 1956 ed., p. 300. In the second edition this point was declared invalid, p. 376.

ian violence and an opposite extreme of an actual breakdown."[22] Abjuring any false modesty, the authors proclaim that the future course of totalitarian foreign policy "can be predicted with some confidence." The future is seen as including the development of "aggressive belligerency in subject populations throughout the world," intensification of "the totalitarianization of the satellite nations," and "foreign expansion, short of war." While the Soviet totalitarians are unlikely, Friedrich and Brzezinski write, to "launch a major and open campaign of aggression because of internal difficulties," the possibility of war will increase as the Communists gain in military preponderance.[23] "The possibility for peaceful coexistence of the nations peopling this world presupposes the disappearance of the totalitarian dictatorships," and consequently, according to these authors, "those who reject the system have no alternative but to strive for its destruction."[24]

Very little happened as anticipated by totalitarian theory. Soviet "totalitarianism" did not become more "total," if by that is meant a heightened use of terror, an extension of the role of the security police (KGB), a more rigorous suppression of dissent. On the contrary, there was a marked tendency in the Soviet Union toward a minimization of police methods of control. Nor have the Soviet Union and similar states oscillated between extremes of violence and total breakdown. The pattern of Soviet foreign policy has scarcely been one of violent aggression or of increased subjugation by the USSR of dependent Communist states. Finally, the increase of Soviet and Warsaw Pact military capabilities has appeared to coincide with a lessening rather than heightening of prospects for the outbreak of general war.[25]

Although an adversary status has continued to characterize Soviet–

---

[22] Friedrich and Brzezinski, *Totalitarian Dictatorship*, 2nd ed., p. 375.

[23] Ibid., pp. 376–77.

[24] Ibid., p. 365.

[25] Anticipating the future is definitely not Professor Friedrich's forte. His analysis of totalitarian prospects in Germany, a country that—unlike Russia—he knew well, was as far off the mark as his analysis of the prospects of totalitarianism in the USSR. Thus, in April 1933 (!), Friedrich assured Americans that whether Germany opted for a U.S.-style presidential republic, muddled along with the Weimar system, or went for a constitutional monarchy, "in any case, Germany will remain a constitutional, democratic state with strong socializing tendencies whose backbone will continue to be its professional civil service"!! See "The Development of the Executive Power in Germany," *American Political Science Review 27*, no. 2 (April 1933): 203.

American relations, negotiations and agreements have become more common than unchecked hostility. Détente has settled in, if on as uneasy terms as in the period of wartime quasi-alliance in 1941–1945. Since the Kennedy administration the former American reluctance to engage in bilateral negotiations with the USSR has almost disappeared. Recurring dangers and opportunities alike made it inexpedient for the superpowers to reject attempts at diplomatic conciliation while waiting for the collapse of the rival.

In short, Soviet internal trends and trends in international relations, including U.S.–USSR relations, made it more and more awkward for the U.S. to hold to the old formula of the free world vs. the totalitarians. Rapprochement with the USSR made pertinent a question: Why was a nice country like the United States keeping company with the totalitarians, exchanging amiable gestures and signing pledges of coexistence? A response might be to drop the theory of totalitarianism down the memory hole. Although a certain trend in this direction can be detected, it is too early to wave good-bye to this central concept of postwar American ideology. The notion of a world divided between free and totalitarian states retains a prominent, if disputed, place in the American ideological arsenal.

The Soviet theory of a world divided between imperialist and antiimperialist states has also run into difficulties. To be sure, this Soviet formula was inherently more dynamic, that is, more capable of accounting for change, than the parallel U.S. formula. Nevertheless, the changes that actually happened were often not those expected in Soviet theory. Thus, sharp divisions in the socialist camp were not foreseen, even if divisions in the adversary camp were anticipated. Moreover, it was expected that when clashes among the imperialists occurred, the USSR and Communists generally would not care much which side won or lost. In fact, the divergences that emerged in the imperialist camp, notably those between France and the United States, were of intense interest to Moscow. Soviet leaders saw in these Franco-American differences an opportunity to develop political, economic, and cultural ties to France, hoping thereby to weaken American domination of Western European policy.

There was a still greater difficulty in reconciling a firm antiimperialist line with the warming of Soviet relations with the United States. It might be awkward to hold hands with the minor-league imperialists, but this could be justified as a way of weakening the major imperialist power, the U.S. But to consort with the big daddy of all imperialists! True, peaceful coexistence with the U.S. and other capitalist nations had long been a prominent formula in Soviet ideology, and tête-à-têtes of Soviet and American leaders could be exploited to show what a long way Soviet power had come from enforced isolation to meeting the U.S. on an equal footing.

But Soviet bilateral relations with the U.S. in the 1960s and 1970s went way beyond that minimum civility and restraint required by the war-avoidance posture endorsed in coexistence theory. The image of hand holding across the ideological gulf that purportedly separated the imperialists from their most resolute opponents seemed especially flagrant on occasions such as the Moscow summit of May 1972. For Brezhnev and his associates welcomed Nixon to Moscow at the very time when the U.S. military forces under Nixon's orders were escalating attacks on North Vietnam, linked in fraternity if not by military alliance with the Soviet Union.

The awkwardness inherent in such Soviet dealings with American imperialists mirrored that of Americans dealing with the hated totalitarians. Naturally, Soviet ideology sought to explain away the seeming contradiction. The USSR was said to be uncompromising in its hostility to imperialism, including the American variety, but perfectly amenable to good relations with the United States government. Soviet compromises with the latter, in a word, did not compromise the principled Soviet opposition to the former. This was a particular application of a more general formula: peaceful coexistence should govern the relations between the USSR and states of a different social system, but there could be no coexistence between socialism, on the one hand, and capitalism (imperialism) on the other. Implicit in the formula was the idea that the Soviet authorities were not about to allow penetration of alien ideas into Russia, nor to renounce support for efforts to eliminate capitalism wherever it existed.

In effect, if not openly, Soviet ideology thus treated imperialism as merely one aspect of American ruling-class behavior, something that did not enter into USSR–U.S. arrangements on a wide span of political-economic-military-cultural issues. An American president could be toasted in Moscow as a coexistent state leader, somehow not quite the same imperialist who was simultaneously directing attacks on or seeking to undermine Soviet Communist ideology and institutions, the same person who was in charge of U.S. efforts to maintain economically weak nations in neoimperialist bondage. But it was, and is, difficult to reconcile this fine distinction with the basic Leninist theory of imperialism. For that theory held, as noted before, that imperialism was not just a policy, not just a result of base leaders holding office, but a stage in the development of capitalism, a stage characterized by certain very determined, and very odious, policy consequences. The salami was being sliced exceedingly thin.

Despite the difficulties of reconciling doctrine with behavior, no inclination has been shown in the USSR toward major alteration, let alone abandonment, of the formula describing the world as caught in a struggle between the forces of imperialism and of counterimperialism. Nor is such abandonment at all likely, even if stability and cooperation were to become the rule rather than the exception in Soviet–Western and particularly Soviet–American relations, a highly improbable prospect. New faces may appear and new accents be heard, but Soviet leaders are not about to undergo a miraculous conversion on the road from their dachas to the Moscow Kremlin.

They will continue to need an ideology, and among other elements a theory like that of imperialism vs. antiimperialism, to justify their efforts to bring about a global victory of communism and to achieve unquestioned Soviet supremacy in the world. They need this just as much as American leaders need an ideology, and a theory like that of totalitarianism vs. the free world, to give meaning and organizational structure to American efforts to solidify the global position of capitalism and to enhance the world role of the United States.

7

U.S.-USSR MILITARY RIVALRY

$\mathbb{S}$ OVIET–AMERICAN military rivalry is distinct from rivalry in other areas because of the intensity of mutual interaction. The possibility of a direct armed clash between the United States and the Soviet Union leads each country, as a first priority, to equip itself with armed forces and armaments capable of dealing with those of the adversary. In other areas of U.S.–USSR competition the reciprocal element is far less important. Economic rivalry is certainly as important as military, and may ultimately be more decisive. But competing economic systems cannot come to grips in a fateful confrontation at a single time and place. Therefore, policy-makers rarely adjust economic policy to anything the opponent does or does not do. The urgency of countering a rival's initiatives and innovations, technological or other, is felt most strongly in the military sphere.

This characteristic of military rivalry encourages a certain degree of symmetry in the two nations' force structures and levels of military effort. Changes in the technological level and gross power of one side call forth responses from the other. True, the symmetry is far from complete. While army divisions and squadrons of fighter planes may be organized to take on rival divisions and squadrons in combat, missile and bomber forces are likely to have as their major missions strikes at targets other than the enemy's missile and bomber forces. A strengthening of offensive arms may be met by a strengthening of defenses. In the "bomber age" the Soviet Union attempted to counter American capabilities for a long-range air attack on the USSR by relying more upon antiaircraft defense than upon a matching deterrent force of heavy bombers.

And there are numerous other conditions that contribute to the maintenance of some asymmetry: differences in geography, in industrial and scientific levels, in tradition, in ideology. Moreover, while the rivalry between the U.S. and USSR plays a major role in determining the size and structure of the respective armed forces, the latter have other assignments, even domestic assignments, that have little to do with countering the principal rival. This is evident in relation to the USSR, which shares a contested border of several thousand kilometers with a hostile state, the Chinese People's Republic; it is also true of the United States, though in a less dramatic way.

Nevertheless, U.S.–USSR symmetry has increased in the three postwar decades. Postwar military history shows that innovations on one side or the other have usually inspired imitative responses, from the development of atomic and nuclear weapons to the perfection and proliferation of rapid delivery systems. Under the Johnson administration the United States explicitly linked a decision to begin deployment of antimissile defenses with the appearance of an ABM defense ring around Moscow. Similarly, the Soviet response to the American MIRV (a system allowing a single missile launcher to fire simultaneously several individually guided warheads) was to proceed on a parallel line of development. Keeping up with the Joneses meant that the Ivanovs usually tried to have whatever the Joneses had, and vice versa; since both had adequate scientific, technological, and industrial resources, neither could expect to maintain exclusive possession for a long time of military innovations.

The subsequent treatment of Soviet–American military rivalry begins with a discussion of some general indices of military efforts, the numbers of persons maintained in the armed forces and the expenditures for military purposes in the two countries. This is followed by an examination of rival forces in three more or less distinct areas, strategic arms, European theater forces, and globally mobile forces. Proposals and negotiations on measures to limit arms competition in these various areas are then taken up, leading to an assessment of the impact of agreements on Soviet and American forces. Because the military position of the two states is strongly affected by their roles as senior states in military alliances, the next section considers the status of bilateral and multilateral alliances in which the two countries participate. In a less direct manner the military position of these great powers is also affected by their activities as the world's greatest arms givers and arms merchants, a topic that is considered in the following pages. In the final section, after rather brief mention of quasi-military competition in intelligence and scientific fields, an attempt is made to assess the postwar changes in correlation of military strength between the United States and the Soviet Union.

Two caveats are in order. One concerns comprehensiveness. Obviously in this chapter, as in others, the treatment aims to present a broad outline of major developments, not a detailed analysis. The other concerns the data base. Almost without exception the data for both American and Soviet forces and for military spending come from U.S. sources, either the Pentagon or the CIA, and this includes data filtered through Western (but non-American) sources such as the London International Institute for Stretegic Studies. The only military figure routinely published in the USSR is an annual lump-sum appropriation for defense; although this figure is probably meaningful, no one not privy to Soviet secrets knows what it means. It clearly does not cover all the expenditures usually associated with military activities in the United States. With only a few minor exceptions in the past, no figures are published on numbers in the Soviet armed forces, or in individual components, or on numbers of missiles, aircraft, tanks, surface ships, and submarines. All of the U.S.–USSR strategic arms negotiations have proceeded on the basis of U.S.-supplied data for both sides; the same has generally been true of the Vienna talks on mutual reductions of forces in north and central Europe, although some data were eventually presented to the conference by the Warsaw Pact countries.

It is recognized in all military powers, including the United States, that secrecy about military and quasi-military affairs contributes to national strength. But the line is drawn at a much different point in the USSR and other Communist states than in Western countries. Nor have Soviet authorities become more forthcoming with the narrowing of the gap in military power between the USSR and the United States. Although there are inconveniences for the USSR associated with this penchant for secrecy, they are apparently far outweighed in the eyes of the authorities by the advantages gained.

Whatever the reasons for the policy, the latter hampers efforts to make accurate comparisons of U.S. and Soviet military strength. It forces reliance on exclusively American figures, i.e., on data and estimates from sources that have a strong interest in inflating figures on USSR military capabilities. This interest is dictated by the heavy use of these data to justify enlargement of American military programs. (In contrast, American data suppliers have an opposed interest in respect to economic developments, where secrecy—though not as complete as in the military sphere—also results in gaps and distortions. They have an interest in deflating figures on Soviet economic achievements so as to buttress an image of socialist inefficiency and failure.) In neither area, and especially not in the military field, is there any way of avoiding reliance on U.S. estimates.

POSTWAR MILITARY TRENDS

Before 1945, when rivalry between the United States and the USSR for the first time began to dominate their military programs, there had been little similarity between American and Russian military structures. For decades before World War II the navy had been the strongest element in U.S. peacetime forces, the standing army in Russian. World War II modified this orientation in the U.S. Aircraft along with surface vessels and submarines played a crucial role in campaigns in the Pacific and European theaters, although ground troops were committed in large numbers, particularly in Europe, during the later war years. Thus, the United States developed and made abundant use of long-range bombers in strikes at Japanese and German targets; these anticipated the strategic forces on which postwar American–Soviet military rivalry was to center.[1] In contrast, naval and air power played a distinctly secondary role in the USSR's wartime forces. Russia in 1941–1945 slugged it out with Germany in epic ground battles that consumed men and matériel in wholesale quantities.

Technologically, therefore, the United States emerged from the war far better equipped than the Soviet Union for the ensuing military competition. At the war's end it possessed the capability of making atomic bombs and a means of delivery on distant targets, plus a navy that could reach the shores of any adversary. The USSR had no such ultimate weapon, no suitable delivery vehicle for such a weapon even if it had it, and no navy capable of distant operations. Strategic rivalry in the years to follow meant intense efforts on the part of the

---

[1] It is ironic to recall the words of the U.S. Army chief of staff in 1936 advising against American procurement of four-engine bombers: "The subject airplane is distinctly an airplane of aggression. It can bomb points in Europe and South America and return without refueling. It has no place in the armament of a nation which has a national policy of good will and military policy of protection, not aggression." Quoted in Robert W. Krauskopf, "The Army and the Strategic Bomber, 1930–1939," *Military Affairs* (Summer, 1958): 85.

United States to maintain and advance its No. 1 military position, and equally intense Soviet efforts to eliminate the American advantage.

Military Personnel

One frequently used measure of military strength is that of total armed forces personnel. It has limited utility, particularly in the context of U.S.–USSR rivalry. Total personnel figures give disproportionate weight to changing numbers of ground troops; they likewise are a most inadequate index of air and naval power, better measured in quantities of variously equipped seagoing vessels and aerospace vehicles. Moreover, personnel totals of the Soviet and American military establishments have been especially subject to increases and decreases that related only indirectly to U.S.–USSR rivalry. Nevertheless, trends in overall personnel numbers deserve some consideration for whatever they are worth as a guide, admittedly inadequate, to total Soviet and American military efforts.

The accompanying chart highlights the trends in manpower, for the years shown usually represent turning points, culminations of upward or downward trends on one side or the other. The reductions depicted after 1945 are relevant to a claim often made in the U.S. that America demobilized after the war but Russia did not. The notion is no less erroneous because widely believed. Both demobilized, if to different degrees, and mostly in ground forces. Neither country returned to its prewar level, about half a million for the USSR and a quarter-million for the United States. In fact, at the very lowest postwar point, in 1948, each state had about six times the size of its prewar forces. This maintenance by both the Soviet Union and the United States of much larger postwar than prewar military forces resulted in part from their deployment abroad of substantial numbers of ground troops and other military personnel. Before World War II such foreign stationing was on a very modest scale. After the war both countries had forces outside national territory that were larger than their entire armed forces of prewar years.

Post-1945 demobilization cut into ground troops much more than air and naval forces, because the latter were central in Soviet–American rivalry. Long before the cold war became intense, President Harry Truman said on October 27, 1945: "When our demobilization is all finished as planned, the United States will still be the greatest naval power on earth. In addition to that naval power, we

Table 6
Armed Forces Personnel Strength
(millions)

U.S.		USSR
12+	1945	12+
1.4	1948	2.9
3.6	1953	6.1
3.	1955	5.
2.6	1958	3.8
2.6	1961	3.8
2.7	1965	3.1
3.5	1968	3.2
3.	1970	3.3
2.1	1975	3.6

SOURCE: International Institute for Strategic Studies, *The Military Balance, 1976–1977* (London: IISS, 1976); John M. Collins and John Steven Chwat, "The United States/Soviet Military Balance," The Library of Congress, Washington, D.C. January 21, 1976. The figures represent U.S. data and U.S. (or Western) estimates, although they take account of the sparse data released by Soviet authorities.

shall still have one of the most powerful air forces in the world."[2] Soviet priorities were different, particularly as to naval power, but Soviet leaders were also intent on maintaining or building the kind of military establishment relevant to postwar (and post-Hiroshima) conditions.

Demobilization of personnel up to 1948 was followed by sharp increases occasioned by rising tension in Europe and then by the sudden outbreak of war in Korea. American forces were more than doubled by 1953, as were Soviet forces, even though the latter did not participate in the Korean fighting except peripherally. The Soviet Union, which raised its armed forces to a total never subsequently

[2] Quoted in A. M. Schlesinger, Jr., ed., *Dynamics of World Power, Documentary History of U.S. Foreign Policy*, Vol. 2, *Eastern Europe and the Soviet Union*, Walter LaFaber, ed. (New York: Chelsea House Publishers, 1973), p. 170.

approached, did, however, face a very real prospect that the fall of North Korea would bring American troops to Soviet Far Eastern borders.[3]

A post-Korea relaxation led to a decline of both American and Soviet armed forces in the late 1950s. But this trend ended as the Berlin issue became acute, heightening prospects of armed confrontation in 1960–1961. Reexpansion occurred, and the subsequently stepped-up American participation in the Vietnamese war brought U.S. forces back up to Korean wartime levels. Soviet totals also increased gradually, probably more as a result of sharpening hostility with China than of events connected with Vietnam or the U.S. This expansion continued even after the U.S. reduced and then withdrew its forces stationed in Indochina and simultaneously cut back the total number under arms.[4]

No one without access to Soviet official data knows exactly how much larger Soviet personnel strength is today than American, but the margin is obviously considerable, as indeed it has been throughout the postwar period. In tsarist and Soviet Russia, unlike the United States, maintenance of a large standing army has been tradi-

---

[3] Soviet participation in, and concern about, the Korean War was publicized more fully after the war than at the time. According to a recent Soviet account, the USSR not only sent military supplies to the North Koreans and Chinese, and advisers to the former, but also stationed several aviation squadrons in northeastern China. The latter took part in air battles and "shot down tens of American planes." If the North Korean situation had worsened, the authors state, the Soviet authorities were ready to send five divisions of ground troops to engage American forces. B. P. Ponomarev, A. A. Gromyko, and V. M. Khvostov, eds., *Istoriya Vneshnei Politiki SSSR, 1917–1970 gg.*, Vol. 2, 1945–1970 gg. (Moscow: Izdatelstvo "Nauka," 1971), pp. 166–167.

[4] Data for the chart and text from the following: *Historical Statistics of the United States, Colonial Times to 1957* (Washington, D.C.: Bureau of the Census, 1960), p. 736; ibid., *Continuation to 1962* (Washington, D.C.: Bureau of the Census, 1965), p. 103; J. G. Godaire, "The Claim of the Soviet Military Establishment," Joint Economic Committee, U.S. Congress, *Dimensions of Soviet Economic Power* (Washington, D.C.: Government Printing Office, 1962), p. 43; Murray Feshbach and Stephen Rapawy, "Labor and Wages," Joint Economic Committee, U.S. Congress, *Economic Performance and the Military Burden in the Soviet Union* (Washington, D.C.: Government Printing Office, 1970), p. 75; Murray Feshbach and Stephen Rapawy, "Labor Constraints in the Five-Year Plan," Joint Economic Committee, U.S. Congress, *Soviet Economic Prospects for the Seventies* (Washington, D.C.: Government Printing Office, 1973), pp. 520–21; Murray Feshbach and Stephen Rapawy, "Soviet Population and Manpower Trends and Policies," Joint Economic Committee, U.S. Congress, *Soviet Economy in a New Perspective* (Washington, D.C.: Government Printing Office, 1976), p. 132; John M. Collins and John Steven Chwat, *The United States/Soviet Military Balance*, A Study by the Library of Congress (Washington, D.C.: Government Printing Office, 1976), p. 16.

tional, with conscripts used to fill the ranks. Exemptions from compulsory military service have been minimal, in contrast to the numerous, and strongly upper-class-oriented, exemptions allowed from the U.S. draft, itself suspended in 1973 with the institution of an all-volunteer military force.

The disparity in size of Soviet and American armed forces is clearly due in large part to previously mentioned different geographical circumstances: the vulnerability of Soviet, and invulnerability of American, territory to invasion, a difference highlighted by the presence on Soviet borders, and absence from U.S. borders, of a strong hostile power (China). In tsarist times, it might be noted, the Russian margin in active-duty forces over American was far greater than in recent years; the ratio was unrelated to Russian–American relations. But other conditions in addition to tradition and geopolitical situation no doubt contribute to the disparity in personnel strength.

Military Spending

A measure of the two countries' military efforts, a better measure than personnel totals, though still inadequate, can be found in the U.S.–USSR expenditures on military establishments, including military-related research and development, nuclear weapons production, and space activities. Of course, these appropriations represent "inputs," and thus are potentially misleading. One country may get a more effective military establishment than another even if it spends much less (because the industry producing military end items is more efficient, or for other reasons). Whether the U.S. or the USSR gets "the most bang for the buck," as the saying goes, cannot be known short of battlefield verification of total effectiveness. Rather than face the prospect of repairing this lack of knowledge through testing in battle the relative efficacy of U.S.–USSR military spending, it is easy to believe that ignorance is bliss.

Postwar military appropriations in both the U.S. and USSR, like armed forces totals, have varied in response to the rise and fall of tension and to rapid or slow procurement of new armaments and vehicles. Although the overall trend in military spending was upward, even with the impact of inflation neutralized, military appropriations as a percentage of Gross National Product displayed no similar rise. In the United States, military spending as a proportion of total product amounted to only 4 percent in the late 1940s, the lowest postwar level. This rose to 12 percent at the postwar peak, during the Korean

War, and then declined in the last half of the 1950s. It rose gradually in the 1960s to almost 10 percent of GNP at the height of the war in Vietnam. Again a decline set in until military allocations amounted to less than 6 percent of GNP in the mid-1970s.

Because there is no agreement between Soviet published figures on military spending and estimates by U.S. analysts (who disagree among themselves), there is no agreement on the ratio of military spending to total output in the USSR. It seems clear, however, that the burden rose in response to international crises, notably in the Korean War years, and to the great expansion of strategic arms in the 1960s. According to one U.S. study, the USSR allocated from 10 to 13 percent of GNP to military purposes each year between 1950 and 1969 (except for 14–15 percent at the time of the Korean War), with a generally lower percentage toward the end of the period.[5] The U.S. Arms Control and Disarmament Agency estimated a range of 6–10 percent in the years 1963–1973.[6] A recent study by the CIA concludes that the Soviet defense effort absorbed some 11–13 percent of GNP in 1970–1975, almost twice as much as the 6–8 percent the CIA earlier estimated for the same period.[7] The Soviet Union claims that only 8 percent of national income went to defense in 1961–1965 and 7 percent in 1966–1970; this is based on a simple ratio between the state budget item for defense and national income calculated according to the Soviet concept, that is, a total that is limited for the most part to material product, excluding services, and is therefore considerably less comprehensive than the U.S. concept of GNP.[8]

Comparisons of defense/GNP ratios do not provide any answer to the question: Which country is spending more on its military establishment? The question is unanswerable in any definitive sense, and not merely because of the paucity of hard data on Soviet military spending. A much greater portion of U.S. spending than of Soviet goes to personnel costs, wages and maintenance of active-duty and re-

---

[5] Stanley H. Cohn, "Economic Burden of Defense Expenditures," *Soviet Economic Prospects for the Seventies*, p. 158.

[6] U.S. Arms Control and Disarmament Agency, *World Military Expenditures and Arms Trade, 1963–1973* (Washington, D.C.: ACDA, 1974), p. 56.

[7] Central Intelligence Agency, "Estimated Soviet Defense Spending in Rubles, 1970–1975," May 1976, p. 16.

[8] TsSU, *Narodnoye Khozyaistvo SSSR, 1922–1972 gg.* (Moscow: Statistika, 1972), p. 362.

tired military personnel. This portion has been rising in the Pentagon budget, partly because of wage increases connected with the shift to volunteer armed forces; the portion has been declining in the Soviet budget as more and more expensive equipment, vehicles, and armaments of advanced design have been procured. From a U.S. perspective, conscripts in Russia have to pay a kind of special "tax" to support the Soviet military establishment because their pay and maintenance is well below what they could command in the civilian economy. Measured in terms of U.S. dollar costs, a recent CIA study has estimated that Soviet defense programs would have required greater expenditures than U.S. defense programs in every year since 1970; for 1975 they would have been about 40 percent higher, or 50 percent if pensions were subtracted on both sides. (For the period 1965–1975 as a whole the dollar costs of Soviet military activities would have been about the same as the actual costs of U.S. activities.)[9] But, of course, this is highly artificial, because the USSR does not operate in a context of U.S. prices; Soviet policy-makers would make different choices if they were responding to a U.S.-type economic environment. Hence a dollar comparison measures neither the burden on the Soviet economy of USSR military efforts nor the relative military capabilities of the two countries.

Despite the inability to attain any precision, it is clear that the United States and the Soviet Union have to devote much treasure and effort to produce, maintain, and develop the large forces equipped with advanced machines, equipment, and destructive devices that enable them to deter each other and remain out in front of other countries in military power. No other advanced countries devote resources to military ends on the scale of the U.S. and USSR.

The United States has been able to afford this military spending better than the USSR because of the much greater productivity of its economy. Only rich countries can bear with equanimity the economic waste of war preparations. Of course, as the economic potential of the USSR in relation to the U.S. increased over the postwar years, so also did the Soviet capability of absorbing with less pain the cost of military competition with the United States. In 1950, when the USSR could produce only a third of what America could produce, military expenditures cut deeply. In 1975, the Soviet burden was less

---

[9] Central Intelligence Agency, "A Dollar Comparison of Soviet and U.S. Defense Activities, 1965–1975," February 1976, pp. 1–3.

onerous. The Soviet problem was not primarily one of choosing between "guns and butter," because rapid expansion of military production was associated with slower increases in the output of producer goods, such as machinery for civilian industrial production, rather than with a pinch in the output of goods for consumers. That is, in the early postwar years capital investment tended to suffer when defense spending spurted, and benefited when such spending stabilized. In more recent years, however, even this economic impact of war preparations has become less noticeable.[10] By the 1970s, with arms competition no longer causing as deleterious an effect on the Soviet economy as earlier, the time was well past for any U.S. attempt to use a speeded-up arms race to force political concessions from the Russians, or, if such concessions were rejected, to impose severe deprivations on the population. This idea had currency at one time in certain influential American business and military circles, but even then it was never translated into consistent action.[11]

If military spending retarded Soviet growth, especially in the early postwar years, it had more ambiguous effects on the United States. The American economic problem was to keep productive capacity utilized and workers employed rather than to sacrifice civilian production for the sake of military. Maintenance of large armed forces (large in relation to previous U.S. levels) and of a relatively high level of military production contributed directly and indirectly, it has been argued, to avoidance of the unemployment and idleness of civilian plant that occurred in the 1930s. In other words, the 1930s army of the unemployed gave way to a post-1945 real army, and formerly idle plants were replaced by factories busily turning out military aircraft and munitions.[12]

The method worked, but all was not rosy. New capabilities to wage war generated a new willingness to engage in distant wars, with some

---

[10] Terence E. Byrne, "Recent Trends in the Soviet Economy," *Economic Performance and the Military Burden in the Soviet Union*, pp. 4–8; Stanley H. Cohn, "Economic Burden of Defense Expenditures," *Soviet Economic Prospects for the Seventies*, pp. 147–55.

[11] A prominent U.S. businessman suggested in 1958 that the United States should double its military budget in order to force the Russians to follow suit and thus "take away from their people the already sparse good things of life they have." The author was William C. Foster, later to head U.S. disarmament efforts! See *General Electric Defense Quarterly* (September 1958), p. 67.

[12] Paul M. Sweezy, "Capitalism for Worse," *Monthly Review* no. 25 (February 1974): 1–7.

negative consequences from the Korean War and even more serious difficulties from the war in Vietnam. Not wanting to raise taxes to finance an increasingly unpopular war, the U.S. government relied on deficit financing. This launched an inflationary trend unparalleled in modern American history, and one that continued even after war spending leveled off. America's capability of affording almost any level of military spending to counter the increase of Soviet or Communist strength and influence turned out to be only theoretical; short of a threat of imminent war, an attempt to regain commanding superiority over the USSR promised to involve consequences as traumatic for the United States as for the Soviet Union.

This brief review of personnel strength and arms expenditures as guides to an assessment of relative Soviet–American military capabilities has ended inconclusively. Even with better data, an analysis using this approach would remain inconclusive. Part of the problem stems from the fact that it is of limited utility to discuss on a general plane the correlations of military force between the United States and the USSR. Much depends on the uses for which the rival military establishments are designed, uses that include, but are not limited to, combat and that are associated with varied weapons systems and are affected by geographical considerations. A better grasp of rival capabilities can be secured by a breakdown into strategic forces, European theater forces, and globally mobile forces. It is to the first of these that the discussion now turns.

STRATEGIC ARMS COMPETITION

Defined simply as the forces that give the two superpowers capabilities of long-distance attacks on each other's homeland, or of defending against such attacks, strategic arms have occupied a novel and dramatic place in Soviet–American postwar military rivalry.[13] Their

---

[13] Identification of strategic arms with long-range weapons systems in somewhat arbitrary, because relatively short-range aircraft and missiles, as well as naval vessels, can, if positioned close enough, attack U.S., or USSR territory just as effectively as intercontinental missiles or bombers. Moreover, aircraft can be refueled in flight, sent on one-way missions, etc., so that their designation as strategic or nonstrategic is itself conditional. The problem has bedeviled U.S.–USSR strategic arms talks, partly because the United States, unlike the USSR, has forward bases from which relatively short-range vehicles can strike Soviet territory.

importance derives, of course, from the development of incomparably more destructive weapons and of incomparably more rapid means
of delivery than any known earlier.

The United States began the postwar period with the capability of
producing atomic bombs like the two exploded over Japanese cities in
the last days of World War II. Production of additional weapons was
not interrupted by the lack of an immediate target, and research continued on their perfection. Although the Soviet Union had begun
research in this field before American success was revealed to the
world, there was a lag of four years after Hiroshima and Nagasaki
before the first Soviet atomic device was successfully tested in 1949.
Even that lag was shorter than American authorities expected. (Such
underestimation of Soviet military capacities, whether of staying
power, mastery of technology, or production potential, has been traditional in the U.S. from 1917 to recent times.)

Even this brief period of American atomic monopoly was not to be
repeated in the development of thermonuclear weapons, successfully
tested in both countries during the same years, 1952–1954. And in
any case the short-lived monopoly of atomic weapons yielded the
U.S. no large returns either militarily or politically. U.S. efforts, by
way of the "Baruch Plan" of internationalizing atomic developments,
to prevent Soviet acquisition of A-bombs failed, and were certain to
fail. The plan required great concessions of the USSR, in terms of
control over Russian domestic resources and enterprises, in return for
a U.S. promise to transfer its atomic weapons and facilities—at some
time in the future wholly determined by American authorities—to an
international agency, an agency that under then-existing conditions
was certain to be dominated by the U.S. and its allies.

Nor did the United States find a suitable occasion, despite a pleth-
ora of tense U.S.–USSR confrontations in the immediate postwar
period, to theaten the use of atomic bombs as a means of changing Soviet behavior. To be sure, the public stance of Stalin and his associates in minimizing the importance of the new weapons, said to be
frightening only to people with weak nerves, clearly represented an
attempt to make the best of a bad situation. Behind the scenes Soviet
scientists and industrial producers were working feverishly to counter
the U.S. advance. Still, in the years of U.S. monopoly it is no doubt
true that American use of A-bombs to dispose of Soviet challenges
would have been risky. As a Soviet writer rather wittily put the mat-

ter, when the United States had a monopoly, it did not have many atomic weapons; by the time it had accumulated an atomic stockpile, it no longer had a monopoly.[14]

Soviet mastery of atomic and nuclear weapons technology in the first postwar decade did not mean, of course, that the USSR was anywhere near the U.S. in strategic capabilities. In both the quantity and quality of such explosive devices the Soviet military establishment lagged far behind the American. More importantly, the USSR was far behind in the development and deployment of appropriate carriers. Long-range bombers suitable for atomic strikes were well represented in the U.S. and allied air fleets of the 1940s and 1950s, and the U.S. developed in-flight refueling techniques to extend the range of aircraft incapable of round trips to Russia and back. Soviet bombers of World War II vintage were basically short-range, so that the USSR had little to build on after the war. Soviet backwardness was illustrated by the fact that the USSR retained and subsequently produced copies of an American strategic bomber, a B–17, that had been forced to land in Siberia in the period of World War II when Russia was neutral toward Japan. Though Soviet adaptations of this model and other bombers entered the Soviet military inventory, the USSR fleet of long-range bombers remained small throughout the period in which the U.S. placed reliance on bombers for delivery of atomic weapons, the U.S. having hundreds of such planes in its intercontinental strike force.

The reasons for this Soviet failure to match U.S. bomber deployment remain obscure. In part it may have stemmed from confidence that a thick antiaircraft defense network could parry a possible American strike. According to a Soviet military writer, a decision to skip the bomber phase in development of deterrent capabilities was taken at the highest level of Soviet leadership, where the bomber was considered a "transitional" means of delivery, too vulnerable and too slow to be matched with nuclear weapons.[15] The "absolute weapon" had to be mated to an absolutely new kind of vehicle.

Whether or not this was the real reason, Soviet intercontinental strike forces began to rival those of the U.S. only after, considerably after, intercontinental ballistic missiles became a reality. The USSR

---

[14] G. Gerasimov, "Pervyi Udar," *Mezhdunarodnaya Zhizn'*, no. 3 (1965): 53.

[15] Lt. Col. V. Bondarenko, in *Kommunist Vooruzhennykh sil* no. 24 (December 1968): 22–29.

was the first country to test such an ICBM, in August 1957; subsequent launches of orbiting space vehicles, beginning in October 1957, reduced U.S. skepticism about Soviet capability to produce ICBMs. Despite the Soviet priority in testing, the United States soon outproduced the USSR in this area under a program that involved the deployment, from the late 1950s through the mid1960s, of something over a thousand surface launchers, mostly Minuteman, a few Titan. The USSR lagged far behind.

It was the United States that pioneered in the development of an underwater missile-launching system, installed on Polaris nuclear-powered submarines. These missile-launching submarines gave a strike capability that was even less vulnerable to counterattack than land-based ICBMs, because of the mobility and concealability of submarines. In this area, also, the Soviet forces lagged well behind, having in 1965 less than a fourth of the U.S. number of submarine ballistic missile launchers; many of these were on diesel submarines, whereas all U.S. launchers were on the much superior nuclear-powered submarines.

When Leonid Brezhnev replaced Khrushchev in the top leadership post, the USSR stepped up production and deployment of ICBMs and missile-launching submarines.[16] In the following decade, 1965–1975, the Soviet Union erased the American lead in both categories. By 1975 it had 50 percent more ICBM launchers than the U.S. and 10 percent more submarine launchers. Only in numbers of heavy bombers did the U.S. retain, and even enlarge, its margin of superiority, though the importance of this arm declined in the decade as both countries reduced their fleets. The Soviet numerical advantage became clear, but this was basically due to an American decision to stay at 1967 levels of land- and sea-based missile launchers and to concentrate on other, so-called qualitative improvements.

Of the latter, the most significant involved a system of lofting several nuclear warheads simultaneously from each launcher. Originated and first introduced by the U.S., MIRV (Multiple Independently targeted Reentry Vehicles) enabled each Minuteman ICBM launcher to strike at three targets rather than one; each launcher on a MIRV-submarine (Poseidon) could place under missile fire ten to fourteen

---

[16] In view of the long lead time required for development, production, and deployment of complex weapons systems, the post-Khrushchev acceleration may have been purely coincidental.

Table 7
Strategic Nuclear Forces

Weapon	Year	U.S.	USSR
Intercontinental ballistic missile	1965	854	234
launchers (ICBM)	1975	1054	1527
Submarine ballistic	1965	496	120
missile launchers	1975	656	845
Ballistic missiles, single-	1965	1702	344
launch capabilities (with	1975	6794	3442
multiple reentry vehicles—			
MRV—and multiple independently			
targeted reentry vehicles—MIRV)			
Long-range bombers	1965	630	210
		463	135
Deliverable nuclear warheads	1976		
ICBM		2154	2195
SLBM		5120	785
Bombers		1256	270
Total		8530	3250
Throw-weight of strategic	1976		
delivery vehicles			
(million pounds)			
ICBM		2.4	7.
SLBM		.9	1.2
Total		3.3	8.2
Bombers[a]		22.8	4.7

[a]This is the theoretical capacity with use of gravity bombs.

SOURCE: International Institute for Strategic Studies, *The Military Balance, 1976–1977* (London: IISS, 1976); John M. Collins and John Steven Chwat, "The United States/Soviet Military Balance," The Library of Congress, Washington, D.C., January 21, 1976. For somewhat different estimates, see Stockholm International Peace Research Institute (SIPRI), *World Armaments and Disarmament: SIPRI Yearbook 1976* (Cambridge, Mass., and London: The M.I.T. Press, 1976), p. 24–25.

targets instead of one.[17] The multiple warheads carried a smaller total charge than that thrown by single-firing launchers, but even these smaller weapons could take out all but heavily resistant installations. There was no doubt that they could transform large urban areas into wastelands.

By the mid-1970s, as a result of this innovation, American missile

---

[17] A less complex system for multiple launching, called MRV, lacked the independent targeting of MIRV; that is, all the weapons were aimed at the same general target.

launchers in silos and on submarines had the theoretical capability to make a simultaneous attack on almost 7000 targets in the Soviet Union, not even counting those that bombers might be able to reach. Naturally, the Soviet Union followed the MIRV path pioneered by the U.S. By 1975 it had adapted the system to its ICBMs, though it had only one-fifth as many ICBMs with multiple-firing capability as the United States, and had installed no MIRVs on its missile-launching submarines. Therefore, despite the USSR superiority in numbers of missile launchers, it had a capability—again a theoretical capability—of simultaneously attacking less than 4000 U.S. targets.

Strategic arms capabilities are also affected by "throw weight," that is, the destructive power that can be carried by missiles or bombs. Ever since the "space age" began in 1957 the USSR has emphasized very powerful launchers, and this emphasis has characterized its missile launchers as well as those used for lofting satellites. In the early stages of deployment all of the Soviet ICBMs were of the heavy variety, and though the 1975 inventory came to include about the same number of light ICBMs (comparable to the U.S. Minuteman) as the U.S. possessed, over one-third of Soviet ICBMs were in the heavy category (590, as against the 54 Titans in the American arsenal). Thus, a simultaneous launch of all Soviet missiles would bring much more destructive power on the United States than a comparable launch of all American missiles on the Soviet Union. Such powerful nuclear warheads are chiefly relevant against highly resistant targets rather than against urban and industrial areas. If heavy bombers were brought into the equation, this would again swing the advantage to the United States, for the U.S. force is not only four times larger but has a seven-to-one superiority in theoretical payload (and considerably more than Soviet missiles and bombers together). Such bombers are, of course, much slower than missiles and much more vulnerable to interference and destruction (particularly since the USSR has an extensive air defense system).[18]

Means of defense as well as strike forces must obviously enter calculations of relative strength in strategic arms. While both the USSR and U.S. have organized more or less elaborate systems of defense against aircraft (the United States much less than the USSR

---

[18] Most of the data are from Collins and Chwat, *United States/Soviet Military Balance;* International Institute of Strategic Studies, *The Military Balance, 1974–1975* (London: IISS, 1974); and IISS, *Strategic Survey, 1972* (London: IISS, 1973).

because of the small role of bombers in Soviet strike forces), neither
has an elaborate system of ballistic missile defense. Technical problems militated against creation of effective ABM defenses, and, as will
be noted later, the U.S. and USSR agreed in 1972–1974 to refrain
from further development in this area.

There are additional considerations that should enter a full discussion of U.S.–USSR rivalry in strategic arms, including questions of ac-
curacy, hardening of missile silos and other military installations, the
role of forward-based aircraft, etc. In addition, the strength contributed by allies, especially by American allies, is relevant to a consideration of U.S.–USSR strength.

But it would be chasing a will-o'-the-wisp to try to make a precise
estimate of relative Soviet–American strength in strategic arms. The
general movement is clear: the Soviet Union has been able substantially to erase the wide gap in strategic capabilities that existed at the
end of World War II and during the two following decades. This was a
period in which the United States lost, but the Soviet Union did not
gain, an invulnerability to attack; it was a period in which each side's
capability of inflicting damage on the other spiraled upward, leaving
stagnant means of defense; and it was a period in which any major innovation of either country inspired the other to match or exceed the
originator.

Anyone who looks with a fresh eye at Soviet–American developments in the strategic arms field has to be struck by a certain unreality. This unreality stems from the discrepancy between the resources, technology, and human skills devoted to the competition and
the absence of any occasion for testing the efficacy of the systems installed. Historically, weapons systems have been produced in order
to be used, and those in charge usually found occasions, rather sooner
than later, for such checking. American and Soviet leaders vie with
each other in solemn avowals that they expend such great resources
on development of nuclear missile systems in order not to use them.
But their reluctance to test such weapons in conflict is only exceeded
by their reluctance to halt their accumulation and improvement, and
their even greater reluctance to abandon them.

While the United States did use two atomic weapons against Japan
at the end of World War II, that use is scarcely relevant to the mutual
use of more powerful nuclear weapons in a Soviet–American engagement. Such an engagement is not ruled out merely because it has
been avoided for the thirty-odd years in which the two countries have

been rivals for world leadership. But a strategic duel has appeared to become less and less likely. The gap between ever-increasing capabilities for warfare many times more destructive than any experienced earlier and the actual prospects of using those capabilities has thus widened over time. Moreover, the inhibitions on nuclear conflict have reinforced inhibitions on subnuclear conflict because of the prospect that either side might escalate under pressure of impending defeat. As a result, the traditional means of proving military superiority and inferiority, on the battlefield, have been ruled out of bounds, for the time being at least. The interested parties have to be content with technological "victories" and with contemplation of their swelling inventories of deadly weapons.

It may not matter much whether or not one state is ahead of the other in strategic forces or the two are more or less equal. Perhaps, it has been urged, all a great nuclear power needs for purposes of deterring an adversary is a relatively invulnerable "second-strike" force, i.e., an offensive force capable of surviving an initial attack, even a surprise attack, and responding with a powerful retaliatory blow. The argument has cogency, because each superpower possesses more than enough weapons to bring devastation to the opponents, and to other countries in the bargain. But the cogency of the argument has not appealed to either Soviet or American leaders when their own country was to accept the safe security of second place. It was not accepted by Soviet policy-makers, despite repeated urging from Washington.[19] And it was not accepted by U.S. leaders as the USSR increased its strategic arms to, and in some cases beyond, American levels.

To be sure, under President Nixon, Washington dropped its earlier insistence on American superiority, particularly in any agreement limiting strategic arms.[20] Nixon substituted the concept of "suf-

---

[19] This line was propounded especially by Robert McNamara when he was secretary of defense, 1961–1967. McNamara convinced himself that the Soviet leaders "have decided that they have lost the quantitative race, and they are not seeking to engage us in that contest." *US News and World Report*, April 12, 1965, p. 52, quoted in Richard J. Whalen, "The Shifting Equation of Nuclear Defense," *Fortune*, June, 1967, pp. 85ff.

[20] McNamara told a Senate committee in 1964 that "as a nation any disarmament treaty or agreement . . . that we participate in must be one in which we maintain what I call our favorable differential balance of power." Quoted in Jeremy J. Stone, *Strategic Persuasion: Arms Limitations Through Dialogue* (New York: Columbia University Press, 1967), p. 137.

ficiency" for that of superiority.[21] The new doctrine was transparently subjective, but provided a formula easing official recognition of the actual change in Soviet–American ratios of strategic forces. But the adoption of sufficiency as the criterion has been coupled with repeated insistence that the United States cannot afford to be No. 2 to a No. 1 Soviet Union. Putting the matter this way served as another backhanded acknowledgement of Soviet attainment of parity; it still left the way open for U.S. efforts, perhaps by way of a technological breakthrough, to regain supremacy. Verbally, the formula ruled out only one possible development, namely, acceptance by the U.S. of an inferiority earlier described as adequate for the USSR.

Soviet leaders, including currently Brezhnev and his associates, usually refrain from discussions of the specifics of Soviet–American ratios of strength in strategic or other forces. While superiority is lauded as a worthwhile goal in Soviet military writings, usually in reference to victory in, rather than deterrence of, war, pronouncements from the Kremlin normally merely stress that the USSR has more than enough strategic forces to defend the country and its allies against attack from any quarter. This formula, anticipatory of the U.S. sufficiency doctrine, is so flexible that Soviet achievement of a rough measure of equality required no doctrinal shift. Whether Soviet decision-makers are intent on efforts to gain strategic superiority is as yet unclear, but they have certainly demonstrated their intention to continue a brisk pace of strategic arms development, as indeed have U.S. leaders.

While the USSR has been adding MIRV capabilities to existing ICBMs, the U.S. has a well-advanced program to install long- and medium-range cruise (air-breathing) missiles on vessels and aircraft; both military establishments have programs for mobile surface-to-surface missiles; both have continued to develop advanced models of bombers; the U.S. has a program for a system involving underwater launches, from waters close to U.S. shores, of missiles capable of reaching targets in the USSR; and both have worked on still more exotic kinds of strategic arms.

Even if the Soviet leadership is intent on gaining a clear-cut superi-

---

[21] See Nixon's press conference of January 27, 1969, reported in the *New York Times*, January 28, 1969; and, for a fuller statement, the president's report to Congress of February 18, 1970, "U.S. Foreign Policy for the 1970s: A New Strategy for Peace," reprinted in *Department of State Bulletin*, March 9, 1970, pp. 319–20.

ority in strategic arms, the United States may not have to tolerate its establishment; the U.S. has economic and technological resources at least to match Soviet efforts. It should be noted, however, that a Soviet aim at strategic superiority would not be, taken by itself, more sinister than the earlier U.S. commitment to the same goal. Both powers can ideologically justify their search for, or maintenance of, military superiority as the surest means of preventing aggression from hostile forces and preserving the peace.

U.S.–SOVIET MILITARY RIVALRY IN EUROPE

If the major Soviet and American strategic forces were kept a safe distance apart, U.S.–USSR rivalry for dominance in Europe brought their theater forces into juxtaposition, separated by a seemingly permanent line of East–West division that cut through Germany. From the end of World War II Europe occupied the central role in American and Soviet military calculations; likewise, the U.S. and USSR were the decisive elements in the European military situation. No European state was any longer capable, without U.S. or Soviet permission, of a serious move to upset the territorial or political status quo resulting from the Second World War.

Both countries sponsored military alliances in Europe to solidify their positions, though the North Atlantic Treaty of 1949 antedated the Warsaw Pact by six years. Alliances in Europe were not new, but these alliances were unique in European history. The continent was polarized as never before, with almost all nations, except for traditional neutrals, brought under the leadership of Washington or Moscow, i.e., of states outside, or on the periphery of, Europe. The alliances were novel in that they served as bases for permanent military staffs in charge of armed forces that were organized on a more or less integrated pattern. This kind of permanent organization was in contrast to the ad hoc arrangements typical of traditional military alliances, and facilitated the maintenance in Europe of substantial American and Soviet contingents, largely concentrated in the two Germanies. Stationing of such U.S.–USSR forces on the front lines of Europe made almost certain the participation of the two powers in any European conflict. The senior role of the two countries in the rival alliances was meant to guarantee the respective American and Soviet spheres of influence from adversary encroachment; to bolster the social order favored by Washington or Moscow, capitalist institutions for the former, socialist for the latter; and to make sure that if a new war broke out it would be on U.S. or USSR initiative, not that of an aggrieved local power.

The United States and the Soviet Union have almost uninterupt-edly maintained powerful military forces in Europe since the war, forces equipped with substantial numbers of vehicles and armor, tanks and artillery, aircraft and ships. Forces on both sides are sup-plied and trained for both conventional and nuclear operations.[22]

Unlike the situation in strategic arms and in globally mobile forces (the latter are discussed in the next section), in European theater forces the Russians did not begin the postwar period in a position of inferiority. They were able to build upon their traditional sources of military strength, that is, ground forces with associated artillery, tanks, other armored vehicles, and tactical aircraft. Such forces re-mained crucial to the European military equation as they were largely irrelevant to rivalry in strategic arms and globally mobile forces. An-other characteristic distinguishing U.S.–USSR rivalry in European theater forces from that in the two other areas concerns the role of allies, important in the former, marginal in the latter. Thus, assess-ment of the military position of the U.S. and USSR in Europe can be usefully approached only in the context of NATO and Warsaw Pact ri-valry.

But the Soviet Union and the United States supply dissimilar pro-portions of alliance strength. The North Atlantic Treaty includes many more countries than the Warsaw Pact, and among the NATO countries are the largest countries of Europe (excluding Russia) as well as the most advanced economically and militarily. European NATO states have three times the population and four and one-half times the economic capacity of Eastern European states in the War-saw Pact. Therefore, Western European countries can and do con-tribute a greater share to NATO manpower and equipment than is contributed to Warsaw Pact strength by Russia's Eastern European allies.

Assessment of the military strength of the rival alliances is compli-cated by a number of ambiguities. Among these, the most important are (1) the treatment of France, a member of the North Atlantic alli-ance but a nonparticipant, or a limited participant, in the integrated military organization established under the treaty; (2) the treatment of Soviet forces stationed in the USSR and of American forces stationed

---

[22] *The Military Balance,* 1974–1975.

outside Europe; and (3) the treatment of NATO–Warsaw Pact forces in southern Europe together with, or separate from, those forces stationed in northern and central Europe. Much discussion in the United States of the European military situation, particularly alarmist appraisals of the Warsaw Pact's growing superiority, is based on calculations that are open to question. Appraisals of this kind often omit French forces in summarizing Western units; include in Warsaw Pact totals large numbers of troops, tanks, and aircraft physically located on Soviet soil but exclude from NATO totals most or all similar U.S. units stationed in the United States; and focus on northern and central Europe, where the balance is least favorable to NATO, to the neglect of southern Europe, where it is more favorable.

Each of these choices has its rationale. French troops are not committed to NATO, and the French do not participate in NATO military planning (though there is scarcely any doubt that they would join NATO forces if there were the kind of invasion from the East so much talked about in NATO circles); it is certainly easier for the Soviet military to bring up forces from the Western USSR than for the Pentagon to deploy units across the ocean; etc. But the dice are a bit loaded; the various exclusions and inclusions all tend, and often are intended, to buttress a case for expanded U.S. and NATO forces in Europe rather than to give an objective appraisal of relative strength.

Taken as a whole, portrayals of the European military balance based on U.S. estimates, and on the treatment of French, U.S., and Soviet forces discussed above, indicate that NATO has approximately the same number of personnel under arms as the Warsaw Pact but many fewer organized in divisions, and has almost as many tactical aircraft as the other side but far fewer tanks. If the northern and central area of Europe is considered separately, the balance weighs more heavily in favor of the Eastern alliance, with NATO having four-fifths the tactical aircraft of the Warsaw Pact, two-thirds the personnel, and about two-fifths the number of tanks and ground divisions (though NATO divisions are typically larger than those of the Warsaw Pact).[23] A calculation limited to the U.S. and USSR shows gross disparities in favor of the latter, which has from two to five times the number of

---

[23] Drawn mostly from Collins and Chwat, *United States/Soviet Military Balance.* Although they have not been made public, data presented by the USSR and Warsaw Pact countries to the Vienna conference on mutual reduction of forces apparently indicated lower totals for Eastern forces in the northern and central European area than the estimates used in the West.

personnel, divisions, tanks, and aircraft in Europe as the United States maintains; this is explained in part by the consideration mentioned above—the USSR relies less on its allies than the United States does.

Both the U.S. (NATO) and the USSR (Warsaw Pact) have the delivery means and more than enough warheads to fight a nuclear war in Europe (about 7000 U.S.–controlled nuclear weapons in Europe, an estimated 3500 under Soviet control). The dependency of European states on the senior alliance members is clearly shown in the arrangements for possible use of these weapons. American nuclear weapons are available in various NATO countries, but their use depends on U.S permission under a double-key system. Soviet nuclear weapons are apparently restricted to Soviet territory, although Russia's allies have nuclear-capable weapons just as American allies do.

In recent years prospects have noticeably declined for early resort to tactical nuclear weapons if hostilities break out in Europe. In the United States an idea was floated in the 1950s, prominently by Henry Kissinger, that the U.S. and NATO could gain a freer hand in Europe if they displayed a willingness to use tactical nuclear weapons, in which the United States had a clear superiority. Supposedly this would have involved no great risks because an understanding could be reached beforehand with Soviet authorities on certain ground rules limiting the use of nuclear weapons to relatively low-yield warheads. Fortunately, cooler heads prevailed. The notion that such an agreement was possible, or that it would be honored by the side facing defeat, was too fantastic to form the basis of serious policy.

Moreover, subsequent war exercises and other appraisals showed that the probable damage to European countries from so-called tactical nuclear warfare was scarcely distinguishable from a war of obliteration, except that the United States and the Soviet Union were to be left untouched.[24] Prospects of nuclear war were so fearsome, in fact, that they tended to discourage not only thoughts of deliberately initiating nuclear war but also any drift to major conventional warfare, because it was not clear that the "fire break" between use of conventional and of nuclear weapons would hold.

---

[24] See the *Report of the Secretary-General on the Effects of the Possible Use of Nuclear Weapons and on the Security and Economic Implications for States of the Acquisition and Further Development of these Weapons* (New York: United Nations, October 10, 1967), Document A/6858.

Nevertheless, Europe remained an armed camp, with the U.S. and the USSR occupying the commanding heights. Discrepancies in the balance of military power existed, but the level of East–West armaments was sufficiently high to deter any major use of force in realization of fond dreams in Moscow and Washington, to push the rival's forces back to the homeland. Neither superpower retreated an inch from the forward positions occupied by mutual agreement in 1945.[25] They could be neither pushed nor enticed to leave.

Of course, both the American and Soviet authorities justified their strong military roles in Europe, as the senior states of adversary alliances, by the need to preserve the peace. According to the Washington version, only NATO prevented war by blocking a Soviet advance on Western Europe (or other use of military pressure to alter political alignments in Moscow's favor), and an American presence was essential for NATO to fulfill this role. According to the Moscow version, Soviet–Warsaw Pact strength deterrred American "hotheads," German "revanchists," and others of that ilk from attempting to roll back Communist gains and thus bring on World War III.

Whether due to the military balance or not, Europe has been relatively stable over the three postwar decades, despite occasional crises and despite the division of the continent between hostile alliances. It has certainly been more stable than most other areas of the globe, particularly the Middle East and South and Southeast Asia. And in the post-1945 period it has been much more stable than the Europe of the interwar period, when Germany and other revisionist states were unchecked by any outside superpower as they went about altering territorial and other arrangements to their advantage. Had the interwar timetable been repeated, World War III would have broken out by the late 1960s. As it turned out, by that time expectations of such a war had receded into the background.

GLOBALLY MOBILE MILITARY FORCES

Rivalry in strategic arms and European theater forces is geared to possible U.S.–USSR hostilities. This prospect of direct confrontation between the superpowers is less central in the development of glob-

---

[25] The mutual withdrawal from Austria in 1955, a consequence of the Austrian State Treaty of that year, constitutes a partial exception to the statement in the text, as does the withdrawal of U.S. (and other NATO) troops from France upon request of the de Gaulle government.

ally mobile military forces, i.e., those forces that give the rival powers capabilities for military intervention in areas distant from home territory, in and around Asia, Africa, and Latin America. This rivalry centers more on conventionally equipped forces than nuclear arms; it involves principally naval and air units, airborne and seaborne troops, plus the home and foreign bases to support these units.

In the years immediately after 1945 only America had the naval and air power to project its influence on a world scale. This capability emerged from the kind of far-flung military operations characteristic of U.S. participation in World War II. Prior to the war the United States had a first-class navy, but its military establishment was generally very small. And before that war the U.S. made only limited use of its military forces outside its territory, chiefly in the Caribbean and, less often, in the rimlands of the Pacific.

The war changed all this. New opportunities and new dangers appeared. The European colonial powers, especially Great Britain and France, were no longer in a position to dominate the underdeveloped world, certainly not without U.S. approval and assistance. Disturbed by the growth of Soviet power and fearful of the spread of communism, American leaders came to be imbued with the ambitious mission of preserving Western positions of strength and saving the world from communism. They saw to the development and maintenance of a worldwide system of military bases that, as a supplement to installations on U.S. territory, enabled powerful American naval, air, and ground forces to reach any spot on the globe.

There was much talk in the United States of the "Soviet menace," not only in relation to Europe—where the USSR had real capabilities—but on a global scale. Yet in the early postwar years the USSR had almost no capabilities to exert military influence in areas distant from the USSR's borders. If the Soviet threat was unreal, the threat to the world predominance of the advanced capitalist states was real enough. Expressed in terms of national independence, anticolonialism, and antiimperialism, this sometimes took the form of radical nationalism, sometimes of communism. Washington administrations, Democratic and Republican alike, not without reason lacked confidence in the staying power of pro-Western indigenous elites in many backward and semideveloped countries. The U.S. was, therefore, determined to supply the missing ingredient by a judicious interjection of military power if other means of bolstering anticommunist régimes proved insufficient.

The policy had its successes as well as failures. Having military bases scattered in dozens of countries and having ready military forces enabled the United States to intervene effectively when favored power holders were in danger, and thus to influence developments in directions sought by Washington. Such military bolstering by the U.S. of right-wing forces in the former Belgian colony of the Congo (now Zaire) serves as one example of successful intervention. But in the two most dramatic applications of U.S. military power the results were disappointing, mildly so in Korea, bitterly so in Vietnam. Taking a major role in the war in Korea (1950–1953), the United States succeeded in preserving anticommunist rule in South Korea, but failed to dislodge the North Korean régime and thus unify the country under Seoul's pro-American leadership. The U.S. took a similarly leading role in the war in Vietnam, particularly in 1965–1972, but withdrawal of American forces was followed by the collapse of the anticommunist governments in South Vietnam and Cambodia and a rapid pro-Communist shift in Laos. Moreover, the American involvement caused such domestic repercussions in the U.S. as to jeopardize the freedom of future administrations to intervene at will wherever and whenever Communist advances threatened the hold of U.S.-oriented governments.

Like the postwar United States, the USSR also had a world mission, i.e., a mission that went beyond safeguarding the homeland and protecting allies on its European and Asian frontiers. For a long time after 1945, however, the USSR had minimal capabilities of projecting its military power to places beyond the marching distance of Soviet troops. The Soviet navy was designed primarily for coastal defense and, in the case of submarines, wartime interruption of enemy shipping, The Soviet air force, like the navy, could not operate far from bases on Soviet territory, and the USSR had no foreign bases outside Europe.

Certainly the Moscow leaders felt less need than their Washington counterparts for capabilities of military intervention in distant areas where no threat to the security of the Soviet homeland could originate. They were just as interested as American policy makers in the orientation of the "third world," but they had a confidence, almost totally lacking in the American capital, that history was on their side, that the famous "balance of forces" was shifting in the direction of socialism and the USSR and away from capitalism and the United States. Little pushes by the USSR to help history do its appointed job

were not ruled out. But the Moscow leaders did not see Soviet projection of military power as the necessary ingredient for the world to
move in the right, that is, the "left," direction.

This ideological slant was in part, but only in part, responsible for
Soviet backwardness in development of globally mobile military
forces. Priorities mattered: accumulating strategic forces to protect
the Soviet Union and maintaining war-ready theater forces in Europe
had a much higher priority for the Kremlin. Nevertheless, experience
showed that Soviet lack of capabilities to project military power at a
distance damaged efforts to present to the world an image of Soviet
military potency, particularly by complicating endeavors to assist
friendly nations confronting external threats. The misbegotten venture to install missile bases on Cuba in 1962 terminated in an embarrassing display of Soviet weakness against overwhelming American
superiority in conventional forces. Though this drama was played out
in America's backyard, even in distant Vietnam the USSR was in no
position to deter U.S. intervention on a grand scale and U.S. attacks
on comradely North Vietnam. In transporting essential military and
civilian supplies to Hanoi the Soviet authorities took pains to avoid a
challenge to locally based U.S. air and naval units. Moreover, the lack
of capabilities for distant application of military force became a more
acute problem as the USSR began to acquire a clientele of non-Communist as well as Communist states in the underdeveloped world.

Although steps were taken earlier, the main Soviet push to build
forces for uses outside the context of a strategic nuclear duel with the
U.S. and of theater operations in Europe occurred in the decade after
Khrushchev's fall from power. This push was especially evident in the
development and expansion of Soviet naval forces, a military arm that
Khrushchev had tended to downgrade. The USSR enlarged and modernized its fleet of surface vessels and submarines, with emphasis on
equipping new models of cruisers and destroyers with missile launchers. Although Soviet naval vessels were generally smaller and less
sophisticated than those of the U.S. Navy, in most of the categories,
such as cruisers, destroyers, escort vessels, and amphibious ships, the
USSR had greater numbers in 1975 than the United States. This
reversed the situation of 1965. Modernization included the introduction of nuclear-powered vessels; this characteristic contributed to an
increase in capabilities for operating at considerable distances from
Soviet ports. The USSR was thereby enabled to maintain a presence

in the Mediterranean, off the coasts of Africa, and in the Indian Ocean.

The Soviet navy had nothing, however, comparable to the large aircraft carriers of the U.S. Navy that, with their powerful complements of fighter bombers, had replaced battleships as the main attack forces of the fleet. (It is known that at times in the past Soviet authorities considered, but rejected building such large carriers.) The only USSR carriers are a few smaller ships designed for helicopters and STOL (Short Take-off and Landing) aircraft. As a consequence, the USSR has capabilities far inferior to those of the United States for projecting air power in distant areas. Almost all of its aviation, including naval, remains ground-based, and therefore cannot operate outside the range of airfields in friendly hands. In a related area, however, the decade 1965–1975 saw a major Soviet effort to build up its capabilities for airlift and sealift of personnel and equipment to distant points, overtaking the U.S. in this category.

For the USSR to have a first-class capability for long-range deployment of military power it would seem almost essential that it have military bases abroad. So far the Soviet authorities have rejected such bases on principle and called for abandonment of foreign military bases by all countries, meaning the United States in particular. This posture was expedient at a time when Soviet facilities for distant operations were minimal, and when there were almost no places where the USSR might acquire base rights. But clearly the USSR, even if it possessed no "extraterritorial" bases as such, made unpublicized arrangements with Egypt, with the Somali Republic (both now in abeyance), and perhaps elsewhere for facilities to serve temporarily or permanently in support of Soviet naval and air units. The rejection of foreign bases may become inconvenient for the Soviet leadership with the buildup of naval and air capabilities for distant projection of military power. It is far from clear, however, that the USSR will move in this direction. Open acquisition of bases in other countries would jeopardize Soviet standing in nonaligned countries and undercut continued Soviet encouragement of moves in "third world" countries to oust American military installations.

If all of the various relevant factors are considered, it is still the United States rather than the Soviet Union that possesses the greater capabilities in the area of globally mobile forces. Nevertheless, the gap between the two states has substantially narrowed, partly because of the Soviet buildup, partly because American forces of this type have been somewhat reduced and the U.S. has been compelled to relinquish bases in various far-flung countries, including Morocco, Libya, Pakistan, Vietnam, Thailand, and Ethiopia.

Moreover, the improvement of Soviet capabilities has made it more risky for the U.S. to intervene in distant areas without thought of Soviet reaction. Thus, the increased Soviet presence in the eastern Mediterranean has become a factor that must be considered by American authorities contemplating the display or use of military force, either in a situation such as that of Lebanon in 1958 or in a situation involving a renewal of Arab–Israeli hostilities. Even in the Indian Ocean the Soviet capabilities for response were probably one element discouraging a more vigorous U.S. military reaction in 1973 to the successful assertion of independence by Bangladesh (East Pakistan), aided by India, against the will of America's ally in the region, Pakistan.

ARMS LIMITATION AND
U.S.–USSR MILITARY COMPETITION

Given the intensity of their rivalry, it would be expected that more Soviet and American effort would go into arming than into disarming, into building rather than limiting armaments. Such an expectation would have proved right. Nevertheless, disarmament and arms limitation have been the topic of frequent U.S.–USSR negotiations. As might be also expected, such negotiations have displayed the fundamental rivalry of the two states for advantage fully as much as other spheres of U.S.–USSR interaction. The fact that negotiations on arms limitations brought a variety of agreements into force is testimony to the existence of certain shared interests, but the extremely limited impact of such agreements on Soviet–American military competition is evidence of the depth and pervasiveness of the rivalry.

A review of disarmament and arms limitation proposals, of agreements reached, and of the impact of agreed arms limitations on military rivalry is in order; the treatment follows the same sequence as that adopted for the discussion of arms rivalry, that is, overall military allocations, strategic arms, European theater forces, and globally mobile capabilities.

It is not necessary to spend much time on proposals for "real" disarmament. They got nowhere, and perhaps were not expected to get anywhere. Representatives of the U.S. and USSR engaged in some discussions of "general and complete disarmament" in the late 1950s and early 1960s, agreed on some vague general principles to govern negotiations, and launched (especially from the Soviet side) some far-reaching plans indicating the successive stages by which the goal was to be reached. But there were never any serious negotiations, and in the last decade general and complete disarmament has not been much talked about in U.S.–USSR meetings.

A less drastic type of proposal, but one still calling for across-the-board arms cuts, has been repeatedly floated by the USSR. The most recent version would require the five nuclear weapons states, all permanent members of the United Nations Security Council, to cut their military budgets by 10 percent with the idea of devoting part of the savings to aid developing countries. The proposal aroused no interest in the United States, and no serious negotiations have occurred.

One reason for American coolness is obvious. For budgetary ceilings to be meaningful, there would have to be agreement on a definition of military expenditures and there would have to be available sufficient data on detailed military appropriations to satisfy suspicious participants. The gross disparity in published Soviet and American expenditure figures puts a burden on "trust," that is, American trust in Soviet fulfillment, that the existing state of U.S.–USSR relations cannot bear.

Apart from the data problem, however, American representatives have suggested that mutual budgetary limitations would be unacceptable without assurance that no "destabilizing imbalances" would occur. Translated from governmentese into plain English, a language often spoken outside Washington circles, this appeared to mean that the U.S. wanted to retain its freedom of military action to counter unfavorable developments abroad, and therefore wanted to be able to adjust appropriations upward as well as downward as international developments dictated. This attitude in turn lessened any possible Soviet interest in the American suggestion that "study groups" might work on problems of data and definition. Regarding secrecy as an asset to Soviet security, the USSR could only lose from an exercise that promised to be purely academic, i.e., would result in no agreement.[26]

---

[26] For statements of the U.S. position, see *Department of State Bulletin*, August 25, 1975, pp. 282–85, and December 8, 1975, pp. 825–26. For the Soviet position, see R. Mikhailov, "Sokrashcheniye voyennykh budzhetov—veleniye vremeni," *Pravda*, October 2, 1973.

Strategic Arms Limitation

Almost all of the various agreements reached between the United States and the Soviet Union have focused on strategic nuclear weapons systems or other means of "mass destruction"; such agreements have marginally affected U.S.–USSR arms competition, leaving untouched, however, so-called conventionally armed forces, the only kind put to military use since 1945. The most important of the treaties negotiated in the 1960s were the partial test-ban treaty of 1963 and the nonproliferation treaty of 1968. The former prohibited for the signatories all but underground testing of nuclear weapons; it was supplemented in 1974 by a U.S.–USSR agreement under which the two powers agreed to end, as of March 31, 1976, even underground tests of weapons yielding in excess of 150 kilotons. The nonproliferation treaty banned states having nuclear weapons from transferring these to any other country and from aiding any non-nuclear weapons state to develop or otherwise acquire such weapons.

The test-ban and nonproliferation treaties were designedly multilateral, and their military consequences for countries capable of developing nuclear weapons were considerably greater than for the U.S., USSR, and other countries that had acquired these arms. For the U.S. and USSR, however, the test-ban treaty was unique among all the arms limitation agreements of the past decade or so in requiring the rival military establishments to retrench from an activity to which they had grown accustomed, namely, uninhibited testing of new devices for nuclear destruction. Although much testing after 1963 was simply transferred underground, the partial test-ban could qualify, in a pinch, as arms reduction. With minor exceptions, none of the others involved any reductions.

Most of the other multilateral arms agreements focused on exotic weapons systems or exotic environments. The Antarctic Treaty of 1959 prohibited all military installations, conventional as well as nuclear, in the region. Similarly, all military installations on the moon and other celestial bodies were banned under a treaty on outer space signed in 1967; the treaty likewise ruled out the orbiting of satellites carrying nuclear weapons. It did not, however, contrary to a widespread belief, prohibit the military use of outer space except for the activities specified. The seabed treaty of 1971 provided that nuclear weapons or other weapons of mass destruction could not be stationed on the seabed or ocean floor; again, it tacitly permitted other military uses of the seabed. The possession as well as the use of biological weapons and toxins were banned under a "convention" signed in 1972. This supplemented the Geneva Protocol of 1925 against the wartime use, but not the possession, of bacteriological *and* chemical weapons, an agreement belatedly ratified by the U.S in 1975.[27]

For the most part in these agreements the United States and the Soviet Union merely assumed obligations to refrain from courses of action that they had shown no disposition to follow irrespective of the treaties. It was no great sacrifice to renounce military bases in the Antarctic, or installation of nuclear weapons on the bottom of the sea or on the moon, or orbiting nuclear warheads in sputniks circulating endlessly around the earth. Neither the Pentagon nor the Soviet military had initiated programs toward such objectives. The seabed and outer space treaties were carefully worded so as not to interfere with existing or contemplated military programs. Even the nonproliferation treaty, though it foreclosed for the duration of the treaty an option of transferring nuclear weapons to other countries, merely ratified a policy of nontransferral that both the United States and USSR had effected while free from treaty obligations. Moreover, nothing in the treaty prevented either the U.S. or the USSR from resuming, or beginning, technical assistance to another nuclear weapons state (Great Britain, France, China) of the kind that the two countries had rendered earlier.[28]

The bilateral strategic arms limitations agreed upon by the U.S. and USSR in 1972–1974 were more important in some respects than any of the multilateral agreements discussed above. They involved no more disarmament, but they centered on the main strategic forces of each side, subjected for the first time to quantitative ceilings. These agreements resulted from the Strategic Arms Limitation Talks (SALT) proposed by President Johnson in 1967 but begun under President Nixon in 1969. Earlier proposals from Moscow and Washington on strategic arms never led to serious negotiations, largely because of the great imbalance in U.S.–USSR ratios of strength. Proposals from

---

[27] For a convenient summary of 1959–1975 agreements, see U.S. Arms Control and Disarmament Agency, *Arms Control and Disarmament Agreements* (Washington, D.C.: ACDA, 1975).

[28] For a fuller discussion of these developments, see Thomas B. Larson, *Disarmament and Soviet Policy: 1964–1968* (Englewood Cliffs, N.J.: Prentice-Hall, Inc., 1969), pp. 125–56.

Moscow sought to achieve Soviet parity with the United States the easy way, by bringing about reductions to zero or to a very low level of arms. They envisaged, therefore, much more severe cuts from actual American forces than from Soviet forces in being. The answer from the U.S. was: "No dice!" American proposals sought to slow the USSR's strategic buildup by gaining Moscow's acceptance of permanent inferiority. The answer was: "Nyet!" It was a dialogue of the deaf.

The Soviet gain of near-parity in strategic arms made feasible agreed limitations, because, although the United States was not prepared to lose at the negotiating table a superiority it had won on production lines, it was prepared to recognize diplomatically the equalization achieved in practice by Soviet arms producers. In an agreement (not a treaty) covering the years 1972–1977, the two states promised to avoid further increases in the number of missile launchers beyond the 1054 ICBM and 656 submarine missile launchers in the U.S. arsenal and the 1618 ICBM and 740 submarine missile launchers operational or under construction in the USSR. The proportion and sophistication of the strategic submarine forces could be increased under the agreement, but only by retiring the equivalent number of older ICBMs or submarines. The numerically higher Soviet ceilings took account of the fact that no restrictions were placed on bombers or on MIRV installations, in both of which the U.S. had a significant advantage. Forward-based aircraft were also left out.

To replace this temporary accord President Ford and General Secretary Brezhnev reached agreement in Vladivostok in December 1974 on the outlines of a pact to cover the period 1977–1985. This was to bring under limitations the bombers and MIRV installations omitted from the 1972 accord. An upper limit of 2400 offensive units, land- and sea-based missile launchers and strategic bombers, was to be placed on each country's strategic offensive forces, with a maximum of 1320 missile launchers to be equipped with the capability of lobbing multiple independently guided warheads (MIRV). This accord on principles, however, has not been translated into a binding agreement, largely because of unresolved issues over the inclusion or exclusion of certain delivery vehicles from the 2400 overall limit. One issue concerned a new type of long-range cruise missile under development in the U.S., a robot aircraft (i.e., air-breathing, nonballistic) capable of being launched from either bombers or naval vessels. Another concerned a new Soviet supersonic bomber, designated by the U.S. as "Backfire," that might be able to reach targets in the United States if flown subsonically. The U.S. insisted that Backfire be counted among Soviet strategic bombers if cruise missiles were counted, as the USSR demanded, within the overall missile–bomber limit of 2400.

The 1972 agreement on strategic offensive weapons was paralleled by a treaty, of indefinite duration, limiting ballistic missile defense systems. Under the agreement each country could install antimissile defenses in two areas, one protecting its capital city and the other an area of ICBM deployment, each to be equipped with no more than 100 launchers and 100 interceptor missiles. At the 1974 Brezhnev–Nixon meeting this arrangement was modified to limit such deployment to one area, the USSR opting for defense of Moscow, the U.S. for defense of ICBM silos in North Dakota. Each was permitted a one-time change of mind between the two options.

Except for the reduced scope of underground nuclear tests, these SALT accords of 1972–1974 were similar to previous arms limitation agreements in requiring no reductions. The ceilings established for missile launchers and bombers, for MIRV applications, and for ABM defenses, were above—and in some cases considerably above—actual force levels. Plenty of room remained for continued technological innovation and strengthening of strategic forces on both sides. It was argued, of course, that the establishment of upper limits might prevent an otherwise considerably greater buildup of offensive and defensive forces. Perhaps. But the two powers showed that they were far from any thought of disarmament, no matter how modest.

If the agreements were a step toward ensuring peace and reducing the risks that nuclear war would occur, they were so primarily on a psychological plane, not that of military capabilities. In a minor way the agreements may even have spurred steps to increase capabilities to the limits allowed. In the Nixon administration various arms development measures were pushed on the stated ground that these were needed as bargaining counters in disarmament negotiations. By the same token, the agreed limitations were not of a character to reduce the military burden on either economy. Throughout the years of negotiation of arms limitation measures, before and during SALT, it was often alleged that the costliness of military competition was driving the heavily armed states, at least the USSR with its less affluent economy, to find means of easing the burden through mutually agreed steps. The record offers little support to this idea. Soviet–American arms competition might have become even more of an "arms race" without the agreements, but economic pressures proved insufficient to force leaders of either country to cut military expenditures.

Arms Limitation Proposals for European Theater and Globally Mobile Forces

Outside the strategic arms field, no Soviet–American agreements were reached, and there have been only a few sustained negotiations. In the 1950s and early 1960s Soviet authorities floated a number of proposals for specifically European limitations, but most aroused little interest in official American circles. No negotiations resulted, for example, from proposals initiated by the then-foreign minister of Poland, Rapacki, that envisaged a "freeze," reduction, or elimination of nuclear weapons on German, Polish, and Czechoslovak soil, with or without accompanying reductions of conventional forces. Measures to avert the danger of surprise attack were, in contrast, the subject of an East–West conference in 1958 that was largely centered on Europe. The conference ended in complete deadlock. The USSR proposed the establishment of a system of control posts on U.S. and USSR territory, and on the territory of other NATO and Warsaw Pact countries, for mutual observation of military movements. The proposal made establishment of such control posts dependent on reductions in the number of foreign troops in European countries and on the removal of nuclear arms from East and West Germany. The United States was hostile to the arms reduction features; U.S. negotiators sought to have the conference agree not on measures against surprise attack but on the kind of measures that might be appropriate *if* the governments subsequently decided on a system to lessen the danger of surprise attack.

Soviet interest in European arms limitations fell off sharply after Khrushchev's deposition in 1964. It appeared that Brezhnev and his associates had second thoughts about proposals in this area, most of which would have given a kind of peace-keeping role to NATO as well as the Warsaw Pact. Under Brezhnev, major emphasis went to the convening of an all-European conference on security and cooperation. Though initially resisted by the U.S. (and therefore by NATO), this eventually met in 1973–1975 and produced the so-called Helsinki Declaration signed by representatives of thirty-three European states plus the United States and Canada. The conference had little to do with arms limitations in a strict sense. However, an old Soviet proposal for a nonaggression pact between NATO and Warsaw Pact countries reappeared in the "Final Act" of the conference in a slightly different form, as a renunciation of "any acts constituting a threat of force or direct or indirect use of force against another participating State."[29] The conference also agreed on mutual notification of major military maneuvers, defined as those exceeding 25,000 troops, with a saving clause, inserted for Soviet benefit, that required notification only if the maneuvers were within 250 kilometers of the state's European frontiers. The "Final Act" also encouraged reciprocal invitations to military exercises, exchange visits of military personnel, and prior notification of major military movements.

The European security conference did not deal, however, with limitation or reduction of military forces and armaments in Europe; a smaller conference, limited to certain NATO and Warsaw Pact nations, was convened in Vienna in 1973 to deal with this subject. Its focus was on central Europe, not the whole of Europe, with central Europe defined to include the two German states plus Poland and Czechoslovakia in the East, and Belgium, Luxembourg, and the Netherlands in the West.[30]

By one of the ironies that has bedeviled arms control negotiations on various occasions, the United States and its allies developed an interest in troop reductions just as the Soviet Union and its allies showed a lessening of enthusiasm. Nevertheless, the U.S. made it a condition, actually if not explicitly, for participation in the European security conference that there be parallel negotiations on mutual reduction of forces, or, as the U.S. described the topic, mutual and *balanced* force reductions (MBFR).[31]

There was an immediate stumbling block, and the years of negotiations have not removed it. "Balanced" in the U.S. description was a

---

[29] Text of "Final Act" in *Department of State Bulletin*, September 1, 1975, pp. 323–50.

[30] In addition to the countries mentioned, other direct participants are the states having forces in the area, i.e., the USSR, the U.S., Great Britain, and Canada. France has declined to take part.

[31] In the jointly agreed language of the conference the talks are described as "Negotiations on the Mutual Reduction of Forces and Armaments and Associated Measures in Central Europe."

shorthand way of saying that reductions should be greater for the East than for the West. American and Western negotiators wanted to bring Warsaw Pact and NATO forces in the defined area down to a common level of 700,000 ground forces, and to begin the process by cutting U.S. and Soviet forces alone. To achieve the 700,000 level would require cuts in Soviet and other Eastern forces over two and one-half times the size of the cuts envisaged for NATO states.

The Soviet (Warsaw Pact) proposal sought equal percentage reductions. After an initial cut of 20,000 on each side, NATO and Warsaw Pact forces were to be reduced in stages ultimately totaling over 15 percent. Both the initial cut and the subsequent percentage reductions were to apply to all participants, not just the senior states, and reductions were to affect air forces and nuclear weapons, not just ground forces.

Soviet and American tactics were consistent with past practices in arms limitation negotiations. The side with larger forces advances proposals designed to perpetuate this superiority, if at changed levels; the side with smaller forces advances proposals to eliminate the adversary's advantage. The Vienna talks have not brought about a major narrowing of the differences. A minor modification was introduced into the Eastern plan so as to permit the initial stage to begin with U.S.–USSR reductions, as in the Western plan. But the principle of equal percentage reductions remained, along with the requirement that all of the countries in the area commit themselves to reductions. The NATO states introduced a modification of the Western plan by suggesting that the U.S. reduce by 1,000 the large number (some 7000) of nuclear weapons on European soil in return for a reduction of Warsaw Pact tank strength. As in the case of the Warsaw Pact modification, this did not alter the basic principle of the NATO approach.

The present outlook for mutual reduction of forces in Europe does not, therefore, seem promising. Neither side appears to be ready for a major compromise. The interest of Washington administrations in negotiations on mutual European force reductions has always been largely a function of the need to head off congressional pressure for unilateral cuts. Such pressure has declined, and with the decline U.S. willingness to give ground at Vienna. As to the USSR, a Vienna agreement might require Soviet compromises of a different kind from those that facilitated earlier agreements, on outer space, the seabed, and chemical-biological weapons. In those, Soviet negotiators initially proposed more far-reaching measures than were acceptable to the

U.S. Eventually the USSR compromised, because it could take a half-loaf without changing Soviet military strength. At Vienna relative military strength, U.S.–USSR and NATO–Warsaw Pact, is very much at issue.

Nevertheless, agreement cannot be ruled out. Over the past fifteen-odd years almost all U.S.–USSR discussion of arms limitation proposals that reached a Vienna-like stage of negotiations eventually led to agreements. And it may be that the Vienna talks are likewise doomed to succeed.

Even if the most ambitious reductions were realized under either the U.S. or USSR proposals, or some compromise between them, the two powers would still have sufficient military strength in Europe to maintain their roles as leaders of rival military alliances, particularly since their strategic arms form an indispensable backup force for the two alliances. Reductions of Soviet effectives on the order of those under consideration would not, for example, seriously affect USSR capabilities of controlling events in the area overshadowed by Soviet military power; that is, they would not incapacitate Soviet authorities for the kind of military intervention *in extremis* undertaken in Hungary and Czechoslovakia. Soviet forces in Eastern Europe are equipped and positioned, like U.S. and NATO forces in Western Europe, for a major war, not to control internal challenges to, or disintegration of, the existing Communist régimes. The capability of handling challenges to the established order is merely a by-product of military forces much too large and heavily armed to have this as their main function.

In the third area of U.S.–USSR military rivalry, that of globally mobile, conventionally equipped military forces, there have been no arms control negotiations of importance, let alone agreements. From time to time proposals have been advanced, mostly by the USSR, that would have affected capabilities for intervention in the "third world." One staple in the Soviet repertory of proposals calls for the mutual renunciation of foreign military bases (and withdrawal of troops to their homelands). This aroused no American interest. Even if the U.S. government were prepared to relinquish foreign bases voluntarily—which it assuredly is not!—there would be no advantage to do so by way of an agreement with the USSR, which has no reciprocal concessions to offer.

Proposals for regional denuclearization have also been advanced from Moscow in relation to various areas. If put into effect in areas outside those where U.S. or USSR forces are heavily concentrated, they would marginally affect the military capabilities of the two countries. But the only zonal denuclearization agreement embodied in a treaty is that concerning Latin America. The 1967 Treaty of Tlatelolco (Mexico) was not entirely satisfactory to either great power, for different reasons, although neither opposed the treaty on principle. In any case, it is of peripheral importance to Soviet–American military rivalry.[32]

In summary, the preceding discussion has indicated that arms limitation agreements have had a most indistinct impact on the pace and direction of military rivalry between the United States and the Soviet Union. If competition was blocked in old channels, it tended to flow into new. Weapons tests in the atmosphere were halted; those underground were pushed. Numbers of missile launchers were limited; their capabilities to take out targets increased. Perhaps Soviet–American military competition would have been more strenuous without the agreed limitations. This will never be known, because levels of effort are determined by a variety of considerations, of which only one, and that not always the most important, is the absence of mutually agreed prohibitions and limitations.

U.S.–USSR RIVALRY IN BUILDING MILITARY ALLIANCES

The United States and the Soviet Union have been rivals not only in the development of their own military forces but also in arranging bilateral and multilateral alliances. Through these they sought access to militarily useful real estate and, sometimes, support in armaments and personnel from junior alliance members. Such alliances were more significant for the American military position than for the Soviet, because the U.S. alliances extended into most corners of the globe whereas Soviet alliances were more restricted.

Washington and Moscow spokesmen frequently allude to the defensive role of such alliances, to the protection of what is called in the U.S. "national security." If by this is meant protection of the homeland against possible attack, then certainly some of the Russian and American alliances can be seen as contributing to the national secu-

---

[32] A less formal agreement for African nonnuclearization was embodied in declarations of the Organization of African Unity and of the United Nations General Assembly. See *Documents on Disarmament, 1965* (Washington, D.C.: ACDA, 1966), pp. 624–26.

rity. By utilizing the territory of allies, the U.S. and USSR are able to extend their military frontiers forward of their national borders, and thereby deny to a potential adversary any chance of moving unmolested up to these borders. Obviously, protection of the homeland looms larger in Soviet than in American motives for alliance building, because USSR territory is much less invasion-proof than that of the United States. Almost all of the Soviet allies share a common border with the USSR, the only exceptions being two Warsaw Treaty members, the German Democratic Republic and Bulgaria. Although the U.S. is allied to the two states bordering American territory on the north and south, these states are of minor importance in the U.S. alliance structure.

There are other interests involved, of course, in addition to direct protection of the homeland. In the U.S. these are frequently brought under the umbrella of "national security," but they are remote from protection of the physical integrity of the United States against a foreign threat. In some cases they have to do with American property interests, widely dispersed throughout the non-Communist world. If there is no Soviet parallel to such foreign holdings, like the United States the USSR is involved in the protection of junior alliance members against external military pressure from the rival camp and in safeguarding the social order in allied states against "subversion," that is, internal disintegration. The first element is primary in the Soviet and American alliances with states of Europe and North Asia, the second in U.S. alliances elsewhere (the USSR has none). But the difference is one of degree. If the North Atlantic and Warsaw Treaties are primarily directed at external dangers, certainly part of their raison d'être is to maintain the kind of social order that Washington and Moscow officials find congenial. Likewise, in the U.S. alliances aimed primarily at internal stability, protection against external military pressure plays a role, but a distinctly secondary role.

This difference in alliance priorities is reflected in different levels of military preparedness for possible interstate warfare. The North Atlantic and Warsaw Treaties serve as foundations for more or less integrated military organizations that exist nowhere else. Such organizations were new even in Europe, although military alliances have been as common in European history as the resort to war among European states. Post–World War II domestication of nuclear weapons imposed higher requirements of war readiness and thus led to the creation, unique in peacetime, of permanent unified command structures. Outside Europe the threat of interstate warfare involving the USSR and the U.S. was not a major concern, except possibly for North Asia. Hence American bilateral and multilateral alliances with countries of South Asia, the Middle East, and Latin America were aimed first of all at preserving the stability of local régimes against internal threats; only in Latin America did the United States make an attempt to have established, under the aegis of the Organization of American States, a permanently ready military force. Undertaken in the aftermath of the 1965 U.S. military intervention in the Dominican Republic, the attempt failed. There was no plausible extracontinental military threat to any Latin American state, and all knew that such an OAS military establishment would almost certainly be dominated by the United States, the only advanced military power in the hemisphere.

The Latin American alliance was distinct from the other two extra-European multilateral alliances in which the U.S. participated, one in Southeast Asia, the other in the Middle East, in its broadly inclusive scope. Antedating (1947) even the North Atlantic alliance, it included all of the independent states of the Western Hemisphere from the U.S. southward. Neither of the others gathered in a representative collection of states in the regions covered: the alliance formed at Manila in 1954 brought in only three "indigenous states," the Philippines, Thailand, and Pakistan; the Baghdad Pact of 1955 lost its single Arab member in 1958 when the British-supported régime was overthrown in Iraq.[33] Largely for this reason, neither of the alliances proved of any use to the United States in dealing with the interstate armed conflicts that erupted in the regions, between Pakistan and India, for example, or between Israel and her Arab neighbors. Nor did these multilateral alliances prove very effective, despite the anticommunist, anti-Soviet thrust that characterized them, in forestalling internal transformations that Washington and other Western capitals regarded with apprehension or hostility.

U.S. failure to get effective anticommunist alliances organized on a multilateral basis has to be balanced against the very real military

---

[33] The Manila treaty included, in addition to the U.S. and the three "indigenous" states, Great Britain and France, plus the two European-settler states, New Zealand and Australia. In the Middle Eastern alliance the U.S. is associated with Great Britain and with Turkey, Iran, and Pakistan; the United States is not formally a member of the alliance, but nevertheless is the most important participant in CENTO (Central Treaty Organization), the organization formed to run alliance affairs.

gains Washington derived from numerous bilateral treaties and agreements. It was on the basis of such agreements that the U.S. was able to station military forces around the globe. Normally the American military could use these foreign bases for extraterritorial purposes, even if formally they were supposed to function for the defense needs of the host countries. Thus, bases in Japan, the Philippines, and Thailand could be used to support military operations in Vietnam and elsewhere in the Far East. U.S. bases in Turkey, Pakistan, and other countries provided convenient locations for monitoring signals emitted from Communist-ruled countries. Even if no extraterritorial element were involved, such alliances gave American military personnel entrée to influential members of local ruling groups, enabled them to influence or control the training and supply of local military and police forces, and allowed them to maneuver inside these countries against adversary elements, domestic or foreign.

Outside Europe the Soviet Union has participated in no multilateral pacts and has had bilateral military alliances with only three states, the Mongolian People's Republic (so-called Outer Mongolia), the Korean People's Democratic Republic (North Korea), and the Chinese People's Republic. In the first, where Soviet troops are stationed, the USSR authorities have a faithful follower for whom the great northern neighbor is mentor and guardian; in the second, where there are no Soviet forces stationed, the USSR authorities have a difficult, wayward ally; and in the third, the same authorities have a sworn enemy along whose border with Russia substantial forces have been arrayed. Though neither Russia nor China has chosen to denounce the 1950 treaty of alliance, for all practical purposes it is now a dead letter.

China's transformation in less than a decade from friend to foe was a drastic enough complication for Moscow military planners. Probably even more disturbing was the gradual shift of Chinese policy as the CPR came to line up increasingly with the United States and its allies against the USSR on key issues of international affairs. China as an adversary within the Communist world was one thing; China as a potential ally, if only a de facto ally, of the United States was something else again. This prospect became more real with the warming of American–Chinese relations in the early 1970s. Though still impeded by unresolved bilateral issues (especially Taiwan), Sino-American rapprochement has a solid grounding in the common opposition of the two states to Soviet power.

In contrast, the United States managed steps toward reconciliation with China without seriously endangering its relations with the other major power of the area, Japan. The latter had oriented its foreign policy on the U.S. from the very end of the war in the Pacific, when American military forces entered the country as the sole occupation force, never again to leave. A peace treaty of 1951 ended the occupation régime, but an accompanying "security" treaty allowed American ground, naval, and air units to be stationed in Japan.

Japanese–American political and economic relations were not, of course, entirely cloudless. The U.S. faced stiff commercial competition from the Japanese—whose economy expanded more rapidly in the postwar decades than that of any other major power—but there was no resurgence of military rivalry. In fact, American authorities came to be in the somewhat paradoxical position, given the experience of the 1930s, of urging the Japanese, like the Germans, to increase their military forces, for the two countries enjoyed an "unfair" economic advantage over the U.S. by wasting a much smaller part of their national income on war preparations. But from a military standpoint the United States succeeded in improving its position in northern Asia over the postwar years at the expense of the Soviet Union. This success had no parallel elsewhere, but bilateral military ties with forty-odd states in various parts of the world yielded important advantages to the U.S.

Away from Soviet borders the USSR had no military alliances even with other Communist-ruled countries such as the People's Republics of Vietnam and Cuba. Abundant military assistance went to both, and was probably crucial in their survival in the face of American pressure and military attacks. Cuban and Vietnamese leaders may have had their own reasons for avoiding the signature of mutual assistance treaties with the USSR, but the Kremlin authorities were also probably reluctant to record formal obligations of support. Soviet military deficiencies counseled a policy of prudence with options left open. Prudence likewise dictated the avoidance of Soviet commitment of military support in the treaties concluded in the early 1970s with Egypt (subsequently renounced by Cairo), Iraq, and India; these treaties called only for consultations if war threatened.

On the whole, therefore, it appears that a worldwide network of military alliances (particularly those of bilateral character) yields advantages to the U.S. in its military rivalry with the Soviet Union, poorly represented globally in this kind of activity. Not all of the consequences for the United States are positive, however. In some less-developed countries the dependence of ruling groups on U.S. military support and the intimacy of their relations with the American military ran counter to nationalist currents. In pushing for such close relationships Washington policy-makers may have sometimes unwittingly made these ruling groups more vulnerable to dislodgement than they otherwise would have been.

U.S.–USSR RIVALRY AS ARMS SUPPLIERS

In addition to maintaining their own military forces at a high level, and using alliances with less powerful states to fortify their military position, the United States and the Soviet Union also carried on a vigorous competition as arms givers and arms merchants. They transferred or sold military equipment and supplies on a scale that no other country could rival. The flow of arms went to support formally allied and other friendly nations, and to influence nonaligned countries.

The United States was in a position to enter this business from 1945; with the USSR, it assumed large proportions outside Europe only a decade later. Economic as well as political considerations encouraged both countries to assume major roles as arms suppliers. Economically, arms sales on a large scale were attractive because they lengthened production runs on military equipment with a reduction of unit costs. This reduced procurement expenses for national military forces, and made it easier for the military establishments to keep their laboratories, production plants, and skilled personnel gainfully occupied in periods of slack domestic demand. In the case of the United States, military sales abroad helped overcome balance-of-payments difficulties.

Even disposals abroad at less than the cost of production might be beneficial economically, provided some return was gained, if the military supplies in question were excess to domestic Soviet or American needs. Otherwise, equipment being phased out of U.S. or USSR inventories would have to be consigned to the junk pile. To be sure, economic considerations of this kind, i.e., those involving economies of scale, are less pressing for the U.S. and USSR than for other countries in the arms trade. American and Soviet military establishments are so large and technologically advanced that internal demand is sufficient to maintain rather large-scale production even without sales abroad.

In any case, economic incentives for arms transfers should not be given undue importance. Neither the USSR nor the United States derived national economic benefits from most such transfers. Until recent years, when arms sales zoomed, most U.S. transfers were on a grant basis, gifts paid for by American taxpayers. Such transfers might be profitable for the corporate producers, if not for the country, because costs were "socialized" and only profits were privately appropriated. Although grants were not characteristic of Soviet military assistance, arms were sold at low prices on easy credit terms, and the credits often went unpaid, as in the case of large deliveries to Indonesia and Egypt.

Political rather than economic considerations were dominant in both American and Soviet policies on arms transfers. Making arms available was seen in both Washington and Moscow as a means of fortifying governments deemed worthy of support, or of gaining influence in countries that could be made dependent on one or the other great power for their security needs. Arms deals thus opened the door to entry of Soviet influence into Egypt and several other Middle Eastern countries. The USSR has even supplied arms to countries allied to the United States, such as Iran and Pakistan, though both of these received many more U.S. than USSR arms. In contrast, the United States has banned transfers to Soviet allies; it was, however, a major supplier to Yugoslavia in the period of most intense Soviet–Yugoslav hostility.

Both the U.S. and USSR have refrained from transfer of such strategic arms as nuclear weapons systems and heavy bombers, but they have supplied their allies and others with sophisticated equipment in the form of advanced fighter planes, short-range missile launchers, tanks, armored carriers, radar, submarines, and other naval vessels, as well as various small arms. The inclusion of technologically advanced equipment gave each power an opportunity to send along technical personnel and instructors as advisers, to train and supervise foreign military staffs.

Exact figures on arms transfers are difficult to come by, but it is certain that in the postwar period transfers from the United States, totaling well over $100 billion, have been much greater than those from the USSR. In the first postwar decade Soviet transfers went only to a relatively small number of allies, whereas the United States had a much greater capability of provisioning its allies and supplying other friendly countries as well. In the next two decades the gap narrowed, although it appeared to be widening again in the first half of the 1970s. A recent U.S. study estimates that Soviet transfers in the period 1961–1970 totaled almost $15 billion, compared to about $23 billion for the United States.[34] American grants of military equipment declined in the 1970s but sales shot up to around $10 billion yearly; the U.S. found newly rich customers among Persian Gulf and Middle Eastern states with the will and means to buy technologically advanced armaments. The USSR, in contrast, was not able to benefit from this bonanza, its transfers in the early 1970s amounting to less than $2 billion annually.

Comparative figures on military assistance only (that is, excluding commercial sales but including types of military assistance other than arms transfers), show a similar U.S. margin over the USSR. In the period from 1955 through 1971 the USSR is estimated to have made available over $8.5 billion in military assistance to less-developed countries, not including aid to Communist states. In roughly the same period the United States gave about $40 billion in military assistance to less-developed countries outside Europe.[35] The recipients of the largest amount of Soviet military aid were Egypt, India, Indonesia (before 1965), and Iraq; of American aid, Vietnam, Laos, South Korea, and Taiwan. Almost all of these countries were involved in external or internal military confrontations or warfare; the large flow of supplies encouraged confrontation and fueled the fighting.

Even a cursory look at the list of favored recipients indicates that military aid in volume often did not achieve the results sought by the suppliers. Almost half of all military assistance from the U.S. to less-developed countries outside Europe went to Vietnam, Laos, and Cambodia, with well-known results. The return on the investment in pro-American régimes was worse than a big fat zero, because the victorious anti-American forces were left in possession of large stocks of U.S. military equipment. Likewise, about 45 percent of Soviet military aid to non-Communist less-developed countries went to Egypt and Indonesia, where subsequent shifts in domestic and foreign policy were adverse to Soviet interests. It is no wonder that Washington

---

[34] U.S. Arms Control and Disarmament Agency, *The International Transfer of Convention Arms* (Washington, D.C.: Government Printing Office, 1974), p. 4.

[35] U.S. Agency for International Development, *U.S. Overseas Loans and Grants, July 1, 1945–June 30, 1973* (Washington, D.C.: AID, 1974), pp. 6–9; Leo Tansky, "Soviet Foreign Aid: Scope, Direction, and Trends," in *Soviet Economic Prospects for the Seventies*, pp. 771–72.

and Moscow policy-makers came to take an occasionally jaundiced view of military assistance as an effective way of promoting their influence.

Despite these disappointments, transfers of arms remain a significant area of U.S.–USSR military rivalry. U.S. transfers have even increased in volume and value, but with a remarkable shift from aid to trade. Twenty years ago the ratio was about ten to one of grants to commercial sales; by the mid-1970s it was about ten to one of sales to grants. As for the USSR, the Kremlin leaders have swallowed their disappointments and continue their modest aid programs. They are conscious of the role played by arms transactions in opening the way for expansion of trade and of political contacts with nonaligned countries, and in binding weaker Communist states to their leadership, even if they recognize that such transfers have proved insufficient to guarantee the continuation of trends in recipient countries that Moscow desires to see.

COMPETITION FOR MILITARY SUPREMACY

The discussion so far of military rivalry has omitted a number of peripheral areas, at least two of which deserve special mention because of the importance they have assumed in the postwar period. One is rivalry in intelligence activities; the other is rivalry in that part of scientific development most closely related to national power considerations. Both countries devoted resources to these activities on a previously unknown scale, a condition induced in part by the revolution in capabilities for warfare associated with the introduction of nuclear weapons sytems, in part by the global character of the struggle between the United States and the Soviet Union for leadership.

Postwar intelligence collection went far beyond its traditional military forms, and both countries maintained large intelligence organizations in the field separate from their military establishments, the U.S. Central Intelligence Agency and the USSR KGB (Committee on State Security). Their organizational scope differed in that the latter combined a domestic with a foreign function, while the former was largely confined to foreign intelligence, with the FBI (Federal Bureau of Investigation) handling the domestic side. There were other organizations involved in addition to these, for example, in deciphering coded communications. Despite the broad scope of postwar intelligence activities, in some respects military intelligence remained primary, and the military establishments controlled (certainly in the U.S., probably in the USSR) the largest staffs and the largest funds.

Some intelligence collection involved processing of openly published sources, but most of it was covert, with varying degrees of "cover." Military attachés functioned as legally recognized and diplomatically protected "spies"; other intelligence agents operated on embassy staffs under "light cover," again with diplomatic protection; and still others assumed a deeper cover to penetrate into areas where identification with a foreign state would be a hindrance to accomplishment of their missions.

The major trend in postwar intelligence rivalry did not, however, revolve around the competition of rival agents but centered on the use of sophisticated equipment for intelligence collection. The two most important of these mechanized activities were the registration of sounds and of images. The former included the registration of coded and uncoded verbal symbols and of electronic signals associated with military-related activities such as rocket firing. Enormous efforts went into the reading of coded messages and scrambled oral communications, and into means of countering such disclosure. The registration of images took various forms; probably the most important was the constant circling of the earth by American and Soviet satellites equipped to photograph adversary or other territory of interest to intelligence agencies.

The other development of particular military importance in the years after 1945 was the organization of science, especially the natural sciences but in a more limited way the social sciences, to serve national power interests. This was not a new assignment for the sciences, but there was a striking change between prewar and postwar military attention to science. This has resulted in increased state funding of science and particularly funding of science directed toward military needs. This is as true of the USSR, where science and education have always been under direct state control and dependent on state appropriations, as of the United States, with its more diversified arrangements for control and support of scientific activities.

Soviet–American rivalry in intelligence activities and in scientific research and discovery has been ancillary to the kinds of military rivalry earlier discussed, that is, competition in strategic arms, European theater forces, and globally mobile capabilities for military intervention. Military rivalry has been a constant of Soviet–American relations over the past three decades. In the early postwar years of intense hostility this rivalry threatened more than once to erupt into open warfare. That danger has receded. But the rivalry persists in a period of greater civility.

In fact, the most significant development in U.S.–USSR military rivalry has not been a change in the tempo of competition but a shift in the standing of the contestants. If it is premature to say that the Soviet Union has attained military parity with the United States, it is not too much to say that it has made substantial strides in approaching a rough kind of equality after beginning a very poor second at the close of World War II.

The overall consequences of this shift in military power relationships can be assessed only speculatively, and remarks on the topic are reserved for the concluding chapter, in which future possibilities are discussed. At this point, however, it should be noted that the most even balance of military capabilities cannot possibly rule out the persistence of significant disparities in the amount and kinds of military power that can be applied in various local situations. Such a balance cannot, therefore, rule out a resort to force if the American or Soviet authorities find such a resort expedient and consider it relatively safe. In this sense, at least, overall parity—were it to be achieved—could not serve as a guarantee of peace.

8

SOVIET-AMERICAN RIVALRY IN INTERNATIONAL RELATIONS

T HE WORLD that emerged from World War II enabled the Soviet Union and the United States to play international roles unprecedented in either's earlier history. Distrust and antagonism were
not new in their relationship, but the scale of their postwar confrontation was unique.

Both powers assumed world missions. They thrust themselves onto
the world scene with all their political, economic, and military capabilities, and sought to organize wide-ranging aggregations of states
and peoples to follow their leadership while abjuring the rival's.

The Bolsheviks of 1917 were also conscious of a world mission, of
course, a revolutionary mission in which the October Revolution was
supposed to spark upheavals in Europe and beyond. But the early
revolutionary élan was not based on the power of the Soviet state but
rather on its mere existence. For Soviet Russia was engaged immediately in a struggle for survival against potent domestic and foreign opponents, including among the latter the United States. Soviet power
survived. But the consolidation of the régime in Russia occurred simultaneously with the dimming of prospects for revolution elsewhere. The USSR could neither inspire the "oppressed masses"
abroad to overthrow the old order nor amass sufficient state strength
to play a major international role in the interwar years. Assumption
by the Soviet Union of such a world role had to wait on the war-in-
duced decline of London, Paris, Berlin, Rome, and Tokyo as centers
for the radiation of power.

The decline of these once-great states also gave opportunity for a
tremendous expansion of the American place in world affairs. No
doubt in the interwar period the United States had unused capacity—
as the USSR did not—to exert its power in European and Asian af-

fairs. To this extent it was isolationist, a term more apt for describing the U.S. position in respect to Europe than to Asia or Latin America, and within Europe more to political-military than to economic affairs. Be that as it may, in the postwar period there was no similar reluctance to make full use of America's capacity to influence international developments.

These new postwar roles were accepted willingly enough in both countries, though the acceptance was sometimes accompanied by ostentatious displays of modesty. Nothing appeared to please Soviet leaders more than to talk of the leading position of the USSR in the postwar world; they often repeated a claim that no important international question could be decided without their participation. In Moscow it was: "Glad we are in the vanguard." In Washington it was: "We regret that we must accept the burden of free-world leadership." Perhaps this "reluctant dragon" style was a spin-off from American domestic political rituals; at any rate, plaintive regrets were voiced over the lost pleasures of absorption in provincial affairs, but America would not fail its responsibility for world leadership.

The postwar dominance of America and Russia is often attributed to their lead over other states in capabilities for warfare, especially their mastery of nuclear weapons systems. Even without the revolution in military affairs, however, the U.S. and USSR would probably have become the power centers of the post-1945 world, because of their industrial strength, the size and vigor of their populations, the resources they commanded. The great powers before World War II were mostly centers of colonial empires, and by 1945 the days of such empires were clearly numbered. New structural relationships, new forms of empire, had to be found. Neither the U.S. nor the USSR had any vested interest in the old forms of colonial relationship. There was, to be sure, an ambivalence in U.S. ruling circles about the disintegration of colonial rule in Asia, the Middle East, and Africa that was not much apparent in Moscow. But this was not due to any American reluctance to see other countries' empires collapse, for the withdrawal opened doors for American political, military, and economic influence to enter. It was due simply to fear that independence might be followed by "chaos," i.e., communism or radicalism. To the extent that such fears could be quieted, U.S. leaders looked with equanimity at the prospect of functioning under conditions favoring colony-less empires.

Reference to the rival world missions should not obscure the fact that the United States occupied a much more global position than the USSR, particularly in the early postwar years but even in more recent times. The regions and countries in which the U.S. could maneuver with ease were more numerous and stronger economically and militarily than those allowing similar Soviet maneuverability. To this extent a description of the U.S. and USSR as world powers must be modified: throughout the postwar years U.S. influence has been felt on a global scale, whereas Soviet influence only gradually assumed a worldwide scope after an initial confinment to the Eurasian continent.

The discussion that follows delineates some of the outstanding characteristics of postwar Soviet and American foreign policy and of the changing conditions that influenced international rivalry between the United States and the Soviet Union. There is no attempt to recount the history of Soviet–American international relations in 1945–1975, though some events and trends are mentioned. Nor is there any effort, obviously, to present a comprehensive treatment of the multitude of issues engaging the attention of U.S. and USSR foreign policy managers, though some of the issues are alluded to.

THE RISE AND DECLINE OF BIPOLARITY

In a study of Soviet–American rivalry it is tempting to emphasize bipolarity, the division of the world into two spheres headed by the U.S. and USSR. A portrayal stressing bipolarity is neat and economical instead of complex and diffuse. Moreover, Soviet and American ideologies have traditionally encouraged a focus on bipolarity, because each has favored a Manichean view depicting a world struggle between the forces of light and darkness.

No doubt in the first postwar decade or so bipolarity reflected reality to the extent that the two countries were unchallenged leaders of diametrically opposed groups of states. Bipolarity lost ground as once-faithful allies took their distances from the two senior states and as nonaligned countries increased in number and influence. Both blocs suffered some fragmentation, but the estrangement of Mao's China from the Soviet Union was the single most striking manifestation of the trend. It not only dealt a crushing blow to Moscow's hopes of leading a unified bloc of Communist states but transformed Peking into a sworn enemy of Moscow: China had the potential of challenging in the future the Soviet world role as it could already threaten the USSR on a local level. Other divisions as well sapped the unity of Communist-ruled countries and of nonruling Communist parties.

Nothing as dramatic weakened the American leadership role. French assertions of independence never brought Paris–Washington relations to the low state of Sino-Soviet relations, and France lacked China's potential for global status. Nevertheless, American allies among the advanced industrial nations began to display a greater assertiveness, and the economic resurgence of Western Europe and Japan cut into U.S. economic dominance. Ties to the U.S. among developing countries also loosened.

These phenomena led to descriptions of the world power structure in terms of tripolarity (American, Russia, and China) or of a pentagonal arrangement (the three above plus Japan and Western Europe). Such conceptions have in their favor a recognition of the divisions cutting across the capitalist and Communist camps, but even they take no account of the autonomous role in world affairs successfully asserted by various less-developed countries.

This fragmentation has altered the environment in which Soviet–American rivalry occurs. Each of the two major states has to maneuver in a new way, to adjust to the crisscrossing lines of accord and discord. Still, the trend has not eliminated the special role of the U.S. and USSR, nor attenuated greatly the extent to which each focuses on the other as its principal rival and adversary. If Japan and the major capitalist countries of Europe have become strong economic competitors of the United States, they have been in no position to mount a political challenge to Washington, in part at least because of their military dependence. In contrast, China was in a position to challenge the USSR and to go it alone, principally because China—unlike Japan and Western European countries—was not dependent on foreign economic exchanges to keep its economy functioning.

CLASHING FOREIGN POLICY OBJECTIVES

It is not necessary to insist at length on the incompatibility of most of the basic objectives dominating postwar Soviet and American foreign policy. The differences were rooted in the permanence of U.S.–USSR rivalry for world primacy, a rivalry persisting through periods of relaxation in bilateral relations as through periods of tension, even movement toward the brink of war. A point of equilibrium was ruled out in a contest of two dynamic states. Following the de

facto alliance of the war years, recognition of the deep gulf between
the U.S. and USSR emerged gradually in the period after 1945. The
ruling elites needed time to adapt to the breach, and public opinion
had to be remolded, a process that in both countries included pressures against those who lagged behind in viewing old friends as new
enemies and old enemies as new friends. By 1948, at the latest, the
basic and largely antithetical purposes animating American and Soviet foreign policy were writ large for all to see. Naturally, much
changed in succeeding decades, but these purposes remained constant.

These differing international objectives can be briefly summarized.
On the American side, the basic elements of postwar foreign policy
were: (1) protection of U.S. territory; (2) expansion of American influence and economic interests abroad, including entry into areas formerly the preserve of other advanced countries; (3) stabilization of the
capitalist order wherever it came into jeopardy; (4) containment and
weakening of Soviet power and influence; and (5) blocking
or erosion of Communist gains outside the USSR. On the Soviet
side the comparable basic elements of foreign policy were: (1) safeguarding the USSR against dangers from abroad; (2) solidification
and extension of Soviet international influence; (3) protection and advancement of Communist gains in other countries, above all the consolidation of Communist rule in Eastern Europe; and (4) restriction or
elimination of the influence of the leading capitalist countries, especially that of the United States, wherever this existed.

One major limiting condition affected the pursuit of their objectives by both the U.S. and the USSR. Even before, but particularly
after, nuclear weapons became standard equipment, risk taking had
to stop short at the brink of war. The outcome of such a war was too
uncertain to permit either Soviet or American policy-makers to follow
Danton's formula: "De l'audace, encore de l'audace et toujours de
l'audace." It was not only the deliberate initiation of war that became
unattractive; care had to be taken against stumbling into war. Neither
power could allow itself, however, to be deterred into political quies-
cence by the war-threatening capabilities of the other. Consequently,
the push of the two states toward incompatible objectives was accompanied by recurrent tugs toward and away from armed conflict.

Situations arose, of course, requiring choices by U.S. and USSR
foreign policy managers among competing goals, not all of which
could be promoted simultaneously. On several occasions, for ex-

ample, the anticommunist thrust of U.S. policy had to be subordinated to anti-Sovietism, or Moscow's anticapitalist orientation softpedaled in order to stress anti-Americanism.

Thus, America's relations with Tito's Yugoslavia were probably worse than with any other Eastern European country, Russia aside, until the Cominform ouster in 1948; almost overnight previously unsuspected virtues were discovered in the same régime that had been regularly denounced before the break with the USSR. In contrast, the shift of U.S. policy on China was much delayed, but the Chinese Communists eventually found themselves appreciated in America after they had showed their willingness to challenge Soviet power by force of arms, to claim extensive territory from the USSR, to support many of the basic elements of Western policy vis-à-vis Russia, and to make anti-Sovietism the central theme in Chinese foreign policy.

In a like manner Kremlin leaders discerned virtues in French policy that had gone unnoticed until de Gaulle's declaration of independence from America. And they gave sympathy to various bourgeois, semifeudal, and dictatorial governments if they adopted an anti-U.S. orientation. Some of these ruthlessly suppressed indigenous Communists, and were precisely the kind of government that would have been targets for outbursts of hostile propaganda had they lacked the saving grace of anti-Americanism.

It is almost unnecessary to note that the guiding lines of Soviet and American foreign policy as summarized above are not spelled out in this form by spokesmen of the two countries. The objectives are deduced from practice rather than copied from pronunciamentos. The latter conceal more than they reveal; they are almost useless for an analysis of Soviet–American rivalry because they are designed to win support, at home or abroad, by appealing to high-sounding principles suffused with the glow of altruism. They pertain, therefore, to ideological competition; in the modern phrase, they are part of the problem rather than of the solution.

OTHER COUNTRIES' INTERNAL AFFAIRS ARE THE BUSINESS OF THE U.S. AND USSR

Most countries have too meager resources to set other than very limited tasks before foreign policy, tasks limited in geographical scope, limited in their concentration on foreign activities of states that impinge directly on their existence and welfare. Not so the United States and Soviet Union. Their foreign policy concerns are global (though obviously some areas are more crucial than others). And the superpowers are as much, if not more, interested in the so-called internal affairs of countries around the world as in their foreign alignment.

Statesmen of the two countries will, of course, swear on a stack of Bibles or Communist Manifestos that they oppose interference in other countries' internal affairs. They sign solemn declarations in this vein, the latest embodied in the "Final Act" of the Helsinki Conference on Security and Cooperation in Europe. Naturally, they do not "interfere," because they define interference to exclude even their armed intervention in other countries, not to speak of less forthright means of influencing trends. President Johnson did not call the U.S. landing of marines in 1965 interference in Dominican Republic affairs, and party General Secretary Brezhnev denied that Soviet–Warsaw Pact introduction of troops into Czechoslovakia in 1968 was interference. Overt military intervention is rare, in any case, and represents merely one extreme of a spectrum of means employed by these great powers to affect the internal political structure and course of development in other countries.

The U.S and USSR have a variety of economic, military, and other instruments for the exercise of leverage. These should not be exaggerated; frequently they are insufficient for ultimate control of events. Moreover, the U.S. and USSR may make gains or suffer losses wholly as a result of the interplay of indigenous forces. The USSR and even the Moscow-allied Cuban Communist party had almost nothing to do with Castro's rise to power, but this redounded to Soviet advantage, though probably in a more expensive way than could have been expected. Similarly, the U.S. appears to have played no significant part in the anticommunist coup d'état that ended Sukarno's grip on power in Indonesia, but the United States could only benefit, and the Soviet Union suffer, from the overturn.

USSR Efforts to Encourage Leftist Trends in Other Countries

It is not likely to be disputed that Moscow policy-makers are keenly interested in the internal power alignments within other countries, and do their level best to encourage Communist, leftist, or anti-U.S. trends. From 1917 to the present, Soviet leaders have not concealed their hopes for the eventual replacement of capitalist by Communist rule on a world scale. Where they had the opportunity, as in Eastern Europe and North Asia in the closing phases of World War

II, they oversaw the gradual accession to power of Communists in replacement of German- or Japanese-installed or pro-Axis régimes.

Beyond the reach of Soviet military preponderance, however, USSR policy in this respect was rather cautious. Even in war-torn areas, such as Yugoslavia and China, the Soviet authorities were reticent toward ambitions of indigenous Communist parties to gain complete control of their countries. In the postwar period as a whole the Russians avoided encouragement of revolutionary seizures of power in the manner of Lenin's Bolsheviks. (The Soviet leadership insisted on the continued and worldwide validity of Leninism, but it is striking that there was not a single Communist party outside Russia that gained power by following Lenin's tactics.) The Soviet party maintained ties with CPs all over the world and was not loath to pass on advice and, sometimes, money, but generally had only modest means of exerting influence in favor of pro-Communist trends. The Soviet emphasis was on Communist use of legal opportunities, including parliamentary institutions, where this was possible, the preservation of Communist cadres, augmentation of strength by collaboration with other progressive forces, and appeals to national as well as class interests.

Soviet solicitude toward changes in the internal alignments of foreign countries has not been wholly concentrated on Communist gains, especially in the last twenty years. As long as Stalin was alive Soviet policy manifested great suspicion of national liberation movements under non-Communist leadership, as in India, Burma, and Indonesia. No doubt Stalin remembered with rancor the crashing failures of the 1920s when hopes were placed on Kemal Ataturk's nationalist movement in Turkey and, even more painful for Stalin personally, the similarly nationalist movement in China led by Chiang Kai-shek, head of the Kuomintang.

This negative orientation toward nationalist movements outside Communist control began to change about 1950, in the course of the Korean War, but it remained for Stalin's successors to activate a policy of support for national liberation movements and newly independent countries under "bourgeois" leadership in the "third world." Soviet officials began the treks to nonaligned and non-Communist states, and the reception of leaders of such states and movements in the USSR, that have continued for the past two decades. The practice contrasted sharply with Stalin's stay-at-home habit and his stay-away attitude toward "third world" statesmen. More important, the USSR after Stalin began to give not only moral but material support, economic and military, to such states. A considerable portion of economic assistance was explicitly directed to the creation of state industry in less-developed countries, partly with the aim of augmenting their typically small working classes. Indirectly, therefore, the USSR sought, even in countries where Communist parties were nonexistent, weak, or repressed, to build bases for future growth of Communist strength. Any anticipated effects from such Soviet efforts would take years to realize (if ever), and in the short term Soviet links to the ruling groups of these countries tended to undercut the revolutionary pretensions of local Communists.

USSR leaders have had to confront the prospect that support of national-democratic or even Communist movements and régimes may not ultimately redound to Soviet benefit and influence. From Ghana to Egypt, from Indonesia to Cambodia, bitter pills have had to be swallowed. In many, perhaps most, cases—China is the outstanding exception, but there are others—Kremlin officials have been able to take some comfort, a rather cold comfort, from the fact that states taking their distance from Soviet patronage do not necessarily move from Moscow's orbit to Washington's. In any event, ways of insuring against disappointment are not apparent. Consequently, Kremlin leaders still appear to rely on successes of foreign Communist parties and national liberation movements as the principal means of gaining on the United States in rivalry for world leadership. Hope springs eternal in Soviet breasts that wayward Communists will return to the fold, and that countries struggling to emerge from underdevelopment will come back to the noncapitalist, socialist-oriented path after dallying with other solutions to their problems. In fact, the USSR has had some success in improving relations, after periods of hostility, with ruling Communists (in Yugoslavia and North Korea, for example) and with radical nationalist but non-Communist governments.

American Efforts to Support Favored Trends in Other Countries

At first glance it might appear that the United States is in a quite different situation from that of the Soviet Union in capabilities to influence political trends within other countries. Clearly, the U.S. leads no organized world movement comparable to the Communist movement, in which to invest hopes, efforts, and resources, and from whose successes it expects to improve or solidify its international position. Soviet–American rivalry is asymmetric on this level. Moreover, it might be thought that the United States is more attuned to a pluralistic world, and therefore lacks the will, even if it possesses the resources, to exert its influence on other countries' internal developments.

But American leaders have been far from indifferent to the domestic alignments of such countries, and far from backward in seeking to influence trends in a favorable direction. The resources that the U.S. can bring to bear are not, on the whole, similar to those within Soviet capabilities, but they are substantial, and on a worldwide scale greater than the Soviet. And, while the U.S. leadership can tolerate a variety of régimes in other countries, this toleration stops well short of Communist or left-leaning governments. Just as Kremlin policy managers can turn a kindly eye on a variety of ruling groups and governments, provided that they array themselves against "American imperialism," so Washington policy-makers can readily accept a variety of governments provided that they are anticommunist and anti-Soviet, or, at the minimum, free of Communist influence.

The record in this area is clear; it antedates the period of intense "cold war." At the close of World War II, for the first time in U.S. history American armies were in a position to have a major impact on the social order in liberated and occupied countries of Western Europe and Asia. Where it had control or influence, the U.S. saw to it that bourgeois groups were in charge and that Communists and leftists were not. In France, Italy, and Germany, in Japan and South Korea, the same pattern prevailed. And in those countries, like France and Italy, where Communists were relatively strong because of their role in resistance movements, and made their way as a minority into early postwar governments, American authorities used their control of badly needed relief and reconstruction supplies to help push them out. The U.S. had, of course, a much easier task in securing the dominance of pro-capitalist, pro-U.S. elements in areas where its military forces functioned than did the USSR in securing the dominance of pro-Communist, or-USSR elements in areas of its military ascendancy. For the United States, this was simply a restoration or consolidation of entrenched elites and established institutions, not their extirpation. Thus, American authorites could rely on strong indigenous forces to a much greater extent than could their Soviet counterparts. They also had, unlike the latter, great economic capabilities to influence trends; these made resort to crude methods of coercion unnecessary.

These early efforts set a pattern followed in later times, in other areas, under quite different circumstances, where there was no U.S. military presence, or, if such existed, it was simply one of several means of forwarding U.S. policy. The U.S. was in a position to favor, finance, and generally assist governments in various parts of the world oriented to institutions and policies of which Washington approved. American efforts were directed at the elimination or curtailment of Communist and radical influence and the promotion of groups considered to be the most staunch opponents of communism and Soviet power. The favored groups were the parties of "order," those sympathetic to business and propertied interests, domestic and foreign, often those linked to American business interests operating in those countries.

A natural reciprocity existed between conservative or rightist forces abroad and American authorities. In Europe, for example, the most ardent and reliable supporters of the U.S. and of NATO have always been found on the "right" flank of the political spectrum. It is not surprising, therefore, that the United States, officially and unofficially, under liberal Democratic and conservative Republican administrations, finds such forces the most deserving of support. The pattern is not all that different outside Europe, in the Middle East, Latin America, and elsewhere. The chief dissimilarity is that most of the advanced capitalist countries where U.S. influence is strong maintain parliamentary, pluralist institutions, whereas these traits are rare among American protégés in the "third world."

U.S. capabilities for influencing internal politics abroad involve somewhat different instrumentalities than those available to the USSR, although there is an overlap. Both countries can exert a general influence stemming from their status as world powers. Both maintain large official missions, where these are permitted, of diplomatic, economic, military, and intelligence personnel. But in most non-Communist states there are also large contingents of American business people, technicians, students and educators, travelers, and residents for whom there is no Soviet analogue. The U.S. economic stake is often substantial, and this entrée into the economy gives the U.S. capabilities of influencing local affairs that the Soviet Union usually lacks. Thus, U.S. firms operating abroad, including so-called multinational corporations, can and do play an important role in binding other countries to U.S.-made policies; the synchronization of efforts against Allende in Chile by U.S. official agencies and the International Telephone and Telegraph corporation is illustrative. In contrast to the USSR, which has to place greater reliance on indigenous elements to advance Soviet interests, because of its generally smaller complements of USSR residents abroad, the United States can and indeed must put greater emphasis on the role of American residents abroad.

COVERT OPERATIONS SUPPLEMENT OVERT

The various means used by the U.S. and USSR to influence domestic and foreign orientations of other countries include not only overt tactics, some of which have been discussed, but also covert operations. Economic, military, and diplomatic support (and sanctions) are usually publicized; Soviet and American propaganda (information) services are active in spreading the word. But such open activities are supplemented by a range of operations whose authorship is meant to remain concealed. These are frequently within the province of intelligence agencies (although the function has nothing to do with the gathering of intelligence).

One variety of such covert operations is the spread of "disinformation," a practice in which both the USSR and the U.S. indulge with the intent of compromising each other or of damaging inimical local political forces and aiding favored opponents. Such tactics include anonymous circulation of forged documents compromising adversaries, broadcasts from clandestine radio stations, and insertion in local communication media of materials originating from U.S. or Soviet sources but purporting to be of local provenance.

Another type of covert activity involves the judicious distribution of money and other rewards to promote favored political leaders or to buy off opponents. Political figures are subsidized, sometimes by payment for secret information. Politicians are not usually bought outright (they are a commodity that does not keep well), but are often rented or leased. Favored parties or individuals may be financed in electoral campaigns or receive subsidies for their publications. Alternatively, a flow of funds to opponents of a régime in bad favor, whether in Washington or Moscow, may contribute to its weakening, by strikes or demonstrations, for example.

Activities such as these are clearly marginal in the sense that none by itself is likely to change the orientation of a country, though in combination with overt means of influence they may produce such an effect. Another kind of covert activity aims at major changes. Efforts on this scale have been identified only with the U.S.; the USSR apparently does not assign such ambitious tasks to its covert forces. Thus, U.S. plans were developed for the "rubbing out" of inconvenient and particularly charismatic adversary leaders such as Fidel Castro and Patrice Lumumba. Attempts to murder Castro failed; plans for the liquidation of Lumumba did not reach the stage of, it might be said, "execution."

Plans for such assassinations have been supplemented by even bolder efforts to bring about the overthrow of governments displeasing to Washington. Thus, the U.S. had a large covert part in the downfall in 1953 of Mossadegh, the Iranian premier who was jeopardizing the cosy ties linking the Shahansha with Anglo-American oil interests and with the U.S. and U.K. governments. A year later, in 1954, the U.S. covertly organized the overthrow of President Arbenz Guzmán's government in Guatemala, utilizing for the purpose rightist Guatemalan military officers based in Honduras. These two successes were followed by two failures. U.S. aid to and participation in a separatist movement in Indonesia, 1957–1959, directed against the government of President Sukarno, did not achieve the intended results. And, in the most dramatic affair of this kind, a U.S.-organized invasion of Cuba in 1961 by Cuban-exile forces, intended to spark a counterrevolution, was crushed at the Bay of Pigs. When another leftist government appeared in Latin America, however, the United States had better luck. Although U.S. efforts to prevent Salvador Allende from coming to power were unsuccessful, the U.S. eventually managed through a combination of open and covert tactics to destabilize the government, which was finished off in 1973 by a reactionary military coup under General Pinochet.

In these episodes, and similar affairs where the U.S. role was more murky, Washington moved against governments that had come under leftist control (though only Castro's was avowedly Marxist-Leninist), and threatened important American business interests. Both conditions were apparently necessary, and probably sufficient, to trigger U.S. covert intervention.

The record of U.S. successes is impressive enough (three out of the five best-known cases), but the successes, not to speak of the failures, were far from cost-free. At any rate, attempts of this kind could not be repeated often. They tended to make other nations, at least those undertaking programs of fundamental social change, wary of allowing the U.S. to maintain *points d'appui* that might spell doom for local régimes. Somewhat paradoxically, the episodes suggested that countries were all the more vulnerable to U.S. designs the more they attempted to maintain pluralist political and economic institutions while implementing programs of radical change. For it was precisely these pluralist features that enhanced U.S. freedom of action.

U.S.–USSR SUPPORT OF DEMOCRACY AND STABILITY

The extent to which the United States and the USSR use their influence to support democratic institutions in other countries has already been discussed, in a different context, where it was noted that democracy is a positive value in both Soviet and American ideologies, though defined in rather contradictory ways. It is only necessary to repeat here that other values usually take precedence over furthering democracy in both countries' foreign policy activities. Anti-Sovietism is much more consistently promoted in U.S. practice and anti-Americanism in USSR practice than support of what each calls democracy. There's no problem for either country in reconciling verbal endorsement of democracy with support of its major allies, because the latter (principally the states of Western Europe for the U.S. and Eastern Europe for the USSR) are regarded as exemplars of democracy, as respectively defined in Washington and Moscow. But discrepancies between principle and practice occur elsewhere.

Thus, many states enjoying favor in Moscow have been worlds away from the Soviet conception of democracy. This was true of Syria, Iraq, and Algeria, even more so of Afghanistan and Haile Selassie's Ethiopia. Whatever the merits of republics such as those of Peru and Burma, their institutions could not qualify as democratic according to Soviet standards. In contrast, two states that qualify as democracies ("bourgeois" democracies to be sure) in the Soviet lexicon, the United States and the Federal Republic of Germany, have been the targets of greater Soviet hostility over the postwar years than almost any other countries in the world. An early episode pointed up the Soviet inconstancy regarding democracy: when the USSR under Stalin fell out with Tito's Yugoslavia, the latter suddenly lost its democratic standing in Soviet eyes even though its political institutions and practices underwent no coincidental shift.

The discrepancy is no less flagrant in American practice. The United States has remained on the best of terms with régimes which American principles would assign to an authoritarian or dictatorial category instead of democratic. In fact, American authorities certainly warmly welcomed military coups d'état ending democratic rule in countries like Brazil in 1964 and Chile in 1973. The Greek colonels who seized power in 1967 using NATO contingency plans abolished the kind of pluralist democracy praised by the U.S.; they were in no danger of losing Washington's support.

Perhaps the most cynical display of U.S. practice in regard to democracy abroad involved Portugal and Spain. No American president or secretary of state showed the slightest dissatisfaction with Portugal in the Salazar–Caetano years of dictatorship and repression at home and in the African colonies. All tolerated use of American military supplies to buttress this regime, including use against independence movements in the colonies. The military-led revolution in 1974 overthrew the dictatorship and introduced a lively pluralism under the loose control of military leaders, generally leftist in orientation but of variegated hue. Under these new circumstances Communists displayed strength that they had acquired underground. Suddenly American voices, silent for years, were heard as defenders of democracy. The editors of the *New York Times* and the *Washington Post*, who had long concealed any concern for Portuguese democracy, overnight became its strong defenders. President Ford and Secretary of State Kissinger orchestrated a campaign of pressure to prevent Portugal from straying out of the capitalist camp. To cap the farce, stern reproaches to the president of Portugal about the threats to "democracy" occurred simultaneously with friendly gestures to the dying Franco in Spain, the good old "democrat" who had allied himself with Hitler, Mussolini, and Hirohito. The performance deserved a Nobel Prize for Hypocrisy.

The "Status Quo" in U.S. and USSR Foreign Policy

It is sometimes asserted that even if attitudes toward democracy are more or less irrelevant to the foreign practice of the United States and the Soviet Union, the two countries are sharply divided in their positions on preservation or overturn of the status quo existing in the world. Or, to put the matter more directly, the U.S. favors stability, the USSR thrives on instability; the USSR is expansionist, the U.S. is content with what it has.

The proposition has a germ of truth. In numbers and in most indices of strength, capitalist countries vastly outweigh Communist-ruled countries, and therefore the U.S. has more to defend, the USSR more that it wants to change, for Soviet leaders avow that socialism and communism are on the agenda for all countries. (Phrases like "overturn" or "preserve" the status quo point to extremes, of course; real-life situations usually involve marginal changes.)

But the differences of U.S.–USSR approach to the status quo are not grounded in principle but relate to situation. Everything depends on whose ox was being gored. American authorities sought to curtail Soviet and Communist power and influence as well as to prevent accretions to strength; Soviet authorities, to undermine the U.S. status in the world along with that of other advanced capitalist countries. Foreign policy planners in Washington were far from adverse to changes in the status quo improving the U.S. world position, even at the expense of allies. They professed to abhor vacuums (great-power vacuums) and believed that such vacuums should be filled by a country uniquely free of self-serving aims. Likewise, Kremlin managers saw opportunities for expansion of Communist Rule and Soviet influence in the collapse of old empires.

Territorial expansion was crucial for neither the USSR nor the U.S. in the postwar spread of their power and influence to far corners of the Earth.[1] Their empires did not flourish because of the incorporation of more and more territory. But both expanded in almost every other dimension—political, economic, military, cultural. If based on combined military-political-economic-cultural indicators, a global map contrasting postwar to prewar conditions would display a tremendous outward expansion of both U.S. and USSR strongholds. Such a map would also show a considerably greater worldwide spread of American than of Soviet positions of strength, not least in the military area, for the Stars and Stripes came to fly over hundreds of military installations scattered over almost all continents.

GAINING ALLIES AND WINNING SUPPORT

Efforts at influencing the trend of internal developments in other countries occur simultaneously, of course, with parallel efforts to in-

---

[1] This is not to say that there was no territorial expansion during the war years, 1939–1945, and in the aftermath. American acquisitions were some small but strategically important islands in the Pacific. The USSR regained once-Russian areas in Europe such as the three Baltic countries (Latvia, Estonia, and Lithuania), Bessarabia, a small part of Finland, and a substantial area in Eastern Poland; in addition, it acquired the Carpatho-Ukraine, a small area from Germany, and Tannu Tuva in Central Asia, territories that had not previously been part of the old Russian Empire. Despite these gains, present Soviet territory is smaller than that of tsarist Russia in 1917.

fluence the international orientation of these countries in favor of Moscow or Washington. It is only an analytic convenience to treat separately these two aspects of U.S.–USSR foreign policy that are intermixed in real life.

Alliance building has played an important role in both countries' world approach, a role that goes beyond the military importance of alliances. While this is true of the North Atlantic Treaty and Warsaw Pact, which are unique in having in place military structures designed for warfare, it is especially evident in other alliances of primarily political importance. The military aspects of Soviet and American alliances have been discussed earlier; here it is only necessary to touch on the political side.

For both the U.S. and USSR the foundation of their postwar alliance structures lay in wartime treaties and agreements, but it was the U.S. which was more ambitious and successful in multiplying postwar alliances, bilateral and multilateral, with advanced and less-developed countries. Permanent peacetime alliances were new for the United States, and required the jettisoning of encumbering ideological baggage. A principle of American foreign policy as old as the republic itself counseled against entrance into "entangling alliances." But postwar Washington, D.C., rejected Washington, George. This was accomplished without engendering wracking divisions inside the country because most of the ex-isolationists were as ardently anticommunist and anti-Soviet as the former interventionists.

The ease and rapidity of the shift was facilitated by two factors. First, American capabilities of maneuver had been enhanced so greatly, and those of prospective allies so diminished, that alliances promised to "entangle" allies more than the U.S. America needed no longer to fear being the tail on the kite of European powers, and being drawn into others' conflicts; allies would have to follow where America led.

Second, only the United States could lead the defense of the capitalist order and the crusade against the Marxist-Leninist heresy. Before World War II the U.S. could rely on European powers and Japan to assume the main burden of blocking Soviet and Communist gains. These states shared an interest in preventing Soviet and Communist consolidation and expansion, even though they were split into "limited adversary" groupings, the Axis expansionist powers against the states satisfied with the territorial status quo. The weakening of every one of these once-great powers meant that they could be relied on after the war to play only a secondary, but not the primary, role in opposition to the USSR and communism.

In Russia, unlike America, there was no historical predisposition against peacetime alliances. Quite the contrary. But for Bolshevik Russia of the interwar period there were no possible allies, and even for post-1945 Russia alliances were possible only with neighboring states, all Communist-ruled except Finland. Not until the 1970s, long after the spurt of U.S. alliance building in the first postwar decade, did the USSR begin to develop a series of alliances with non-Communist states, and even these involved no mutual-defense obligations.

Almost without exception the rival alliances dominated by the U.S. and USSR had an explicit or implicit political thrust, pro- or anticommunism, pro- or antiimperialism. Formally, it is true, neither the North Atlantic nor the Warsaw Pact alliance put forward any ideological qualification for membership, and the Warsaw Treaty explicitly proclaimed that it was "open to the accession of other states irrespective of their social and political systems." The alliances cannot be understood, however, except as aggregations of the principal capitalist (or Communist) states against their rivals. Khrushchev and his Politburo colleagues could not have been serious when they applied in 1954 for USSR entry to NATO. Undoubtedly they sought to show that the North Atlantic alliance was not a collective security system but something more familiar in European history, a bloc of states banded together to oppose another group of states. The requirement for correct political-ideological qualifications was again illustrated later when Washington inspired threats to deprive Portugal of participation in NATO affairs if it came under Communist influence.[2] On the Eastern side, it is certainly difficult to conceive the highly politicized Warsaw Pact as functioning with even a single non-Communist participant, because the principle of unanimity is even more important in Warsaw Treaty affairs than in those of NATO.

If the ideological bent has to be read between the lines of the rival European treaties, and is expressed very discreetly in the Rio treaty establishing the Organization of American States, it is more explicit in

---

[2] The ideological requirement was also illustrated when the U.S. led a successful move to exclude Cuba under Castro from participation in affairs of the Organization of American States.

other U.S. treaties of alliance, notably that for Southeast Asia. The Manila treaty refers to the cooperation of member states to "prevent and counter subversive activities directed from without against their territorial integrity and political stability." By definition, Communist activities were regarded as always directed from without, and in this context "political stability" means nothing more or less than preservation of non-Communist rule. To dot the "i"s, the U.S. attached a protocol making it clear that the American concern was with "Communist aggression," not just any old aggression; here again, Communist aggression meant any Communist activities, internal as well as external.

Over the postwar period as a whole the United States and the Soviet Union encountered difficulties as well as successes in organizing and maintaining alliances designed to solidify their claims to world leadership. In the period of Dulles's so-called pactomania the United States sought to link non-Communist states the world over in U.S.-led alliances against "international communism." The hopes were doomed to failure, for too many countries said "No, thank you." In South Asia and the Middle East there were so many rejections that the poor representation of indigenous states rendered the alliances ineffectual. This was not true in Europe, where the rival alliances enhanced U.S. and Soviet military capabilities, though both suffered from some fragmentation and, in the case of the Warsaw Pact, one minor defection (Albania). Some bilateral as well as multilateral alliances turned sour, the notable examples being the Soviet pacts with China and Egypt. Even when alliances persisted, none proved of decisive importance to Washington or Moscow as an instrument for maintenance of the kind of political order in member nations that they sought. Moreover, the decline of alliance unity meant that American and Soviet authorities were increasingly compelled to maneuver within their alliances, not always successfully, to achieve their objectives, rather than simply to lay down a line commanding instant acceptance.

Of course, the U.S. and the USSR had a wide range of techniques apart from treaty ties to advance their foreign policies, not only in regard to the numerous states outside their alliance systems, but also to those within. They had, though in unequal degree, economic advantages to offer to cooperative states and economic pressures that could be brought to bear against states in disfavor. Most countries were dependent on external markets for the maintenance of economic activity and on external sources of supply for economic development. By virtue of their economic power, therefore, the United States and, to a much lesser degree, the Soviet Union could use investment (U.S. only), trade, credits, and aid to implement their foreign policies. But this has been discussed in the chapter on economic rivalry and need only be recalled here.

Their great military capabilities also gave the U.S. and the USSR means of forwarding foreign policy objectives on a scale that no other country could match. Again, their ability to deploy military power in various parts of the world was unequal, as was their utility as sources of arms and equipment. But both made frequent use of their supply and deployment capabilities to advance and maintain their world position, in ways described in the earlier section on U.S.–USSR military rivalry.

In addition to the economic, military, and other means utilized in bilateral and multilateral dealings with individual countries, the U.S. and USSR have also maneuvered in the United Nations so as to implement national policies through the world organization, or at least to gain UN endorsement of U.S. or USSR policies. The UN has never occupied a crucial place in the foreign policy of either country, both having preferred to rely on more wieldy instruments. Still, the United Nations (here meaning the General Assembly and Security Council) is of sufficient importance to the U.S. and USSR to require some discussion.

It should come as no surprise that the esteem enjoyed by the UN in Washington or Moscow policy circles is correlated with their chances of securing favorable decisions on contentious issues. In the early postwar years, the United States held a dominant position in the United Nations, in both the broadly representative General Assembly and in the select Security Council, the only UN organ having authority—a largely theoretical authority—to institute coercive action. The USSR was protected, of course, like the other four permanent members, against decisions of which it disapproved by the rule that any action of the Security Council required not only a majority vote but the concurrence of all the permanent members.

Despite frustration over Soviet "abuse" of its veto power, in the first postwar decade or so American authorities were able to mobilize international pressure against the USSR and its few allies by winning lopsided majority votes in the General Assembly and Security Council. In fact, in the Security Council the U.S. repeatedly forced votes, knowing the outcome in advance, in order to demonstrate Soviet intransigence. The issues displaying Western strength and Eastern weakness covered a wide range, from control of atomic developments and other military matters to the behavior of Communist states, the appropriate representatives of China, and admission of additional states to the UN. The last issue elicited the bulk of Soviet vetoes, as the U.S. and its allies attempted repeatedly to gain admission for pro-Western states without admitting those sponsored by the USSR.

American dominance of the UN was most complete when membership was smallest. In the beginning there were only fifty-one member states, mostly from Europe and Latin America. By 1955 the membership had increased to more than 75, by 1960 to more than 100, and subsequently grew to almost 150, or about three times the original number. The preponderance, especially in the General Assembly, shifted from Europe and the American hemisphere to Asia and Africa, from states long independent to those just emerging from colonial subservience, from economically advanced or semideveloped countries to those struggling against backwardness.

The change drastically altered the roles of the U.S. and USSR in UN affairs and consequently Soviet–American official attitudes toward the virtues and vices of the organization. In earlier years Soviet authorities often evinced distrust of the UN and complained of the "mechanical majorities" that the U.S. assembled in support of American policy. As Soviet negativism gave way to a more positive approach, American official favor for the UN cooled. It was now the turn of the U.S. to complain of "bloc voting" and automatic majorities in the General Assembly, meaning the frequent association of Communist states with nonaligned Afro-Asian countries in an antiimperialist majority. The change was less marked in the Security Council, among whose permanent members the U.S. continued to have two allies, even after the Chinese People's Republic took over the representation formerly accorded the Taiwan-based Republic of China, whereas the Soviet Union faced four adversaries. But the expansion and change in complexion of the UN affected the Security Council as well. USSR vetoes (over a hundred in earlier years) became a thing of the past, while the United States began, admittedly on rare occasions, to exercise its own right of veto.

The decline in U.S. ability to use the UN in foreign policy implementation can be traced in three episodes of East–West confrontation, in all of which the USSR was on the defensive: the Korean War beginning in 1950, the 1956 Soviet intervention in Hungary, and the Soviet-led Warsaw Pact intervention in Czechoslovakia in 1968. In 1950 the U.S. was able to gain overwhelming support for a condemnation of North Korea as an aggressor, secured use of the UN name and flag for U.S.-led military forces entering the war, and even won General Assembly endorsement of the U.S. objective of unifying Korea under the Republic of (South) Korea, i.e., of eliminating Communist rule in North Korea. Admittedly, insofar as the Security Council was involved, U.S. success was due to the "accident" of temporary Soviet absence. In 1956 U.S. capabilities of maneuver were already less potent than in 1950, but American authorities were still able to get a General Assembly resolution of censure against the USSR passed, though by a thinner margin than in the Korea case, and won support for other measures discomfiting to Budapest and Moscow. By 1968 even such steps were impossible in relation to Soviet actions in Czechoslovakia. The newly dominant forces in the General Assembly were not especially concerned about this kind of quarrel, and the United States did not have the votes for action in the General Assembly or, of course, in the Security Council.

The issues of concern to the new UN majority centered on relations between the developed and less-developed countries, particularly those of colonialism and racism. On these the USSR could find common ground with the militant régimes of Africa and Asia, while the United States was on the defensive. But this did not mean that the tables had been turned from American dominance of the UN in the early years to Soviet dominance in recent years; the balance of forces is much more equal than that. That kind of balance was illustrated in United Nations consideration of the Arab–Israeli dispute following the 1967 war. Despite a major effort, the USSR could not marshal enough support for a pro-Arab resolution condemning Israel and calling for a complete withdrawal of Israel from conquered Arab territory, and neither could the United States muster enough votes for a resolution favoring Israel.

In this instance, and indeed in others before and afterward, the balance of forces encouraged more real negotiations between the major protagonists than had been characteristic of the earlier situation. Thus, a negotiated resolution on the Arab–Israeli question was passed by the Security Council after the fiasco in the General Assembly. It has played an important part in subsequent Middle East negotiations, though it is sufficiently ambiguous to permit of rather different interpretations by the U.S. and USSR, not to speak of the Arab states and Israel.

This U.S.–USSR willingness to negotiate differences on a variety of issues, rather than be satisfied with abusive propaganda exchanges, has been increasingly evident in the past decade or so. It has gone well beyond negotiations in UN organs and other multilateral forums to find expression in bilateral contacts, including those involving top leaders of the two countries. There were, to be sure, nonnegotiable issues, and neither the quickening of negotiations nor the greater civility of contacts diminished the pervasiveness of U.S.–USSR rivalry. But it is necessary to discuss these changes in American–Soviet relations and their impact on that rivalry.

SOVIET–AMERICAN BILATERAL RELATIONS

The statement of basic foreign policy objectives at the beginning of this chapter emphasized the anti-Soviet, anticommunist thrust of Washington policy and the anti-US, antiimperialist thrust of Moscow policy. Such Soviet and American orientations were compatible, however, with varying kinds of bilateral relations, with few or abundant contacts, with little or much tension in U.S.–USSR encounters. In fact, the postwar years have witnessed significant shifts in the interaction of the two states as they moved from the limited partnership of the war years to the bitter hostility of the late 1940s and early 1950s and then to a gradual, frequently interrupted, enlivenment and regularization of contacts.

To illustrate the great change in the U.S. approach to the USSR a single example will suffice. In the late 1940s, George Kennan—regarded justly then and later as a sober and moderate exponent of American policy toward Soviet Russia—could introduce into his celebrated discussion of postwar American strategy a reference to "a power of life and death over the Communist movement," and could pose the U.S. objective as one to "bring about the early fall of Soviet power in Russia."[3] A quarter-century later, Richard Nixon—who, in contrast to Kennan, had made a career exploiting fears of communism

---

[3] George F. Kennan, "The Sources of Soviet Conduct," *Foreign Affairs* 25 (July 1947). Kennan, to be sure, makes the point negatively, that is, the United States "unassisted and alone" could not accomplish the stated objectives. Presumably, if the United States coped with what Kennan described as "the responsibilities of a World Power," i.e., organized a coalition of major Western states against Russia, then it would be able to accomplish these ambitious goals.

and of Soviet power—was hobnobbing with the No. 1 card-carrying Communist of the Soviet Union and signing agreements with him pledging peaceful coexistence between America and Russia.

On the Soviet side, also, much had changed. Fears receded that American or German imperialists were thirsting for a military attack on Russia, and Kremlin hopes for an early collapse of the capitalist order likewise diminished. The advanced capitalist countries, including the colonial powers allied to the United States, had even absorbed the decomposition of colonial empires without great internal disturbance and without being drawn into wars for access to markets. Such intraimperialist wars had been anticipated by Stalin as late as 1952, in his pamphlet entitled "Economic Problems of Socialism in the USSR." The gravediggers of capitalism were short of corpses to inter.

Nevertheless, communism continued to be the specter haunting American policy-makers from the Truman–Acheson era to the most recent times. Likewise, imperialism, above all American imperialism, continued in Brezhnev's day as in Stalin's to be viewed in Kremlin offices as the main threat to the USSR. The basic change did not concern Soviet–American struggle and rivalry but the means of carrying these on, and in particular the perceptions in Washington and Moscow of the likelihood and imminence of war as a way of resolving the clash of irreconcilable objectives.

European Developments and U.S.–USSR Relations

Postwar American–Russian conflict had initially erupted over the fate of Eastern Europe. It was in Eastern Europe that U.S.–USSR expectations about the future of countries freed from Axis control clashed most sharply, for in Western Europe the Russians (and pro-Moscow Communist parties) were ill-equipped to challenge the dominance of the U.S. and U.S.-dependent ruling groups. The Soviet leadership wanted something more in Eastern Europe than merely the replacement of hostile by friendly governments, which the U.S. was prepared to accept. Moscow had no assurance that the Eastern European political elites might not restore an anti-Soviet orientation if the capitalist economic base remained intact. The capitalist order had to go. Hence, military dominion over Eastern Europe allowed USSR leaders to provide the shield for installation of leftist coalition governments that within a few years became thoroughly Communist-dominated. And these governments proceeded at varying paces to carry out "revolutions from above," instituting the characteristic features of Soviet-style socialism.

Washington circles interpreted the role of Soviet military power in promoting USSR influence and Communist rule in Eastern Europe as merely an initial step toward military conquest and communization of Europe all the way to the Atlantic. In that context the future of Germany became the central European issue (and remained so for two decades). The United States and the Soviet Union each organized German client states with ambitions to gain control of all German territory, including, for the Federal Republic, the lands beyond the Oder-Neisse absorbed by Poland. West Germany was in a much better position to entertain pan-German ambitions than East Germany, because the Western German state had the larger and more developed area, and three times the population of the Eastern zone. With war seeming to lurk around the corner, Western Germany as an American ally assumed signal importance. German anticommunist, anti-Soviet credentials could not be challenged: Germany had initiated an anti-Comintern pact long before NATO, and German soldiers had killed more Russian Communists than had any other army, a record to which German Chancellor Adenauer once discreetly alluded in recalling Germany's role in saving "Western civilization."

Moscow's Germans not only cut a poorer figure internationally than U.S.-allied Germans, but the Communist leadership encountered great difficulty in stabilizing the new order in East Germany. It could not make as effective use of nationalism as other régimes in Eastern Europe, and instead had to try to counteract the greater weight and magnetism of the other German state, which mobilized its efforts to isolate and disrupt the German Democratic Republic. The USSR and GDR were, therefore, in a disadvantageous position to promote Communist influence in the country as a whole when Communist rule in East Germany was weakly rooted in the society.

Lacking other means of improving the situation, Moscow tried to use the vulnerability of West Berlin as a pressure device. In 1948–1949 all but air routes to West Berlin were cut off in an attempt to preserve some USSR leverage over all German affairs. The effort failed. In the second Berlin crisis, 1958–1961, a different objective lay behind Soviet pressure: to fortify the independent status of East Germany by eliminating exclusive Western control over West Berlin. This did not succeed either. The effort essentially ended with the erection of the Berlin "wall," which, however, succeeded in stanching the flow out of East Germany by way of West Berlin of substantial numbers of citizens, mostly young people with advanced training seeking their fortunes in the West.

Subsequently, Germany and Berlin lost their immediacy as issues arousing fears of East–West armed conflict; there was increasing acceptance of the division of Europe and of Germany into more or less permanent spheres of capitalist and Communist domination. Facilitated by the coming to power in the Federal Republic of Social Democrats led by Brandt, who enunciated a new Eastern policy, a series of agreements centering on Germany was negotiated. These involved, at various points, the U.S. and USSR, the two German states, Great Britain and France, Poland and Czechoslovakia. They provided for (1) recognition of the Oder-Neisse line as the German border on the east, (2) recognition of the existence of a separate state in East Germany, (3) establishment of bilateral diplomatic relations between the two German states and between these states and NATO–Warsaw Pact nations, and (4) redefinition of the status of West Berlin vis-à-vis the four powers with special rights in Berlin as a whole (the USSR, U.S., Great Britain, and France) and in respect to the Federal Republic of Germany.

These agreements amounted to a substitute for a never-concluded German peace treaty, constituting for the most part a diplomatic ratification of the territorial changes and alignments that had existed in fact since the end of World War II. To bring about this settlement the USSR was forced to compromise on a number of points, particularly on the status of West Berlin. On the whole, however, the agreements served objectives pursued by the USSR for almost two decades. In contrast, the agreements signaled the failure of the West Germans, supported faithfully by the U.S., to dislodge Communist rule over Eastern Germany and reunite the country under pro-Western leadership, thereby enabling NATO forward lines to be extended at least to the Oder-Neisse border, if not beyond.

With this resolution of some of the most acute problems relating to Germany, a calm descended on Europe. This in turn contributed to a change in the focus and character of U.S.–USSR rivalry as bilateral relations became more civil and involved more frequent and higher level contacts. Before examining the nature of Soviet–American relations under détente, however, it is necessary to recapitulate briefly the impact of postwar developments outside Europe, particularly in Asia.

Soviet–American Relations Outside Europe

Two characteristics of the European scene as a theater of U.S.–USSR competition and struggle were absent elsewhere. First, in Europe the peoples falling under Communist control were, with few exceptions, those who were in the line of Red Army advance. It was, to say the least, the Soviet military presence that made possible local Communist gains; to say what American authorities said, Russia used its military forces to communize Eastern Europe against the will of the local populations. Second, since Soviet and American armies were never to leave Europe, they faced each other directly at the East–West dividing line that cut through Germany. In Europe, therefore, the issue of Communist or non-Communist rule was linked inextricably with the U.S.–USSR military confrontation.

Nowhere else did this situation prevail. Communist gains in other parts of the world were not, by and large, a function of Soviet military power; they occurred, or loomed as possibilities, in areas where there was no juxtaposition of Soviet–American forces. To be sure, Soviet troops facilitated the establishment of Communist control in North Korea and Manchuria, but did not remain in either. Only an incidental part in the Chinese Communist conquest of power could be attributed to the Soviet Union. And outside the North Asian rimlands of the USSR, the Soviet leadership lacked the capability, even if it had possessed the will, to deploy military forces to assist local Communist advances, as in Asia, Latin America, and Africa. Indigenous Communists were on their own.

If the USSR could not intervene in these areas in favor of communism, the United States could intervene against any Communist threat that seemed likely to get out of hand. For such intervention it possessed a variety of means and the will to use them. They included military capabilities for worldwide operations that gave the U.S. an option, if worse came to worst, of committing its own military forces. In most countries where Communist advances threatened, the U.S. could accomplish its purposes without resort to military operations, but in Korea and Vietnam it became involved in what turned out to be the most bitterly fought wars of the post-1945 period, with differing results for the United States.

The Korean War of 1950–1953 could be termed a qualified success from Washington's point of view. It was a success insofar as American-led forces succeeded in driving North Korean armies out of South Korea after a deep penetration and capture of Seoul. The success was qualified, however, because in the flush of the above achievement the United States elevated its goal from merely the repulsion of invasion and preservation of the existing South Korean state to something more ambitious, the liquidation of the Communist régime in North Korea and the unification of the country under the American-installed Seoul government. This did not occur. Introduction of Chinese troops turned the tide, and the war ended as it had begun, with Communists in control of North Korea and anti-Communists of South Korea.

The Korean War had seriously negative consequences on Soviet–American relations, although the USSR was not an official participant. The main Russian role was to supply equipment from Soviet arsenals for the armies of North Korea and China (incidentally, making the latter pay for the deliveries, and thus contributing to Chinese resentment against Russia). In the period of U.S. military advance to the Yalu River the Russian leaders appear to have worried not only about a prospective rollback of territory under Communist rule but, more concretely, about the imminent lodging of U.S. forces on USSR borders, a situation that did not exist anywhere else, even in Europe.

As to the U.S. side, American leaders had no doubt that the war in Korea was part of a larger undeclared war that Russia was orchestrating, with Koreans and Chinese serving as proxies. There were divisions, certainly, in the American political-military leadership between those who were willing to widen the war beyond Korea (to accept engagements on the Chinese mainland, for example, or even on Russian Far Eastern territory), and those who thought that the real war with Russia should be fought later and in Europe, rather than there and then in Asia. But no real difference of interpretation existed as to the "Russian" nature of the war and its character as initiatory stage of a more general U.S.–USSR conflict.

The Korean War also heightened an already-existing tendency of Washington policy managers and ideologists to see local Communists as Russian agents in foreign dress. The same interpretation was applied globally, so that Communist activities in Tokyo, Cairo, Santiago, or Johannesburg were seen as responses to signals from Moscow. In fact, there was an inclination to attribute to the USSR responsibility for any kind of radical or anti-American manifestation wherever it occurred and whatever form it took, armed struggle, strike, demonstration, riot, or signature of antiwar appeals. Thus, the undoubted role of Soviet power in promoting communization of Eastern Europe was translated into a concept of "international communism" in which the Kremlin pulled strings around the world to destroy or discomfit the United States and other rightfully ruled countries. The outstanding case was that of China. It did not require any occult intelligence sources or even great perspicacity to discern the low level of Soviet participation in Chinese Communist affairs. Yet American policy-makers saw Russians wherever they saw Communists. Thus, for Dean Rusk, a prominent figure in the foreign policy establishment under all the Democratic administrations of the quarter-century after World War II, the Chinese Communists were not really Chinese at all but Russian agents in disguise.

If this was madness, there was a method to it. U.S. policy-makers had a strong interest in identifying communism with Russian power. Fear of or antipathy to Soviet Russia could then reinforce hostility to Communists in countries far from Soviet influence, and apprehension toward Communist activities elsewhere could reinforce hatred and fear of the USSR. It would be wrong, however, to intimate that the portrayal represented merely cynical manipulation by U.S. foreign policy managers of notions they themselves did not believe (although certainly there was an element of this). Acceptance was easy because the idea appealed to a deeply ingrained U.S. perception of communism in all countries as an importation of alien doctrine and practice. In the early years of the Russian Revolution the idea was popular among American ruling circles that communism in Russia resulted from a German or Jewish plot. With the consolidation of Bolshevik rule the source of the Communist infection could be firmly located in Soviet Russia, held responsible for Communist activities everywhere.

In postwar America this interpretation had a particular appeal as an explanation of the resistance that U.S. foreign policies and programs encountered at various times and places. By definition such policies and programs were benign and selfless; therefore, opposition had to be unnatural and unnational. The viewpoint served instrumental purposes as well. It meshed nicely with the strong U.S. commitment to active use of its power against communism on a world scale, to employment of overt and covert means, of military and economic resources. If Communists could be portrayed as an alien force in the very countries where they lived and whose language they spoke, then the U.S. could hope to deflect onto communism any xenophobia or ultranationalism that might otherwide be directed against the U.S. and U.S. personnel stationed in other countries. Americans involved in foreign countries, even Americans carrying guns and engaged in armed conflict, could then, despite their evident foreignness in terms of local ethnic characteristics, language, and culture, appear as quasi-natives, and local Communists, despite their indigenous qualities, could then be regarded as quasi-foreigners.

This ideological and policy orientation contributed to U.S. involve-ment in Vietnamese struggles, in which an anticolonial movement was organized and led by Communists. The U.S. supported the French attempt to subdue the independence movement, though only by financial aid, but after French withdrawal and the temporary parti-tion of the country in 1954 the U.S. began to introduce military forces, at first gradually and then, from 1965, in great numbers. Si-multaneously, American ground forces were committed to battle in South Vietnam and American air and naval units began attacks on targets in North Vietnam. But the resistance escalated concurrently with the stepping up of U.S. activity, and by 1968 the failure to achieve results commensurate with the costs in American lives and treasure elicited such strong domestic repercussions as to compel a retrenchment. Restrictions on bombing were followed by gradual and finally complete withdrawal of American fighting forces, steps facili-tated by certain agreements with the North Vietnamese authorities. The corrupt, inefficient, and unpopular Saigon régime could not hold its own, however, in a "Vietnamized" war, and its forces were routed in disorder coincident with the cut-off of American supplies. The gov-ernment collapsed, as did shortly thereafter the pro-American, an-ticommunist government of Cambodia. Communists soon controlled all three states of Indochina, for in Laos as well there was a rapid shift, largely peaceful, to Communist domination.

The only important Soviet role in Vietnam, as in Korea earlier, was to supply military and economic assistance to the Communist-led forces. Although the war complicated Soviet–American relations, it did not have the dramatic impact of the Korean War. In part this was due to the fact that the Russians could not plausibly be depicted by the U.S. as the villains of the piece; in fact, there were efforts by Washington to use the Russians as intermediaries with the North

Vietnamese. (President Johnson and, once again, Dean Rusk, this time as secretary of state, made a feeble effort to portray the Vietnamese Communists as proxies of foreign masters, only now the Chinese. In contrast to Korea, the latter did not participate in the fighting, although they also—like the Russians—gave military and economic assistance).

The Soviet authorities, for their part, clearly did not feel that the USSR was threatened, as they had in Korea, by the massing of American troops in warfare against a fraternal state, because Vietnam was thousands of kilometers from Soviet borders. If during the Korean War Russian troop strength shot up rapidly to an unparalleled peacetime high, the large-scale fighting in Vietnam in the 1960s produced no comparable increase in Soviet strength.

The change in American posture on Russian responsibility for Communist activities around the world was obviously a response to the appearance and perpetuation of sharp divergences not only between the Soviet Union and China but among other ruling and nonruling Communist parties. Until the end of the 1950s the relative unity of Communist parties had lent plausibility to U.S. portrayal of non-Russian Communists as puppets pulled by strings from the Kremlin, although the Yugoslav example told against the proposition. By the 1960s, however, the evidence of internecine strife was too strong to permit continued U.S. exploitation of the old line. In addition, it was difficult for the U.S. to make use for its own purposes of the Sino-Soviet split and other disharmonies if their existence was not explicitly recognized. And American policy-makers were moving toward a position from which they could take advantage of the dissension, as the warming up of Chinese–American relations in the early 1970s was to demonstrate.

The "tool of Moscow" emphasis in the U.S. anticommunist rationale had tended to obscure a significant feature of U.S. policy, namely, that the United States was just as much opposed to "national" communism as to Soviet or Soviet-linked communism. United or disunited, pro-Moscow or anti-Moscow, Communists were anathema to Washington because they threatened important American interests, governmental and private, whether economic, like investments and trade, or military, like bases for troops, aircraft, and ships, and installations for collection of intelligence. In a more general way, any Communist advance anywhere threatened U.S. prestige as the reliable and successful guardian of the non-Communist world. And it did not matter much whether the Communist success resulted from electoral or other peaceful methods or from use of force.

This American viewpoint ruled out any graceful acceptance of Communist gains; it did not rule out a differentiated U.S. approach to Communists in power. The situation was complex. Even though the Soviet Union remained the No. 1 adversary of the United States, the U.S. had to exercise great caution in applying military power where there was considerable risk of Soviet (or even Chinese) counterforce. Military activities against Communist or leftist régimes or movements distant from Soviet power bases were within the scope of acceptable options. Even if such activities were ultimately unsuccessful in preventing Communist victory, as in Vietnam and Cambodia, they could wreak such destruction on people and places as to both seriously impair the "assets" inherited by the victors and make other countries cautious about incurring similar American vengeance.

There was no similar reluctance to employ economic pressure against the Soviet Union (or China), but there was increasing realization in Washington that such pressure against large, and largely self-sufficient, countries like Russia and China would be insufficient to undermine their institutions. Such pressures exerted on small countries dependent on foreign trade, and particularly on countries where native or foreign (U.S.) capitalists still controlled key economic sectors, offered much better chances of success for the United States.

The differentiated U.S. approach to Communist states was most evident, however, in the favor shown Communist régimes on the outs with Moscow, Yugoslavia in the late 1940s, Rumania from the 1960s, and China in the 1970s. China was the crucial example, because U.S. gestures of sympathy involved the most profound break with past policy and at the same time promised the greatest returns, because China potentially could seriously rival the Soviet Union. The China switch was instructive as to the priority of anti-Sovietism over anticommunism among a considerable number of American right-wingers (former secretary of defense James Schlesinger, Senator Henry Jackson, and Joseph Alsop, for example) who combined vociferous attacks on the USSR with kind words for the Peking authorities.

The anti-Soviet priority in American policy-making could be partly explained by the relatively small capabilities of China to influence events in areas such as Latin America, Africa, and the Middle East, and the considerably greater influence that the USSR could wield.

This is not to say that the Soviet impact was very strong, let alone decisive, but whatever external Communist influence existed came from Moscow rather than Peking. (In any case, Peking increasingly seconded U.S. policies in these areas.)

Latin America in the 1970s came to be much less a bone of Soviet–American contention than it was in the 1960s, when Cuba under Castro (whose band overthrew Batista in 1959) evolved gradually into a full-fledged Marxist-Leninist state with close—though occasionally troubled—ties to Moscow. The evolutionary character of the transition complicated and finally defeated American efforts to find a way of ridding the Western Hemisphere of this first Communist state without resort to open warfare. Surviving the U.S.-sponsored invasion by exile forces at the Bay of Pigs in 1961, and surviving the missile crisis of 1962 that brought the U.S. and USSR to the brink of war, the Castro government subsequently consolidated its position but did not succeed in sparking a revolution elsewhere in Latin America. Clearly, the revolutionary potential in various Latin American countries had not disappeared, but the general trend in the late 1960s and early 1970s—despite some countercurrents, especially in the Caribbean—was toward rightist dictatorships, whose ranks were increased with the overthrow of the left-leaning Allende government in Chile. This calmed American official anxieties about the forward march of Communist and Soviet influence, and permitted preliminary steps toward a normalization of U.S.–Cuban relations.

If Latin America, Cuba aside, was not a major area of U.S.–USSR conflict and competition, the same could not be said about Africa, where decolonization created in the two decades 1955–1975 more than a score of newly independent states to join the very few that existed in 1945. Neither the U.S. nor the USSR had military allies in Africa, and neither deployed there any sizeable military forces. But instability made the continent an area of intense Soviet–American rivalry, for the orientation of African countries was in flux, both internally—as to the choice between capitalist and socialist institutions and development paths—and externally—as to reliance on Western powers, including the U.S., or on the USSR. In general, the United States and its allies fared best in countries where colonial rule (British, French, Belgian) was dismantled more or less voluntarily, i.e., without armed struggle. And the Soviet Union made gains largely—again, there were exceptions—in ex-colonial territories where resistance movements were well-organized and tempered by armed struggle. These included Algeria in North Africa and Mozambique and Angola in South Africa. Soviet prospects were also favorable in countries like Libya and Ethiopia in which semifeudal autocracies, oriented toward the U.S., finally were overthrown after stubbornly resisting for long years any concessions to modernization.

As to the South African areas remaining under white rule after the Portuguese withdrawal, the prospective arrival of black rule in Rhodesia (Zimbabwe) and Southwest Africa (Namibia) promised to further the radicalization of the area that was already evident in Mozambique and Angola, and thus increase Soviet and diminish American influence. The situation was different in the Republic of South Africa only to the extent that black rule was farther off. The white minority was more numerous and more strongly entrenched than in Rhodesia; it was ruthless in its opposition to majority rule; and so far it had not had to confront an armed resistance movement.

In regard to all three white-ruled states, the United States was in a policy bind that resulted in considerable wavering between equally unpromising alternatives. In order to respond to pressures from black African states to the north (and, to a lesser extent, pressures from American blacks), the United States had gradually dropped its earlier tacit support of lily-white rule and apartheid. Yet it opposed an armed liberation struggle, even though the South African authorities and, to a lesser extent, those of Rhodesia appeared to prefer to take their chances on the outcome of armed conflict rather than yield to majority rule. In addition, American economic interests in the area, particularly in the Republic of South Africa, were large and profitable, second only to those of the British, and seemed to be more secure under white rule than they might be when, and if, the black majority was in control.

In contrast, the USSR could forthrightly support those struggling against minority white rule in southern Africa, whether the struggle took the form of armed conflict or not. Moreover, Soviet representatives were in a position to draw comfort from American embarrassment when militant African states with USSR encouragement pushed for UN measures against the Rhodesian or South African states that went beyond American tolerance. The USSR lacked, however, as the U.S. did not, any means of pressing changes in Rhodesian or South African policies except through support of black guerrillas or UN condemnations.

U.S.–USSR rivalry in the Middle East was as intense as in Africa but took a different form. True, in the 1950s and early 1960s American policy-makers were concerned about the possibility that one or another country in the region would come under Communist rule. The alarm first centered on Iran and subsequently on Syria and Iraq. But such possibilities dimmed, even though the USSR—defying American warnings to stay out of Middle Eastern affairs—established its influence in the region by becoming the principal diplomatic supporter and arms supplier of Arab countries on the front lines of the conflict with Israel. Despite its initial support for the creation of Israel, the USSR soon became an inveterate foe, having no diplomatic relations after 1967. This meant, however, that the Soviet Union lacked leverage on Arab–Israeli issues, and Soviet diplomatic-military support was insufficient to enable the Arabs either to stem Israeli conquest of Arab lands or to achieve a satisfactory modus vivendi.

The United States, in contrast, not only welcomed the creation of Israel in 1948 but after the 1956 fiasco (the coordinated Israeli–French–British invasion of Egypt, opposed by both the U.S. and the USSR) adopted Israel as a quasi-ally that it lavishly financed and equipped militarily. Though U.S. support was crucial to Israeli success in the wars of 1967 and 1973, following the latter conflict the U.S. maneuvered to improve its relations with front-line Arab states and to edge the Soviet Union out of an influential position in the area. It had considerable success. The U.S. had numerous assets with which to work, not least its capability of putting pressure on Israel to make accommodations with the Arab neighbors. But American success was determined in part by the fortuitous shift of Egypt under Sadat from friend to foe of the USSR. Nasser's Egypt was oriented toward socialism (though Communists were restricted in their activities), and toward reliance on Soviet arms. Sadat plumped for capitalist development and opened the door for an anticipated—but so far unrealized—influx of foreign (American) capital; simultaneously he renounced dependence on Soviet military assistance, broke the treaty of friendship with the USSR, and sought arms supplies from the United States and its allies.

Withdrawal from Vietnam left the U.S. no longer engaged anywhere in armed conflict with Communist-led forces, and disinclined to commit its forces quickly in similar ventures elsewhere. The time had long passed, as noted, when American authorities could view all Communist activities, wherever in the world they occurred, as evidence of Moscow's long reach. By the 1970s, also, the prospect of a direct military confrontation between the United States and the Soviet Union was in abeyance, especially with European skies clearer than they had been at any time since 1945. Under these circumstances, incentives existed to put U.S.–Soviet relations on a new footing.

"NORMALIZATION" OF SOVIET–AMERICAN RELATIONS

From the perspective of Soviet–American rivalry for world leadership, it is easier to account for hostility and tension in U.S.–USSR relations ("cold war"), than to explain the relaxation ("détente") that began in the 1960s and assumed a qualitatively new form in the 1970s. Détente was characterized by the toning-down of polemics, by repeated meetings of the two countries' leaders, by the signature of general agreements attempting to define the way in which the U.S. and USSR should coexist, and by the conclusion of specific agreements not only on strategic arms but on trade, exchanges, and other areas of mutual interest.

In the justifications for détente proffered by American and Soviet spokesmen there is a strong emphasis on the need to avoid nuclear war. Peaceful coexistence, it is said, is the only alternative to such a war, one that would devastate both countries. But there are problems with this interpretation. Normalization of relations is not a substitution of peace for war. The "cold war" was also a state in which the two countries never let their antagonisms drive them over the brink; it involved almost all the characteristics of war except the fighting and dying. Moreover, it was precisely the decline in anticipation of U.S.–USSR warfare that allowed the ruling circles in Washington and Moscow to move toward more civility and concord in their dealings with each other.

This interpretation is also weakened by lack of evidence that contemporary U.S. and USSR leaders have been more aware of the dangers of war than those of earlier years. Stalin, for example, was in many respects the soul of caution on war risks. His early minimization of the importance of atomic weapons did not indicate a casual attitude toward war, but involved a perfectly rational stance (later to be imitated by the Chinese) for a country temporarily lacking a military innovation possessed by its main adversary. As to the U.S., no doubt the minimal magnitude of World War II losses and the early atomic monopoly made President Truman and his associates less concerned about an outbreak of war than their opposite numbers in the USSR. But apprehensions existed, and became more acute as the U.S. came to be vulnerable to attack. American and Soviet leaders alike sought to best the adversary, not, as the Germans say, *so oder so,* but without war and all its expected traumas.

Another explanation attributes the tendency to normalize U.S.–USSR relations to the weakening of the position of the U.S. and USSR as unchallenged leaders of two rival camps. Simply stated, the Soviet Union moved toward détente in order to buttress itself in the West against a threat in the East from China, and the United States—which faced no such threat—to meet the economic and political competition of other major capitalist powers. Sharp border clashes in 1969 between Soviet and Chinese forces on the Ussuri River were the sole occasion since 1945, except for Chinese–American fighting in Korea, when battlefield clashes occurred between great powers. They suggested, as did other episodes of Sino-Soviet confrontation, the possibility of a war between the two largest Communist states. Facing that possibility, the Soviet authorities purportedly sought to mend fences in Europe and with the U.S. in order to avoid a dreaded two-front war.

As to the United States, it lagged behind Western Europe and Japan in expanding the volume of East–West trade, and lagged behind its European allies in reshaping political relations with the Russians (notably the French, who began regular visits back and forth between Soviet and French leaders in 1966, and the Germans, whose opening to the East under Brandt had a decisive impact on the frozen European situation). With the American economy buffeted in the 1970s by severe internal and international difficulties, the U.S. was in a poor position to renounce trade opportunities in the Soviet and Eastern markets while such opportunities were being seized by America's capitalist competitors. And maintenance by the U.S. of hostility or icy indifference to the USSR as Western European countries were improving their political relations would have deepened existing rifts among the NATO allies. Of course, American problems with allies were of a different, less serious order than those of the Soviet Union with its ex-ally, China.

It must be noted, however, that initial Soviet moves toward a rapprochement with the U.S. preceded rather than followed the definitive break with China. Thus, the Khrushchev visit to the United States in 1959 and Khrushchev's rather benign treatment of American policy immediately prior to the U-2 incident of 1960 contributed to the Chinese unhappiness with Soviet behavior. Soviet signature in 1963 of the treaty with the U.S. and U.K. partially banning nuclear weapons tests, a blow to China, preceded China's improvement of relations with the leading captialist countries, preceded China's successful testing of nuclear weapons, and preceded Peking's assertion of claims to territory held by Russia. The chronology tells against the idea that the China factor was decisive in the Kremlin leaders' search for accommodations with the U.S. and the West. Nevertheless, the deepening of Chinese hostility toward Moscow must certainly have reinforced Soviet inclinations to get on a better footing with the North Atlantic countries.

Actually, there is less need of subtle reasoning to explain Soviet interest in détente than to account for the American shift from "cold war" to more amicable relations. It was the U.S. which had sought to isolate the USSR as much as possible from "normal" interstate relations, bilateral and multilateral, economic exchanges especially but other kinds as well. By maintaining and encouraging other countries to maintain restrictions on trade, the U.S. sought to force on Russia a kind of autarchy, rebuffing Soviet efforts to expand economic exchanges. (To add insult to injury, American ideologists then promoted a theory that Soviet striving for economic independence, *samostoyatel' nost*, meant a commitment to autarchy, i.e., renunciation of trade.) In the political realm, also, the United States was reluctant to recognize that Russia had any legitimate interests outside issues such as disarmament and outside the geographical limits of Europe. The right of the U.S. to a role in Asian, Latin American, African, and Middle Eastern affairs was vigorously asserted; the right of the USSR to a similar role denied.

By the late 1960s and early 1970s, however, it was plain that the Soviet Union had to be dealt with, not ignored or merely anathematized. The idea surfaced that U.S. aims of deflecting Soviet policies from courses deemed in Washington to be harmful or dangerous might be better served through bilateral contacts, participation in trade, and in general through diplomatic maneuvers than through reliance on external pressures. For the USSR had strengthened its capabilities despite U.S. efforts at isolation, had become a significant factor in world trade, including trade with Western Europe and Japan, and had established its influence in various parts of the world.

Establishment of "normal" relations with the United States was, as mentioned, a Soviet objective long antedating détente, Behind this objective lay a yearning to gain acceptance of the USSR as a world power on the same general level as the United States. Moreover, the campaign for recognition of peaceful coexistence as the principle that should govern relations between states with different social orders was directed first of all at the U.S. (which until the 1960s rebuffed all Soviet proposals for mutual endorsement of the principle). But if the objective was traditional, certainly interest in better relations with America increasingly characterized Soviet policy in the post-Stalin years, especially under Brezhnev's tenure as party chief. This was partly due to economic considerations, as the slowing of the USSR's rate of economic growth in the 1960s made doubly attractive the idea of gaining access to American technology, the most advanced in the world. No doubt Soviet interest in détente and better relations with the U.S. accounted in part for a change in tactics under Brezhnev, for the USSR carefully avoided crisis-provoking initiatives of the kind that Khrushchev launched on Berlin in 1958 and on Cuba in 1962.

The new stage in Soviet–American relations marked by the summit meetings of 1972 and succeeding years did not end rivalry and struggle between the two countries but merely altered the conditions under which the contest was carried on. One obvious alteration, in fact, was the possibility that détente offered American and Soviet authorities to claim that the adversary was abusing détente by continuing to do what it had always done, that is, attempt to expand its own power and influence and simultaneously block the maintenance or aggrandizement of the rival's!

Each of the powers continued, for example, to build up its military forces, including the forces designed for destruction of the adversary, while complaining that the adversary's efforts were scarcely consistent with détente. Each continued to woo and aid clients and allies abroad, complaining all the time that the rival's similar efforts threatened relaxation of tension. There was, in other words, much business as usual.

But not all was business as usual. The SALT agreements of 1972–1974 were qualitatively different from earlier agreements on arms limitation in establishing upper limits on major Soviet and American forces, those maintained by each country for deterrence of, or strikes against, the other. By subjecting this sensitive area to diplomatic regulation, the adversaries renounced some freedom of action to pursue unilateral programs of military development. Implicitly endorsing the principle of strategic parity between the U.S. and USSR, the agreements offered the rival political leaderships a means of braking pressure from their military and industrial establishments for increasing the tempo of strategic competition. But the inhibitions on strategic arms competition should not be exaggerated; apart from the fact that no reductions were contemplated, the agreements left open a wide area for introduction of new weapons systems and other qualitative strengthening of strategic strike forces, a topic discussed in the military chapter. Moreover, the general agreement reached in the Ford–Brezhnev meeting at Vladivostok in December 1974 (for a follow-up to the temporary, 1972–1977, limitations on strategic offensive weapons systems) was not subsequently translated into a binding accord.

If negotiations and limited agreements on main strategic forces were central to the new phase of Soviet–American relations, there were other changes in the two countries' relations made possible by transcendence of extreme cold war hostility. Probably the two most important of these changes centered on European affairs and economic exchanges.

As indicated earlier, agreements focusing on Germany quieted at least temporarily some of the most acrimonious disputes plaguing East–West, and U.S.–USSR, relations in Europe. The eased atmosphere made possible unprecedented negotiations among almost all European states, East and West, plus the United States and Canada, in a Conference on Security and Cooperation that met intermittently from 1972 to 1975. The conference was a Soviet idea, promoted energetically by the Brezhnev leadership group for almost a decade. The whole idea had been resisted by Washington, which looked on the proposal as one designed to weaken the U.S. role in Europe and loosen the ties binding NATO nations to American leadership. Although some Western countries showed greater receptivity, it became clear to the Russians that such a conference could not take place against American opposition and without American participation, so they dropped the idea of making it a purely European gathering.

The Russians and their allies had to make other concessions. They agreed, with a noticeable lack of enthusiasm, that there should be concurrent negotiations, in a separate forum, between NATO and Warsaw Pact powers on mutual reduction of military forces in Central

Europe. Such talks began in Vienna in 1973, but in over four years have gotten nowhere.

Another Soviet-bloc concession on the European security conference involved their acceptance, with still less enthusiasm, that the conference should deal not only with interstate questions but also with questions of "human rights." The Soviet Union and its allies had wanted the conference to center on such matters as the obligation of participating states to refrain from the threat or use of force in their mutual relations, to respect the inviolability of frontiers and the territorial integrity of states, and to avoid intervention in the internal affairs of other states. The cooperation that the conference should promote centered, in the Soviet view, on economic cooperation and exchanges in the field of culture, etc.

Although clauses on these topics formed the major part of the "Final Act" of the conference, the so-called Helsinki document, the latter also included a number of clauses regarding movement of people across state frontiers, the reunion of families, the rights of foreign journalists, circulation of foreign publications, and exchanges of information.

With each side able to point to favored sections of the Helsinki agreement, the consequences could easily be imagined. USSR mass media published the entire long text of the agreement but focused propaganda on the political security and economic cooperation sections, though they also responded with polemical counterattacks to U.S. and Western charges that Warsaw Pact countries were violating the human rights clauses. American mass media, though not publishing the agreement, launched a full-scale propaganda campaign attacking the practices of Communist states and conveying an impression that the role of the United States in regard to the agreement was simply to monitor Soviet and East European fulfillment of the human rights clauses. The situation was somewhat ironic; if, as this campaign suggested, the agreement required major changes in Soviet behavior and none in American, why did U.S. authorities resist for so long the movement that resulted in the Helsinki accord? In any case, despite the initial focus on security questions, the conference achieved nothing concrete to alleviate the division of Europe into opposing military blocs, and it appeared that the ultimate contribution of the Helsinki exercise might be an intensification rather than a lessening of mutual hostility.

The atmosphere of discord over the fulfillment of the Helsinki agreement centered on state treatment of individuals, and therefore was qualitatively different from the atmosphere of tension of earlier years, usually involving apprehensions of interstate armed conflict. A somewhat similar change was noticeable in the kind of alarm expressed in the United States over the possibility of Communists coming to power in states of the Western alliance, and, to a lesser extent, in Soviet concern over the persistence of Western-oriented dissenters in the USSR and other socialist countries. In neither case were the apprehensions connected with use of military force, to spread communism or to roll back communism by force. The United States appeared determined to block Communist domination of governments in Portugal, Italy, and France, for example, whether Communist gains were secured by elections or other routes, even if this required support—as in Italy—to right-wing elements attempting to replace constitutional government with an anticommunist dictatorship. Europe was not Africa, and thwarting Communist advances in Europe was a cause to which moderates in the United States, the so-called cold-war liberals, would be likely to rally in the company of the more militantly global anticommunists.

The other major area of change in Soviet–American relations in the 1970s involved commercial and other economic exchanges. U.S. government and business circles finally began to reciprocate, if not with equal fervor, the persistent Soviet interest in expanding trade levels, which had remained extremely low throughout the postwar years, even after Western European and Japanese trade with the USSR had become sizeable. This enlivening of U.S. interest was partly due to a decline in belief that the severe U.S. restrictions on trade with the USSR were achieving their purpose, and partly to the internal and international problems besetting the American economy, problems which impelled a new look at the policy of renouncing trade opportunities in the East.

And trade levels increased, particularly American exports to the Soviet Union, as restrictions were eased, though such restrictions on both exports and imports remained more stringent than those of America's capitalist competitors, much more aggressive in seizing openings for trade. As part of an American–Soviet agreement to expand trade, the USSR promised to settle its old Lend-Lease debt (at a reduced sum, of course, following the example of other Lend-Lease settlements) in return for elimination of discriminatory duties levied on goods of Soviet origin imported to the U.S. The grant of "Most

Favored Nation" (MFN) treatment, accorded to almost all countries except those under Communist rule, would have been of more symbolic than practical importance, unless the pattern of goods imported from the USSR changed. Traditional imports have been of commodities with zero or low duties. But the agreement was never implemented, because forces hostile to the USSR in the U.S. Congress, led by Senator Jackson, succeeded in attaching a condition for extension of MFN treatment and also, far more important, for extension of credits to the USSR, namely, that the USSR should regulate emigration of Soviet citizens abroad in a way satisfactory to Washington. The Soviet authorities refused to accept this condition.

While the issue centered on Jewish emigration, and the principal lobbying effort against easing trade restrictions was led by powerful Zionist organizations, the episode revealed the split in the American business community on the advisability of increasing trade with the Soviet Union. Some important elements favored expansion, but there were others, especially in the defense-supplying industries, that were either indifferent or opposed. The latter were unlikely to benefit directly from such trade, and might ultimately suffer if trade expansion reinforced détente. Prospects for peaceful relations with the USSR could then get out of hand, and threaten continuation of the high level of U.S. military appropriations on which Pentagon-oriented industry thrived.

Even if the artificial barriers to trade were eventually eliminated, and even if exchanges assumed volumes proportional to those attained in Western European and Japanese trade with the Soviet Union, this would not mean a subsidence of U.S.–USSR economic rivalry, but merely its rechanneling.[4] Gains from such trade would presumably flow to both the USSR and the U.S., and this would be true even if expanded trade had to be financed through U.S. loans. In international as in domestic transactions, friendly merchants extending credit do so for their own profit, not for the good of the purchaser—who must pay extra for paying later. But the gains of the two countries would be rather different.

Soviet leaders make their thinking plain. As discussed in the chapter on economic rivalry, they expect trade with the United States

---

[4] Even if the U.S. relaxed trade restrictions to Western European–Japanese levels, its possibilities for trade with the USSR are limited because the U.S. cannot absorb Soviet imports of a type and in a volume that is possible for these other advanced economies.

to help speed Soviet economic development and the eventual achievement of an economy more powerful than the American.

Although American interest in trade with the Soviet Union, to the extent that it existed, obviously involved the attraction of profit-making opportunities for U.S. industrial and agricultural businesses, American policy-makers advanced certain long-term political expectations to justify expansion of trade with the Russians. Increased trade and other economic ties, it was thought, would create a dependence on the American market that would deter the Soviet authorities from political actions harmful to U.S. interests, because they would not want to jeopardize the trade linkage. This idea was almost directly contrary to the ruling principle of U.S. policy over the postwar period, when Washington sought to isolate the USSR economically.

Of course, opponents within the U.S. did not buy the notion, and indeed it was far from certain that economic linkage would tie the USSR any more than the United States. If exchanges attained a volume sufficient to create important vested interests in the USSR committed to their continuation, they would almost certainly create similar interests in the United States. Moreover, American business and agricultural enterprises have shown a capability of deflecting U.S. policy in favor of their profit-making ventures for which there is no Soviet parallel. Already in 1975, farmer opposition caused the Ford administration to back away from use of a cut-off of grain sales to Russia as a means of influencing Soviet policy in Africa.

In sum, U.S.–USSR trade negotiations in the 1970s were fraught with difficulty, and, just as in the case of negotiations on strategic forces and European security, highlighted the underlying animosity so often expressed in relations between the two powers. Even without settlement of the issues about legal restrictions, however, maintenance of a higher level of Soviet–American exchanges seemed likely.

Lessening of U.S.–USSR tensions made possible not only discussions and certain agreements on specific topics such as those treated above, but also general agreements defining the principles by which the two states were to conduct their mutual relations. An agreement of May 1972 recognized "peaceful coexistence" as the norm for these relations, and characterized efforts to obtain unilateral advantage by either side, directly or indirectly, as inconsistent with this norm. Recognition of the security interests of the two countries was said to be "based on the principle of equality and the renunciation of the use of force or the threat of its use."[5] The following year an agreement was signed on the prevention of nuclear war in which the two parties agreed to act so as to prevent "the development of situations capable of causing a dangerous exacerbation of their relations, as to avoid military confrontations, and as to exclude the outbreak of nuclear war. . . ." They promised to "immediately enter into urgent consultations" if a "risk of nuclear war" appeared.[6]

The importance of such agreements is difficult to evaluate, because the obligations are of such a general nature that the line between adherence and violation is unclear. The ruling circles in neither capital are likely to expect any substantial modification of behavior from the other side as a result of the agreements. Thus, the entire history of U.S.–USSR negotiations on arms limitations and other matters is shot through with attempts to gain unilateral advantages, and no noticeable change occurred after the agreements were signed. About all that can be said is that "atmospheric" agreements probably have some importance of a psychological variety, in altering popular and elite expectations regarding war, for example. Indeed, some of the more specific agreements on arms control reached in the 1960s and 1970s were more significant because of their psychological impact than their impact on warmaking capabilities.

SOVIET AND AMERICAN INTERNATIONAL STANDING AFTER THREE POSTWAR DECADES

After thirty years of intense postwar competition for world leadership, no one—well, hardly anyone—doubts that the world standing of the Soviet Union has become stronger relative to that of the United States, even though the latter still occupies a superior position. Perhaps this trend favoring the USSR was inevitable in the absence of any cataclysmic turn of events, if only because the impact of the lopsided distribution of World War II costs and benefits was certain to fade as the war became ancient history. The United States could not retain its overwhelming dominance of the first postwar years. And the Soviet Union was bound to recover from the hurts of war and push

---

[5] *Pravda*, May 30, 1972; and *Department of State Bulletin*, June 26, 1972, pp. 898–99.

[6] *Department of State Bulletin*, July 23, 1973, pp. 160–61.

out from the circumscribed area to which its power and influence were confined in those same years.

This change in relative U.S.–USSR world status owed much, but not everything, to the geographical spread of Communist rule over most of Eastern Europe, over much of North Asia, over Indochina, and even into the Western hemisphere. The advance occurred with Soviet support and against American resistance, for the U.S. saw progressively restricted the areas where American economic, military, and political forces could freely operate.

But U.S. losses were not necessarily USSR gains. The expanded world of Communist states turned out to resemble nothing as much as the traditional world of states divided by conflicting interests, incompatible ambitions, and old or new antagonisms. It was not at all the ideal world envisaged by Marx and even Lenin, a world in which class linkages across national frontiers would submerge ethnic and other divisive elements. Recognition that the expansion of Communist rule had some negative consequences for the USSR should not, however, obscure the fact that on balance the trend was unfavorable to the United States and favorable to the Soviet Union, because each of the rivals had a stake not only in improving its own position but in weakening its adversary's.

Both countries were able to profit from a second major postwar development, the decolonization which simultaneously shortened the reach of America's major allies and led to the creation of scores of newly independent states, mostly in Asia and Africa. In many areas the U.S. could take over some of the external responsibilities and privileges formerly exercised by Western European countries and Japan. By and large, however, the USSR profited more from decolonization than did the U.S. With few exceptions, these new states did not "go Communist," but they displayed an inclination toward nonalignment and antiimperialism that suited Soviet purposes much more than American. This was not primarily a matter of speeches and votes in the United Nations, but of more practical steps in their domestic and foreign policies, particularly those infringing on prerogatives exercised by foreign (notably American) investors and enterprises.

In the industrially advanced countries, however, the overall trend of events was more favorable to American interests and less to communism and Soviet power. The U.S. contributed to the stabilization of war-shaken capitalist rule in Western Europe and Japan, established firm politico-military alliances with almost all of the governments in these regions, and helped prevent intercapitalist rivalries, including competition for markets, from exploding into the kind of conflict that had punctuated their pre-1945 history. On the other side, in the early postwar years Communist strength declined in countries like France and Italy where their leading role in wartime resistance movements appeared to give them initial advantages, nor were they able to build up strength in the other major capitalist states where their end-of-war position was weak (the U.S., U.K., West Germany, Japan).

It took more than a quarter-century after 1945 for Communist rule in an advanced country to become a serious possibility. Such possibilities were confined for the most part to countries in the Mediterranean basin. Because these were among the least developed of the advanced countries, the trend reinforced a phenomenon announced by the Russian Revolution and authenticated by subsequent Communist takeovers, that communism had more appeal to relatively backward than to highly developed countries, that is, had more appeal as a mechanism for economic development and protection of national autonomy than as a system for redistribution of economic and political power.

In the first postwar decade or so the USSR did poorly in the developed capitalist world not only in advancing the Communist cause but also in maintaining, let alone increasing, Soviet Russian influence. Partly as a result of growing economic and military power, however, and partly because of a change in tactics, from the late 1950s on the Soviet Union managed to improve its political and economic relations with most of the developed world. Still, the USSR was unable to dislodge the United States from its dominant position in Western Europe and Japan.

To take the international scene as a whole, the balance of forces between the United States and the Soviet Union, and between capitalism and communism, underwent significant changes in the three decades under review. Nor did the changes come to an end; no equilibrium was in prospect. But the record strongly suggested that Russia and America, and the adversary systems of which they were prototypes, possessed considerable staying power, and that further shifts in the power equation would assume the form of incremental steps rather than an avalanche sweeping one or the other to universal predominance.

9

TOWARD THE NEW
CENTURY: THE FUTURE OF
SOVIET-AMERICAN RIVALRY

THE SOVIET UNION has been shown to have made significant gains toward a long-sought objective, to equal and indeed eventually displace the United States as the most powerful country in the world. This shift in the balance of power is not just a change in the relative standing of two nations. It also involves a shift in the power balance between two different and opposed social orders, capitalism and socialism. Its consequences, therefore, go beyond those resulting from such previous shifts in power relationships as the displacement of Great Britain by the United States as the leading industrial power of the world.

Exaggeration should be avoided: in most of the areas considered earlier, Soviet capabilities still lag behind American. In fact, it is impossible to single out a single area of competition in which the Soviet Union is obviously equal or superior to the United States. In military capabilities, where parity is often assumed to prevail, the USSR has some way to go before it can match the United States. Its inferiority is still more pronounced in economic capabilities. Although objective indices are not available to measure relative strength in projection of political influence abroad or in exertion of ideological sway, even in these spheres the Soviet Union probably lags behind the U.S. The events that startled America into an appreciation of Soviet technological advances, the launching of the first intercontinental ballistic missile, of the first earth-circling satellite, and of the first man in outer space, were insufficient to give the USSR dominance in space activities; the United States belatedly gained a priority position.

It might be argued that comparisons of Soviet–American strength and of trends affecting relative strength are too esoteric to occupy the attention of any but a few specialists. Certainly neither John. Q. Citizen nor Ivan Ivanovich Ivanov goes to bed each night wondering about standings in the International Strength League. Nevertheless, such changes in the relative power of nations ultimately affect the lives and welfare of plain people as well as rulers. Politicians on both sides of the ideological divide find it possible and useful to galvanize hopes and fears about who's ahead and who's behind. And they are able to energize particular concern about relative military power, even in countries like the U.S. and Russia with no tradition of enmity, and even though the manifestations of military strength are remote enough from everyday life.

PAST TRENDS AND FUTURE PROJECTIONS

If there were, as there is not, complete agreement on the trend lines of the postwar decades and on the current relative strength of America and Russia, this would still not offer any sure handle on the future. The direction and rapidity of change in 1945–1975 are not certain to characterize coming decades. Accidents happen, new leaders appear, systems of coping with difficulties and opportunities are modified. The interstate environment changes; new contenders push for a place in the sun. And many of the conditions destined to affect Soviet–American competition are not amenable to control by either country.

Moreover, perceptions of changes in the power ratios of the rivals may themselves alter the course of competition. A competitor's spurt may inspire a redoubling of effort. Soviet–American strategic rivalry offers a current example. In the 1960s the American lead first advanced and then dwindled. But in the 1970s, American leaders, undistracted after the write-off of Indochina as a lost cause, began to express renewed determination to keep the United States as No. 1, and to back these expressions with an increase of resources for development of armament systems relevant to the Soviet challenge. Détente was not allowed to interfere with this process, as indeed it did not divert Soviet leaders from their own programs of military buildup. The end of the story is not known, of course; the United States may find itself unable to maintain its military position without endangering prospects in other areas of competition. Whatever the results in this sphere, the perception of shifts in the balance of power can affect future courses of action.

Two assumptions underly the following discussion of American–

Soviet prospects. One is that both countries preserve their respective social systems, whatever modifications the latter undergo. The assumption seems safe, because in neither country is a powerful challenge to the established order visible. Such a challenge might appear, and the extraordinary events in France and Czechoslovakia in 1968 suggest that it might rise rather suddenly. But the Soviet and American establishments appear to have sufficient reserves of strength to preclude any overthrow of the system. The two countries are the strongest links in the capitalist and socialist chains, to apply a variant of Lenin's theory that identified revolutionary possibilities as greatest in the weakest link of the capitalist state system.

A second assumption rules out a major war involving the United States and the Soviet Union. This seems a somewhat less safe assumption than that ruling out revolutionary shifts, because it depends on cooperation of two basically hostile ruling groups, reinforced by whatever pressure for war avoidance the concerned populations bring to bear. Even if it is accepted that nuclear war would be irrational, since not only the losers but the victors would lose, the thought offers limited reassurance. Sober calculations matching possible benefits to possible costs have never been typical of statesmen contemplating war-risky moves. No doubt the unique devestation in prospect from nuclear war forces on state leaders a powerful concentration of mind, much as the prospect of hanging, according to Samuel Johnson, forced such concentration of mind on condemned men. But the manipulation of military force, including implied threats of resort to nuclear weapons, is likely to characterize Soviet–American relations in the future as in the past. If the danger of war has receded, it has not disappeared.

ECONOMIC PROSPECTS

Economic developments in the last quarter of the nineteenth century will be fundamental in determining the relative world standing of the U.S. and USSR when the twenty-first century begins on January 1, 2001. Needless to say, no one "knows" how the rival economies will develop. The record of past predictions, including those of economists and political leaders, is uninspiring. Soviet projections of growth almost invariably assume fulfillment of ambitious USSR programs and crisis after crisis in the United States. The reverse is true of most American projections, which assume steady progress for the U.S. and aggravation of difficulties for the Soviet economy.[1]

There is, certainly, no dearth of obstacles standing in the way of Soviet efforts to overtake the United States in economic power. Some of these already made their appearance in the 1960s, when the USSR rate of overall growth noticeably slipped compared to the 1950s. Investment has become less productive, as indicated by an increase in the amount of capital needed to produce a given unit of output. Opportunities have diminished for the Soviet economy to maintain rapid growth by large expansion of the labor force, especially the industrial labor force. True, agriculture is still overpopulated by the standards of advanced countries, even though numbers of farm workers have been significantly cut back over past years. But sharp withdrawals from farm labor would put in jeopardy already unstable levels of farm output.

Finally, administrative reforms to improve economic efficiency do not promise great benefits. The reforms of 1965 were modest in conception, implementation, and results. The autonomy granted enterprises remains very limited, as does the use of profits as a major criterion of performance. Much reliance is still placed on such indicators as total ruble value of output, physical weight of output, and number of physical units produced, all of which lead to distortions affecting production and distribution, distortions of which Soviet au-

---

[1] Tendentiousness is flagrant in Soviet discussions, but it is not a Soviet monopoly. A U.S. example can be cited from one of the generally sober reports prepared periodically for the Joint Economic Committee of the U.S. Congress, which traditionally treat as sacrosanct U.S. official projections of growth while heavily discounting USSR planned targets. In the 1973 volume the paragraphs on Soviet prospects are peppered with words like "risks," "difficulties," "bottlenecks," "dilemmas," and "failures." Those on U.S. prospects, under the heading "A Period of Accelerated Recovery," were to sound ironic only months later. They describe the soon-to-be-forgotten "New Economic Policy" of the Nixon administration as a "revolutionary" program; anticipate a combination of balanced budgets and full employment, nothing less; and conclude with a gem of clouded crystal ball gazing: the U.S. "appears to be entering a period of more stable growth following the transition from a period of high inflation, high unemployment, and dislocations resulting from changing priorities." All this just as the United States was entering the worst postwar recession, with unprecedented unemployment and inflation! See Robert W. Campbell, M. Mark Earle, Jr., Herbert S. Levine, and Francis W. Dresch, "Methodological Problems Comparing the U.S. and U.S.S.R. Economies," in *Soviet Economic Prospects for the Seventies*, Joint Economic Committee, U.S. Congress (Washington, D.C.: Government Printing Office, 1973), pp. 139–46.

thorities are well aware but for which they have found no solution.

These and other difficulties have led many American students of the Soviet economy to discount prospects of the USSR's gaining substantially on the United States in the future, even if they recognize—as most do—that the Soviet Union has narrowed the economic gap in the past quarter-century. But there are reasons to believe that the Soviet economy will continue to grow more rapidly than the American, partly because the USSR can still tap sources of strength, partly because the U.S. also confronts serious difficulties.

1. The Soviet authorities are able to see to it that productive investment receives a very large share of economic resources, historically a much larger share than in the American economy. Even if the unfavorable trend in the Soviet capital/output ratio is not overcome, it seems likely that the burden of defense production—whatever its precise weight at present—will become less onerous in the coming decades. In putting higher priority on matching U.S. military capabilities than on equaling U.S. economic potential, the USSR had to devote great effort to building up its military "capital" and mastering the production of sophisticated arms output requiring scarce skills and scarce equipment and supplies. Keeping up with further advances will probably be less of a drag than catching up with a far-ahead rival.

2. The Soviet Union has an internal source of growth which is no longer available, at least on a major scale, to the U.S. This lies in the still large proportion of total output contributed by agriculture, and the even larger proportion of the total labor force occupied in farming. Despite problems noted earlier, the gradual shift from agriculture to industry, from a slow-growing to a more rapid-growing sector, should contribute substantially to efforts by the USSR to maintain a more rapid rate of overall growth than is to be expected in the United States, where agriculture contributes a small percentage to GNP and where farming occupies a small percentage of the work force. Prerequisites for this shift in the USSR will be either, or both, greater "industrialization" of agriculture with provision of more industrially produced equipment and supplies (including fertilizers and herbicides), and consequent mechanization, chemicalization, and electrification of farm operations, or greater dependence on farm imports from countries where natural conditions are more favorable to agricultural bounty. Most signs point to continued Soviet reliance on the former course, but there are some indications of interest in the latter.

3. Some international trends will probably benefit Soviet efforts to catch up economically with the U.S. One of these is the withering of American efforts to block Soviet economic advancement by forcing autarchy on the Communist world. Although U.S. and allied restrictions have already lessened, in coming years the USSR will probably have still more access to advanced Western technology, even though its capability of paying for this through exports remains a problem, as does its capability of making efficient use of such imports. To be sure, the United States may be able to maintain its own restrictions on imports and exports, if not those of allied states. But the American international economic position is no longer so strong that it can, at least without some sacrifice and without worsening its competitivity with capitalist rivals, pass by opportunities to take advantage of the Soviet market.

4. Another international trend favoring the USSR more than the United States, or damaging the USSR less than the U.S., is a shift in the terms of international trade increasing prices of primary products relative to those of fabricated goods. The most dramatic example involves petroleum products; sharp price increases beginning in 1973 imposed a substantial burden on the U.S. but not on the USSR. Other raw materials, foodstuffs, and fuels have also been affected, though this may be a short-term fluctuation because producer nations arc not in as good a position to impose price discipline as the oil-exporting countries. To the extent that a shift in world market prices of primary and finished products lasts, the Soviet Union is likely to benefit and the United States to suffer. The USSR is more self-sufficient than the U.S., and primary products play a smaller role in its imports and a larger role in its exports than is the case with the United States.

5. The shift in these price ratios is not unrelated to a trend toward greater control on the part of developing countries of production of fuels, raw materials, and other export commodities. This takes different forms, from sharing ownership and management with foreign enterprises to complete state control. This trend, encouraged by Soviet authorities, is potentially unfavorable to the United States, in view of the far-flung American investments abroad. The high American standard of living is in part dependent on the exploitation of cheap raw materials and cheap labor in less-developed countries. Their declining availability would have negative consequences for the American economy.

6. Finally, the Soviet Union has a potential source of growth in making greater use of the so-called international division of labor, that is, substituting imports for domestic production in areas of Soviet disadvantage, and expanding production for export in areas of Soviet advantage. Of course, the United States also has the possibility of expanding the role of foreign trade in its economy. The gains to be expected, however, would almost certainly be less than those available to the USSR, in view of the larger volume of U.S. foreign trade and the fact that such trade has not been hindered as much by artificial barriers as Soviet foreign exchanges. Greater Soviet participation in a global division of labor would supplement an already considerable participation in the socialist division of labor, that is, exchanges among countries participating in the Council of Mutual Economic Assistance.

Even if it were assumed, for whatever reasons, that the USSR would not be able to sustain as rapid growth in the next quarter-century as in the last, this would not necessarily prevent an overtaking of the United States. The outcome would depend on how well the U.S. as well as the USSR performs in the coming years. It is appropriate, therefore, to turn from a consideration of economic prospects largely focused on the Soviet Union to one centered on the United States.

Despite the notes of gloom and doom frequently sounded in Soviet discussions and occasionally even in American, there is no sign that capitalism in the United States has played itself out. There appears to be little likelihood that the American economy will stagnate and become moribund or, alternatively, arouse such opposition as to bring about fundamental change. Even the unusually sharp recessionary slide which began in 1973 ended in an upturn, as was true of earlier postwar recessions, not a deep depression. And it must be recalled, with a glance back to the 1960s, that American growth rates increased over those of the preceding decade, while those of the USSR slackened.

Nevertheless, serious contradictions made themselves felt, particularly in the 1970s, and it seems unlikely that the American economy will advance steadily and rapidly enough to maintain the existing lead over the rival system. The 1970s dealt a staggering blow to confidence in the possibility of "fine-tuning" the economy. Intervals between recessions shortened; recessions lasted longer and cut deeper. And at the moment when even conservative leaders—allergic in their souls to unbalanced budgets—became converts to Keynesian principles of economic adjustment, these principles demonstrated their ineffectiveness to deal with the combination of inflation, stagnation, and high unemployment.

The difficulties stemmed in part from the international economic situation, which promises to remain troublesome for the American economy. Here if anywhere the days of wine and roses appear to be gone. Japan and Western Europe provide stiff competition for the U.S. in world markets. Unfavorable trade balances persist. Protectionism appears to be on the rise, in the U.S. as outside, as national authorities attempt to preserve markets for their less competitive industrial and agricultural producers. Other unfavorable international trends have already been mentioned; in addition; there was a prospective shrinkage of the capitalist world, and with it a shrinkage of the areas in which American business could operate with a free hand.

Domestic prospects are also clouded. No means of seriously and permanently reducing high unemployment levels loom as likely to be acceptable to those controlling American institutions. Structural rigidities prevent a concerted attack on problems of poverty, racial stratification, urban decay, and deterioration of many qualitative aspects of American life. Chief among these rigidities are the great disparities in wealth and income that have persisted despite long years of talk about, and programs promising, relief for the "one-third of the nation" that is "ill-housed, ill-clad, ill-nourished." Moving in this direction promises little profit to American business, which turns elsewhere for opportunities. Nor has the government been able to accomplish what entrepreneurs on their own rejected. President Johnson's highly touted War on Poverty ended in unconditional surrender—on the part of Washington.

The role of war and war preparations in sustaining American growth may also be changing. Theoretically, American capitalism could continue to expand without war preparations. Indeed, military spending was unimportant in American economic development over the long period from the end of the Civil War to the late 1930s. But it has played a significant role in the maintenance of relatively full employment of resources from the end of World War II to the end of the war in Vietnam. But the failure of the Vietnam venture led to disillusionment about U.S. recourse to military intervention to stop the spread of communism, and resistance to spending for this purpose. It has not as yet led, however, to resistance to spending for military forces more directly related to great-power rivalry, and powerful military and industrial interests have mounted a campaign on the Soviet menace designed to make sure that such appropriations do not suffer.

These current or impending obstacles to maintenance of prosperity should not obscure U.S. strengths. The impact of developments abroad is somewhat limited because the United States is relatively self-sufficient compared to most other advanced states, if less so than the USSR; and the failure to extend the gains of economic progress and modernization to a deprived underclass has not prevented their wide distribution to other population sectors. The market system of the U.S. encourages a flexibility in production and distribution, notably in the prompt adoption and diffusion of new technology, that has so far not been demonstrated in the more cumbersome centrally planned economy of the rival. In contrast, however, Russia has not had to face in the past, nor is likely to face in the future, the crises of underconsumption that have interrupted economic growth in the United States.

If all these conflicting trends are taken into account, it is reasonable to expect a continued gradual narrowing of the gap between Soviet and American production capabilities, with the USSR equaling the United States in total output of goods and services around the turn of the century. This would follow a rise from less than one-third of American output a quarter-century ago to almost two-thirds at present. The catching-up would occur slightly earlier if the relative rates of growth of 1950–1975 were reproduced, somewhat later if the relative growth rates approximate those of only the last fifteen years. In either case the USSR would still lag behind the United States in per capita output because of the Soviet Union's almost one-fifth greater population.

Whether measured in terms of national or per capita output, such an equalization would not mean that the Soviet population would be supplied with as many consumer goods and services as the American; the very large current discrepancy would be reduced but by no means erased. Of course, Soviet priorities may very well change, that is, in the coming years provision to consumers of both socially distributed and individually purchased goods and services could be given more emphasis in economic policy, in line with a somewhat inconsistent trend of recent years. But a major shift in economic policy toward consumer welfare would in all likelihood depress the rate of growth of the economy as a whole. Whatever gains in labor productivity were achieved through enriched incentives would thus be counterbalanced by a slackening of the rate of expansion of productive capacity. Because Soviet leaders are allergic to growth slowdowns, a marked shift in priorities between output of means of production and provision of consumer items does not seem to be in the cards, at least in the imminent future.

The prospect outlined may be challenged, indeed challenged from different directions. It can be hardly doubted, however, that Russia's equaling of the United States economically, if such occurs, would have profound consequences on the two states' across-the-board rivalry. The achievement would increase Soviet capabilities to rival the U.S. as a world power, especially militarily (both in the status of its own forces and in military supply and support of other states) and economically (increased impact of the USSR abroad as a market and source of supply, including development assistance). Internally, it would lend material substance to long-repeated claims of socialism's dynamism, strengthening acceptance of distinctive Soviet institutions and reducing the appeal of foreign alternatives. And ideologically such an achievement would refurbish the tarnished image of socialism (Soviet-style) as the most progressive social order.

THE PROSPECTIVE MILITARY BALANCE

By 1975 the USSR was approaching parity with the United States in military capabilities, a goal sought ever since 1945. Changing the unfavorable military balance was *a* or *the* top Soviet priority, which required sacrifices of otherwise attainable programs of civilian economic development. The relative weight of the military burden lessened, of course, as the Soviet economy narrowed the productivity gap; unless there is a great spurt of military spending in the next quarter-century, the burden will be further reduced as the USSR approaches equality in economic strength. It is barely conceivable, moreover, though not too likely, that Soviet–American arms limitations, or more generally détente, will reduce the proportion of resources the U.S. and USSR devote to military ends in the coming decades, and thereby ease the economic burden of war preparations.

Because of the greater size of the American productive plant and its higher technological level, the United States in theory might be able to regain a clear military superiority over the Soviet Union by upping the ante in military spending. In practice, however, this might be difficult under the existing political system. Consumption would

probably suffer with a commitment to a steep rise in defense allocations, and plentiful supplies of consumer goods play a larger role in
U.S. "system maintenance" than in Soviet. Consequently, it is doubtful that American nostalgia for the good old days of unchallenged
military dominance will be translated into a program to resurrect a
lost superiority.

The next quarter-century is likely to see additional Soviet efforts to
substantially improve capabilities in the one military sphere in which
the United States remains clearly dominant, that of military forces,
chiefly air and naval, designed for long-range operations using conventional weapons. Moscow has been poorly equipped, despite recent improvements, to bring military pressure to bear in support of
allies and protégés in distant parts. Clearly, Soviet authorities want to
rectify this situation. As pointed out in the chapter on military rivalry,
however, matching American forces in this sphere would probably
require a difficult political decision, to abandon a long-promoted
campaign against foreign military bases that has had considerable
resonance in militarily weak nations.

The prospective attainment by the Soviet Union of parity with the
U.S. in military power raises a number of questions to which
definitive answers cannot be given. Two such questions may be posed
here: Will the Soviet leadership be content with a rough equality with
the United States in overall military capabilities or strive for clear-cut
superiority? Will improvement of Soviet military capabilities to or
beyond the American level lead to greater risk taking on the part of
Moscow, and thus increase the likelihood that war will break out?

In economic rivalry with the United States, Soviet leaders do not at
all hide their ambition to have the USSR gain superiority over, and
not merely establish equality with, the U.S. Likewise, in their perception of the struggle between rival social systems, Soviet authorities express hope and expectation that socialism will survive and capitalism perish. No such clear-cut avowal of military superiority over
the United States is advanced in authoritative USSR discussions of
the military balance. There are several reasons for this reticence. Posing an objective of military superiority would lend color to assertions,
strongly denied in Moscow, that the USSR is bent on military conquest, on Soviet imposition of Communist rule by force in other
countries. Military superiority in this respect is in contrast to economic superiority, which cannot threaten or harm any other country.
Soviet statements insist that the USSR devotes resources to military

preparations only for the purpose of defending the country and its allies, and only as much as is needed to provide a reliable defense. Soviet doctrine holds, moreover, that arms spending is intrinsically undesirable (though necessary) in the sense that diversion of resources to military ends reduces possibilities for more rapid economic development, and thus more rapid betterment of living standards, goals regarded as intrinsically desirable.

Considerations such as these help explain why the USSR makes no avowals of intentions to achieve military superiority; they do not foreclose the possibility that such intentions lie behind quantitative increases or qualitative betterment of Soviet military forces. The question remains open, and may never be answered, in view of the reciprocal element in arms competition.

The question of superiority in the bilateral context is complicated by the fact that both countries' military programs are affected by the existence of other adversaries besides the main rival, and other situations open to use of military force besides Soviet–American mutual deterrence or armed conflict. This is particularly true of the Soviet Union, which has a strong antagonist in China; the United States has none of this caliber. While the Chinese factor obviously influences the size and deployment of Soviet military forces, Russian discussions of military programs allude only *sotto voce*, as it were, to requirements for countering the Chinese militarily. They cannot, therefore, use this consideration of a two-front menace to justify larger Soviet than American military forces.

One final point needs to be made. Anxiety in regard to possible Soviet attainment, or attempt to attain, military superiority is understandable from a United States perspective, or from the perspective of countries shielded by American nuclear or conventional military strength. But designation of the United States as the principal military power of the world is not decreed in tablets of the universe; the American dominance is strictly a historical phenomenon with a definite beginning and a possible ending. Nor would Soviet ascendancy, or striving for ascendancy, by itself prove anything about Soviet intentions regarding the use of that superior position, any more than American interest in remaining No. 1 militarily proves anything about U.S. intentions. But this leads to the next question, about possible Soviet use of military parity with, or superiority over, the U.S.

Countries pay for armies, air forces, and navies to buy benefits from their existence and presence, not exclusively or even necessarily—and less so today than in earlier times—in order to commit these forces to use in conflict. At least this is the rationale offered for expenditures on strategic nuclear forces, and it applies in some degree to other forces whose engagement in fighting portends less ominous consequences. It applies to the USSR as well as to the United States. In fact, for reasons advanced earlier, Soviet authorities have been less inclined than American to commit their forces to armed conflict outside homeland defense perimeters. (It must be recognized, however, that past inferiority of military capabilities, slowly and still incompletely overcome, powerfully reinforced Soviet caution).

In strategic nuclear forces the Soviet attainment of near parity has brought about a kind of neutralization of such forces, in which neither superpower has any substantial freedom of action. It has certainly not led to greater Soviet risk taking, but to less, while making even more unattractive for the U.S. the so-called nuclear option; rejected in crises of the 1950s but seriously considered at the time. The principal Soviet objective in the buildup of forces available for distant military operations is probably the neutralization of American capabilities for long-range intervention. Throughout most of the past three decades Washington has not had to pay much attention to possible Soviet response before deciding to intervene militarily in countries such as Lebanon, the Congo (Zaire), Indonesia, Vietnam, and Cambodia. Only in areas where USSR ground forces could be easily committed, especially in Eastern Europe, was the prospect of Soviet involvement a decisive hindrance to U.S. freedom of action. This freedom to disregard Soviet response is no longer true of U.S. calculations about military intervention in Middle Eastern countries, and probably not about intervention in Africa. And in the next decades it will no doubt become more risky for the U.S. to apply military muscle in Asia without taking into account Soviet capabilities for counteraction.

The probable gravitation toward U.S.–USSR military equality is not likely to eliminate disparities between Soviet and American capabilities for unchallenged application of military force in areas bordering on the respective homelands, including Latin America, much of the Pacific Ocean area, and perhaps other places for the United States; Eastern Europe, and possibly other border areas for the USSR. Of course, other disincentives to intervention may become stronger, including prospects of strong indigenous military resistance.

As with the question of Soviet aims in military development, equality or superiority, no definitive answer can be given to the question of

Soviet use of a new-found parity or superiority in military power, if such were to be realized. But the result would probably be a kind of mutual stymieing, or neutralization. If this proves to be correct, then the military competition between the Soviet Union and the United States—while continuing to absorb substantial resources in both countries—will prove to be less decisive than rivalry in economic and other areas.

STRUGGLE FOR INTERNATIONAL INFLUENCE

The earlier discussion of U.S.–USSR international rivalry in 1945–1975 stressed the duality of objectives sought by each power. First, each attempted to expand its national influence, frequently at the expense of the other, and to bring as many states as possible into alignment with the policies of Washington or Moscow. And this applied fully as much to "nonaligned" nations as to allies: Soviet authorities wanted them to be nonaligned in favor of Moscow, American authorities in favor of Washington. Second, each of the rivals sought at the same time to solidify or extend the world scope of its socioeconomic system, capitalism or socialism, and of the kind of rule, Marxist-Leninist or bourgeois, of which it served as examplar and guardian.

For neither country were these perfectly compatible objectives, and sometimes hard choices had to be made as to priorities. It had always been clear that capitalist states could be at odds with one another, and American efforts to bolster the capitalist order in countries where it was challenged did not assure a pro-American orientation. Though not clear earlier, it became evident in the postwar years that "socialism in many countries" did not mean everlasting harmony but the recurrence of old and the appearance of new conflicts among these states. In favoring the spread of Marxist-Leninist rule, therefore, the Soviet policy managers could not count on a pro-Soviet orientation on the part of states newly converted to Communist rule. This blow to cherished visions of international concord under socialism was only partially mitigated by the discovery that Soviet influence could expand in countries where socialism was anathema, just as—though to a much lesser degree—American influence could expand in countries where capitalism had been banished.

As in economic and military potential, so as a world power the USSR has gained substantially on the U.S. in the last three decades. At the war's end only the Soviet Union (save for the Mongolian Peo-

ple's Republic) was under the rule of a Marxist-Leninist party, and
the USSR had relatively little influence internationally beyond the
confines of Europe and Soviet border areas. In contrast, great economic and military resources gave the United States an opportunity
to exert influence on a world scale, an opportunity seized with relish.
The ensuing thirty years brought immense changes in the distribution of international power and influence. Communist rule spread
spasmodically until it extended over a vast area of the Eurasian continent from Berlin to Saigon (now Ho Chi Minh City) plus Cuba in the
Western Hemisphere. Though in Africa there are no full-fledged
Communist régimes, ruling groups friendly to Moscow and professing attachment to Marxism-Leninism have emerged in Angola, Mozambique, Ethiopia, and elsewhere.

Obviously, the spread of Communist rule was not the same thing as
the spread of Soviet influence. China is the glaring example of the
contrary, but Yugoslavia, Albania, and Cambodia also illustrate the
discrepancy. Nevertheless, all such countries, taking their distance,
sometimes an angry distance, from Moscow, have been removed
from the capitalist sphere, and thus from the sphere in which the
U.S. usually has carte blanche to establish a solid presence.

Even apart from gains derivative of Communist accessions to
power, Soviet world influence has expanded greatly, if also unevenly.
Soviet diplomatic missions, spotty outside Europe thirty years ago,
are now installed in almost as many capitals as American missions. Soviet influence in the UN has grown as the USSR emerged from isolation; simultaneously the U.S. position in the UN has weakened. The
situation in the United Nations is not representative, however, of the
international order generally, because in most affairs there is no principle of one state, one vote. Despite a rise of Soviet international
power, the United States still occupies a more dominant position than
the USSR. This is most evident in international economic affairs, such
as finance and trade. If the American economy ails, the sickness
spreads; if the Soviet economy is afflicted, the infection stops at the
border. But American preponderance goes beyond economic affairs
to include cultural, political, and other spheres.

How will the next quarter-century alter the alignment of states between those oriented toward the United States and those toward the
Soviet Union, between the capitalist and socialist areas of control? To
begin with a brief summary answer, it is probable that there will be a
further shift in the direction of the socialist and Soviet camp, though

not on the scale of the shift in the first postwar decades. The dislocations resulting from war engendered most of the post-1945 shifts, and
the assumed absence of a major war in the next quarter-century
would mean the absence of a force generating widespread political
upheavals. However, decolonization may turn out to be a similarly
upsetting force; instability has been rife in postcolonial states.

Communist successes have occurred mostly in underdeveloped
countries, a pattern first set with the Bolshevik victory in Russia, a
relatively underdeveloped great power of Europe. The well-known
link between communism and underdevelopment was reinforced, in
defiance of Marx, with the spread of Communist rule to still less industrially developed countries in Europe, Asia, and Latin America,
including semicolonial states and states freeing themselves from colonial domination.[2] The Communist appeal showed strength less in
divisive calls to the kind of class struggle emphasized in traditional
Marxism, more in calls for national unity so as to pursue struggles for
independence or autonomy from foreign control. Likewise, the appeal centered less on redistribution of income and wealth between
favored and deprived population sectors, more on programs for national development and escape from age-old backwardness and dependence on advanced countries.

The link between communism and relative or absolute underdevelopment is not likely to be broken in the coming quarter-century.
In other words, communism is unlikely to make significant headway
in the most advanced capitalist nations (the United States, Japan,
West Germany, or Great Britain) or to lose its appeal outside this
realm. The novelty of the 1970s is the broadening of the regions
where a Communist orientation looms as a possibility. This affects
countries at both the upper and lower margins of "underdevelopment." The upper margin includes countries in Europe that are
among the less advanced countries of high capitalism; the lower
margin includes, for example, African nations which are among the
least developed of the world. It is no accident that the Communist potential in Europe is strongest in the Mediterranean states of Italy,
Spain, Portugal, and Greece; nor is it entirely coincidental that all but
Italy have just emerged from long periods under anticommunist dictatorships strongly supported by the United States.

---

[2] Of Communist implantations outside Russia, only those in Czechoslovakia and
East Germany involve societies generally more advanced than the Soviet Union.

This does not mean that Communist successes are probable even in these more backward of relatively developed European countries. The bourgeois order has strong roots; not only the upper crust of society but a large middle class has strong ties to the existing order; and, finally, the United States and major West European states have economic, military, and political capabilities for intervention (and little reluctance to use such capabilities) to prevent Communists from assuming power, peacefully or otherwise. Communists in coalition reformist governments are one thing, unwelcome but tolerable; Communists in a position to undermine the capitalist order are something else again.

Even in African countries and other countries much less developed than the most backward European countries there is likely to be no sweep toward communism. The pattern is complicated, permitting no simple generalization. But postcolonial régimes congenial to the United States and to the former metropolitan powers have, on the whole, held their own in areas where independence was granted more or less peacefully. Governmental instability found expression in repeated coups and countercoups, frequently involving military officers, but left untouched the basic social structure and external orientation of the countries. In such countries no national liberation movement was tempered in armed struggle. As a result, there was no need to look for external support from the Soviet Union or other Communist states, and there was no process of internal differentiation in which pro-Western, conservative elements were marked off from radical, pro-Soviet elements.

The chances of a pro-Soviet and pro-socialist orientation were greater in areas where nationalists had to fight for independence from colonial rule or foreign domination. In French Indochina national liberation movements came under Communist leadership, but this was exceptional. In Algeria, where the similar movement did not, the newly independent country was set on a course toward socialism under radical nationalist leadership, and developed generally warm relations with the Soviet Union.

But in the southern part of the African continent the struggle against Portuguese colonial rule led to an even clearer orientation of the liberation movements toward Moscow and toward acceptance of Marxism-Leninism as the ruling ideology. Even in Angola and Mozambique, the most important countries energing from the collapse of Lisbon's empire, the leadership was not Communist and the socioeconomic order was not modeled on that of the USSR. But the USSR became the most influential external power, and quickly negotiated friendship treaties with the new states.

Moreover, prospects for Soviet and Marxist-Leninist gains looked reasonably bright in the remaining strongholds of white rule in southern Africa. In Rhodesia and Namibia (Southwest Africa) the days of white minority rule are clearly numbered, as black liberation movements using guerrilla tactics already make life uncomfortable for the authorities. A shift to black majority rule is certain to add to the pressure on the Republic of South Africa, already placed in a weakened position by the changes in Angola and Mozambique. In all these countries the Soviet Union was in a position to support, and benefit from, a shift from white to black control without the ambivalence that characterized American policy, torn between apprehensions of radical change and of again backing a losing cause.

It would be a leap in the dark to prophesy that such and such a country, whether among the less-developed of the European capitalist nations or among the semiindustrial or primitively agricultural countries of Africa, Asia, or Latin America, will "go Communist" in the next decade or quarter-century. Going Communist does not here mean merely the entry of Communist ministers into governmental cabinets; this has occurred before in various governments in Europe and elsewhere without any long-term impact on institutions or policies. The phrase implies a more fundamental break with capitalist institutions and at least the beginning of their replacement by socialist institutions.

There are good reasons for reticence. While it is possible to outline conditions propitious for a shift to a Communist, pro-Soviet orientation, the history of Communist accessions to power since 1917 reveals that there have been almost as many Communist routes to power as there have been takeovers. About all that can be said is that future revolutionary shifts, like all those after 1917, are unlikely to follow the Bolshevik pattern, and that the Soviet promotional role will, somewhat paradoxically, probably count for less than American blocking efforts. If Soviet power was decisive for the ascendancy of Communist parties in most Eastern European countries, as earlier in Outer Mongolia, the United States played a more decisive role—to the extent that foreign influence was a factor—in the establishment of Communist states in Asia, from China to Vietnam, and in Cuba. For the U.S. supported and came to be identified with colonial powers,

America's allies in NATO, or with corrupt or dictorial régimes, against which Communists or radical nationalists could organize mass support. And if in the next twenty-five years new Communist or pro-Moscow states emerge in Mediterranean Europe, Africa, or elsewhere, it seems probable that anti-U.S. sentiments, nourished by American identification with oppressive rule, will have had more causative influence than any Russian activities.

Often past situations of this kind were not to the liking of Washington authorities, who would have preferred, for example, that the Portuguese allies had ceded independence gracefully, instead of hanging on to their African possessions; who would have preferred that the Saigon ruling group had been free of corruption; and, nowadays, who would prefer that the white leaderships in southern African states make concessions to black populations by drawing them into established forms of political participation. But the United States has to take its allies where it finds them, and cannot play God, creating *de novo* the most efficient instruments for its purposes. And in the crunch the commitment to anticommunism and anti-Sovietism has usually prevailed over whatever repugnance was aroused in Washington by corruption, dictatorship, or racism.

This account of conflicting tendencies in the international rivalry of the United States and the Soviet Union, and in the related efforts to defend or extend the spheres of capitalism and socialism, leads to a conclusion previously indicated, that additional countries are almost certain to come under Communist or quasi-Communist rule in the next quarter-century. American claims to world leadership will thus suffer, and Soviet claims improve. Changes in the direction of communism are most likely in Africa and perhaps also in Asia. No one should be surprised to see by the beginning of the twenty-first century additional Communist or quasi-Communist states in Africa and Asia, in addition to those now present on the latter continent. Such Communist gains are a good deal less likely, though they cannot be ruled out, in Latin America. They are probably not to be expected in even the relatively poorer parts of Europe, and almost certainly not in the most advanced nations of Europe or North America, or in Japan.

Soviet as well as Communist gains are also to be expected, partly as a consequence of the presumed development of USSR economic and military strength to American levels. For the rise in the Soviet world position over the past years has not been wholly dependent on the spread of Communist rule. With added assets at their command,

Kremlin authorities will undoubtedly be able to make their influence felt in situations where Communist rule is not a factor, as they have in the past on Middle Eastern questions. But leftward shifts in various areas and countries are likely to have the weightiest impact on Soviet–American spheres of influence. Even if there is no automatic connection between USSR gains and gains by Communist or radical-nationalist forces, some if not all of any emerging left-oriented states are almost certain to rely on Soviet support and to welcome close ties with the USSR—political, military, or economic, or all three.

Objections may be raised to this all-too-summary analysis indicating the probability of a further shift in the world balance of forces favoring the USSR rather than the United States. These anticipations concern human affairs, not geological processes immune from human control. Why should not the United States avoid what destiny has cooked up? Cannot Americans, seeing their lead slip, summon up reserves of strength and wisdom and "Try Harder"? Similar questions can be posed about the Soviet Union. May not it bungle favorable chances or, alternatively, make more startling gains than the modest ones suggested? In brief, is the prospect inevitable?

The answer must be a ringing "Yes and No!" Policies can be changed, within limits; leaders can be replaced by others who are wiser (or more foolish) or who take different tacks. But societies, like the American and Soviet, are organized in certain ways that change only slowly except in revolutionary periods; they concentrate power and influence in certain sectors and not in others; they engender certain courses of action and not others. A constellation of political-economic forces in each system establishes the orbit within which national policy is made and the leadership moves. And in both systems the boundaries are reinforced by the dominant ideologies.

In foreign policy the boundaries of the feasible are narrow enough to rule out all sorts of theoretical possibilities. In America, for example, a president has only limited freedom of maneuver in regard to foreign policy, despite the fact that his constitutional prerogatives are immense. In practice he must tailor policy to satisfy important American interest groups who have a stake, sometimes a very large stake, in policy concerning various geographical areas or functional issues. Their interests may diverge, thereby widening an administration's room for maneuver. But no president can afford to ignore such interests, because they have clout in the bureaucracy, Congress, and communications media. Although the top Soviet leadership and the party general secretary probably have greater autonomy, similar systemic limitations on policy choices operate within the Soviet system as well. In fact, the existence of such systemic limitations in both countries is the principal, though not the sole, reason for the large element of consistency in Soviet and American foreign policy over the postwar years, despite shifts in the top leadership which brought rather varied types of persons to the fore. As long as these rival systems continue without major transformation, therefore, it can only be expected that the strengths and weaknesses, the policy preferences and antipathies, they have displayed in the past quarter-century will continue to be manifest in the next.

IDEOLOGICAL PROSPECTS

The prospects for a further shift in the world balance of forces pertain fully as much to Soviet–American ideological struggle as to other arenas of contest. Whether the view focuses on the competition between these ideologies as totalities, or on key propositions discussed earlier, the verdict is the same: the Marxism-Leninism propounded by the USSR has gained adherents over the liberal capitalist ideology backed by the U.S.

In part, the diffusion of Marxism-Leninism has been a direct result of the spread of Communist rule to additional areas in 1945–1975. Whatever else Communist leaders did on coming into power, they placed a high priority on achievement of an ideological monopoly and on thorough indoctrination of their populations. But this is not the whole story, because Marxism also made inroads in societies where Communists were not in power, where they constituted a substantial or tiny minority, even where they had to function underground.

The rise in influence of Marxism-Leninism will no doubt continue in the next quarter-century, and not only as a result of gains to Communists in control of territory and population, if such gains are realized as foreseen. Détente has facilitated the spread of Marxism-Leninism in the more or less advanced industrial nations—if often a Marxism diverging from Soviet orthodoxy—because relaxation of Western governmental hostility to the socialist East made it more difficult to maintain a quarantine on the ruling ideology of the area. In the less-developed world it is the popularity of antiimperialism that facilitates the spread of Marxism-Leninism, the only current ideology to accord imperialism a central place in its description of the twentieth-century world.

The rival American theory which depicts the world as split between totalitarian and free states, in essence, between Communist and non-Communist, never had much resonance outside the advanced industrial countries where capitalism could deliver the goods, i.e., a relative abundance of worldly goods. The theory of the free world vs. totalitarianism had nothing to offer peoples struggling for independence or for escape from backwardness except the assurance that they were already free, and the warning that the only danger confronting them came from internal or external communism. Even in the United States and its allies among advanced capitalist countries the theory lost popularity as the cold war waned. Its prospects of acceptance in the coming decades do not look promising, either, though U.S. ideologists have found no substitute to promote.

Apart from the free world vs. totalitarianism formula, the main postulates of American ideology have lesser relevance than those of Soviet ideology to the circumstances of nations facing enormous development tasks. U.S. ideology centers on individual initiative, individual or private ownership, individual expression, with the corollary that freedom is identified with absence of governmental interference, whether in economic affairs, political organization, or the communication of ideas and information. Such emphases have appeal to the populations of highly advanced countries, though they are challenged even there. But for many societies these prescriptions are irrelevant or dysfunctional: they do not speak to their major problems. Economically weak countries, agricultural or semiindustrial, cannot hope to compete successfully with advanced capitalist powers in their own markets, let alone on world markets, yet they are advised to give free rein to foreign as well as indigenous capital. Economically, the prospect that adherence to American precepts lays before them is not of independent development but of perpetuation of their status as raw material appendages of the developed world. Politically, also, the American emphasis on pluralism and diversity runs counter to aspirations for national unity, regarded as essential both to protect their autonomy against powerful external forces and to facilitate programs of national development.

These American vulnerabilities on the ideological front should not obscure difficulties attending Soviet efforts to achieve worldwide adherence to the Kremlin's version of Marxism. The divisions that have sapped Communist unity mean that the gospel according to Moscow will continue to be challenged by other versions. Soviet Marxism looks very different from the Maoist ideology of China, and the Maoist is only one, though the most important, of the Communist ideologies diverging from the Russian. Just as Communist accessions to power do not automatically add to Soviet influence, so the diffusion of Marxism-Leninism does not necessarily carry with it gains for the Soviet version of the ideology.

Ideological fragmentation appears to be on the rise in the Communist movement; almost every party, from the very important to the most miniscule, now seeks to define a unique "personality" distinct from and sometimes counter to the Soviet model. It is possible that the coming period will see some reunification as well as further splintering, but it is impossible to imagine a restoration of an ideologically harmonized Communist world. Obviously there is also ideological diversity among and within capitalist nations, but this does not damage U.S. leadership in the way that divergence of doctrine among Communist states and parties damages the Soviet cause. For the USSR strains for monolithic unity, while the United States advertises its toleration of ideological pluralism, though the toleration stops short of subversive, i.e., Communist, ideology.

In addition to rival Marxist orthodoxies outside the country, the USSR also has to contend with challenges to the reigning ideology from within the country. And in some respects the problem these pose has become more acute. In the early years of Bolshevik rule opposition manifestations could be explained as phenomena of not-yet-concluded class warfare. But sixty years after the Revolution their persistence is an embarrassment, if not a threat, to a leadership celebrating the maturity of the socialist order. Rejection of Soviet socialism, Soviet institutions, Soviet policies cannot easily be attributed to class antagonisms, supposedly long departed from the scene along with the exploiting classes that nourished opposition to the new order. They cannot even be explained as a reaction to the mistakes and crimes of Stalin, if such an explanation were not ruled out on other grounds. Stalin has been dead for a quarter-century and, in most cases, present-day oppositionists focus on post-Stalin practices, not primarily those of the "cult of personality."

The Soviet leadership is thus faced with a choice of almost equally unpleasant and damaging alternatives. It can step up repression of dissidents internally and clamp down on channels of communication with the outside world; the price is to display the régime's failure to enjoy the wholehearted support of the population and its need to rely on compulsion. If, however, it lightens pressure on dissidents internally and allows relatively free external communications, then dissidents can gain additional circulation inside and outside the country for expression of anti-Soviet and anti-Communist ideology.

In fact, the leadership has vacillated between the two courses without achieving any solution to the problem. And the problem has been rendered more difficult for the régime by the efforts of Western European Communist parties, on the one hand, and of adversary states like the U.S., on the other, to make use of the situation to promote their own purposes. Still, these various difficulties encountered by the Soviet Union on the ideological front should not be given exaggerated importance. The Soviet order faces no possibility of being swept away under the influence of an anticommunist ideology defiantly propagated by a small group of dissidents. And while the image of the USSR may suffer in the leading capitalist counries, Soviet chances of promoting the Moscow version of Marxism-Leninism in the world contest of ideologies will be largely unaffected save in Europe and the Americas. In most areas and among most peoples of the world there are more pressing concerns than the right of emigration from the Soviet Union or the right to express hostility to socialism.

CHALLENGES TO SOVIET AND AMERICAN LEADERSHIP

A discussion of American–Soviet rivalry and prospects for the next quarter-century cannot pass silently by the possibility that another state or group of states may challenge Soviet and American dominance. The obvious candidates are China, Japan, and the Western European countries forming the European Economic Community. This is not to say that a so-called north–south division may not place the most developed capitalist and Communist states in opposition on certain issues to less-developed countries predominant in the Southern Hemisphere. But the latter group cannot exert unified power, except in the most special circumstances, and lack the economic, military, and political capabilities to radiate influence on a worldwide scale.

Of these possible challengers to U.S.–Soviet world leadership, China under Communist rule presents the greatest difficulty for assessment. China has long been a great power *manqué*. With its large territory and enormous population, China certainly has the potential for superpower status, and has made some strides on the route, notably by entering the exclusive club of states possessing nuclear weapons. The precondition for China to become a center for the radiation of power was realized after World War II when the Communist conquest of power unified mainland China under a single system of authority for the first time in ages. Simultaneously, the Chinese authorites were able to oust from their strongholds the foreign powers, including Russia and the United States, whose position had given the country a semicolonial status.

But China is the least developed economically of the contenders for world primacy, and this backwardness is only partially compensated by China's mass. The Chinese Communists under Mao Tse-tung inherited this economic backwardness, but fits and starts of party politics and party policies since 1949 have impeded progress in overcoming it. Consequently, present-day China is not as yet able to exert strong military, political, or economic influence on a world scale, that is, far from its periphery. Given its present level of industry and agriculture, and the uncertainty of chances for rapid modernization, China will probably require more than the next quarter-century to emerge as a genuine superpower on the American–Soviet level.

Japan, unlike China, is a great power déclassé, remembered for if not remembering its one-time domination of almost all the Asian rimlands of the Pacific Ocean. Japan, unlike Western Europe, faces no problem of unification; the Japanese state has a long history of control over the home islands, and the Japanese political-economic order was subject to less upheaval as a result of the war than that of China or even of Germany, the most important country in the European Economic Community. But postwar Japanese efforts have gone almost exclusively into economic recovery and development. The rapidity of this development has allowed Japan to rival, in different ways, both the Soviet Union and the United States as an economic power; it ranks a respectable third behind the two. Nevertheless, it is a somewhat fragile economy, more vulnerable to international upsets than either the American or Soviet economy. Because of this vulnerability, and because Japan has virtually renounced ambitions for great-power political or military status, postwar conservative governments in Japan have relied almost entirely on the United States for military security and political leadership. This could change, of course, and indeed would have to change if Japan were to strike a course in international affairs independent of the United States. Even if that were to occur, and there are no signs of Japanese ambitions for independent great-power status outside the economic sphere, certain vulnerabilities would continue to limit the Japanese challenge to the U.S. or the USSR.

Although the Western European states of the European Economic Community cover the most highly developed area of the world, and have considerable potential in the military and political fields, they cannot maneuver on the international scene as a unified whole. The weakness is in organization rather than resources. Economic unification is still limited, even fragile; there is an almost complete absence of political integration; and the grouping as such has no military capabilities. The whole is less, a good deal less, than the sum of the individual parts. And resistance to integration within this group of nine long-established nations with proud individual traditions is so strong as to make unlikely any quantum leaps toward creation of a single Western European power.

In view of the above, it is China which can mount a challenge to the present world leaders, and it is Russia which is immediately menaced by the possible Chinese challenge. Western Europe and Japan have remained generally in the American orbit and almost wholly dependent militarily on the U.S. China, in contrast, has not only asserted an independence of the Soviet Union economically, politically, and militarily, but has made the USSR its prime enemy.

The United States, in contrast, is not immediately threatened by any Chinese ambitions. The United States has increasingly received support from China, because of Peking's anti-Soviet orientation, on U.S. positions regarding international issues centering not only on Asia but as to Europe, Latin America, and Africa; specifically, the U.S. maintenance of a worldwide system of military bases and alliances has received Chinese endorsement. On issues concerning Angola or Egypt, for example, Washington can be more certain of Peking's support than the support of formal allies.

But Washington cannot be entirely nonchalant about a future challenge from a rising China to the dominance of the present superpowers, feeling that only Moscow need worry. The Chinese Communists were not always pro-American and anti-Soviet, and the present orientation is not necessarily permanent. It might be argued, even, that in historical perspective the net effect of Communist control of China has probably been more adverse to the U.S. than to the USSR. Its most profound effect was to close the open door to China for direct U.S. investment, trade, and influence that Washington had long sought to maintain and widen. The door was shut on Russia, too, with an even louder slam, but the interests affected were of more marginal importance to the USSR than to the U.S. Elsewhere in Asia, also, the Chinese authorities have played a part in frustrating American objectives, in Korea in the early 1950s and, to a much smaller degree, in Vietnam in the 1960s.

Moreover, questions of China's orientation toward the Soviet Union and toward "imperialism," i.e., the United States, appear to have been involved in leadership crises concerning, first, China's president, Liu Shao-chi, then Lin Piao, the erstwhile successor to Mao Tse-tung, and more recently Teng Hsiao-ping, putative inheritor of Chou En-lai's post as premier. There is much that is murky about all these affairs, and the net result was a hardening of China's anti-Soviet orientation. Nevertheless, they suggest that it is still too early to assume a permanent orientation of China's policy in favor of the United States and its allies and in stark opposition to the USSR and its allies.

CONCLUSION

The shift in U.S.–USSR correlations of strength over three postwar decades has been absorbed without major repercussions and without heightening interstate tensions. Indeed, Soviet–American relations improved as the USSR narrowed the large end-of-war gap in economic, military, and other capabilities. That shift occurred simultaneously, however, with a very marked expansion of both countries' power potential (partly at the expense of other countries), a circumstance that might, but need not, recur. The shift also left the United States well ahead of the Soviet Union at the end of the period in all areas of competition save rivalry in military power. That, too, may not be true, or as true, of the anticipated situation at the beginning of the twenty-first century.

Nations, like individuals, must learn to absorb losses as well as gains, defeats as well as victories, and the lessons are not necessarily easier in the one case than in the other. Dizziness from success, engendering national hubris, may be as dangerous for the future welfare of a country (and other countries as well!) as frustration over failure, engendering irrational impulses for retaliation. National rivalries, however, work themselves out slowly, unless they eventuate in war, a receding but not absent prospect in the Soviet–American contest. Gradualness thus cushions whatever tremors are produced by changes in strength ratios.

However, any shocks are almost certain to result not from long-term trends as such, no matter how clearly apprehended, but from specific episodes in the relations of the two countries that display shifts in their relative capabilities, whether the episodes involve military, scientific, economic, or political activities. Therein lies the hazard inevitably associated with the changing fortunes of rival states, each armed to the teeth, each confident of its strength, each secure in the rightness of its cause.

But it is impossible to foresee U.S. and Soviet responses at some time in the future to developments that have not yet occurred. This work on U.S.–USSR rivalry has focused mainly on past developments, that is, from the end of World War II to 1975, in some of the crucial spheres of competition. It would be surprising if the evaluation offered of the direction and extent of changes in the two countries' competitive standing were to command universal agreement, not least because the topics engage deep sympathies and antipathies, strong hopes and fears. The sketch in this chapter of the probable state of Soviet–American rivalry in the next quarter-century is still more hazardous, and more open to challenge by other anticipations of the future.

BIBLIOGRAPHY

Abendroth, Wolfgang. *A Short History of the European Working Class*. New York: Monthly Review Press, 1972.

Adler-Karlsson, Gunnar. *Western Economic Warfare, 1947–1967: A Case Study in Foreign Economic Policy*. Stockholm: Almqvist and Wiksell, 1968.

Adler, Lester K., and Paterson, Thomas G. "Red Fascism: The Merger of Nazi Germany and Soviet Russia in the American Image of Totalitarianism, 1930's–1950's." *American Historical Review*, 75, no. 4 (April 1970): 1046–64.

Agency for International Development, U.S. *US Overseas Loans and Grants: July 1, 1945–June 30, 1973*. Washington, D.C.: AID, 1974.

Allison, Graham T. *Essence of Decision: Explaining the Cuban Missile Crisis*. Boston: Little, Brown and Company, 1971.

Angell, Robert C., and Singer, J. David. "Social Values and Foreign Policy Attitudes of Soviet and American Elites." *Journal of Conflict Resolution*, 8 (December 1964): 329–491.

Arblaster, Anthony. "Liberal Values and Socialist Values." In *Socialist Register 1972*, edited by Ralph Miliband and John Savile, pp. 83–104. London: The Merlin Press, 1972.

Arendt, Hannah. *The Origins of Totalitarianism*. New York: Harcourt, Brace & World, 1951; new ed., 1966.

Arms Control and Disarmament Administration, U.S. *Arms Control and Disarmament Agreements*. Washington, D.C.: ACDA, 1975.

———. *International Transfer of Conventional Arms*. Washington, D.C.: GPO, 1974.

———. *World Military Expenditures and Arms Trade, 1963–1973*. Washington, D.C.: ACDA, 1974.

Baskin, Darryl. *American Pluralist Democracy: A Critique*. New York: Van Nostrand, Reinhold Company, 1971.

Bell, Coral. *Negotiation from Strength: A Study in the Politics of Power.* New York: Alfred A. Knopf, 1963.

Bell, Daniel. *The End of Ideology.* Rev. ed. New York: Collier Books, 1962.

Bergson, Abram. "Toward a New Growth Model." *Problems of Communism,* no. 2 (March–April 1973), pp. 1–9.

————. "Development under Two Systems: Comparative Productivity Growth since 1950." *World Politics,* 23, no. 4 (July 1971).

Bloomfield, Lincoln P.; Clemens, Walter C., Jr.; and Griffiths, Franklyn. *Khrushchev and the Arms Race: Soviet Interests in Arms Control and Disarmament, 1954–1964.* Cambridge, Mass.: M.I.T. Press, 1966.

Brzezinski, Zbigniew. *Between Two Ages: America's Role in the Technetronic Era.* New York: Viking Press, 1970.

————, and Huntington, Samuel P. *Political Power: USA/USSR.* New York: Viking Press, 1963.

Buchheim, Hans. *Totalitarian Rule: Its Nature and Characteristics.* Middletown, Conn.: Wesleyan University Press, 1968.

Bull, Hedley. *The Control of the Arms Race.* 2nd ed. New York: Praeger, 1965.

Burlatskii, F. M. *Lenin, Gosudarstvo, Politika.* Moscow: 'Nauka,' 1970.

Burrowes, Robert. "Totalitarianism: The Revised Standard Version." *World Politics,* 21, no. 2 (January 1969): 272–94.

Carral, Jean. *La prise du pouvoir mondial: Vers la domination Americano-Sovietique de la planète.* Paris: Editions Denoël, 1971.

Carter, James Richard. *The Net Cost of Soviet Foreign Aid.* New York: Praeger Publishers, 1971.

Central Intelligence Agency, U.S. *The Soviet Economy: Performance in 1975 and Prospects for 1976.* Washington, D.C.: CIA, May 1976.

————. *A Dollar Comparison of Soviet and US Defense Activities, 1965–1975.* Washington, D.C.: CIA, February 1976.

————. *Estimated Soviet Defense Spending in Rubles, 1970–1975.* Washington, D.C.: CIA, May 1976.

————. *Handbook of Economic Statistics, 1975.* Washington, D.C.: CIA, August 1975.

Clayton, James L., ed. *The Economic Impact of the Cold War: Sources and Readings.* New York: Harcourt, Brace & World, 1970.

Cohn, Helen Desfosses. "Soviet-American Relations and the African Arena." *Survey,* no. 1 (Winter 1973), pp. 147–64.

Cohn, Stanley H. *Economic Development in the Soviet Union.* Lexington, Mass.: D. C. Heath and Company, 1970.

Collins, John M., and Chwat, John Steven. *The United States/Soviet Military Balance.* Washington, D.C.: Library of Congress, 1976.

Dallin, Alexander, and Larson, Thomas B., eds. *Soviet Politics Since Khrushchev*. Englewood Cliffs, N.J.: Prentice-Hall, Inc., 1968.

Dukes, Paul. *The Emergence of the Superpowers: A Short Comparative History of the USA and the USSR*. New York and Evanston, Ill.: Harper and Row, 1970.

Duncan, W. Raymond, ed. *Soviet Policy in Developing Countries*. Waltham, Mass.: Ginn-Blaisdell, 1970.

Edwards, Richard C.; Reich, Michael; and Weisskopf, Thomas I.; eds. *The Capitalist System*. Englewood Cliffs, N.J.: Prentice-Hall, Inc., 1972.

Eissenstat, Bernard W., ed. *The Soviet Union: The Seventies and Beyond*. Lexington, Mass.: D. C. Heath and Company, 1975.

Erickson, John, ed. *The Military-Technical Revolution*. New York: Frederick A. Praeger, 1966.

Feinstein, C. H., ed. *Socialism, Capitalism and Economic Growth: Essays Presented to Maurice Dobb*. Cambridge: Cambridge University Press, 1967.

Feis, Herbert. *From Trust to Terror: The Onset of the Cold War, 1945–1950*. New York: W. W. Norton & Co., 1970.

Franck, Thomas M., and Weisband, Edward. *Verbal Strategy Among the Superpowers*. New York: Oxford University Press, 1972.

Friedrich, Carl J., ed. *Totalitarianism*. Cambridge, Mass.: Harvard University Press, 1954.

————, and Brzezinski, Zbigniew. *Totalitarian Dictatorship and Autocracy*. Cambridge, Mass.: Harvard University Press, 1956; 2nd ed., revised by C. J. Friedrich, 1965.

————. *Man and His Government: An Empirical Theory of Politics*. New York: McGraw-Hill Book Co., 1963.

————; Curtis, Michael; and Barber, Benjamin R. *Totalitarianism in Perspective: Three Views*. New York: Praeger Publishers, 1969.

Gaddis, John Lewis. *The United States and the Origins of the Cold War, 1941–1947*. New York: Columbia University Press, 1972.

Gillison, Jerome M. *British and Soviet Politics*. Baltimore and London: The Johns Hopkins University Press, 1972.

Glezerman, G., and Kursanov, G., eds. *Historical materialism: Basic problems*. Moscow: Progress Publishers, 1968.

Goldmann, Kjell. "East-West Tension in Europe, 1946–1970: A Conceptual Analysis and a Quantitative Description." *World Politics*, 26, no. 1 (October 1973): 106–25.

Gouré, Leon, et al. *Convergence of Communism and Capitalism: The Soviet View*. Miami: Center for Advanced International Studies, 1973.

Gregory, Paul. *Socialist and Nonsocialist Industrialization Patterns: A Comparative Appraisal.* New York: Praeger Publishers, 1970.

Griffith, William E. *Cold War and Coexistence: Russia, China and the United States.* Englewood Cliffs, N.J.: Prentice-Hall, Inc., 1971.

Herrick, Robert W. *Soviet Naval Strategy: Fifty Years of Theory and Practice.* Annapolis: U.S. Naval Institute, 1968.

Hollander, Gayle Durham. *Soviet Political Indoctrination: Developments in Mass Media and Propaganda Since Stalin.* New York: Praeger Publishers, 1972.

Hollander, Paul, ed. *American and Soviet Society: A Reader in Comparative Sociology and Perception.* Englewood Cliffs, N.J.: Prentice-Hall, Inc., 1969.

————. *Soviet and American Society.* New York: Oxford University Press, 1973.

Iakovlev, A. N., ed. *SShA: Ot "Velikogo" k bol'nomu.* Moscow: Izdat. Polit. Literatury, 1969.

————. *Ideologiia Amerikanskoi "Imperii": Problemy voiny, mira i mezhdunarodnykh otnoshenii v poslevoennoi amerikanskoi burzhuaznoi politicheskoi literature.* Moscow: 'Mysl', 1967.

International Institute for Strategic Studies, London. *The Military Balance, 1976–1977.* London: IISS, 1976. (Annual review)

Jensen, Lloyd. *The Postwar Disarmament Negotiations: A Study in American–Soviet Bargaining Behavior.* Ann Arbor, Mich.: Center for Research on Conflict Resolution, 1962.

Joint Economic Committee, U.S. Congress. *Dimensions of Soviet Economic Power.* Washington, D.C.: Government Printing Office 1962.

————. *Economic Performance and the Military Burden in the Soviet Union.* Washington: GPO, 1970.

————. *Soviet Economic Prospects for the Seventies.* Washington: GPO, 1972.

————. *Soviet Economy in a New Perspective.* Washington: GPO, 1976.

Joshua, Wynfred, and Gibert, Stephen P. *Arms for the Third World: Soviet Military Aid Diplomacy.* Baltimore: The Johns Hopkins University Press, 1969.

Jukes, Geoffrey. *The Soviet Union in Asia.* Sydney: Angus and Robertson, 1973.

Julien, Claude. *America's Empire.* New York: Pantheon Books, 1971.

Juviler, Peter H., and Morton, Henry W., eds. *Soviet Policy-Making.* New York: Frederick A. Praeger, 1967.

Kalenskii, V. G. *Politicheskaia Nauka v SShA (Kritika burzhuaznykh kontseptsii vlasti).* Moscow: 'Iuridicheskaia Literatura,' 1969.

Kennan, George F. *Russia and the West under Lenin and Stalin*. Boston: Little, Brown and Company, 1960.

Kiernan, Bernard P. *The United States, Communism, and the Emergent World*. Bloomington, Ind., and London: Indiana University Press, 1972.

Kim, Young Hum. *Patterns of Competitive Coexistence: USA vs. USSR*. New York: G. P. Putnam's Sons, 1966.

Kolko, Gabriel. *The Roots of American Foreign Policy*. Boston: Beacon Press, 1969.

Krasin, Y. *Lenin, Revolution, and the World Today*. Moscow: Progress Publishers, 1971.

LaFeber, Walter. *America, Russia and the Cold War, 1945–1966*. New York: John Wiley and Sons, 1967.

Larson, Thomas B. *Disarmament and Soviet Policy, 1964–1968*. Englewood Cliffs, N.J.: Prentice-Hall, Inc., 1969.

Liston, Robert A. *The United States and the Soviet Union: A Background Book on the Struggle for Power*. New York: Parents' Magazine Press, 1973.

Luard, Evan, ed. *The Cold War: A Re-appraisal*. New York: Praeger, 1964.

Maddison, Angus. *Economic Growth in Japan and the USSR*. New York: W. W. Norton & Company, 1969.

Mattick, Paul. *Marx and Keynes: The Limits of the Mixed Economy*. Boston: Porter Sargent Publisher, 1969.

Mehlinger, Howard D. *The Study of Totalitarianism: An Inductive Approach*. Washington, D.C.: National Council for the Social Studies, 1965.

Naess, Arne. *Democracy, Ideology and Objectivity: Studies in the Semantics and Cognitive Analysis of Ideological Controversy*. Oslo: Oslo University Press, 1956.

Narodnoye Khozyaistvo SSSR, 1922–1972 gg. Iubileinyi Statisticheskii Yezhegodnik. Moscow: 'Statistika,' 1973.

Narodnoye Khozyaistvo SSSR v 1975 g. Moscow: 'Statistika,' 1976. (Annual volume)

Oxenfeldt, Alfred R., and Holubnychy, Vsevolod. *Economic Systems in Action: The United States, the Soviet Union, and France*. 3rd ed. New York: Holt, Rinehart & Winston, 1965.

Parker, W. H. *The Superpowers: The United States and the Soviet Union Compared*. New York: John Wiley and Sons, 1972.

Parkin, Frank. *Class Inequality and Political Order: Social Stratification in Capitalist and Communist Societies*. London: MacGibbon & Kee, 1971.

Paterson, Thomas G. *Soviet–American Confrontation: Postwar Reconstruction and the Origins of the Cold War*. Baltimore and London: The Johns Hopkins University Press, 1972.

Peterson, Peter G. *U.S.–Soviet Commercial Relationships in a New Era.* Washington, D.C.: Department of Commerce, 1972.

Ponomarev, Boris P., ed. *Istoriia Vneshnei Politiki SSSR, 1917–1970 gg.*, II: *1945–1970 gg.* Moscow: 'Nauka,' 1971.

Problemy Demokratii v Sovremennom mire. Moscow: 'Mezhdunarodnye Otnosheniia,' 1967.

Rapoport, Anatol. *The Big Two: Soviet–American Perceptions of Foreign Policy.* New York: Pegasus (Bobbs-Merrill Co.), 1971.

Roberts, Henry L. *Russia and America: Dangers and Prospects.* New York: Harper & Brothers, 1956.

Rosen, Steven, ed. *Testing the Theory of the Military-Industrial Complex.* Lexington, Mass.: D. C. Heath and Company, 1973.

Rossides, Daniel W. *The American Class System.* Boston: Houghton, Mifflin Co., 1976.

Sarkisyan, G. S. *Uroven', Tempy i Proportsii Rosta Real'nykh Dokhodov pri Sotsializma.* Moscow: 'Ekonomika,' 1972.

Shershnev, Ye. S. "K istorii Sovetsko-Amerikanskikh ekonomicheskikh otnoshenii." *Voprosy Istorii*, no. 1 (1973), pp. 19–29.

Shulman, Marshall D. *Stalin's Foreign Policy Reappraised.* Cambridge, Mass.: Harvard University Press, 1963.

SSSR, SShA, i Razoruzhenie. Edited by I. S. Glagolev. Moscow: 'Nauka,' 1967.

Stanley, John, and Pearton, Maurice. *The International Trade in Arms.* New York: Praeger Publishers, 1972.

State, Department of, U.S. *The Planetary Product at Near Zero Growth in 1975.* (By Herbert Block.) Washington, D.C.: Department of State, March 1977. (Annual report)

Tansky, Leo. *U.S. and U.S.S.R. Aid to Developing Countries: A Comparative Study of India, Turkey, and the U.A.R.* New York: Frederick A. Praeger, 1967.

Thurow, Lester C., and Lucas, Robert E. B. *The American Distribution of Income: A Structural Problem.* (Prepared for the Joint Economic Committee of the U.S. Congress.) Washington, D.C.: Government Printing Office, 1972.

Triska, Jan F., and Finley, David D. *Soviet Foreign Policy.* New York: The Macmillan Co., 1968.

Tucker, Robert C. *A Preface to U.S. Policy toward Russia.* Santa Monica, Calif.: The Rand Corporation, 1958.

Turgeon, Lynn. *The Contrasting Economies: A Study of Modern Economic Systems.* Boston: Allyn and Bacon, Inc., 1963.

Ulam, Adam. *The Rivals: America and Russia Since World War II*. New York: Viking, 1971.

Vladimirov, B. "Polveka ekonomicheskogo sorevnovaniya dvukh sistem," *Kommunist*, no. 1, 1968.

Walters, Robert S. *American and Soviet Aid: A Comparative Analysis*. Pittsburgh: University of Pittsburgh Press, 1970.

Weeks, Albert L. *The Other Side of Coexistence: An Analysis of Russian Foreign Policy*. New York: Pitman Publishing Corp., 1970.

Welch, William. *American Images of Soviet Foreign Policy*. New Haven: Yale University Press, 1970.

Wiles, Peter J. D. *Communist International Economics*. Oxford: Basil Blackwell, 1968.

Wolfe, Thomas W. *Soviet Power and Europe, 1945–1970*. Baltimore and London: The Johns Hopkins University Press, 1970.

Wolfgang, Marvin I., ed. *USA–USSR: Agenda for Communication*. Philadelphia: Annals of the American Academy of Political and Social Science, July 1974.

Zinn, Howard. *Postwar America: 1945–1971*. Indianapolis and New York: The Bobbs-Merrill Co., 1973.

INDEX

ABMs (antiballistic missiles), 168, 184, 201
Acheson, Dean, 6, 148, 154, 156, 240
Adenauer, Konrad, 241
Africa:
  colonial issue in, 153–54, 218, 280, 282
  Communists in, 279, 280–81, 282
  Soviet–U.S. relations and, 249–50
Afro-Asian bloc, UN, 237, 238
agricultural labor force:
  income of, 50–51, 58
  productivity of, 37, 46, 49
  reduction of, 46–48, 267
agricultural output, 17, 45–52, 267
  explanations of Soviet lag in, 49–52
  labor productivity in, 37, 46, 49, 268
  machinery in, 48, 50, 51, 268
  surplus in, 49–50, 65
  U.S. industrialization and, 51
  before World War I, 24–25
agriculture:
  climate and, 17, 48
  collectivization of, 25–26, 27, 39, 46, 48,
    49–51, 58
  investment in, 46, 48, 53
  market forces in, 45–46, 49
  organizational differences in, 45–52
  post-Stalin expansion of, 46, 50–51
  Soviet dependence on, 37, 39, 46
  table, 47
  in world capitalist depression, 25
air power, aircraft, 170, 171, 172, 189,
    190, 192, 193, 195, 204, 246, 274
  see also bombers, long-range
Albania, 70, 235, 278
Algeria, 230, 250, 280
Allende, Salvador, 227–28, 229, 249
alliances, 61, 168, 206–11

in Europe, 187–91, 207
ideological rivalry in, 232–35
political aspects of, 232–39
purposes and role of, 187–88, 206–7
superpower advantages in, 235–36
Americanization, 21–22
Angola, 13, 250, 280–81, 289
Antarctic Treaty (1959), 198, 199
anticommunism, 132, 192–93
  in U.S. policy-making, 110, 113,
    147–48, 222, 244–46, 247–49, 258,
    282
Arab-Israeli conflict, 196, 208, 238–39,
    251
Arendt, Hannah, 149, 150–51
arms limitations, 9–10, 196–206
  "atmospheric" agreements on, 261
  budgetary ceilings and, 197
  for European theater, 202–5
  on globally mobile forces, 205–6
  strategic, 198–202, 205–6, 255–56
arms transfers, 13, 211–14, 251
Asia:
  rise of Communist rule in, 277–82
  Soviet–U.S. relations and, 243–49, 276,
    281
assassinations, political, 27, 229
atomic bomb attacks (1945), 3, 8, 179, 184
atomic weapons, 168, 170, 179–80, 252
  "Baruch Plan" and, 179
authoritarian rule, totalitarianism vs.,
    152–53
automobile ownership, 53–54

Backfire bombers, 201
Baghdad Pact (1955), 208
Berlin issue, 173, 241–42, 255

bipolarity, 5–6, 219–20
blacks, 14, 110, 111, 122, 127, 155–56
    in African states, 124, 153–54, 250, 281,
    282
Bohlen, Charles E., 149
Bolshevik Revolution, *see* October Rev-
    olution
Bolshevism, 21, 217
    early U.S. views on, 3–4, 6
    Russian–American rivalry affected by,
    26–27
    see also Communists, communism
bombers, long-range (strategic), 167, 170,
    180, 183–84, 186, 200, 201, 212
"bourgeois" institutions, society, 119, 124,
    125, 127, 157, 158, 226, 277, 280
Brandt, Willy, 242, 253
Brezhnev, Leonid, 31, 46, 94, 98, 99, 165,
    181, 186, 200, 201, 202, 223, 240,
    255, 256
Brzezinski, Zbigniew, 116n, 126, 149,
    150, 158, 162–63

Cambodia, 193, 213, 246, 248, 276, 278
Canada, 17, 18, 61, 203, 256
capital investment, 46, 48, 53, 267, 268
capitalism:
    "imperialism" and, 157–60, 165–66
    inequalities justified in, 55–56
    international role of, 59–60, 61
    political pluralism and, 83–84
    prospects for, 270–72
capitalist classes, 140
    political domination by, 89–91, 128–29
capitalist countries, advanced, 38, 42, 57,
    59, 69, 75, 83, 159, 160, 231, 232,
    240, 263, 279, 284, 285
capitalist institutions, 28, 112, 117, 187
capitalist-socialist rivalry, 159–60, 165,
    193–94, 226–28, 231–32, 242, 264,
    266, 277–83
    alliances in, 232–36
    economic achievements and, 35, 55,
    74–77, 272
    see also ideological rivalry
Castro, Fidel, 69, 223, 229, 234n, 249
censorship, government, 29–30, 105, 138,
    140
chemical-biological weapons, convention
    on (1972), 199, 204
Chiang Kai-shek, 224
Chile, 69, 227–28, 229, 230, 249

China, nationalist, 224, 237
Chinese People's Republic (CPR), 118,
    149, 237, 243, 244, 245, 247, 286
    leadership role of, 287–88, 289–90
    Soviet economic role in, 66, 70
    as Soviet rival, 5, 66, 168, 173, 209,
    219–20, 222, 247, 253–54, 275, 278,
    289–90
    U.S. rapprochement with, 209–10, 222,
    247, 248, 249
Chou En-lai, 290
CIA (Central Intelligence Agency), 175,
    176, 214
civic indoctrination, 103–8
civil liberties (political rights), 29–30, 102,
    123, 131, 134, 135, 136, 143
Civil War, U.S., 27
class dictatorship, 125
classes, class structure, 86–91, 103, 135,
    159n
    capitalist, 140, 89–91, 128–29
    elections and, 90, 91, 128–29
    proletariat, 28, 87–89, 125, 126–27
classless societies, 124
class struggle, 28, 87, 286
    human rights and, 131–32
climate, economic effects of, 17–18, 48
coexistence, 252–61
    ideological rivalry vs., 162–66
    see also arms limitations; trade, East-
    West
"cold war," 9, 110, 148, 162, 226, 252, 254,
    256, 258
collectivization, *see* agriculture
colonial rule, 152, 153–54, 218, 231, 238,
    240, 249–50, 262, 279, 280, 281–82
Cominform, 160n, 222
commodity production (*table*), 44
communications media, 83, 93, 257
    control of, 90–91, 110, 116, 141
    in ideological rivalry, 112, 116, 286–87
    indoctrinational role of, 85, 103, 105–7,
    111
Communist-led countries, 60–61, 62, 75n,
    83, 147, 149–50, 209, 231
    economic warfare on, 67–69
    Soviet aid to, 63–64, 244
    Soviet economic pressures on, 69–70
    spread of, 277–83, 284
Communist parties, indigenous, 223, 224,
    225
Communist party, Soviet (CPSU), 21,
    28–29, 79, 80, 112

Central Committee of, 88, 91–92
general secretary of, 78, 91, 92, 93, 94, 95–96, 283–84
image of unity in, 82–83
indigenous CPs linked with, 224
leader's role in, 13–14, 30–31, 78, 80, 88, 91–93, 94, 95
proletariat dictatorship in, 87, 126–27
Communists, communism:
in Europe, 60, 223–24, 241, 258, 263, 279–80, 287
fragmentation of, 285–87
global, U.S. view of, 147–56, 244–46, 247–49, 285
Moscow-allied, encouragement of, 112, 113, 223–25, 240–41
Naziism equated with, 151–52
as totalitarian, 144–66
in U.S., 110, 132, 140
Conference on Security and Cooperation (1972–75), 256–58
Congress, U.S., 62, 79, 94–95, 97, 98, 117, 259, 267n
conservatives vs. liberals, U.S., 117, 148, 155, 270–71
Constitution, U.S., 97, 122, 132–33, 134, 135
Constitution, USSR, 30, 133–34, 135
consumer goods and services, 35, 37–38, 43, 45, 52–55, 58, 105, 140
military spending vs., 273–74
producer goods vs., 52, 177
table, 54
consumer welfare, 52–55, 272–73
reward distribution in, 55–59
transportation in, 53–55
consumption levels, 38, 52–53, 55, 59, 272, 273–74
conventional forces, 190, 191–96, 198, 205–6, 274
corporations, 56, 74, 90–91, 92, 102, 227–28
courts, 97, 98, 108, 109, 139
covert operations, 228–30
criminal laws, 108, 109, 110
cruise missiles, 200, 201
Cuba, 13, 64, 65, 75n, 150, 210, 223, 234n, 278, 281
Bay of Pigs invasion of (1961), 229, 249
missile crisis in (1962), 194, 249, 255
U.S. economic warfare on, 68–69
cyclical fluctuations, 38–39
Czechoslovakia, 150, 202, 203, 242

Soviet intervention in (1968), 82, 205, 223, 238, 266

decolonization, 249–50, 262, 279
de Gaulle, Charles, 222
democracy:
foreign policy aims and, 230–32
rival claims to, 115, 121–29
rival meanings of, 118–19
"democratic centralism," Soviet, 88–89
Democratic party, U.S., 27, 79, 80, 81, 90, 110, 111, 129, 148
denazification, 60, 61
denuclearization, zonal, 205–6
Depression, Great, 25, 34, 39, 42
détente, 9, 164–65, 252–61, 265, 284
developed countries, 75, 113, 238, 263
see also capitalist countries, advanced
dictatorships, 125–27
meanings of, 124–25
of proletariat, 87–89, 125, 126–27
right-wing, U.S. links with, 112, 227, 229, 230–31, 282
disarmament, failure of, 196–97
see also arms limitations
dissent, 82–83, 84, 85, 102–3, 104, 286–87
post-Stalin, 108–9, 162
repression of, 101, 103, 108–11, 128, 163
dollar, international standing of, 41–42, 59
Dominican Republic, 208, 223
Dulles, John Foster, 148, 235

Eastern Europe, 67, 150, 151, 257
Soviet and Communist role in, 6, 7, 59, 62, 67, 112, 149, 160, 205, 221, 230, 240–41, 243, 262, 276, 281
economic assistance, 59, 60, 61–62, 246, 247, 270
to less-developed countries, 63–66, 225
surplus food stocks in, 65
to USSR, 32, 60, 62, 67
economic capabilities, 101
European recovery and, 60–62
internal affairs abroad affected by, 226–28
military spending and, 174–78, 268
outcome of rivalry determined by, 33
in sanctions and pressures, 66–70, 235–36
economic cooperation, Soviet–U.S., 256, 257, 258–61

economic development, 23–26, 36–59
  bilateral trade and, 71–72, 259–60
  as foreign aid goal, 65
  future of gap in, 267–73
  GNP and national income in, 34, 37,
    39–42, 43
  industrial base of, 43–45
  in interwar period, 25
  military priorities and, 19, 177–78, 268,
    271–72, 273–74, 275
  1950: strengths compared, 36–39
  1950–75: trends in, 39–43
  total output in, 39–43, 45, 268, 272
  U.S. lead in, before Revolution, 24–25
  see also agricultural output: agriculture;
    industrial development; industrial
    output
economic geography, U.S. favored by,
  17–18
economic growth rates (table), 42
economic models, 35, 38, 74–76, 77, 277
economic rights, 134–36, 143
economic rivalry, 11, 13, 14, 33–77, 167,
  259–60
  dimensions of, 34–35
  distributive systems in, 55–59, 102–3
  domestic comparisons and, 36–59
  future of, 266–73
  international, 35, 59–76, 226, 227–28,
    235–36, 258–61, 269–70, 278
  output stressed in, 267–68
  policy response to, 33–34
  primacy of, in overall rivalry, 33–34, 41
  see also consumer welfare; economic
    development
economic sanctions, 66–70, 228, 235–36,
  248
economic strength (table), 40
educational levels, 22–23
educational systems, indoctrinational role
  of, 15, 103–4
Egypt, 64, 66, 195, 210, 212, 213, 235,
  251, 289
Eisenhower, Dwight D., 94–95
elections, 79, 80, 86, 90, 91, 92, 109, 228
  in ideological rivalry, 127–29
Engels, Friedrich, 3, 142
equalization, income-wealth, 55–59
equal rights, 28, 118, 124
Ethiopia, 230, 250
ethnic diversity, 19–22
Europe:
  economic recovery of, 60–62, 262–63
  military rivalry in, 187–91, 202–5

  occupation policies in, 60, 61
  Soviet–U.S. relations and, 240–43,
    256–58
  see also East Europe; Western Europe
European Economic Community, 287,
  289

fascist regimes, 60, 112, 145n, 147, 151,
  158
FBI (Federal Bureau of Investigation),
  110, 148, 214
February Revolution (1917), 28
Federalist Papers, 97, 134–35
Finland, 71, 234
Five-Year Plans, 50, 51
Ford, Gerald R., 200, 231, 256, 260
foreign policy:
  clashing objectives in, 220–22
  economic rivalry and, 59, 64–70,
    226–28, 235–36
  ideological rivalry and, 145–46, 152–54,
    156, 159–61, 223–28, 244–46, 247–49
  presidency and, 97–98
  Soviet vs. Chinese threats in U.S. view
    of, 247–49
  "status quo" in, 231–32
  UN role in, 236–39
  U.S. anticommunist attitudes in, 5–6,
    113, 147–48, 221–22, 244–46,
    247–49, 258, 282
  U.S. theory of totalitarianism and,
    152–54
  see also international relations
France, 71, 158, 159, 188, 189, 242, 253,
  266
  colonial losses of, 5, 192, 246, 280
  Communists in, 226, 258, 263
  U.S. differences with, 164, 222
freedom, 119, 129–37
  of assembly, 136, 137–38
  of press, 130, 134, 136, 137–42
  of religion, 136–37
  of speech, 130, 133, 136, 137, 140
free enterprise system, 90, 113, 135
free world/totalitarian formula, 144, 146,
  147–56, 159, 164, 166
  domestic impact of, 154–56
  racism and, 153–54, 155–56
Friedrich, Carl J., 126, 149, 150, 156n,
  158, 162–63

geographic contrasts, 16–19
German Democratic Republic (East), 202,
  203, 207, 241–42

Germany, Federal Republic of (West), 71,
    202, 203, 230, 241–42, 253
  reparations and, 60–61
Germany, Nazi, 32, 147, 149, 151, 163n,
    170, 241
  defeat of, 3, 5, 6, 12, 61, 85
government interference:
  in economic affairs, 38–39
  limits on, 29–30, 90, 102, 131, 132–33,
    139, 285
grain output, 46, 47, 48
grain trade, 73, 260
Great Britain, see United Kingdom
"Great Russian chauvinism," 21, 111
Greece, 61, 113, 231, 279
Gromyko, Andrei A., 94
Gross National Product (GNP), 34, 37,
    39–42, 43, 47, 72, 174–75, 268
ground forces, 170, 171, 204, 246, 276
Guatemala, 229

Hamilton, Alexander, 97
Helsinki agreement, 202–3, 257–58
Hitler, Adolf, 3, 147, 149, 151
Hobbes, Thomas, 138–39
Honduras, 229
Hoover, J. Edgar, 148
housing, 52, 53, 54
human rights, 129–43, 257
  class struggle and, 131–32
  as deserving of protection, rival views
    on, 134–37
  international agreements on, 136, 257
  material prerequisites for, 133, 134
  in U.S. value system, 132–34
Hungary, 75n, 150, 205, 238

ICBMs (intercontinental ballistic mis-
    siles), 180–83, 186, 200, 201
ideological rivalry, 12, 114–66, 264
  coexistence, détente and, 162–66,
    239–40
  "democracy" in, 121–29
  domestic impact of, 154–56, 161–62
  economic models in, 35, 38, 74–76, 277
  "freedom" in, 129–37
  future of, 284–87
  history's judgment on, 119
  in overall rivalry, 115–21
  pluralism vs. monolithism in, 79–86, 87,
    107, 112
  policy orientations in, 145–46, 152–54,
    156, 159–61, 239–40, 244–46
  in political background, 26–31

political models in, 111–13
press freedom in, 137–42
Soviet view of conflict in, 156–62
"totalitarianism" vs. "imperialism" in,
    144–66
U.S. view of conflict in, 147–56, 244–46,
    247–49, 285
value symbols in, 115, 120, 130, 144–45
ideology:
  death of, announced, 117–18
  meanings of, 115–21
immigration, 20, 22, 31, 75
"imperialism," 111, 144–46, 226
  antiimperialism vs., 159, 160–61,
    164–65, 166, 226, 237, 240, 284
  Soviet political life and, 161–62
  in Soviet usage, 156–59
income:
  distribution of, 55–59
  farm, 50–51, 58
  industrial, 57
  real, 52–53
income groups, gains of, 58
income taxes, 58
India, 63, 64, 66, 74, 196, 208, 210, 213
individual rights, 131, 135
Indochina, 65, 160, 173, 246–47, 262, 265,
    280
Indonesia, 66, 70, 213, 223, 229, 276
industrial development, 23, 32, 33
  consumer goods stressed in, 37–38, 43,
    52, 53
  heavy-industry emphasis in, 33, 38, 48,
    51
  reforms as spur to, 24, 267
industrial output, 43–45
  agricultural output vs., 37, 268
  climate and, 17–18
  of consumer goods, 35, 37–38, 43, 45,
    177
  in interwar period, 25
  of producer goods, 43–45, 52, 177
  rates of increase of (1950–75), 43–45
  before World War I, 24, 25
inflation, 41–43, 174, 176, 267n, 270
intelligence activities, 214–15, 228
international relations, 217–63, 264
  alliance building in, 232–39
  bipolarity and, 219–20
  covert operations in, 228–30
  democracy and stability in, 230–32
  future of, 277–84
  internal affairs of other countries in,
    222–28, 230–32

international relations (*continued*)
  political models in, 111–13
  Soviet–U.S. relative standing in,
    261–63
  world missions in, 217–19
  see also foreign policy; Soviet–American
    (bilateral) relations
Iran, 64, 212, 229, 251
Iraq, 64, 66, 208, 210, 213, 230, 251
Israel, 63, 208, 238–39, 251
Italy, 62, 71, 147, 148, 151, 226, 258, 263,
    279

Jackson, Henry, 248, 259
Japan, 83, 149, 152, 158, 159, 170, 179,
    184, 209, 226, 233, 287
  defeat of, 3, 5, 12
  leadership role of, 288–89
  Soviet trade with, 71, 73, 254, 258, 259,
    263
  U.S. economic relations with, 59, 67,
    68, 210, 220, 253, 262, 271
Jews, Soviet, 109, 259
Johnson, Lyndon B., 168, 199, 223, 247,
    271

Kennan, George F., 239
KGB (Committee on State Security), 163,
    214
Khrushchev, Nikita S., 31, 46, 70, 94, 99,
    100, 126, 159, 181, 194, 202, 234,
    253–54, 255
Kirilenko, Andrei P., 94
Kissinger, Henry, 190, 231
Korean War, 71, 160, 172–73, 174–75,
    178, 193, 224, 238, 253, 290
  consequences of, 244–46
  Soviet role in, 243, 244, 247
Kosygin, Alexei N., 94, 95

labor camps, USSR, 108
labor force:
  expansion of, 41, 267
  wage differentials and, 57, 58
  see also agricultural labor force
languages, in national unification, 21–22
Laos, 193, 213, 246
Latin America, 208, 227, 229, 237, 243,
    248, 282
  denuclearization in, 206
  Soviet–U.S. relations and, 249
leadership, single-person vs. collective,
    96–100

Lebanon, 196, 276
Lecky, W. E. H., 123
Lenin, V. I., 3, 4, 5, 6, 28, 29, 31, 82, 99,
    121, 127, 224, 262, 266
  on imperialism, 156, 157–58, 165–66
less-developed countries (LDCs), 194,
    238, 263, 269, 287
  Communist appeal to, 279–82
  Communist vs. non-Communist, 63–64
  economic aid to, 59, 63–66, 225
  ideological rivalry and, 75–76, 77,
    112–13, 159–61
  military role of, 64–65
Lin Piao, 290
literacy rates, 22
Liu Shao-chi, 290
living standards, 53–55, 57, 102, 269, 275
  in birthplace of socialism, 74–75
  economic models and, 74–76
Lumumba, Patrice, 229

McCarthy, Joseph R., 110, 148
Mandeville, Bernard de, 72
Manila treaty (1954), 208, 235
Maoist ideology, 286
Mao Tse-tung, 288, 290
Marshall Plan (European Recovery Pro-
    gram), 61–62, 67
Marx, Karl, 3, 75, 82, 116, 119, 122, 125,
    126, 142, 161, 262, 279
Marxism, 4, 34, 57, 116, 123–24, 126, 142,
    146, 279, 285–86
Marxism-Leninism, 61, 64, 80, 82, 104,
    116, 149–50, 161, 162*n*, 233, 277,
    278, 284, 286–87
mass media, *see* communications media
Middle East, 208, 227, 235
  Soviet role in, 66, 195, 196, 210, 212,
    250–51, 276, 283
  UN role in, 238–39
Mikoyan, Anastas I., 94
military aid, 194, 210, 211–14, 246, 247,
    251
military bases, foreign, 195, 198, 199, 209,
    274, 289
military capabilities, 101, 163, 264
  Communist gains due to, 243
  dollar-comparison measures of, 176
  sources of data on, 169–70, 173*n*
military rivalry, 10, 13, 14, 167–216, 255
  in alliance building, 206–11, 236
  in arms supplying, 211–14
  demobilization and, 171–72

in Europe, 187–91, 202–5, 256–58
future of, 265, 266, 273–77
geographic vulnerability and, 16
in globally mobile forces, 191–96,
    205–6, 274
in overall rivalry, 167–68
personnel strength in, 171–74
postwar trends in, 170–78
spending and economics in, 169–70,
    174–78, 197, 201–2, 212–13, 268,
    271–72, 273–75
supremacy as goal in, 214–16, 274–75
symmetry in, 167–68
see also arms limitations; strategic
    rivalry
MIRVs (Multiple Independently targeted
    Reentry Vehicles), 168, 181–83, 186,
    200, 201
missile-launching systems, 181–83, 186,
    200–201, 206
Mongolian People's Republic, 64, 209,
    277–78, 281
monolithism vs. pluralism, 79–86, 107,
    112
Mozambique, 250, 280–81
Mussolini, Benito, 147, 149
mutual and balanced force reductions
    (MBFR), Vienna conference on, 169,
    189n, 203–5, 256–57

Namibia (Southwest Africa), 250, 281
National Income (USSR), 34, 39–42, 175
nationalist movements, 224–25, 241
"national security," 206–7
NATO (North Atlantic Treaty Organiza-
    tion), 61, 187, 188–90, 191, 202–3,
    204, 205, 207, 208, 231, 233, 234,
    242, 253, 256
naval forces, 170, 171, 172, 192, 193, 249,
    274
    Soviet expansion of, 194–95
Nazis, 60, 61, 151–52
Nazi–Soviet Nonaggression Pact (1939),
    147
negotiations, Soviet–U.S., 9–10, 164, 169,
    196–206, 239, 255–56, 261
newspapers, 105–6, 107, 116, 140, 141,
    142
Nicholas II, 30
Nixon, Richard M., 82, 111, 118, 119n,
    148, 165, 185–86, 199, 201, 239–40,
    267n

nonaligned countries, 159–61, 224–25,
    262, 277
nonproliferation treaty (1968), 198, 199
North Korea, 65, 68, 149, 173, 193, 209,
    238, 243, 244
North Vietnam, 64, 65, 68, 82, 149, 165,
    194, 210, 246
nuclear war, 8, 33, 190, 201, 252, 261, 266
nuclear weapons, 114, 168, 174, 178–87,
    198–202, 204, 207, 212, 221
    nonuse of, 184, 275–76
    tactical, 190
    see also strategic rivalry

October Revolution (1917), 3, 27, 28–29,
    52, 57, 93n, 119, 139, 245
aims of, 28–29
role of state before and after, 29–31
oil, 18, 73–74, 229, 269
oil-producing nations, 42, 269
Organization of American States (OAS),
    208, 234
Origins of Totalitarianism, The, 149,
    150–51

Pakistan, 63, 64, 196, 208, 209, 212
peasantry, collectivized, 25–26, 27, 50, 87,
    128
Philippines, 66, 208, 209
Podgorny, Nikolai V., 94
Poland, 150, 202, 203, 241, 242
Politburo, 92–93, 95–96, 98, 99–100
political campaign contributions, 81, 90,
    92
political geography, 18–19
political models, contest of, 111–13
political parties, 27, 79–83, 90, 127–28
political systems, 78–113
    class basis of, 86–91, 128
    government-to-citizen relations in,
        101–8
    in historical perspective, 26–31
    leadership in, 13–14, 30–31, 78, 80, 81,
        88, 91–100
    in overall rivalry, 78, 107–8
    repression in, 108–11
    two-party vs. one-party, 27, 79–80, 81,
        110, 127–28
    unity and diversity in, 79–86, 107
population growth, decisive factors in,
    19–20
population size, 16–17, 20
Portugal, 113, 231, 234, 258, 279, 280, 282

presidency, U.S., 13–14, 30, 78, 91,
    93–95, 96, 97–98, 100
press, 83, 105–7
    freedom of, 130, 134, 136, 137–42
private entrepreneurship, 55–56
    in farming, 45–46, 49
private ownership, 84, 87, 88, 135
producer goods, 52, 43–45, 177
proletariat class, 28, 87–89, 125, 126–27,
    142
profit incentive, 55, 260
propaganda, 111, 114–15, 228, 257
property ownership, 57, 84, 89–90, 113,
    122, 135
property rights, 134, 135

racial problems, racism, 14, 15, 27,
    110, 111, 124, 127, 238, 250, 281, 282
    free world/totalitarian contrast and,
    153–54, 155–56
railroad system, Soviet, 55
recessions, postwar, 267n, 270
redistributive measures, 55–57, 58
religious freedom, 136–37
Republican party, U.S., 27, 79, 80, 90,
    110, 129, 148
revolutions, contrasts in, 27–28
reward distribution, 25, 88
    equity and efficiency in, 55–59
    social order maintained by, 102–3
Rhodesia (Zimbabwe), 124, 250, 281
right-wing dictatorships, 112, 227, 229,
    230–31, 282
Roosevelt, Franklin D., 148
ruling class, 86–91, 123–24, 125, 128, 165
ruling groups, elites, 90, 103, 105, 109,
    111, 114, 211, 221, 266
    ideologies used by, 117, 118
Rumania, 248
rural-urban population ratios, 23
Rusk, Dean, 245, 247
Russian Empire, 3, 4, 6, 18–22, 26–28,
    108, 122, 232n
    economic development in, 24–25
    expansion of, 19–20
    hereditary principle in, 30
    Soviet state compared with, 29–31
    wars of, 20, 36
Russian language, 22

Sadat, Anwar es-, 66, 251
Salazar, Antonio de Oliveira, 113, 231

Schlesinger, James, 248
science, 23, 215
sea access, 18, 19
seabed treaty (1971), 198–99, 204
serfdom, 24, 26, 27, 130
services, see consumer goods and services
slavery, abolition of, 24, 26, 130, 133
Smith, Adam, 34
socialism, 35, 55, 127, 138, 187, 277
    as developmental goal, 101
    real vs. ideal, 74–75
    Soviet monolithic order and, 84
    third-world vs. "scientific," 76
    see also capitalist-socialist rivalry;
        Communists, communism; Marxism;
        Marxism-Leninism
soil conditions, 17, 48
South Africa, Republic of, 124, 154, 250,
    281
South Korea, 63, 66, 193, 213, 226, 238,
    244
South Vietnam, 63, 246, 282
Soviet–American leadership, challenges
    to, 287–90
Soviet–American (bilateral) relations,
    239–61
    in areas outside Europe, 243–52
    background of, 31–32
    Europe and, 240–43, 256–58
    ideological rivalry complicated by,
    162–66, 239–40
    normalization of, 252–61
    see also arms limitations; trade,
        East–West
Soviet–American rivalry:
    future of, 264–91
    geographical-historical background of,
    16–32
    in interwar period, 4–5, 6, 233–34
    national differences vs., 13–15
    post-1945 vs. post-1918, 3–8
    see also specific areas of comparison and
        rivalry
Soviet Union:
    historical continuities in, 29–31
    see also Russian Empire; and specific
        topics
space programs, 174, 181, 183, 264
    treaty on (1967), 198, 199, 204
Spain, 113, 231, 279
Stalin, Joseph V., 3, 6, 29, 50, 57, 75, 149,
    150, 151, 159, 160, 179, 224, 240, 286

authority of, 30, 95, 99, 125, 144
industrialization under, 44, 46
repression under, 93n, 108, 147, 148
Strategic Arms Limitation Talks (SALT),
    199'–200, 255–56
strategic rivalry, 170–71, 174, 178–87,
    194, 205, 265
    arms limitations and, 198–202, 205–6,
        255–56
    defense systems in, 183–84
    delivery systems in, 114, 168, 170, 186,
        200–201
    in postwar period, 178–80
    Soviet parity or superiority in, 275–77
    sufficiency doctrine in, 185–86
    table, 182
    unreality in, 184–87
submarine missile launchers, 181, 182,
    200
Sukarno, 66, 70, 223, 229
Supreme Soviet, USSR, 88, 92
Suslov, Mikhail A., 94, 95
Syria, 66, 230, 251

Taiwan, 63, 65, 66, 209, 213, 237
tax laws, U.S., 56
technology, 264, 269
    Soviet lag in, 23, 75, 272
    in weaponry, 114, 168
television, 105, 106, 107, 116, 137
Teng Hsiao-ping, 290
territories:
    expansion of, 19–20, 231, 232
    size of, 16–17
test-ban treaty (1963), 198
Thailand, 66, 208, 209
third world:
    globally mobile forces and, 192–94
    ideological rivalry and, 159–61, 193–94,
        224–25, 227–28
    internal affairs in, 224–25, 227–28
    see also less-developed countries
Tlatelolco Treaty (1967), 206
Tocqueville, Alexis de, 31
"totalitarianism," 119, 125–26, 144–46
    meanings of, 147–51, 158
    "merely" authoritarian states vs.,
        152–53
    postwar theory of, 149–56, 162–63, 164
trade, East–West, 59, 70–74, 253, 254,
    258–60
    individual deals in, 72

"Most Favored Nation" (MFN) in, 67,
    258–59
Soviet vs. U.S. goals in, 71–72, 73,
    259–60
U.S. restrictions on, 67–69, 258, 259,
    260, 269
trade, international:
    economic sanctions and, 66–69, 248
    global division of labor in, 270
    prices in, 72, 73–74, 269
transportation, 53–55
    public, 54–55
Truman, Harry S., 3, 6, 63, 148, 154,
    171–72, 240, 252–53
tsars, tsarism, 21, 24, 29–32
Turkey, 61, 209, 224

un-American doctrines, 117–18
unemployment, 25, 42, 136, 177, 267n,
    271
United Kingdom, 33, 71, 158, 159, 192,
    242, 254
    postwar decline of, 5, 12, 192
United Nations, 236–39, 250, 278
    General Assembly of, 236, 237, 238
    Security Council of, 197, 236–37, 238
universal vs. class-based rights, 131–32,
    142
urban decay (central cities), 54
urbanization, 22, 23

Vietnam, war in, 41, 82, 110, 114, 155,
    166, 173, 178, 193, 209, 248, 271
    Soviet role in, 194, 210, 243, 246–47,
        276
Vladivostok agreement (1974), 200, 256
voting, 80, 85, 87, 122, 127–29, 156n

wage differentials, 57, 58
war, warfare, 20, 36
    avoidance of, 10, 33, 165, 184–85, 190,
        201, 221, 260–61, 266
    conventional vs. nuclear, 190
    economic aspects of, 19, 177–78, 268,
        271–72, 273, 274
    political geography and, 18–19
Warsaw Pact, 163, 187, 188–90, 191, 202,
    203, 204, 205, 207, 233, 234, 235,
    242, 256, 257
Western Europe, 220, 240, 287
    Communists in, 258, 263, 279–80, 287
    leadership role of, 289

Western Europe (*continued*)
  Soviet trade with, 71, 73, 253, 254, 259
  U.S. role in, 61, 112, 113, 230
Wilson, Woodrow, 3–4, 5, 6, 8
World War I, 3–4, 5
World War II, 3, 25, 26, 60, 147, 151–52, 170–71, 233

Soviet–U.S. emergence from, 6–8, 12, 32, 59–60, 217, 261–62, 277

Yugoslavia, 69–70, 150, 212, 222, 224, 230, 247, 248, 278

Zaire (Congo), 193, 276